NUCLEAR WEAPONS AND
FOREIGN POLICY

NUCLEAR WEAPONS
and
FOREIGN POLICY

By HENRY A. KISSINGER

Foreword by GORDON DEAN

Published for the
COUNCIL ON FOREIGN RELATIONS
by
HARPER & BROTHERS
New York
1957

623.45

X64n

The Council on Foreign Relations is a nonprofit institution devoted to study of the international aspects of American political, economic and strategic problems. It takes no stand, expressed or implied, on American policy.

The authors of books published under the auspices of the Council are responsible for their statements of fact and expressions of opinion. The Council is responsible only for determining that they should be presented to the public.

36521

July 1958

COUNCIL ON FOREIGN RELATIONS

FOREWORD

THERE are those who believe that the principal objective of this generation should be peace at any price. For such people the capacity of the Russians to bring on an atomic holocaust should not be particularly disturbing since peace can probably always be secured—on Russian terms. But for most of us the mere survival of ourselves and our children is not sufficient. We think more in terms of surviving in freedom, and we believe that on this fast-shrinking globe our freedom is somehow bound up with the freedom of all people and particularly of those who have it today or are determined to have it some day.

For those of us who hold this philosophy, the Russian military threat with all it entails in terms of nuclear weapons, fast delivery systems and long-range missiles, does in fact pose the problem of the age. Abhorrent of war but unwilling to accept gradual Russian enslavement of other peoples around the world, which we know will eventually lead to our own enslavement, we are forced to adopt a posture that, despite Russian military capabilities and despite their long-range intentions, freedom shall be preserved to us. We face a great dilemma, and Dr. Kissinger analyzes this dilemma in fine detail. In my own words and with oversimplification, I would express it this way:

For all practical purposes we have in terms of nuclear capabilities reached a point which may be called "parity." We have long known that such a time would come. It is now upon us. I do not mean necessarily parity in numbers of large bombs. Numbers become less important when the point is reached where both sides have the capability to annihilate each other. So long as this condition is coupled with a fear that any strong action on the part of the United States anywhere in the world may ignite a full-

scale nuclear war, we find ourselves more and more reluctant to frame a strong foreign policy or implement it
so as to preserve the vital interests of the free world. We
fear force as never before, and we even fear economic and
political measures which might lead to the use of it. In
the meantime, however, the Soviet leaders do not seem
to have been similarly deterred. They have spilled across
the territories of free and uncommitted countries, capital-
izing on unrest, using all the devices short of war to perform the acts of conquest—infiltration, incitement to civil
war, threats of war, and supplying materials of war to anyone who will use them in the Soviet cause. This conquest
has proceeded in spite of our ominous atomic stockpile
which for various reasons we have been unable or unwilling to employ against conquests of the Soviet variety. This,
then, is our dilemma.

Three years ago, the Council on Foreign Relations
called together a panel of exceptionally qualified individuals to explore all factors which are involved in the making and implementing of foreign policy in the nuclear age.
I was asked to chair this panel. Among the members and
invited guests were framers of our military and foreign
policy, experts knowledgeable in the effects of modern
weapons, persons in responsible positions in government,
persons who had held such positions in the past, persons
less preoccupied with the day-to-day administrative decisions of government who brought to us the benefit which
comes from reflective thinking within the confines of our
universities, persons who had been hardened by the realities of the business world and upon whom we had so
heavily relied in past wars to help outproduce the enemy.*

After almost eighteen months, we decided that we had
gone as far as we could by means of discussion. Before
this time, however, we had secured the services of Dr.
Henry A. Kissinger as study director. Recognizing that our
mission was first to get the facts and secondly to explore
the implications of these facts, we decided that we would
not attempt to secure a consensus of the group, all of us

* The regular members of the group are listed in the author's *Preface*,
p. xiii.

having had experience with large committees which attempted to produce a draft agreeable to all. Instead we asked Dr. Kissinger, fully exposed to the facts and the views of the group, to write a book for which he alone would be responsible, and we ended our deliberations fully respectful of each other and with a final exhortation: "Good luck, Dr. Kissinger. If you can make anything out of the efforts of this panel we will be eternally grateful."

Speaking, therefore, only for myself, I believe that he has done just this. Certainly this book is not an end to thinking in this field. But if it will make people think it has been good in itself. I feel that it has done much more than this. Dr. Kissinger ploughs right into one of the heart areas of our dilemma. Assume a situation where the vital interests of the United States are at stake, if for no other reason than that the U.S.S.R. is attempting to take over another small but strategic area of the world. Would the United States be prepared to use force? Would it be prepared to use tactical atomic weapons to prevent such a conquest if the employment of such weapons were best suited to end quickly a local aggression?

Dr. Kissinger sets a framework for the evaluation which must be made in such a situation. Today we have a complete spectrum of weapons which could be used against the Soviets or a Soviet-inspired operation. These range from the bullet in a rifle through machine guns and artillery, through small atomic weapons and eventually up to thermonuclear weapons which, because of their destructive force, can destroy deployed armies in the field and entire cities. This spectrum is continuous. The destructive power of some atomic weapons is less than that of some conventional high-explosive weapons. The destructive power of some thermonuclear weapons is less than the destructive power of some of our fission weapons. Many efforts have been made in recent years to seek a break in the spectrum and to produce rules of conduct in international behavior which somehow recognize morality in one type of explosive and immorality in another. But obviously immorality arises not from the type of explosive or the explosive power. It arises from the use to which weapons are put. I think it important above all that we convey to our potential enemies our determination that if we must use force it will be used with discrimination; that our objective will always be to restrict the area of conflict and to destroy military targets which threaten the freedom we must preserve.

Dr. Kissinger argues for much more communication of our intentions to the enemy. He believes that it must know that our strength is great or we have lost the asset of a deterrent. He believes also that it must know that our objective is to end the aggression quickly by eliminating military targets lest we bring on an all-out thermonuclear war through a misunderstanding of our intentions. He believes that if this message is not conveyed to the Soviet leaders we shall give ammunition to the advocates of peace at any price who are ready to accept any fate which does not involve force. I share this thesis with him.

Dr. Kissinger's book is not easy reading if for no other reason than that the subject is highly complicated. He has produced, however, what is in my opinion the best single volume on this the hardest problem facing us. There is a way out of our dilemma if we keep our heads, and Dr. Kissinger's book is an appeal to the head and to the way to keep it.

GORDON DEAN

PREFACE

IT WOULD BE difficult to think of a subject with more of a built-in inducement to humility than that of nuclear weapons and foreign policy. Mankind has at its disposal the means to destroy itself at the precise moment when schisms among nations have never been deeper. And the attempt to come to grips with the horrors of the new technology confronts the additional handicap that we can draw only limited guidance from previous experience because much of it has been made irrelevant by the very enormity of modern means of mass destruction.

The challenge of the nuclear age is not only enormous but also inescapable. Within a generation the peaceful uses of atomic energy will have spread across the globe. Most nations will then possess the wherewithal to manufacture nuclear weapons. Foreign policy henceforth will have to be framed against the background of a world in which the "conventional" technology is nuclear technology.

Contemporaries are in a peculiarly difficult position to assess the nature of revolutions through which they are living. All previous experience will tempt them to integrate the new into what has come to seem familiar. They will have difficulty understanding that what is most taken for granted may be most misleading because a new order of experience requires new ways of thinking about it. A revolution cannot be mastered until it develops the mode of thinking appropriate to it.

So it is with the impact of nuclear weapons on foreign policy. Nostalgia for a more secure and less cataclysmic past is understandable. But facts cannot be changed; they can only be used. Many familiar assumptions about war, diplomacy and the nature of peace will have to be modi-

fied before we have developed a theory adequate to the
perils and opportunities of the nuclear age.

This book attempts to be a first step in that direction. I
have sought to set forth the considerations on which policy and strategy may be based and the pitfall of many of
our traditional concepts about the nature of security. To
be useful a work of this kind must indicate the nature of
possible choices, if only because the dilemmas of policy
appear in the resolution and not in the contemplation of
problems. To govern, it has been said, is to choose. A book
about foreign policy which refused to state its position
would seem to me to beg the principal question. Humility
cannot take the form of recoiling before the consequences
of every course of action.

The awful responsibility for the ultimate decision on
which our survival may depend rests, of course, on other
shoulders and statesmen are permitted only one guess. To
some extent, however, those who have to make the final
decisions can be aided by dispassionate public discussion.
If this book does no more than elicit fuller and wiser statements of our strategic problem, it will have been well
worthwhile.

An author who is invited by the Council on Foreign
Relations to work under its auspices is in a fortunate position. He can draw on the experience of an extraordinary
group of individuals who have been exposed to the practice of the problem with which he is dealing. And he has
at his disposal scholarly facilities, including a library service of exceptional efficiency, which guarantee that the inadequacies of his work must be his own.

The Council procedure is particularly helpful in a book
such as this because published material on the strategic
and diplomatic implications of the new technology is scant.
The wisdom we possess is largely in the minds of those
who have been placed in positions of responsibility where
they have had to guide our policy even while the new
technology was daily changing its presuppositions. I have
profited more than I can say from the discussions of the
extraordinary group of men assembled by the Council on
Foreign Relations under the wise and patient chairman-

ship of Gordon Dean. Their deliberations gave me a sense of the dimensions of the problem and of the considerations on which policy is based; this I could have acquired in no other way. It was my good fortune to work with Gordon Dean, the chairman of the over-all group, and with Joseph E. Johnson, William A. M. Burden and Frank Pace, Jr., who headed subcommittees. I am deeply indebted to them, not only for what they have taught me personally, but for the skill and dedication with which they guided the deliberations of the various groups. To enumerate the many ways in which this book profited from the counsel of members of the study group either jointly or individually would transcend the bounds of a preface. I hope they will forgive me if I use this opportunity to express my gratitude to them collectively. The members of the group were:

Gordon Dean, *Chairman*

Frank Altschul
Hamilton Fish Armstrong
Hanson W. Baldwin
Lloyd V. Berkner
Robert R. Bowie
McGeorge Bundy
William A. M. Burden
John C. Campbell
Thomas K. Finletter
George S. Franklin, Jr.
Lieutenant General
  James M. Gavin
Roswell L. Gilpatric
N. E. Halaby
Caryl P. Haskins
James T. Hill, Jr.
Joseph E. Johnson
Mervin J. Kelly

Major General
  Richard C. Lindsay
Major General
  James McCormack, Jr.
Frank C. Nash
Paul H. Nitze
Charles P. Noyes
Frank Pace, Jr.
James A. Perkins
Don K. Price
I. I. Rabi
David Rockefeller
Oscar M. Ruebhausen
General Walter Bedell Smith
Henry DeWolf Smyth
Shields Warren
Carroll L. Wilson
Arnold Wolfers

In fairness to the study group I must emphasize that while this book has grown out of its deliberations, the conclusions, judgments and analysis are my own. The manuscript itself was never considered by the group as a whole, and some members would undoubtedly dissent from even its major conclusions. I am deeply indebted to members of the study group who have read individual chapters and who have made exceedingly helpful suggestions. They include: Frank Altschul, McGeorge Bundy, James T. Hill, Jr., Frank Nash, Henry DeWolf Smyth, Carroll L. Wilson and Arnold Wolfers. Merle Fainsod was extremely helpful with the chapters on the Soviet Union. Caryl P. Haskins has read the entire manuscript and his friendship and encouragement have been a constant inspiration to me. None of these individuals is responsible, however, for the conclusions of this book.

The atmosphere at the Council on Foreign Relations, in my opinion so largely due to the influence of Walter H. Mallory, is particularly conducive to producing the best work of which one is capable. Advice and assistance are always available and all the more helpful for being so unobtrusive. If I were to list my indebtedness, I should have to mention the entire staff. In a subtle and civilized way they create an environment in which ideas are absorbed almost by osmosis and in which one draws the strength which comes from being with a group of individuals who form a community in the best sense. I have profited greatly from the encouragement of John C. Campbell, William Diebold, Jr., and Melvin Conant. Philip E. Mosely, Philip W. Quigg and George S. Franklin, Jr., have read the entire manuscript and have made innumerable helpful suggestions. Philip Quigg, in addition to his invaluable substantive advice, has put his subtle editorial pen to my resistant style. Portions of this book have appeared in *Foreign Affairs* and, as any author who has contributed to this distinguished journal knows, I owe a great deal to the incisive judgments of Hamilton Fish Armstrong.

The library of the Council on Foreign Relations, under the able direction of Miss Ruth Savord, has performed miracles in collecting material and checking references. Its clipping files of newspapers are unique.

I am grateful to Kurt de Witt and to Harold Fletcher, Jr., who helped with the research on German and French material respectively. Elizabeth Valkenier, Randolph T. Major, Jr., and Paul Willen assisted in the collection of Soviet sources. Rear Admiral Sir Anthony W. Buzzard made available his exceptionally useful clipping files on British strategic problems. Corinne Lyman and Nicholas Nyary were extremely helpful in organizing the material from Congressional hearings. Margaret Dreyfus was a patient and efficient research assistant and secretary.

Without the quite extraordinary dedication of Lorna Brennan who helped me on many aspects of the manuscript, the publication date of this book would have been postponed literally for months.

The understanding and devotion of my wife Ann were a constant source of encouragement.

HENRY A. KISSINGER

CONTENTS

PART ONE
THE PROBLEMS OF SURVIVAL

PART TWO
TECHNOLOGY AND STRATEGY

PART THREE

STRATEGY AND POLICY

TABLES

MAPS

PART I

THE PROBLEMS OF SURVIVAL

1

THE CHALLENGE OF THE
NUCLEAR AGE

IN GREEK MYTHOLOGY, the gods sometimes punished man by fulfilling his wishes too completely. It has remained for the nuclear age to experience the full irony of this penalty. Throughout history, humanity has suffered from a shortage of power and has concentrated all its efforts on developing new sources and special applications of it. It would have seemed unbelievable even fifty years ago that there could ever be an excess of power, that everything would depend on the ability to use it subtly and with discrimination.

Yet this is precisely the challenge of the nuclear age. Ever since the end of the second World War brought us not the peace we sought so earnestly, but an uneasy armistice, we have responded by what can best be described as a flight into technology: by devising ever more fearful weapons. The more powerful the weapons, however, the greater becomes the reluctance to use them. At a period of unparalleled military strength, President Dwight D. Eisenhower summed up the dilemma posed by the new weapons technology in the phrase "there is no alternative to peace."

It is only natural, of course, that an age which has known two world wars and an uneasy armistice since should have as its central problem the attainment of peace. It is paradoxical, however, that so much hope should concentrate on man's most destructive capabilities. We are told that the growth of the thermonuclear stockpiles has created a stalemate which makes war, if not too risky, at least

3

unprofitable. The power of the new weapons technology is said to have brought about a tacit nonaggression treaty: a recognition that war is no longer a conceivable instrument of policy and that for this reason international disputes can be settled only by means of diplomacy. And it has been maintained that the peaceful uses of nuclear energy have made irrelevant many of the traditional motivations for wars of aggression because each major power can bring about a tremendous increase in its productive capacity without annexing either foreign territory or foreign labor.

These assertions fit in well with a national psychology which considers peace as the "normal" pattern of relations among states and which has few doubts that reasonable men can settle all differences by honest compromise. So much depends, however, on the correctness of such propositions that they must be subjected to close scrutiny. For if recourse to force has in fact become impossible, diplomacy too may lose its efficacy. Far from leading to a resolution of tensions, the inability to use force may perpetuate all disputes, however trivial. It may be a strange fulfillment of the hopes of centuries for universal peace, that, when finally realized, it should contribute to the demoralization of the international order and that diplomacy, so long considered the alternative to war, should emerge as its complement.

It is an illusion of posterity that past international settlements were brought about entirely by reasonableness and negotiating skill. In a society of "sovereign" states, a power can in the last resort vindicate its interpretation of justice or defend its "vital interests" only by the willingness to employ force. Even during the period of seemingly greatest harmony, it was understood that a negotiation which failed did not return matters to their starting point but might call other pressures into play. The motive force behind international settlements has always been a combination of the belief in the advantages of harmony and the fear of the consequences of proving obdurate. A renunciation of force, by eliminating the penalty for intransigence, will therefore place the international order at the mercy of its most ruthless or its most irresponsible member.

This becomes a particular problem in a revolutionary period like the present, because the distinguishing feature of revolution is the priority it gives to change over the requirement of harmony. Contemporary international relations would therefore be difficult at best, but they take on a special urgency because never have so many different revolutions occurred simultaneously. On the political plane, the postwar period has seen the emergence into nationhood of a large number of peoples hitherto under colonial rule. To integrate so many new states into the international community would not be a simple matter at any time; it has become increasingly formidable because many of the newly independent states continue to inject into their policies the revolutionary fervor that gained them independence. On the ideological plane, the contemporary ferment is fed by the rapidity with which ideas can be communicated and by the inherent impossibility of fulfilling the expectations aroused by revolutionary slogans. On the economic and social plane, millions are rebelling against standards of living as well as against social and racial barriers which had remained unchanged for centuries. And these problems, serious enough in themselves, are manipulated by the Sino-Soviet bloc which is determined to prevent the establishment of an equilibrium and which is organized to exploit all hopes and dissatisfactions for its own ends.

All these revolutions have been taking place, moreover, at a moment when international relationships have become truly global for the first time. Classical history was confined to the Mediterranean basin with little awareness of events in the rest of the world. In the Middle Ages, the policy of the European powers was conducted in almost complete isolation from that of the Asian empires. And when in the eighteenth and nineteenth centuries the European powers developed world-wide interests, they were enabled by the temporary passivity of the Asian states to conduct their affairs as an extension of European diplomacy. With modern technology, and in the face of the contemporary intellectual ferment, there are no longer any isolated areas, however. Any diplomatic or military move immediately involves world-wide consequences.

Statesmanship has never faced a more fearful challenge. Diplomacy is asked to overcome schisms unparalleled in scope and to do so at a moment when the willingness to utilize the traditional pressures available to it—even during periods of harmony—is constantly diminishing. To be sure, the contemporary revolution cannot be managed by force alone; it requires a consistent and bold program to identify ourselves with the aspirations of humanity. But when there is no penalty for irresponsibility, the pent-up frustrations of centuries may seek an outlet in the international field instead of in domestic construction. To the extent that recourse to force has become impossible, the restraints of the international order may disappear as well.

Moreover, whatever the possibilities of identifying ourselves with the aspirations of the rest of humanity, we are confronted by two revolutionary powers, the U.S.S.R. and Communist China, which pride themselves on their superior understanding of "objective" forces and to which policies unrelated to a plausible possibility of employing force seem either hypocrisy or stupidity. Because harmony between different social systems is explicitly rejected by Soviet doctrine, the renunciation of force in the face of it will create a vacuum into which the Soviet leadership can move with impunity. Because the Soviet rulers pride themselves on their ability to "see through" our protestations of peaceful intentions, our only possibility for affecting their actions resides in the possession of superior force. For the Soviet leadership has made every effort to retain its militancy. It has been careful to insist that no technological discovery, however powerful, can abolish the laws of history and that real peace is attainable only *after* the triumph of communism. "We will bury you," [1] Nikita S. Khrushchev has said, and the democracies would have been

---

[1] Reception at the Polish Embassy on November 17, 1956, given in honor of Wladyslaw Gomulka's visit to Moscow, quoted in the *New York Herald Tribune*, November 19, 1956.

spared much misery but for their penchant on insisting that dictators do not mean what they say. "Political power," Mao Tse-tung has said, "grows out of the barrel of a gun. . . . Yes . . . we are advocates of the omnipotence of the revolutionary war, which . . . is good and is Marxist." [2]

The dilemma of the nuclear period can, therefore, be defined as follows: the enormity of modern weapons makes the thought of war repugnant, but the refusal to run any risks would amount to giving the Soviet rulers a blank check. At a time when we have never been stronger, we have had to learn that power which is not clearly related to the objectives for which it is to be employed may merely serve to paralyze the will. No more urgent task confronts American policy than to bring our power into balance with the issues for which we are most likely to have to contend. All the difficult choices which confront us—the nature of our weapons systems, the risks diplomacy can run—presuppose an ability on our part to assess the meaning of the new technology.

This task is complicated by the very novelty of the challenge. Until power is used, it is—as Colonel George A. Lincoln, of the United States Military Academy, has wisely said—what people think it is. But except for the two explosions of now obsolete weapons over Hiroshima and Nagasaki, no nuclear weapons have ever been set off in wartime; there exists, therefore, no body of experience on which to draw. To a considerable extent the impact of the new weapons on strategy, on policy, indeed on survival, depends on our interpretation of their significance.

II

It is the task of strategic doctrine to translate power into policy. Whether the goals of a state are offensive or defensive, whether it seeks to achieve or to prevent a transformation, its strategic doctrine must define what objectives are worth contending for and determine the de-

_____

[2] Mao Tse-tung, *Selected Works* (New York: International Publishers, 1954), v. 2, p. 272; for a fuller discussion of these ideas, see below, Chapters 10 and 11.

gree of force appropriate for achieving them. As a *status quo* power, the basic strategic problem for the United States is to be clear about what strategic transformations we are prepared to resist. The crucial test of our strategic doctrine is, therefore, what it defines as a threat.

In assessing what transformations to resist, our strategic doctrine has been inhibited, however, by the seeming lessons of our history. We have confused the security conferred by two great oceans with the normal pattern of international relations; we have overlooked that concepts of aggression developed in a period of relative safety may become dangerously inadequate in the face of a new type of challenge. A power favored by geography or by a great material superiority, as we have been through most of our history, can afford to let a threat take unambiguous shape before it engages in war. And the most unambiguous threat is overt military aggression against its territory. It can do so as long as the outcome of a war cannot be decided against it by a single battle, or by the loss of an objective located outside its territory which would cause national catastrophe, such as the loss of Middle Eastern oil would be for Western Europe. A nation which does not have this margin of safety is forced to conduct a more precautionary policy. It cannot permit a significant change in the balance of forces, for, to the degree that the equilibrium is disturbed, it surrenders control over its security, indeed over its ability to assure its own survival. A precautionary policy resists the change in the balance, even if this change is not put to any immediately hostile use. As long as the European balance of power dominated world affairs, any accretion in the strength of one state led to an ever wider circle of adjustments, either until all nations had made an equivalent gain, or until the old balance was restored by depriving the first power of its spoils through war.

This strong resistance to seemingly minor changes in the balance of power tends to appear to a less exposed nation both as petty and as a contributing cause of war, as is demonstrated by the traditional American reaction to European diplomacy. But the differences between our approach to foreign policy and that of the European states was primarily a matter of degree. The increment of power required to upset the European balance was relatively small. The margin of safety of the individual nations was, therefore, correspondingly narrow; they tended to resist transformations which could appear to be of only marginal significance to our security. By contrast, under conditions of pre-World War II technology, the increment of power required to upset the world balance of power and thus to threaten the United States was considerable; it could be achieved only by destroying so many nations that no doubt was left about the threat to our security. And because many other states had to be attacked long before the threat to our security became apparent, we could always be certain that some powers would bear the brunt of the first battles and hold a line while we mobilized our resources. Thus we came to develop a doctrine of aggression so purist and abstract that it absolved our statesmen from the necessity of making decisions in ambiguous situations and from concerning themselves with the minutiae of day-to-day diplomacy.

But the destructiveness and speed of modern weapons have ended our traditional invulnerability, and the polarization of power in the world has reduced our traditional margin of safety. The intermediary states having lost either the power or the will to resist aggression by themselves, we can no longer count on other powers to hold a line while we are assessing events and making up our minds on whether a threat has become unambiguous. Resistance to aggression henceforth is no longer a problem of our coming into a battle long in progress in order to tilt the scales, as was the case with our entry into World War I and World War II. It depends not only on our strength, but also on our ability to recognize aggression. In the nuclear age, by the time a threat has become unambiguous it may be too late to resist it.

Moreover, nuclear technology makes it possible, for the first time in history, to shift the balance of power solely through developments *within* the territory of another sovereign state. No conceivable acquisition of territory—

not even the occupation of Western Europe—could have affected the strategic balance as profoundly as did the Soviet success in ending our atomic monopoly. Had a power in the past sought to achieve a comparable strategic transformation through territorial expansion, war would have been the inevitable consequence. But because the growth of nuclear technology took place within sovereign territory, it produced an armaments race as a substitute for war. And immediately before us is the prospect of many other powers upsetting the strategic balance in this manner. Within another fifteen years the diffusion of nuclear technology will make inevitable the possession of nuclear weapons by many now secondary states.

Finally, as the power of weapons has increased, the forms of attack have multiplied, not only militarily, but also politically and psychologically. The age of the hydrogen bomb is also the age of internal subversion, of intervention by "volunteers," of domination through political and psychological warfare.

In such circumstances, our notion of aggression as an unambiguous act and our concept of war as inevitably an all-out struggle have made it difficult to come to grips with our perils. Because the consequences of our weapons technology are so fearsome, we have not found it easy to define a *casus belli* which would leave no doubt concerning our moral justification to use force. We have been clear that we would resist aggression, the goal of which we have identified with world domination, and our military policy has prescribed all-out war for meeting this contingency. But, faced with the implications of our power, we have had to learn that world domination need not be aimed at directly by means of final showdown. Even Hitler's attack on the international order took the form of such issues as his claims to Danzig and the Polish Corridor, which at the time seemed to the United States not to warrant embarking on war. In the face of the methodical, almost imperceptible advances of the Kremlin, subtly adjusted so that no one of its individual steps seems "worth" an all-out war, it has become even more apparent that resistance to aggression depends importantly on the price that must be paid. The dilemma of our postwar policy can be described as the quest for the "pure" case of aggression, in which our military doctrine, the provocation and our principles would be in harmony.

We have, therefore, been vulnerable to Soviet maneuvers in two ways. Because we have considered the advantage of peace so self-evident, we have been tempted to treat each act of Soviet intransigence as if it were caused by a misunderstanding of our intentions or else by the malevolence of an individual. There is a measure of pathos in our continued efforts to discover "reasonable" motives for the Soviet leaders to cease being Bolsheviks: the opportunities to develop the resources of their own country, the unlimited possibilities of nuclear energy, or the advantages of expanding international trade. The Kremlin has been able to exploit this attitude by periodically launching policies of "peaceful coexistence," which inevitably raised the debate whether a "fundamental" shift has occurred in Soviet purposes, thus lulling us before the next onslaught. On the other hand, because our strategic doctrine recognized few intermediate points between total war and total peace, we have found it difficult, during periods of Soviet belligerency, to bring the risks of resistance into relationship with the issues which have actually been at stake.

Much has been made of the "nuclear stalemate" which is supposed to have come about with the development by the Soviet Union of thermonuclear weapons and a long-range air force to deliver them. But so far as the effect on our national policy is concerned, the stalemate is nothing new. In fact, it has been with us ever since the explosions over Hiroshima and Nagasaki. To be sure, in the first postwar years it was not a physical stalemate. For nearly a decade the United States was virtually immune to Soviet retaliation. It was a stalemate, none the less, in the sense that we never succeeded in translating our military superiority into a political advantage. This was due to many factors: a theory of war based on the necessity of total victory, the memory of the wartime alliance with the Soviet Union, humanitarian impulses, lack of clarity about the process in which we found ourselves involved. Whatever the reason, our atomic monopoly had at best a deterrent effect. While it may have prevented a further expansion of the Soviet sphere, it did not enable us to achieve a strategic transformation in our favor. Indeed, even its importance as a deterrent is questionable. Assuming that there had never been an atomic bomb, would we really have acquiesced in a Soviet occupation of all of Europe? And would the Kremlin have risked a general war so soon after having suffered large-scale devastation by the Germans and having lost, by the most conservative estimate, ten million dead? Not even a dictatorship can do everything simultaneously.

Apart from the questionable assumption that an all-out war was prevented by our atomic monopoly, the decade witnessed the consolidation of Soviet control over the satellite orbit in Eastern Europe, the triumph of communism in China and, most fundamental of all, the growth of the Soviet atomic stockpile. Those who think that the problems of the nuclear period are primarily technical would therefore do well to study American reactions after Nagasaki and Hiroshima. No foreseeable technological breakthrough is likely to be more fundamental than our discovery of the atomic bomb. Yet possession of it did not enable us to prevent a hostile power from expanding its orbit and developing a capability to inflict a mortal blow on the United States.

How did this come about? Primarily because we added the atomic bomb to our arsenal without integrating its implications into our thinking. Because we saw it merely as another tool in a concept of warfare which knew no goal save total victory, and no mode of war except all-out war.

The notion that war and peace, military and political goals, were separate and opposite had become so commonplace in our strategic doctrine by the end of World War II that the most powerful nation in the world found itself hamstrung by its inability to adjust its political aims to the risks of the nuclear period. In every concrete instance, even in the matter of the regulation of the atom which affected our very survival, we found ourselves stalemated by our preconceptions. The consequences of military

actions which seemed open to us always appeared to out-
balance the gains to be achieved. Thus our policy became
entirely defensive. We possessed a doctrine to repel overt
aggression, but we could not translate it into a strategy
for achieving positive goals. Even in the one instance
where we resisted aggression by military power, we did
not use the weapons around which our whole military
planning had been built. The gap between military and
national policy was complete. Our power was not commensurate with the objectives of our national policy, and
our military doctrine could not find any intermediate application for the new weapons. The growth of the Soviet
atomic stockpile has merely brought the physical equation
into line with the psychological one; it has increased our
reluctance to engage in war even more. It has not, however, changed the fundamental question of how our political and military doctrines can be harmonized, how our
power can give impetus to our policy rather than paralyze
it.

III

Perhaps this quandary is inherent in the new weapons
themselves, rather than in the strategic doctrine? In the
face of the horrors of nuclear war, perhaps force has ceased
to be an instrument of policy save for the most naked
issue of national survival? Here it may be useful to touch
on some of the fundamental characteristics of the new
technology.

Nuclear weapons, only a short decade ago a difficult and
delicate engineering feat, have now become plentiful.
They can be produced in all sizes, from weapons of a fraction of the explosive power of the bombs used over Hiroshima and Nagasaki, to thermonuclear devices (popularly
called H-bombs) which represent the same increase of explosive power over the Hiroshima bomb as the original
atomic bomb did over the largest "blockbusters" of World
War II: a thousandfold increase. The Hiroshima and
Nagasaki bombs had an explosive equivalent of 20 thousand tons TNT (20 kilotons). Today "tactical" nuclear
weapons as small as 100 tons of TNT equivalent have

been developed. Thermonuclear devices exist which have an explosive equivalent of 20 million tons of TNT (20 megatons), and there is no upper limit: thermonuclear and nuclear weapons can be made of any desired explosive power.

Moreover, there is no "secret" about the manufacture of nuclear weapons or even of thermonuclear devices. Given a certain level of technology, any industrialized state will be able to produce them. With the spread of the peaceful uses of atomic energy, it can be expected that many secondary powers will enter the nuclear race by either making their own weapons or purchasing them from the constantly growing list of countries which will possess a nuclear armaments industry. For better or for worse, strategy must henceforth be charted against the ominous assumption that any war is likely to be a nuclear war.

And the new technology *is* awesome. The lethal radius of the weapons dropped over Hiroshima and Nagasaki—the area within which destruction was total and the proportion of fatalities was in excess of 75 per cent—was 1½ miles. Their blast and heat effects destroyed or set fire to buildings within a radius of another 4.4 square miles in Hiroshima and 1.8 square miles in Nagasaki. The explosions of the first atomic bombs killed between 70 thousand and 80 thousand in Hiroshima and 35 thousand in Nagasaki; the direct injuries were between 100 thousand and 180 thousand in Hiroshima and between 50 thousand and 100 thousand in Nagasaki. The collateral effects of radiation may not become fully apparent for several decades.

For all their horror the atom bombs dropped on the two Japanese cities were puny compared to present weapons. The damage they caused was restricted to a relatively small area, and even the effects of radiation were generally confined to the area covered by heat and blast damage. The thermonuclear weapons, on the other hand, do not possess this relative measure of discrimination. Theoretically, their explosive power is unlimited. A 20 megaton weapon, which is easily within the range of our capabilities and will soon be within that of the Soviet Union, has a lethal radius of 8 miles; its area of total destruction is 48 square miles.[3] Within that area at least 75 per cent of the population would be killed and all the remainder severely injured.

Nor are the damage and casualties exhausted by the direct effects. If it touches the ground, the fireball of a megaton weapon sucks up particles of earth and buildings and deposits them downwind as radioactive material. Depending on meteorological conditions, the radioactive fall-out may cover an area of 10,000 square miles or a territory larger than the state of New Jersey. A successful attack on fifty of the most important metropolitan areas of the United States would thus bring under fire 40 per cent of our population, 50 per cent of our key facilities and 60 per cent of our industry.[4]

At this scale of catastrophe, it is clear that the nature of war has altered. Our traditional insistence on reserving our military effort for an unambiguous threat and then going all-out to defeat the enemy may lead to paralysis when total war augurs social disintegration even for the victor. During the period of our atomic monopoly, it was possible to rely on our nuclear stockpile to deter all forms of aggression because we could inflict punishment without fear of retaliation. But in the face of the new-found Soviet capability to inflict devastating damage on the United States, our reluctance to engage in an all-out war is certain to increase. To be sure, we shall continue to insist that we reject the notion of "peace at any price." The price of peace, however, cannot be determined in the abstract. The growth of the Soviet nuclear stockpile is certain to widen the line between what is considered "vital" and what is "peripheral" if we must weigh each objective against the destruction of New York or Detroit, of Los Angeles or Chicago.

It can be argued that the fear of all-out war is bound

---

[3] U.S. Senate, *Study of Airpower,* Hearings before the Subcommittee on the Air Force of the Committee on Armed Services, 84th Cong., 2nd Sess. (Washington: GPO, 1956), p. 900.

[4] Same, p. 307 (testimony of General Earle E. Partridge). For a fuller discussion of the effects of weapons and their implications, see below, Chapter 3.

to be mutual, that the Soviet leaders will, therefore, share our reluctance to engage in any adventures which may involve this risk. But because each side may be equally deterred from engaging in all-out war, it makes all the difference which side can extricate itself from its dilemma *only* by initiating such a struggle. If the Soviet bloc can present its challenges in less than all-out form it may gain a crucial advantage. Every move on its part will then pose the appalling dilemma of whether we are willing to commit suicide to prevent encroachments, which do not, each in itself, seem to threaten our existence directly but which may be steps on the road to our ultimate destruction.

The growing Soviet nuclear stockpile, coupled with the diversification of nuclear technology, places precisely this possibility in the hands of the Soviet leadership. It can engage in military actions ranging from the employment of conventional forces to the use of "tactical" nuclear weapons of a size which will raise serious doubt as to whether they "warrant" the resort to all-out war. Every Soviet move of this nature will provide us with an incentive to defer a showdown to a more propitious moment or to a clearer provocation. An all-or-nothing military policy will, therefore, play into the hands of the Soviet strategy of ambiguity which seeks to upset the strategic balance by small degrees and which combines political, psychological and military pressures to induce the greatest degree of uncertainty and hesitation in the minds of the opponent. Moreover, to the extent that we become dependent on the most absolute applications of our power, even the secondary states may be able to blackmail us: because the force suitable for an all-out war is not really designed for dealing with local wars, or because we will be inhibited from using it by the fear of its impact on world opinion.

The attempt to develop a doctrine for a more flexible application of our power is inhibited by many factors, however, the chief of which is the very technological race which makes it necessary. Were technology stable, an equilibrium might come about between the power of the new weapons and the fear of their consequences. Technology is far

from stable, however; it is advancing at a constantly accelerating rate. Almost up to the outbreak of World War
II, a weapons system would be good for a generation at
least. In 1939 the equipment of a United States rifle
company hardly differed from its predecessor in 1918.
Today a weapons system begins to be obsolescent
when it has barely gone into production. The B-17 Flying
Fortress of World War II remained in operational use for
a decade; the B-36 intercontinental bomber was obsolescent within less than seven years; and the B-52 heavy jet
bomber, the most recent addition to our strategic striking
force, will probably be outdated within five years. As
weapons must be replaced at ever shorter intervals, their
complexity increases. The F-51, a late World War II fighter
plane, required 154 thousand engineering man-hours to
build and cost $21,000; the F-100, its 1957 equivalent, re-
quires 404 thousand engineering man-hours and costs
$486,000 to perform a similar strategic mission.[5]

The technological race also multiplies the choices which
must be made by the military services. As late as World
War II, at most two or three weapons systems were available for each service. In the 1950's, the number has risen
to scores of different types, each with differing characteristics and implying differing strategies. By the 1960's,
choices will have to be made among hundreds of weapons
systems. Moreover, each choice permits a wide variety of
combinations, so that the number of conceivable weapons
systems reaches fantastic figures.

The obverse of this multiplicity of choices is an unparalleled specialization of functions. Traditionally, weapons
which were useful for offense were broadly useful for defense as well. Today this equation no longer holds true to
the same extent. A superior tank could dominate the battlefield, but a superior bomber does not necessarily dominate the skies. For bombers do not fight each other. Their
performances can be compared only in terms of their ability to reach their target and this depends on superiority
vis-à-vis the opposing defensive system. The test of a mod-

[5] Same, p. 549 (Lieutenant General Donald L. Putt).

ern weapon is not so much whether it is better than its equivalent on the other side, but whether it can perform its strategic mission. The victim of an H-bomb will find small consolation in the knowledge that the delivery system which dropped it was inferior to that of his own country. If two hostile bomber fleets pass each other in the sky, the superior performance of one will be meaningless if both are able to reach their targets.

This is not to argue that we can afford to fall behind in the technological race. It is simply to emphasize the complexity of the current strategic problem. The technological race is not between weapons which have the same mission; rather it is between offensive and defensive capabilities. And because the offensive and defensive weapons systems have different characteristics, one of the most important problems for strategy is to decide on the relative emphasis to be given to each and on the "mix" which will provide the greatest flexibility.

In these circumstances it is not surprising that there exists more concern with technology than with doctrine. The penalty for miscalculation in the technical field is obvious and demonstrable. The penalty for falling behind in the field of strategic doctrine, though catastrophic, is not immediately discernible. Mastering the technical problems is so difficult that it leaves little time for considering the strategic implications of the new technology. It gives rise to the notion that strategy is identical with the technical analysis of weapons systems, obscuring the fact that both the development and the use of weapons systems are impossible without strategic doctrine.

Strategy cannot avoid the problems of the nuclear age by identifying military policy with the maximum development of power, for with modern technology such a course must paralyze the will. In the nuclear age, flexibility depends on the ability to meet the whole spectrum of possible challenges and not only the most absolute one. To be sure, the first charge on our resources must be the capability for waging all-out war, because without it we would be at the mercy of the Soviet rulers. But, while our strategic striking power represents the condition which makes

possible all other measures, it cannot be the exclusive preoccupation of our military planning. Given the power of
modern weapons, it should be the task of our strategic
doctrine to create alternatives less cataclysmic than a
thermonuclear holocaust.

Whether strategy gives an impetus to policy or inhibits
it depends, therefore, on the alternatives which it presents
to the policy-makers. In 1936, the French General Staff
possessed no doctrine for any conflict except all-out war,
and it believed in no strategy save the defensive. It failed
to provide against strategic transformations which stopped
short of violating the boundaries of France. Nor did it anticipate that the strategic balance might be upset by small
stages, each of which, in itself, did not seem "worth" all-
out war. As a result, when Hitler remilitarized the Rhineland, French leadership was paralyzed. It recoiled before
the consequences of full mobilization, but its strategic doctrine provided for no other military measures. Faced with
the prospect of all-out war and obsessed by the memory of
1914, France could not decide whether to rely on Germany's professions of peaceful intent or on its own military
strength. In order to justify its vacillations, the French
General Staff ascribed to Germany a military capability
it did not possess. By adjusting its estimates of the enemy
strength to its strategic doctrine, instead of the reverse, the
French General Staff vindicated its theory of all-out war,
the very war which the country dreaded and which France
was unable to wage except with allies that proved reluctant
or ill-prepared. Finally, torn between its premonitions
of disaster and the inhibitions produced by its strategic
doctrine, France recoiled before the alternatives presented
by its strategic doctrine. Instead, it sought refuge in yet
another guarantee of its frontiers, which substituted a legal
for a physical safeguard and contributed to France's sense
of impotence even while its Army was still thought to be
the world's finest. Only four years later, when France faced
the unambiguous aggression for which French strategic
doctrine had provided, the attack, even then, was not directed at the Maginot line on which France had expended

so many resources. The penalty for doctrinal rigidity was military catastrophe.[6]

The basic challenge to United States strategy is to formulate a military policy which will avoid this very dilemma. Simply because we are strongest in strategic striking power, we cannot base all our plans on the assumption that war, if it comes, will be inevitably all-out. We must strive for a strategic doctrine which gives our diplomacy the greatest freedom of action and which addresses itself to the question of whether the nuclear age presents only risks, or whether it does not also offer opportunities.

This is a complex task, different from any before in our history. For there is little experience to guide us. The theory we develop will determine our response to the challenges which will inevitably confront us. The Soviet capability to inflict a catastrophic blow on the United States is increasing year by year, and just beyond the horizon lies the prospect of a world in which not only two superpowers will possess nuclear weapons, but also many weaker, and perhaps more irresponsible nations, with less to lose.

However complex the task, the test of our strategic doctrine will be its ability to meet it. History will not excuse the inadequacy of the response by the enormity of the challenge. Our past invulnerability has fostered the illusion that there are "purely" military answers to the problems of our security and that policy ends where strategy begins. But the luxury of such an approach ended with our atomic monopoly. Henceforth, our problem will be one long familiar to less favored nations: how to relate the desirable to the possible and above all how to live with possible catastrophe.

---

[6] For a splendid discussion of the interplay between the French General Staff and the Foreign Office in 1936, see B. A. C. Parker, "The First Capitulation: France and the Rhineland Crisis of 1936," *World Politics*, v. 8 (April 1956), pp. 355-73.

2

THE DILEMMA OF AMERICAN SECURITY

ONE OF THE MOST difficult challenges a nation confronts is to interpret correctly the lessons of its past. For the lessons of history, as of all experience, are contingent: they teach the consequences of certain actions, but they leave to each generation the task of determining which situations are comparable. So long as development is gradual, no particular problem arises. New problems will be sufficiently similar to past experience so that even inaccurate analogies will have a certain validity. It is different, however, when events occur which transcend all past experience. Then the very success of the past may inhibit an understanding of the present. An era of unparalleled success may make it difficult to come to grips with a period of possible disaster. The fact that every problem has found a final solution in the past may stand in the way of the realization that henceforth only partial remedies are possible.

This has been the problem which has haunted American military thinking since World War II. Its dilemma can be defined as the conflict between the quest for absolute answers and the risks of the nuclear age, between the realization that we have become infinitely vulnerable and our rebellion against it.

Because we have won two world wars by outproducing our opponent, we have tended to equate military superiority with superiority in resources and technology. Yet history demonstrates that superiority in strategic doctrine has been the source of victory at least as often as superiority in resources. In 1940 superior doctrine enabled the Germans to defeat an allied army superior in numbers, at least equal in equipment, but wedded to an outmoded concept of warfare. Superior mobility and superior use of artillery, a better relationship between fire and movement, provided the basis of Napoleon's victories. Similar examples were the victories of the Roman legions over the Macedonian phalanx, of the English archers against the medieval knights. All these were victories not of resources but of strategic doctrine: the ability to break the framework which had come to be taken for granted and to make the victory all the more complete by confronting the antagonist with contingencies which he had never even considered.

Thus the key to a proper doctrine is the correct understanding of the elements of one's superiority, and the ability to apply them more rapidly than the opponent, whether through the choice of an advantageous battlefield or through the superior utilization of available weapons systems.

Our effort to assess the meaning of the new technology has been difficult, however, because our history makes us more comfortable with technology than with doctrine and because such strategic doctrine as we *had* developed has been made irrelevant by the power and speed of the new weapons. The traditional expression of our strategic doctrine was the allocation of roles and missions among the military services—until the end of World War II, the Army and the Navy. Each of these services had the mission of defeating its enemy counterpart: the Army had primary responsibility for the land battle and the Navy for control of the seas. Although these missions were based, in effect, on means of locomotion with everything moving on land assigned to the Army and everything moving by water assigned to the Navy, they represented meaningful and distinguishable strategic tasks. The Army was powerless on the sea beyond the range of its coastal artillery, and the Navy was unable to project itself far inland. The Air Force was not yet independent, and the range of its planes was sufficiently short to permit the division of functions between the Navy and Army air arms to follow roughly that between the senior services. Each service was, therefore, able to control all the weapons it considered essential for achieving its mission. It could in effect develop its own strategy without too much concern with that of the sister service or without too much dependence on the interpretation of a sister service as to what constituted an essential target.

But the long-range airplane, the ballistic missile and the incomparable destructiveness of weapons have almost obliterated the traditional boundaries among the services. Today, no service can achieve its primary mission without either trespassing on the role of the other services or calling on them for assistance. And cooperation among the services is difficult unless there is an agreement on doctrine, the practical manifestation of which would be that all services hold the same view as to what constitutes an essential target. Is the sea controlled by bombing shipyards from carriers or by destroying the enemy's industrial potential? Is a land battle possible without having won air supremacy, and is it necessary after the air battle has been won?

So long as there is no agreed strategic doctrine, each service will give its own reply. And the reply will be an effort to treat new weapons by analogy to familiar functions: Are missiles analogous to artillery because they are fired like shells, or to aerial warfare because they fly through the air?—this is a bone of contention between the Army and the Air Force. Is the carrier a naval weapon or do the resources devoted to it detract from our long-range striking force?—this is the source of wrangling between the Navy and the Air Force. Is a 1,500-mile ballistic missile a tactical or strategic weapon? In the absence of a doctrinal answer, each service is pushing its own research in the hope that the service which develops a weapons system first will also control its use in combat.

This concern with the control of new weapons systems is the reverse side of the attempt to achieve a perfect division of functions. So long as each service has the primary mission of defeating its enemy counterpart, and so long as there does not exist an agreed strategic doctrine, no service can afford to relinquish control over a weapon which it considers essential for the performance of its mission. For the Navy's conception of what is essential to win control of the seas may conflict with the Air Force's notion of its requirements for winning the air battle. And in view of the necessity for quick reaction imposed by the increasing speed and power of modern weapons, each service will seek to escape this dilemma by hoarding as many weapons as possible. Thus the Army and the Navy are developing a 1,500-mile missile; the Navy is developing a long-range seaplane which our mechanistic approach to doctrine treats as a naval weapon because it takes off from water; and the Strategic Air Command is reported to have established a kind of ground force of its own to protect its air bases.

A duplication of weapons systems and a proliferation of partially conflicting doctrines is inevitable. The division of functions which worked relatively smoothly for a century and a half has become a source of bitter rivalry in the nuclear age. Each new weapon has led to a bitter wrangle as to which service should control it. It was thus with the A-bomb; it is now the case with missiles. And in each instance the doctrinal issue was evaded by permitting each service to develop its own weapon even if it duplicated the efforts of a sister service.

Such a solution is costly. It also defers coming to grips with the doctrinal problem until some crisis brooks no further ambiguity or until some other pressures bring the interservice dispute into the open. Thus the chief impetus to our strategic thought has come from international crises, particularly from the Korean war, and even more importantly from the periodic economy drives of the Administration and of the Congress. At intervals either the Executive or the Congress has proclaimed that bankruptcy was a more immediate threat than military defeat and that our economy would collapse under the burden of defense expenditures if they exceeded a theoretical ceiling variously estimated at $11 billion in 1946, $14.5 billion in 1949, and $35 billion in 1953.

Nothing has so stimulated strategic thought as these periodic economy drives. In a period of national emergency when budgets were plentiful, each service has protected itself by procuring the entire gamut of possible weapons, a course which, whatever the budgetary level, will soon be foreclosed by the extraordinary variety of possible choices. During periods of budgetary squeeze, each service must make a choice among the weapons systems available to it because it cannot afford them all and it can make this choice only in terms of a doctrine. When funds are scarce, each service faces the problem not only of establishing priorities among the weapons available to it, but of justifying its role vis-à-vis the other services. When the services become competitors for available appropriations, an incentive is provided for developing a doctrine about the purpose of war and about the contribution which each service can make to our security.

While budgetary pressures have spurred consideration of strategic doctrine, their influence has not been entirely wholesome. They have fostered a tendency to create doctrines as tools in the interservice battle for appropriations; the incentive they have provided is for a theoretical elaboration of a service view and not of an over-all doctrine. Moreover, the periodic economy drives have confirmed our predilection for final solutions. They have usually been justified with an argument well attuned to our national psychology: that the tremendous destructiveness of modern weapons makes a diversified capability unnecessary. Both the Army and the Navy have been victims of the argument, colloquially expressed as "more bang for a buck," the Navy in 1949, when its giant carrier, the "United States," was canceled by administrative fiat, and the Army since 1953. Only the Air Force has escaped an attack on its mission, if not always budgetary cuts. Alone among the services its Strategic Air Command has been able to maintain the "pure" doctrine, the secret dream of American military thought: that there exists a final answer to our military problem, that it is possible to defeat the enemy utterly, and that war has its own rationale independent of policy.

Because of their awareness that the budgetary rewards are in the field of strategic striking power, the other services have in turn been tempted to emphasize that part of their mission which approximates long-range warfare. In budgetary hearings, at least, the Navy has stressed the offensive power of its carriers over its less dramatic antisubmarine role, and since 1955 the Army has emphasized its medium-range missiles as much as the subtler applications of its power. This has set up another vicious circle. The more the other services have extended the range and power of their weapons, the more closely they have approached what the Air Force considers its primary mission, thus opening the way to endless jurisdictional disputes. In the process, the basic strategic problem of the nuclear age has rarely been faced up to explicitly: whether it is possible to find intermediate applications for our military strength; whether our strategic thinking can develop concepts of war which bring power into balance with the willingness to use it.

Against the background of interservice rivalry, the attempts to reconcile clashing views have resulted in instruments more akin to an agreement among sovereign states than to a workable doctrine. They have had the same vagueness, leaving each service free to interpret them largely according to its own preconceptions. The present assignment of roles and missions among the services dates from 1948, when Secretary James Forrestal took the Joint Chiefs of Staff to Key West in order to formulate common doctrine. What emerged as the Key West agreement was little more than a reformulation of traditional roles. The primary mission of the Air Force was restated to be control of the air, that of the Navy control of the seas, and that of the Army to defeat the enemy ground forces. This formula missed the essential point of interservice rivalry, perhaps deliberately. The disputes have arisen not because the services have sought to take over each other's primary mission—although this too has happened occasionally—but because in pursuit of their *own* missions they have been impelled by the conflicting pressures of technology and of budget-making into developing overlapping weapons systems. The real difficulty has been that the power, speed and range of modern weapons have obliterated the traditional distinctions between ground, sea and air warfare. It is no longer possible to define a distinguishable strategic mission on the criterion of different means of locomotion.

As a result, the Key West agreement could receive concrete meaning only in terms of the dispute that had produced the interservice wrangling in the first place: the disagreement over which service should control the nuclear weapons. This was an important issue because possession of nuclear weapons was the prerequisite to any claim to be able to contribute to the strategy of an all-out war and was, therefore, the best support for budgetary requests. The upshot was a compromise which demonstrated that the neat distinctions set forth in the general principles of the Key West agreement were inapplicable in practice: the Air Force was recognized as possessing the sole right to maintain a strategic air arm, but the Navy was granted the use of the A-bomb against specifically naval targets. It was also permitted to proceed with the construction of its giant aircraft-carrier, designed to handle planes capable of carrying the A-bomb. No effort was made to define what constituted a "naval" target or to distinguish the use of atomic bombs against port facilities from strategic bombing. And, like many diplomatic instruments, the Key West agreement contained an unwritten understanding—the concept of balanced forces, in which significantly the balance was achieved not by doctrine but by the budget: each service was promised approximately the same yearly appropriation. In short, the Key West agreement had not been the expression of a strategic doctrine but a way to postpone difficult choices.

Within eighteen months even the vague division of functions established by the Key West agreement had disappeared in the explosion produced by the "revolt of the admirals" against Secretary Louis A. Johnson's edict canceling the construction of the giant carrier. And within another year, the Korean war revealed that our almost exclusive concern with all-out war and with the most de-

structive type of strategy had obscured the most likely
security problem: the attempt by the Soviet leaders to
upset the strategic balance, not at one blow, but piecemeal.

Most of these rivalries and frustrations have found their
expression at some time in hearings before Congressional
committees. Impelled by the need to justify their requests
for appropriations, to vindicate the mission of their service, or to explain the conduct of a war, the service chiefs
and their civilian superiors have found themselves obliged
to engage in a theoretical defense of their positions. While
they may not always have given public expression to the
full range of their views, their statements do permit a brief
survey of the dilemmas of developing a strategic doctrine
adequate to the challenges of the nuclear age. It is with
this quest for doctrine that this chapter deals.

II

It has often been remarked that nothing stultifies military thought so much as a victorious war, for innovation
then must run the gamut of inertia legitimized by success.
It was no different with United States military thought
after World War II. The war had not only been won, but
its course had run true to our notion of what a war should
be. The aggression had been unambiguous and had been
directed against United States territory. We had brought to
bear our superior resources and inflicted a terrible ret-
ribution. The enemy had been utterly defeated by a
strategy of attrition unencumbered by political considerations. No wonder that we tended to elevate a particular
set of circumstances into general maxims and to turn the
strategy applied in defeating Germany and Japan into
universal military doctrine. "In case of another major
war," testified Lieutenant General Raymond S. McLain
in defense of the Army appropriation for 1948, "the pattern would probably take the following form: First
the blitz, using all modern means. If this should succeed,
the war would be over. . . . If the blitz, however, is
stopped the second phase would be a softening-up phase

in which bases, industries, and ports would be bombarded. The final phase would be a struggle between complete teams, air, sea, and ground, in which the accompanying attrition would finally point to the victor." [1]

Thus, whatever the technological transformations of the postwar period, we sought to fit them into a concept of war which we had perhaps learned too well. Our strategy was based on resisting an overt attack; its political corollary of what might constitute on overt attack was rarely analyzed. The lessons of the two world wars had convinced us that we would have to resist a military onslaught against Western Europe. "The first line of defense," said Secretary Dean Acheson, "is still in Europe." [2] Beyond this, our consideration of the strategic shifts which we would resist by force was inhibited by a doctrine which left no room for intermediate positions between total peace and total war. In fact, because we thought of any war as inevitably all-out, we tended, with every increase in the horror of our advancing weapons technology, to define in more and more drastic terms the provocation considered necessary for us to go to war. Instead of adjusting our capabilities to the likely challenges, we tended to adjust our concept of the likely challenges to the enormity of the new weapons. ". . . any aggressor nation seeking domination of the earth," said General Dwight D. Eisenhower in 1947, "must defeat the United States and must defeat us before we can achieve our maximum strength. Therefore, if global war comes to us again, the first blow will be struck not at Warsaw but at Washington; not at London but at Los Angeles; not even at Pearl Harbor but at Pittsburgh." [3] "It is inconceivable," said Major General Otto P. Weyland, "that the United States will start an aggressive war. Hence, it is obvious that at the start of a war, we will be the recipient of an all-out

---

[1] U.S. House, *Military Establishment Appropriation Bill for 1948*, Hearings before the Subcommittee of the Committee on Appropriations, 80th Cong., 1st Sess. (Washington: GPO, 1947), p. 1,241.

[2] U.S. Senate, *Military Assistance Program*, Joint Hearings before the Committee on Foreign Relations and the Committee on Armed Services, 81st Cong., 1st Sess. (Washington: GPO, 1949), p. 7.

[3] U.S. House, *Military Establishment Appropriation Bill for 1948*, cited, p. 77.

surprise attack. From the air, such an attack will be against the industry and economy of the continental United States." [4]

The notion that a new war would inevitably start with a surprise attack on the United States has been basic to postwar United States strategic thought. Reinforced by the memory of Pearl Harbor, it has provided the background for our preponderant concern with the problem of all-out war. Thus a vicious circle has been set up. The more total the sanctions of our weapons technology have become, the more absolute we have imagined the provocation that would alone justify unleashing it. The more we have become convinced that a war would start with an attack on the continental United States, the more fearsome the strategy we have devised to resist it. In the process, we have not realized how abstract and one-sided the notion of a surprise attack has been, particularly at a time when the Soviet Union possessed neither a nuclear arsenal nor a long-range air force. We have failed to see how vulnerable it has left us to the preferred form of Soviet aggression: internal subversion and limited war. By concentrating on measures to defeat a Soviet attempt to neutralize us physically, we have given the Soviet leadership an opportunity to strive to neutralize us psychologically by so graduating their actions that the provocation would never seem "worth" an all-out war, the only form of war our doctrine took into account.

If our military doctrine in the immediate postwar period had difficulty in coming to grips with our most likely dangers, it had few doubts about the strategy for conducting any war that might break out. A war would be global and it would be won by our superior industrial potential.[5] Since war would start with a surprise attack, our best defense lay in "our ability to strike back quickly with a counteroffensive, to neutralize the hostile attack at its

4 Same, p. 642.

5 Among many examples, see the Forrestal testimony in the *National Defense Establishment—Unification of the Armed Services*, Hearings before the Committee on Armed Services, U.S. Senate, 80th Cong., 1st Sess. (Washington: GPO, 1947), p. 21 ff.

source . . . by striking at the vitals of the aggressor." [6] The doctrine of massive retaliation was far from new at the time Secretary John Foster Dulles proclaimed it.

The postulate that deterrence was to be achieved by strategic striking power and that victory depended on inflicting maximum destruction on the aggressor was never questioned. On the contrary, each service justified its requirements by the contribution it could make to a strategy of strategic bombing. ". . . at the beginning of hostilities," said Secretary of the Navy John L. Sullivan in 1948, "and until the Air Force could acquire operating bases within flying range of the enemy we must fight with whatever we have. In such a situation carrier-based Navy air[craft] could and would deliver attacks that would certainly slow up an enemy attack upon our homeland and might throw that attack off-balance." [7] "Plans for the national security," said General Omar N. Bradley in 1948, "must consider the possibility that the United States will be subject to air and air-borne attack at the outset. The likelihood and the practicability of this kind of attack increases daily. . . . We would [therefore] have to immediately secure bases from which an enemy might attack us by air. Next we will have to launch an immediate counterattack . . . predominantly through the air. . . . To make our counterblows we will need bases which we do not have now. The seizing and holding of [these] bases . . . will require Army combat elements. . . . Lastly comes the phase of total mobilization and maximum offensive efforts. In conjunction with the air and naval arms, the Army will engage in joint operations designed to carry the war to the enemy with ever-increasing intensity. The closer we get to the enemy, the more determined will be his resistance. . . ." [8] Even our

6 General Carl Spaatz before the Subcommittee of the Committee on Appropriations, *Military Establishment Appropriation Bill for 1947*, U.S. House, 79th Cong., 2nd Sess. (Washington: GPO, 1946), p. 402.

7 U.S. House, *Department of the Navy Appropriation Bill for 1949*, Hearings before the Subcommittee of the Committee on Appropriations, 80th Cong., 2nd Sess. (Washington: GPO, 1948), p. 6.

8 U.S. House, *Military Functions, National Military Establishment Appropriation for 1949*, Hearings before the Subcommittee of the Committee on Appropriations, 80th Cong., 2nd Sess. (Washington: GPO, 1948), pp. 3-4.

alliances were justified primarily in terms of the air bases they afforded us.

Thus the strategy developed in the immediate postwar period did not depend on nuclear weapons. Rather it added them almost as an afterthought to a familiar military doctrine, as a more efficient explosive to destroy enemy industrial centers. There were several reasons for this: a feeling of moral revulsion about the destructiveness of nuclear weapons, a fear that the weapons, if flaunted, would make an understanding with the U.S.S.R. more difficult, and real uncertainty about the meaning of the new technology. Above all, the nuclear weapons were taken as another indication of our inherent technological superiority. At least subconsciously, it was felt that as long as we retained our atomic monopoly, we could not possibly be faced with an overt challenge.

There was, to be sure, an awareness that our monopoly would be fleeting. But there was also an air of unreality about these prophecies. In 1945 it was said that the Soviet Union would break our atomic monopoly within five years, and the prediction remained the same with each passing year.[9] Hanson Baldwin estimated in 1947 that the Soviet Union would produce one atomic bomb some time between 1950 and 1957, that it would then take it another twenty years to build up a significant stockpile, and that in any case the U.S.S.R. was not likely to develop a delivery system for a long time.[10] These views reflected the realities of the national psychology, if not necessarily the intelligence reports. (On the other hand, intelligence estimates often exaggerate perils because their author is not likely to get into difficulties if a pessimistic prediction turns out wrong.)

Our complacency with respect to Soviet progress in the nuclear field, coupled with the notion that war was likely to start with a surprise attack on us, lent a quality of abstractness and unreality to all thinking about military

---

[9] See testimony by Dr. Isidor I. Rabi, *In the Matter of J. Robert Oppenheimer*, Transcript of Hearing before Personnel Security Board (Washington: GPO, 1954), p. 452 ff.

[10] *New York Times*, November 9, 1947.

problems in the immediate postwar period. It gave rise to this syllogism, psychologically, if not actually: (1) War must start with a surprise attack; (2) the Soviet Union will not possess an atomic capability for a long time; (3) therefore, there will not be a war.

As a result, our thinking about nuclear weapons oscillated between exaggerating their horror (which was to some extent reassuring) and underrating their strategic significance. The latter was particularly noticeable among the traditional services which were afraid that their roles would be impaired by the new technology. In 1947 the Army and the Navy made known their assessment of the impact of the new weapons on strategy.[11] Both insisted that nuclear weapons had not made their services dispensable. They maintained that although our best strategy involved the nuclear bombardment of the enemy's industrial potential, each service had a role to play in this task—the Navy that of precision bombing and projecting our power visibly, the Army through holding and garrisoning the bases from which strategic strikes could be launched. Both services assumed a prolonged period of nuclear monopoly; the Army statement thought it would last from between eight to fifteen years. Neither service considered that nuclear weapons would affect its tactics fundamentally. The Navy, in particular, deprecated the implications of the new technology. A 1,000-mile missile, it argued, was almost impossible. Such a weapon did not simply represent an extension of the German experience with rockets in World War II, but required an altogether new order of physics. This merely repeated a statement previously made by Admiral Chester W. Nimitz that he did not expect to see intercontinental ballistic missiles in his lifetime.[12] In short, for the next ten to

---

11 See "Navy Department Thinking on the Atomic Bomb," *Bulletin of the Atomic Scientists*, v. 3 (July 1947), p. 177 ff.; "War Department Thinking on the Atomic Bomb," *Bulletin of the Atomic Scientists*, v. 3 (June 1947), p. 150 ff. These statements were written by Bernard Brodie but cleared with responsible officials in each department.

12 U.S. Senate, *Navy Department Appropriation Bill for 1948*, Hearings before the Subcommittee of the Committee on Appropriations, 80th Cong., 1st Sess. (Washington: GPO, 1947), p. 5.

fifteen years any new war would not only be fought with a World War II strategy, but with World War II weapons, with the atomic bomb merely added to increase the power of our strategic arsenal.[13]

Had technology remained static and had we not been challenged in Korea, an uneasy equilibrium might have been established between the claim of the Air Force that it possessed the decisive weapon and that of the other services that they were essential to make this weapon effective. But the advent of the long-range bomber, the B-36, upset the finely wrought concept of the "balanced forces" which permitted each service to do what it had always done, only with more powerful weapons. For, if deterrence was to be achieved by retaliatory power and if retaliatory power was identical with offensive air power, the only justification for the other services was their utility in providing or holding air bases. But if it was possible to launch long-range attacks from the United States, the doctrine of balanced forces might represent a diversion of resources.

Had defense appropriations been larger, this argument might not have been pressed to its logical conclusion. But with a new Secretary of Defense, Louis Johnson, convinced that one of Stalin's aims was to induce the United States to spend itself into bankruptcy,[14] the allocation of missions and with it the availability of scarce defense dollars became a matter of overriding concern. When the Defense Department stopped the construction of the Navy's 65,000-ton aircraft-carrier "United States" and ordered the procurement of additional B-36 bombers, the first important postwar debate on strategic doctrine was inevitable. No longer restrained by an uneasy partnership with the Air Force in the possession of long-range air power, the Navy now gave full expression to the disagreement among the services over the nature of strategy, the

---

13 Statement by Rear Admiral A. G. Noble, U.S. House, *Department of the Navy Appropriation Bill for 1949,* cited, p. 743. Many similar statements were made by other Army and Navy spokesmen.

14 U.S. Senate, *Military Situation in the Far East,* Hearings before the Committee on Armed Services and the Committee on Foreign Relations, 82nd Cong., 1st Sess. (Washington: GPO, 1951), pp. 2,626-7.

definition of essential targets, and the best means for attacking them.

The debate over the B-36 would have taken on added significance had it not been bound up so intimately with the battle for appropriations. As matters stood, the Navy's case, which attacked the efficacy of strategic bombing, gave the impression of having been constructed out of pique at the decision to end its equivalent of long-range aviation, the giant carrier "United States." And the Navy's case was further weakened by the fact that the Chief of Naval Operations had not dissented from any of the formulations of strategic doctrine during the postwar period. Nevertheless, the Navy case, ably marshaled by Admiral Arthur W. Radford, for the first time raised issues which have become the core of present disputes about military policy. It attacked the notion of a quick war to be won by air power alone. It emphasized the importance of working out the relationship between military and political objectives, and it rejected the doctrine that a massive retaliatory attack represents our primary deterrent. "One member of the defense team in one branch of the Government asserts," said Admiral Radford, "that the best guaranty for America's security lies first in preventing war by the threat of atomic annihilation, and second in prosecuting such a war of annihilation if we have to fight. . . . This theory of warfare is not generally concurred in, I believe, by military men. Aside from any moral or political considerations. . . . many reject the theory on the grounds that it will fail to bring victory. . . . [Moreover], future war will extend far beyond the province of the military. In planning to wage a war . . . we must look to the peace to follow. . . . A war of annihilation might possibly bring a Pyrrhic military victory, but it would be politically and economically senseless. . . . the results of two world wars have demonstrated the fact that victory in war is not an end in itself." [15]

---

[15] U.S. House, *The National Defense Program—Unification and Strategy,* Hearings before the Committee on Armed Services, 81st Cong., 1st Sess. (Washington: GPO, 1949), pp. 50-1. (Will be referred to as B-36 hearings.) See also subsequent statements by Admirals Ralph A. Ofstie, William H. P. Blandy, Chester W. Nimitz, Ernest J. King, Louis E. Denfeld.

In the process, the Navy brought into the open for the first time the inadequacies of our method of arriving at strategic decisions. According to this procedure, three service chiefs, whose primary task is the maintenance of the morale and efficiency of their respective services are also required to make over-all strategic judgments which may well run counter to their basic task. As long as the views of the three services on the most effective strategy are in accord, this presents few problems. If they are at variance—as they have been since 1949—only two solutions are possible. In periods of budgetary plenty, as between 1951 and 1954, each service will build up the weapons systems it considers appropriate for its mission without a too careful concern with doctrinal harmony or overlapping functions. In periods of relative budgetary scarcity, it will lead to bitter rivalry over the assignment of missions. And since the presentation of a budget is facilitated by maintaining the *appearance* of interservice harmony, there usually occurs just enough compromise to prevent a resolution of the doctrinal conflict. The necessity of fighting doctrinal battles at intervals set by the budgetary process, with appropriations as the prize, almost insures the perpetuation of the doctrinal disagreements behind the scenes.

To be sure, the "revolt of the admirals" did no more than raise these issues, and the proposed solutions were not adequate to the boldness of the challenge. They demonstrated that the Navy's disagreement was not so much with doctrine as with the technical implementation of a strategy which could not envisage any form of conflict short of all-out war. The Navy had posed the question of the relationship between political and military objectives, but not because it doubted that every war would be a war of unconditional surrender. Rather, it insisted that unconditional surrender should be achieved by a strategy which did not inflict so much devastation that the victor would be forced to rehabilitate occupied enemy territory. It raised for the first time the issue whether our strategy should be nuclear or conventional, and it opposed what it considered the overemphasis on strategic air power. But it did so primarily because carrier planes were said to be able to perform the same missions more effectively and more economically. The B-36 was termed a billion-dollar blunder, but only because Navy fighters and therefore presumably the Soviet defense could outmaneuver it.

The B-36 controversy thus only hinted at the outline of the American strategic dilemma. Our military policy was directed to only two contingencies: a direct attack on the United States and a direct attack on Western Europe. It offered no solutions either to Soviet moves in other areas or to the gradual overturning of the balance of power through subversion, guerrilla activity, or indeed the ending of our atomic monopoly. In fact, it denied that these were the concern of our military policy. In its insistence on a "pure" cause of war, it had developed a *casus belli*, surprise attack on the territorial United States, which did not happen to fit any of the issues actually in dispute, from the division of Germany, to the satellite orbit, to international control of the atom. This was the real gap between our military policy and our diplomacy, and compared to it the dispute between the Air Force and the Navy over allocation of missions paled in significance.

The B-36 hearings were, therefore, chiefly important for affording yet another forum for perhaps the most inclusive restatement of what had become truisms of American strategic thought. So much were they in accord with the sense of the country that they gained the support of almost the entire press and of even so staunch an opponent of the Truman Administration as former President Herbert Hoover. Secretary of the Air Force Stuart Symington denied that the Air Force was putting all its eggs in one basket. He insisted that the United States could not hope to match the Soviet Union man for man and that it would have to place reliance on superior technology, the best instrument of which was the Strategic Air Force. He did not deny that such a policy would cause a heavy loss of civilian life, but he defended it with the statement that "if civilians are going to be killed, I would rather have them their civilians than our civilians." [16]

16 Same, p. 434

This too was the argument of the Chairman of the Joint Chiefs of Staff, General Bradley. He insisted that our military policy was entirely defensive, a view which hardly required reiteration in view of the national objectives he defined: the preservation of peace and of our way of life; the raising of our standard of living and the achievement of world prosperity. His statement was notable for the fact that it listed the collapse of our economy under the burden of defense budgets of $14.5 billion as a danger equally real as the Soviet threat. And it contained perhaps the fullest exposition of our strategic doctrine yet made. All the truisms of American strategic thought were reiterated—the concern with Europe, the war won by superior productivity, the identification of deterrence with maximum destructive power.

We have assumed . . . that the only dangerous force . . . in the world today is Communism, and the only nations whose postwar actions have indicated an opposition to the tranquillity we seek are the Soviet Union and her satellites. . . . Opposing this, the North Atlantic powers . . . now combine in natural resources more of the vital factors for defense than the Soviet combination, except in the case of manpower. . . . Geographically . . . Russia and her satellites stand next door to western Europe and which is undoubtedly a desirable commercial, industrial and cultural prize. The American people have joined with allies . . . to save this prize from interests opposed to our own.

Let us first discuss the basic concept of our defense planning. . . . our basic concept for defense includes protection of the United States and this continent, in case we are attacked. It provides for early retaliation from bases which we hope to have ready at all times. This concept includes a decision that we shall have to be ready to seize other bases . . . so that we may attack the enemy country at shorter ranges. . . . Strategic bombing has a high priority in our military planning because we cannot hope to keep forces in being of sufficient size to meet Russia in the early stages of war. This is particularly true since we are never going to start the war. . . . Finally, if the military continues to effect more economies in defense measures . . . there will be little danger of economic collapse and our over-all risk will be less and less.[17]

III

This was the strategy of a satisfied power, content with its place in the world, eager to enjoy its benefits undisturbed. Its defensiveness was a symptom of our desire to project the pattern of our domestic affairs abroad, to construct an international order animated entirely by the consciousness of the evident advantages of harmony. But the tragic element of our struggle with the U.S.S.R. resided in the insistence of the Soviet leaders on treating the protestations of our peaceful intentions as due to ignorance or hypocrisy, which caused them to seek to neutralize our power by all means. Thus the more we protested our horror of war, the more we removed the Soviet leaders' inhibitions against expanding their influence. Because we could think of no positive goals for which to contend (two of the national objectives listed by General Bradley concerned the preservation of the *status quo* and the other two dealt with economic matters), there was a quality of abstractness about our military planning which was only barely obscured by our concern with technical problems. "Everything the enemy has we must have bigger and better," said Representative Paul J. Kilday during the B-36 hearings, and his views reflected an attitude which inhibited consideration of doctrine by confusing it with our technological achievement.

Our reaction to the ending of our atomic monopoly, was, therefore, as ambivalent as our doctrine of power. On the one hand, we postulated a nuclear stalemate which was still far from real and used it as one more justification for our existing inhibitions against using force.[18] On the other hand, we hastened to create an even more powerful weapon, the thermonuclear bomb, which in turn caused us to defer the consideration of the strategic transforma-

---

17 Same, pp. 517, 520-2, *passim.*
18 For examples of the assertion of nuclear stalemate, see Admiral Radford, B-36 hearings, cited, p. 75; General George C. Marshall testimony, U.S. Senate, *Military Situation in the Far East,* cited, p. 489.

tion wrought by the disappearance of our atomic monopoly.

The literalness of our notion of power made it impossible to conceive of an effective relationship between force
and diplomacy. A war which started as a surprise attack on
us had of necessity to be conducted in a fit of righteous in-
dignation and the proper strategy for waging it was one
of maximum destructiveness. By the same token, now that
the risks of war had grown so fearsome, the task of diplomacy was to attempt to settle disputes by the process of
negotiation and this, in turn, was conceived as a legal
process in which force played a small role, if any. Our
diplomacy and our military policy, therefore, tended to
reinforce each other's abstractness. The objective of war
was conceived to be victory, that of diplomacy, peace.
Neither could reinforce the other, and each began where
the other left off. We proved unable to use our atomic
monopoly to exert pressure or to exploit our unilateral
disarmament as a symbol of our peaceful intentions. Since
our atomic monopoly was considered to be in the realm
of strategy and our unilateral disarmament in the realm
of domestic policy, these were treated as unsuitable for
being injected into the process of negotiation. This attitude was well expressed when General Marshall said
that he would be reluctant to risk American lives for
purely political objectives.

This approach to the problem of power and its uses
came to full expression in our key postwar policy. The
policy of containment was based on the assumption that
military strategy and diplomacy represented successive
phases of national policy: it was the task of military policy
to build strength and thereby to contain Soviet aggression.
After containment had been achieved, diplomacy would
take over. ". . . what we must do," testified Secretary
Acheson at the MacArthur hearings, "is to create situations
of strength; we must build strength; and if we create that
strength, then I think that the whole situation in the world
begins to change . . . with that change there comes a difference in the negotiating positions of the various parties,
and out of that I should hope that there would be a will-

ingness on the side of the Kremlin to recognize the facts
. . . and to begin to solve at least some of the difficulties
between east and west." [19]

But international relations do not permit such absolute
divisions. Secretary Acheson's definition of containment
implied that strength was self-evident, that power would
supply its own rationale. It did not deal with the question
of how the position of strength was to be demonstrated
in the absence of a direct attack on us or on our allies. It
did not supply a doctrine for translating our power into
policy except as a response to Soviet initiative. Nor did it
make clear what would happen if the Soviet leaders refused to negotiate after we had achieved a "position of
strength" and instead concentrated their efforts on eroding
it or turning its flank.

Moreover, the identification of a position of strength
with a military position and of resistance to aggression
with all-out war led to a psychological distortion in two
ways: On the part of our allies, our reliance on an all-out
strategy reinforced the sense of impotence which was one
of the main obstacles to an effective military effort on their
part. Our justification of alliances as providing bases for
our Strategic Air Force offered small consolation to partners whose primary concern was to avoid foreign occupation. Before the Soviet Union broke our nuclear
monopoly, our allies had no military objection to
our base system, provided we gave them sufficient protection against the danger that our use of these bases might
result in their being overrun by the Red Army. After the
Soviet Union developed a nuclear capability, our allies
went along with an all-out strategy only as a deterrent to
war, not as a strategy for fighting it. Our allies were willing to accept the deterrent value of our nuclear capability.
They were reluctant to invoke it in an all-out war and they
did not see its relevance to any other form of conflict.

Our coalition policy had thus put the cart before the
horse. It had conceived its task as primarily technical: to
create an adequate defense force. But, in fact, the problem

19 U.S. Senate, *Military Situation in the Far East*, cited, p. 2,083.

proved to be primarily psychological and doctrinal: to develop a climate of opinion and a strategic doctrine which would make such a force meaningful. At the same time, we never tired of declaring that we would not use force except in resistance to aggression, and we thereby removed any Soviet incentive for making concessions on the issues actually in dispute: the satellite orbit, German unification and, above all, international control of the atom. In short, our posture was bellicose enough to lend color to Soviet peace offensives, but not sufficiently so to induce Soviet hesitations.

These then were the dilemmas of our military doctrine in the immediate postwar period, and they are still with us today. They have been due to our belief in final answers, to our overemphasis on technology, and above all to our concern with "pure" solutions both in our diplomacy and in our military policy. But the test of a doctrine is the marginal case—the situation for which doctrine does not provide and which has to be improvised under the pressure of events. A strategic doctrine is successful to the extent that it provides for the widest range of challenges and to the extent that the marginal case is in fact an unusual situation. The difficulty with United States military doctrine was that all situations actually in dispute were marginal to it. The only contingency for which it provided was all-out war, and even there its goal was modest: to prevent disaster. ". . . our forces," said General Bradley in 1950, less than three months before Korea, "are not sufficient now to fight a major war. . . . Our present thinking on our own contribution is to build up gradually our forces in being to a strength which can prevent disaster . . . and which can strike a retaliatory blow that will be strong enough to slow down the aggressor while we mobilize." [20]

20 U.S. Senate, *Department of Defense Appropriations for 1951*, Hearings before the Subcommittee of the Committee on Appropriations, 81st Cong., 2nd sess. (Washington: GPO, 1950), p. 67. This was reflected also in the Key West agreement among the services apportioning missions. It established three priorities for our defense establishment: (1) the forces required to avoid defeat; (2) what would be necessary next; (3) the requirements if each service could have all the weapons it wanted. It was found that the budget was hardly sufficient to take care of the first priority: to avoid defeat.

So it came about that the only time we resisted aggression by force, we did so in an area which our doctrine had hardly taken into account and by means of a strategy it had explicitly rejected less than a year before. The problem of limited war was forced on American strategic thought despite itself.

IV

When reality clashes with our expectations of it, frustration is the inevitable consequence. For Korea caught us completely unprepared not only militarily but above all in doctrine. Our strategic thinking had defined but two causes of war: a surprise attack on the continental United States and military aggression against Western Europe. It had foreseen all-out war as the only solution, and it had relied on our industrial potential, backed by strategic air power, as the means to victory. Secretary Acheson's speech of January 12, 1950, which excluded Korea from our defensive perimeter, was no more than an application of fundamental United States strategy, no different in content and almost identical in language with a statement made by General Douglas MacArthur nine months previously.[21] In an all-out war with the U.S.S.R. Korea was indeed outside our defensive perimeter, and its fate would depend on the outcome of a struggle fought in other theaters. As a result, the Korean war fitted no category of our strategic thought. It was not initiated by a surprise attack against the United States, nor directed against Europe, nor did it involve the U.S.S.R. It was a war to which an all-out strategy seemed peculiarly unsuited. It has been remarked more than once that had the Korean war not actually taken place, we would never have believed that it could have.

It was a courageous decision to resist an aggression so

---

21 In March 1949 General MacArthur told a reporter: "Now the Pacific has become an Anglo-Saxon lake and our line of defense runs through the chain of islands fringing the coast of Asia. It starts from the Philippines and continues through the Ryukyu archipelago which includes its broad main bastion, Okinawa. Then it bends back through Japan and the Aleutian Island chain to Alaska." *New York Times*, March 2, 1949.

totally at variance with all previous planning. The penalty we paid for the one-sidedness of our doctrine, however, was the necessity for improvising a new strategy under the pressure of events, as well as a growing difficulty in harmonizing our political and military objectives. Throughout the Korean war we were inhibited by the consciousness that this was not the war for which we had prepared. The result was an endless conflict between the commanders who, being responsible for fighting the war, sought to apply literally the doctrine that victory means crushing the enemy, and the responsible officials in Washington who, in the light of their preconceptions and the global nature of their responsibilities, could only consider the Korean war a strategic diversion or a deliberate feint on the part of the adversary.

It would be a mistake, however, to consider the controversies produced by the Korean war as a dispute about the efficacy of an all-out strategy. On the contrary, both advocates and opponents of a greater effort in Korea agreed that war, by its nature, was an all-out struggle that could be won only by crushing the enemy totally. Where they differed was not in their notion of the nature of war, but in their interpretation of the significance of the Korean war. MacArthur advocated a showdown in the Far East and specifically with China. His critics believed we must conserve our strength for a possibly imminent all-out test with the U.S.S.R. and specifically over Europe. To MacArthur the Korean war was frustration because it was not enough of a war in terms of our concept of war; to his opponents because it was too big a war in terms of the strategy on which they had built their defense plans. The dispute over the Korean war was, therefore, less a conflict over the nature of strategy than a disagreement over the *area* in which it could best be applied.

MacArthur was only expressing accepted doctrine when he asserted that "the general definition which for many decades has been accepted was that war was the ultimate process of politics; that when all other political means failed, you then go to force; and when you do that, the balance of control . . . the main interest involved . . . is

the control of the military. . . . I do unquestionably state
that when men become locked in battle, that there should
be no artifice under the name of politics, which should . . .
decrease their chances for winning. . . ." [22] Precisely because
they accepted this notion of war, MacArthur's opponents
sought to keep the Korean war to the smallest proportions
and to reserve our strength for the "real" test which by
definition had to involve the Soviet Union: ". . . enlarge-
ment of the war in Korea to include Red China, would
probably delight the Kremlin more than anything else we
could do," argued General Bradley. "It would necessarily
tie down . . . our sea power and our air power. . . . in an
area that is not the critical strategic prize. Red China is
not the powerful nation seeking to dominate the world.
Frankly, in the opinion of the Joint Chiefs of Staff, this
strategy would involve us in the wrong war, at the wrong
place, at the wrong time, and with the wrong enemy." [23]

The literalness of our notion of power is well expressed
in our certainty that a war *against* the U.S.S.R. must necessarily take the form of a battle *with* the U.S.S.R., probably
over Europe. This was the real bone of contention between MacArthur and his opponents, and it was also reflected in their disputes over the nature of preparedness.
"You have got a war on your hands," MacArthur maintained, "and you can't just say, 'Let that war go on indefinitely while I prepare for some other war.' . . . Does
your global plan for defense of this United States . . . consist of permitting war indefinitely to go on in the Pacific?
. . . If you are not going to bring the war to a decisive conclusion, what does the preparedness mean?" [24] The difficulty was, of course, that it was precisely the global nature
of our defense plans which left us unprepared for the challenges of the Korean war. The assumption behind our
military planning had been that our wars would be fought
against a principal enemy and a major challenge, but that
our forces-in-being need only be powerful enough to gain
us the time to mobilize our industrial potential. This doc-

[22] U.S. Senate, *Military Situation in the Far East,* cited, p. 45.
[23] Same, pp. 731-2.
[24] Same, pp. 75-6.

trine presupposed two related contingencies: that other powers would bear the initial brunt of aggression and that the threat would be unambiguous.

But in the aftermath of World War II, this doctrine was no longer adequate to the situation because the smaller states had lost either the strength or the will to resist by themselves. Since their ability to resist aggression had now come to depend on our willingness to commit our forces at the very beginning of any war and their decision to resist at all depended more and more on their confidence in our ability to act at once, our forces-in-being would have to be strong enough to absorb the first blows and to strike back effectively without delay. The quandary presented by a limited war turned out to be that its challenge was either not made by a principal enemy or that it did appear as an all-out challenge. In Korea the opponent was first a satellite of the third order and then Communist China. The attack was directed not against us or our installations, but against a remote area from which we had withdrawn our troops scarcely a year before. In such a situation, it is little wonder that our preoccupation with an all-out strategy caused us to consider the Korean war as an aberration and a strategic diversion.

The notion of all-out war against a principal enemy coupled with the reliance on "purely" military considerations exaggerated the inherent conservatism of our strategic planning. It is almost axiomatic that military planners are never satisfied with their "readiness." War always has an element of uncertainty, because victory depends not only on the power available but on the manner in which the factors of power are combined. Within limits, superior leadership and doctrine can compensate for inferior resources. It is the temptation of military planning to seek to escape this element of uncertainty by assembling overwhelmingly preponderant force, to substitute power for conception. But it is difficult to assemble overwhelming force against a major enemy in peacetime, particularly while relying on a defensive strategy which concedes the first blow to the adversary. For, by definition almost, the opponent will not strike the first blow if the force arrayed against him appears to him to be overwhelming. Reliance on "purely" military considerations can, therefore, only heighten the conviction of the military planners that they are not "ready" and will induce them, in all situations short of a direct attack on the United States, to advocate postponing a showdown to a more propitious moment. "We feel that we are not in the best position to meet a global war," said General Bradley. ". . . we would like very much to avoid a war at this time, not only as to our own readiness, but the longer you can avoid a war the better chance you have of avoiding it altogether. . . ." [25] ". . . we certainly do not want to become involved in a world struggle at any time," said General Marshall, "and certainly not prior to the time we are reasonably prepared to meet it." [26]

The Soviet thrust in Korea had thus been directed at the point where we were weakest psychologically, at the gap between our all-out strategy, our forces-in-being and our inhibitions. It is remarkable that the Administration spokesmen were unanimous about our strategic superiority vis-à-vis the Soviet bloc, but they were also agreed that we must avoid an all-out war. The postulate that an all-out war had to be avoided short of an overt attack by the U.S.S.R. on us or on Europe was the reverse side of our inability to conceive goals of war other than the total defeat of the enemy. It represented an effort to elaborate a cause of war commensurate with the enormity of our weapons technology and with the only strategy we were prepared to pursue.

Given the threat which we knew the Soviet Union must soon pose when it had developed its nuclear capability further, it is possible to doubt the premise which lay behind the desire to avoid all-out war, the assumption that time was on our side, or at least to raise the question whether the U.S.S.R. did not have more to lose from an all-out war than we did. Be that as it may, our announced reluctance to engage in all-out war gave the Soviet bloc a psychological advantage. In the face of the inhibitions

[25] Same, p. 896.
[26] Same, p. 479.

produced by our strategic doctrine, we tended to be more aware of our risks than of our opportunities; in fact, in our eyes even opportunities became risks. ". . . Russia possesses a very valuable ally in China," said General Marshall. ". . . . Now in view of their treaty with the Chinese Communist regime . . . if it appears that they have failed to support that government in its fight in Korea, we have a very special situation because it affects every other satellite of the Soviet. . . ." [27] ". . . whether or not the Soviet government can afford to have China defeated decisively by the Allies and put in a position where the reaction of China toward the Soviet Government might be one of deep distrust because they were not fully supported, that introduces a [new] factor in a current active situation. . . ." [28] In short, we thought we could not afford to win in Korea, despite our strategic superiority, because Russia could not afford to lose.

The Korean war was a peripheral war, therefore, not only because of its geographic location, but because of our difficulty in coming to grips with it. We kept it limited, not because we believed in limited war, but because we were reluctant to engage in all-out war over the issues which were at stake in Korea. Whatever aspects of the Korean war we considered—geographic location, strategy for conducting it, or our preparedness—we resolved them into arguments for keeping it to the smallest possible proportions.

As a result, many of the disputes produced by the Korean war were as abstract as the concept of power which produced them. They turned less on the opportunities presented by limited war than on the possibility of achieving all-out victory. MacArthur argued as if the Soviet timetable could not be affected by *any* measures the United States might take and that we could, therefore, crush China completely without fear of Soviet intervention.[29] His opponents argued as if the U.S.S.R. were wait-

---

[27] Same, p. 594.
[28] Same, p. 432.
[29] Same, pp. 9, 69, 130, 198.

ing for an excuse either to intervene in Asia or to launch forces against Western Europe.[30]

By thus posing absolute alternatives as our only choices, by denying the existence of any middle ground between stalemate and total victory, both MacArthur and his opponents inhibited a consideration of strategic transformations which would be compatible with a policy of limited objectives. It was perhaps true that the U.S.S.R. would not permit an unambiguous defeat of China in an all-out war leading to the overthrow of the Communist regime. But it did not follow that the U.S.S.R. would risk everything in order to forestall *any* transformations in our favor, all the more so as our nuclear superiority was still very pronounced. Had we pushed back the Chinese armies even to the narrow neck of the Korean peninsula, we would have administered a setback to Communist power in its first trial at arms with the free world. This might have caused China to question the value of its Soviet alliance while the U.S.S.R. would have been confronted with the dilemma of whether it was "worth" an all-out war to prevent a limited defeat of its ally. A limited war is inconsistent with an attempt to impose unconditional surrender. But the impossibility of imposing unconditional surrender should not be confused with the inevitability of a return to the *status quo ante*.

Our strategic doctrine made it very difficult, however, to think of the possibility of intermediary transformations. Its defensive assumptions led us to analyze Soviet reactions as if every move were equally open to the Kremlin. And the divorce between force and diplomacy tended to paralyze both. The objective of our campaign was varyingly stated as repelling aggression, resisting aggression, punishing aggression, or as the security of our forces.[31] Each of these objectives was defined in military terms and each assumed that diplomacy would take over only *after* a position of strength had been established.

---

30 Same, pp. 593, 594, 687 and 942.
31 Same, p. 478 (General Marshall); p. 937 (General Bradley); pp. 1,225 and 1,191 (General J. Lawton Collins); p. 1,717 (Secretary Acheson); p. 570 (General Marshall).

The Korean war thus represented an application of the doctrine of containment. In fact, it was explicitly justified in those terms.[32] But it suffered from the same drawbacks. Throughout the Korean war we made our objectives dependent on the military situation: they fluctuated with the fortunes of battle between repelling aggression, unification, the security of our forces, and a guaranteed armistice.

The fluctuation of our objectives demonstrated that it is impossible to conduct limited wars on the basis of purely military considerations. After Inchon, at a moment of maximum strength, we proved unable to create a political framework for settling the Korean war, and we thereby provided the enemy with an incentive, if any was needed, to seek to restore the military balance as a prerequisite to any negotiation. It is not clear that a generous and comprehensive offer, for example, to stop at the narrow neck of the peninsula and to demilitarize the rest of North Korea under United Nations supervision, would have been accepted; for purposes of this argument, it is sufficient to note that it was never made. The attempt by both sides to achieve a position of strength *prior* to negotiation resulted in a vicious circle of gradually expanding commitments which was brought to a halt only because an equilibrium was gradually established between the physical inability of Communist China to invest more resources in the conflict and our psychological unwillingness to do so.

The same attitude toward power which kept our diplomacy from setting limits to our military aims after we had the upper hand also prevented us from drawing strength from our military posture after we had opened negotiations for an armistice. Our decision to stop military operations, except those of a purely defensive nature, at the *very beginning* of the armistice negotiations reflected our conviction that the process of negotiation operated on its own inherent logic independently of the military pressures brought to bear. But by stopping military operations

---

[32] Same, p. 886 (General Bradley).

we removed the only Chinese incentive for a settlement;
we produced the frustration of two years of inconclusive
negotiations. In short, our insistence on divorcing force
from diplomacy caused our power to lack purpose and our
negotiations to lack force.

v

The same literal approach to power which affected our
views about the strategy for fighting the Korean war also
shaped our coalition policy. Our alliances were based on
the same assumption as our strategic doctrine: that aggression is deterred by assembling the maximum force. As
a result, we tended to equate deterrence with a system of
general collective security which gave rise to the notion
that, unless all allies resisted aggression jointly, no resistance was possible at all. "The basis upon which we are
building our security, in addition to the strength of our
own Armed Forces, is collective security," said Secretary
Acheson. ". . . . [Our allies] are the most fundamental
forces in the security of the United States. Therefore, it
is of transcendent importance that in our policies *in all
parts of the world, where danger of war may be created,
we work absolutely hand in hand with our allies.*" [33]
By such a course the inhibitions produced by our military policy were compounded by the vulnerabilities of
our allies. A system of general collective security is effective only against a threat so overpowering that it obliterates all disputes about the nature of the threat or about
the strategy for dealing with it. And it presupposes a military policy which offers each major ally a measure of protection against what it considers its greatest peril.
Neither condition held true in the Korean conflict. The
attack was directed at a point at which the interests of our
European allies were involved indirectly at best; yet our
coalition policy treated the Korean war as if it were of
world-wide concern. Our allies, conscious of the ability
of the Red Army to overrun them, therefore magnified

---

[33] Same, p. 1,764; emphasis added.

our own tendency to consider the Korean war only in terms of risks. No conceivable gains in Korea seemed "worth" the danger to their national existence which was implicit in the risk, however slight, that the Korean war might spread to Europe.

Thus our efforts to assemble the maximum number of allies was the obverse of our all-out strategy, and it involved the same problems: the greater the force, the greater the reluctance to employ it. Both our military and our coalition policy tended to make it difficult to undertake decisive action against peripheral threats: the former by posing risks disproportionate to the objectives in dispute, the latter by causing us to limit our actions to what could gain allied support. "This is the first time," said General Bradley, "we have had a United Nations field command . . . [we should] do anything we can to keep from breaking up a United Nations [field] command and discouraging them from taking United Nations action in the future." [34] For this reason, we rejected any expansion of the Korean war. Even "hot pursuit" of enemy planes beyond the Yalu seemed too risky in the face of the opposition of six of our allies.[35]

To be sure, in the early stages of the Korean war the hesitations of our allies were not apparent; indeed the eagerness with which they offered military assistance seemed to prove the contrary. But the willingness of our allies to participate in the Korean war reflected their uncertainty as to whether we had actually outgrown our traditional isolationism and whether we could, in fact, be relied on to help them defend their homelands. Their interest in Korea was, therefore, largely symbolic: to commit us to the principle of collective security. Beyond this, their willingness to run risks was inhibited by the consciousness of their weakness. Since our commitment to the principle of collective security was established with our entry into the Korean war, the pressure of our allies from then on was in favor of a strategy of minimum risk. This is not to say that our allies were "wrong," only that they

---

[34] Same, p. 1,077.
[35] Same, p. 2,078.

tended to look at the Korean war from the perspective of their vulnerabilities rather than from that of strategic opportunities.

Moreover, the alternatives of our coalition policy were posed in the same absolute terms as those of our military strategy. In fact, however, the choice in Korea was not necessarily collective action or isolation in a global war, as was so often maintained during the MacArthur hearings. Had we set ourselves more ambitious goals in Korea, one of two things might have happened: the war would have spread in the Pacific without becoming all-out; or it might have led to an all-out war between the United States and the Soviet bloc. In the former contingency allied support would have been unnecessary; a war in the Pacific from which our European allies remained aloof would have achieved through a political device what we strained every effort to accomplish by force: Europe would have been protected by its neutrality instead of by our alliance, but the accretion to Soviet power represented by Europe's industry and skilled labor—the contingency we feared most —would have been averted none the less. In a limited war we did not need the increment in strength represented by allied support, while the attempt to obtain it tended to undermine the psychological framework for dealing with an all-out threat.

In an all-out war, on the other hand, our allies would have had no choice as simple as that between neutrality and commitment. It was one thing for them to refuse to support us in a limited war; it would have been quite another to stand by while we lost a total war, for this would have left them at the mercy of the U.S.S.R. Moreover, had the war been turned into an all-out one through a Soviet attack on Europe, NATO would have come into operation automatically, and our allies would have been confronted by a naked threat to their survival. This is not to imply that it would have been wise to expand the war in Korea. It is simply to indicate that, by leaving no room between total war and stalemate and between complete allied support and neutrality, we posed alternatives for ourselves which did not, in fact, exhaust the gamut of our options.

VI

Our reactions to the frustrations of the Korean war have illustrated the manner in which strategic and political concepts tend to linger on even after they have outlived their usefulness. Instead of reassessing our strategic doctrine, we have shown a strong inclination to ascribe our difficulties to a departure from our traditional policy. Limited war has tended to be identified with a strategically unproductive holding operation. We have refused to admit that our strategic doctrine had created a gap between our power and our policy. Rather, our experience in Korea has reinforced our determination to reserve our all-out power for use in contingencies in which it could be utilized without restraint.

Whether interpreted in Secretary Dulles' statements on "massive retaliation," [36] in Vice President Richard M. Nixon's speech of March 13, 1954,[37] or in Thomas K. Finletter's lucid study of *Power and Policy*,[38] these postulates of American strategic thinking have amounted to the assertion that the chief deterrent to Soviet aggression resides in United States nuclear superiority. From this reaffirmation of strategic orthodoxy we have drawn the conclusion that the United States should not exhaust itself in a war of attrition over peripheral areas nor keep in being forces so large as to drain our economy without adding to our effective strength on A-day (the hypothetical date of the outbreak of the nuclear war).[39] Since the Sino-Soviet bloc possesses interior lines of communication and is therefore able to choose the point of attack, we should, according to the predominant view, not let ourselves be lured into areas where we would be operating at a strategic disadvantage. Instead, we should inhibit aggression at its source by the threat of general war. To be sure, there are some areas where we might resist aggression on the

---

[36] John Foster Dulles, "Policy for Security and Peace," *Foreign Affairs*, v. 32 (April 1954), pp. 353-64.

[37] *New York Times*, March 14, 1954.

[38] New York: Harcourt, Brace, 1954.

[39] Same, p. 231.

ground, at least initially—the NATO region, for example—
and for their defense, it is argued, ground forces, perhaps
backed by nuclear weapons, are essential. But in the remainder of the world, the part which Mr. Finletter has
called the "Gray Areas," Sino-Soviet moves can be prevented only by the threat of a general war.

The distinguishing feature of this strategic doctrine is
not its novelty but its orthodoxy. Here is the pre-Korea
United States military doctrine buttressed by the lessons
we have drawn from the Korean conflict, which have come
to symbolize the frustrations to be experienced in waging
peripheral wars. And it contains all the inconsistencies of
the pre-Korea thought, sharpened by a renewed economy
drive and by the realization that another technological
revolution—the discovery of thermonuclear weapons—has
occurred.

Thus, the most recent public consideration of strategic
concepts, the hearings on air power conducted by Senator
Stuart Symington's Senate subcommittee, turned into restatements of familiar doctrine. All the services, except
the Army, were in accord that the next war would start
with a suprise attack; all agreed that it would be won by
maximum offensive power.[40] It was little wonder therefore
that deterrence was again identified with strategic striking
power, as if the Korean war had never taken place. ". . . the
key to the enemy decision [to attack]," said the Strategic Air Command briefing, "is our relative strength in
1958-65. We use the word 'relative' because our strength
as compared to his determines what he has to pay in excess
costs as to whatever action he undertakes. . . ."[41]

The notion that the decision between peace or war
depends on the ability to inflict a greater level of damage
than the enemy, demonstrates the traditionalism of our
military thinking. True, when the power of individual
weapons was relatively small, the side which could deliver

---

40 U.S. Senate, *Study of Airpower*, Hearings before the Subcommittee
on the Air Force of the Committee on Armed Services, 84th Cong., 2nd
Sess. (Washington: GPO, 1956), p. 50 (General Spaatz); p. 184 (Major General Curtis E. LeMay); p. 1,055 (Rear Admiral C. D. Griffin); p. 1,845
(General Nathan F. Twining).

41 Same, p. 185.

the greater weight of offensive effort would generally win, because damage would not be so drastic as to affect the ability of the stronger side to continue the war. But the strategic transformation caused by nuclear weapons derives from the fact that the notion of "relative damage" may have become meaningless when applied to all-out war. For even the side which has mounted the stronger offensive may have to absorb a level of damage which drains its national substance. With modern weapons, even an inferior retaliatory capacity may deter, not because it can inflict disproportionate damage, but because it can inflict unacceptable losses. This, if anything, should have been the lesson of the Korean war, which we refused to expand despite Soviet strategic inferiority.[42]

To be sure, General LeMay has also stated that deterrence is achieved by the capacity to inflict a level of damage which an enemy would consider unacceptable. In practice, however, he has seen no way of achieving this result except through absolute numerical superiority of our long-range striking force.[43] This in turn involves the following syllogism. (1) Deterrence is produced by absolute superiority in long-range air power. (2) Only one side can deter. ". . . I think I pointed out," said General LeMay, "that in 1958 [the Soviet Long-Range Air Force] were going to be stronger, and from then on getting stronger. . . . And that the deterrent force would then transfer to Russia from the United States." [44]

This definition of deterrence includes all the dilemmas of our pre-Korea doctrine. It does not consider whether a deterrent force adequate to prevent all-out war can also deter limited aggression. It does not deal with the question of what constitutes aggression short of a direct attack on the United States. Above all, it contains the seeds for endless interservice rivalries, for the only war with which this doctrine of deterrence is comfortable is a contest of stra-

---

[42] This should not be construed as an argument for inferior retaliatory capability; it is merely to indicate that we have to be clear about the nature of deterrence and the significant factors of military superiority. See below, Chapter 5.

[43] U.S. Senate, *Study of Airpower*, cited, p. 220.

[44] Same, p. 213.

tegic striking forces. "All modern military men, whether they be airmen, soldiers, or sailors, agree that no surface military tasks can be undertaken until air superiority is achieved," General LeMay testified. "Therefore, the first thing that must be done in modern war is to win the airpower battle." [45]

If land operations are impossible before victory in the air battle, however, they are unnecessary afterwards. Once it is possible to roam the enemy's skies at will, there are more efficient ways to impose surrender than by land operations.[46] By the same token, the carrier forces designed to destroy shipyards and port facilities,[47] can, in terms of Air Force doctrine, represent only a diversion of resources. For, as will be seen in the following chapters, the punishment which has to be inflicted in order to gain uncontested air supremacy makes it highly unlikely that port facilities will still have any strategic value after the air battle has been won or lost.

Thus the clash of strategic doctrines which marked the pre-Korea period has continued. The three services, in pursuit each of its primary mission as laid down in the Key West agreement, have developed partially overlapping, partially inconsistent, strategies. The Air Force speaks of winning the air battle, the Navy of keeping the sea lanes open, and the Army of conducting brushfire wars. And because their force levels are set on the basis of their primary missions, all the interservice pressures operate to perpetuate a division of functions which the power of modern weapons had rendered almost meaningless. In the absence of an agreed doctrine, the conflict of missions is irreconcilable. The Army request for more airlift is correct in terms of its need for greater mobility in dealing with peripheral wars. But the Air Force retort that the resources can better be devoted to procuring additional combat aircraft is equally justified in terms of its mission of winning the air battle. The Navy's insistence on a long-range airplane

---

[45] Same, p. 102.

[46] This view was made explicit in "The Army's Atomic Dilemma," in the semi-official *Air Force*, v. 39 (May 1956), p. 40.

[47] U.S. Senate, *Study of Airpower,* cited, p. 1,028.

is wise, if bombing facilities can affect the course of a general war. It is unnecessary if the Strategic Air Command is able to decide the issue in a relatively short period.

The Symington hearings revealed an attempt by each service to hoard weapons of maximum range and destructiveness, because, in the absence of an agreed over-all doctrine, no service can rely on a sister service's interpretation of what constitutes an essential target. The only way a service can be certain that its targets will in fact be attacked is to seek to obtain every weapon which can be used against them. ". . . if I was assured," said General Twining, "when we wanted to attack Russia on a strategic mission, that the naval carriers were assigned to General LeMay . . . fine. But that is not the case, and I don't know where those carriers are going to be. . . . So the Strategic Air Force has to be just as big, just as strong, and just as ready, regardless of this Navy contribution on these targets. . . ." [48] ". . . the primary function of the Army is the destruction of the enemy army," said General Maxwell D. Taylor in justifying the Army's development of a 1,500-mile missile. "The primary function of the Air Force is to destroy enemy air power and for the Navy to destroy enemy naval power. . . . if you accept the fact that the Army exists to destroy hostile armies, then any missile which will destroy hostile ground forces should be available to the Army." [49] "To control the sea," said Rear Admiral Arleigh A. Burke, "the Navy must be capable of destroying the source of weapons which threaten ships and operations at sea—submarine bases, airbases, missile bases and any other bases from which control of the sea can be challenged." [50]

Thus each service seeks to get under its control every weapon it requires to attack the targets it considers essential, even if such a weapon already exists in a sister service and even though it is almost impossible to draw a definite line between essential targets for

---

[48] Same, p. 1,840; see also p. 178 (General LeMay).
[49] Same, p. 1,285, p. 1,287.
[50] Same, p. 1,343.

air, land and sea warfare. The doctrinal split among the services can be measured in General Twining's assumption that it would be simpler to permit a duplication of effort between the Air Force and the Navy than to secure an adaptation by either to the other arm's strategic doctrine. "Each of the armed services," said Secretary Charles E. Wilson, "has its own particular military philosophy . . . [about] how wars should be fought." [51] But three strategic doctrines, each partially inconsistent with the others, increase the dilemmas of policy. At each crisis they force the political leadership to resolve the inconsistencies under the pressure of events. The disagreements of military experts magnify the insecurity of the policy-makers, for they symbolize the uncertainty of any proposed solution.

The power and speed of modern weapons have made almost irrelevant the rigid division of functions among the services and the literal interpretation of separate missions. A 1,500-mile missile equipped with a thermonuclear warhead can destroy enemy armies. From present free-world bases, or from ships, it can also reach almost all of metropolitan Russia. A multimegaton weapon, an effective tool for cratering enemy airfields, is also certain to obliterate an area much larger than that of a traditional target. In each case, the indirect effects of the weapons system go far beyond the primary mission for which it was originally created and which is the justification for its existence.

The setting of force levels on the basis of each service's primary mission inhibits the consideration of these collateral effects. The primary missions become ends in themselves, and this in turn exaggerates the abstract quality of our military doctrine. Given the range of modern weapons, the attempt to develop a weapons system capable of destroying every target that can affect a service's primary mission must lead to an attempt by each service to develop a strategic striking force. It prevents an adequate consideration of intermediate applications of power which in the nuclear age may bring

51 Same, p. 1,618.

much higher political returns than resort to all-out war.

The importance of a strategy of intermediate objectives is now all the greater because of the changing nature of deterrence. The notion that deterrence can be achieved by only *one* of the two superpowers is no longer applicable, if it ever was. So long as the United States enjoyed an absolute atomic monopoly, even a small number of nuclear weapons exercised a powerful deterrent effect. Then we could protect many areas by the threat of massive retaliation. But, as the Soviet nuclear stockpile has grown, the American strategic problem has been transformed. No matter how vast our remaining margin in the number and refinement of weapons, henceforth not only *they* but *we* must fear them. In this situation deterrence can no longer be measured by absolute numbers of bombs or planes. To seek safety in numerical superiority, or even in superior destructiveness, may come close to a Maginot-line mentality—to seek in numbers a substitute for conception. Moreover, in many fields where our present weapons system is already adequate to its mission, new technological advances will add much less to our effective strength than to that of the Soviet bloc. This seems to be true for the Intercontinental Ballistic Missile and the atomic submarine. And when weapons can be made of any desired degree of destructiveness a point will be reached at which additional increments of destructive power yield diminishing returns. What is the sense in developing a weapon that can destroy a city twice over?

Thus for the first time in military history we are facing the prospect of a stalemate, despite the absolute superiority of one side in numbers of weapons and in their technology. It is a stalemate not so much in equality of power as in the assessment of risks; an uneasy balance which shifts from region to region with the importance which the contenders attach to each and with the alternatives which their strategy and their weapons systems present them. To be sure, the key to survival is the possession of an adequate retaliatory force. Without a powerful Strategic Air Force no other measures are possible. But all-out surprise attack does not exhaust the range of our perils; although the greatest threat, it may, in fact, be the least likely danger. Mastery of the challenges of the nuclear age will depend on our ability to combine physical and psychological factors, to develop weapons systems which do not paralyze our will, and to devise strategies which permit us to shift the risks of counteraction to the other side. The pernicious aspect of the absence of doctrinal agreement among the services is that it tempts each of them to aim for absolute solutions in purely military terms. And it therefore inhibits the attempt to bridge the gap which has opened between power and the objectives for which power can be used.

A revolution cannot be mastered until it is understood. The temptation is always to seek to integrate it into familiar doctrine: to deny that a revolution is taking place. Nothing is more important, therefore, than to attempt an assessment of the technological revolution which we have witnessed in the past decade, in order to determine its impact on our, by now, traditional concepts of surprise attack, deterrence, coalition policy, and all-out war.

PART TWO

TECHNOLOGY AND STRATEGY

3

THE FIRES OF PROMETHEUS

For many centuries, the legend of Prometheus, who sought to steal the secret of fire from the gods and who was punished by being forced to spend the rest of his life chained to a rock, has been the symbol of the penalties of presumptuous ambition. It was not understood that the punishment inflicted on Prometheus was an act of compassion; it would have been a much more severe penalty had the gods permitted their fire to be stolen. Our generation has succeeded in stealing the fire of the gods and it is doomed to live with the horror of its achievement.

Any examination of the strategic revolution brought about by nuclear technology must start from a discussion of the increased destructiveness of modern weapons. Since our strategic doctrine assumes that the targets will include industrial facilities, air bases, and ports, and since most of these are located in or near big cities, the first consideration must be the effect of thermonuclear and nuclear weapons when used against urban concentrations.

The growth of the city is perhaps the distinguishing characteristic of modern civilization. It is the expression of its power and its vulnerability. In a primitive society the basic unit is the family which is largely self-sufficient, producing its own food supply and containing the skills required for its survival. Its margin of subsistence being generally low, it is more vulnerable to natural catastrophes which affect its food supply than to the actions of its neighbors. The modern city, on the other hand, is made possible by specialization. Because of it, the individual

65

in modern society develops a substantially greater pro-
ficiency in his skill than his counterpart in primitive
groups. By the same token, his dependence on other parts
of the society becomes more pronounced. He is less vulnerable to natural catastrophes, but more vulnerable to events
which affect the performance of his fellows.

Specialization makes possible a greater degree of material well-being than is even conceivable in primitive
societies. But it also defines the vulnerability of a city,
both physically and psychologically. Most of the skilled
population of a modern country will be found in cities.
The leading hospitals and medical schools, many of the
universities, the banks and credit institutions, and most
of the exchanges which form the essential links of modern
society are concentrated in cities. The city is thus the
repository of a nation's capital and skills.

Any breakdown in one of the innumerable links of a
city's "nervous system" can produce paralysis: an elevator
failure, a subway strike, even a stoppage of traffic signals,
can materially slow down the economic machine. More
serious still is a failure of essential supplies. The entire
economic life of the city is dependent on the uninterrupted
supply of energy, of which fuel energy is the single most
important item. Above all, a city is held together by an
intangible quality: the confidence of its inhabitants that
the highly articulated mechanism will continue to function; the conviction of the individual that the machine
will serve and not destroy him. The highest expression
of this confidence is the degree to which it appears inconceivable that the intricate relationships which define
a city could ever be destroyed. The penalty of a loss of
confidence is illustrated by the depression of 1929. The
physical plant of our society did not shrink, the skills of
the people did not grow less, yet production fell by more
than 40 per cent and millions were unemployed.

In planning for the contingency of an attack on our
cities, the Federal Civil Defense Administration in 1955
made the following assumptions: (1) The U.S.S.R. has the
capability of attacking any target within the United States
with nuclear weapons, including thermonuclear types de-

livered through the air and detonated above ground, during normal working hours. Its targets will be our centers of industry and population. (2) Initial attacks will include sufficient nuclear weapons to hit all of our critical target areas, to be followed by other less heavy attacks. (3) Bomb sizes will vary from a few thousand to millions of tons of TNT equivalent. Any city attacked, with very few exceptions, can be substantially destroyed by one bomb. (4) The principal city in each critical target area will be hit. The daytime centers of population will be the aiming points within the city. (5) Any city attacked will need outside help to meet the emergency. (6) A warning time of one hour in most areas is expected but cannot be guaranteed. (7) Evacuation of people from downtown areas in cities is to commence upon the first warning.[1] They are expected to have moved two miles from their offices by the time the attack becomes imminent.

While some of these assumptions, particularly with respect to evacuation, are now outdated, they suffice to describe the magnitude of the threat. The Federal Civil Defense Administration has identified 92 critical target areas with a total population of 68 million inhabitants. The Air Defense Command has described 170 standard metropolitan areas, each with a population of 50,000 or more. These areas contain 55 per cent of the population and 75 per cent of the industry of this country. An attack on the most important 50 of them would bring under fire 40 per cent of the population, 50 per cent of the key facilities and 60 per cent of the industry of the United States.[2]

Nuclear technology, furthermore, has advanced to a point at which weapons of any desired explosive power

---

[1] U.S. House, *Civil Defense for National Survival*, 24th Intermediate Report of the Committee on Government Operations (Washington: GPO, 1956), pp. 1-33.

[2] U.S. Senate, *Study of Airpower*, Hearings before the Subcommittee on the Air Force of the Committee on Armed Services (Washington: GPO, 1956), pp. 239, 307. Population density in the U.S.S.R. is somewhat less, but this would be compensated by the effects of fall-out and, in the immediate future, by the superiority of our strategic striking forces. The effects of a thermonuclear attack on the U.S.S.R. would therefore be comparable to those on the United States.

can be produced. The atomic bombs of the Hiroshima type now range from the equivalent of below 1 kiloton TNT equivalent (or one-twentieth of the explosive power of the Hiroshima bomb) to close to 1 million tons (1 megaton) TNT equivalent (or fifty times the explosive power of the Hiroshima bomb). Thermonuclear weapons have no inherent upper limit. The U.S.S.R. will, therefore, be able to attack each target with a weapon of whatever size is most suitable for its destruction. Since a 10 megaton weapon is by no means the most powerful weapon available, a description of the damage caused by it will err, if at all, on the side of conservatism. The effects of such a weapon can be classed under three headings: blast and heat, radiation and fall-out, genetic effects.

The destruction by heat and blast inflicted by a 10 megaton weapon would extend over three circles of decreasing damage. Within a radius of 3 miles there would occur total destruction of all buildings and a mortality rate of 75 per cent, with all the survivors severely injured. Within a radius of 7 miles, all buildings would be heavily damaged and the most conservative estimates indicate a mortality rate of 30 per cent, with at least 40 per cent of the remainder injured to varying degrees of severity. Heavy damage is defined by the Federal Civil Defense Administration as structural damage that would result in the collapse of buildings. Beyond this a circle of light damage would extend over a radius of 10 miles. At the outer edge of this circle, the heat and radiation would be sufficient to kill or injure severely individuals caught outside of shelters and to set fire to buildings. Since the suburbs of most American cities are constructed of wood, a devastated city may find itself encircled by a wall of flames.[3]

The proportions of such a disaster thus become fairly clear. A 10 megaton bomb exploded over New York City, at Forty-second Street and Fifth Avenue, would include in its 3-mile radius of total destruction all of Man-

---

[3] It must be repeated that a 10 megaton weapon represents by no means the upper limit of possible weapons. The device set off at Eniwetok in 1954 was 20 megatons; its radii of destruction would be 10 and 14 miles respectively.

hattan south of Ninety-sixth Street, parts of Jersey City, all
of the cities on the west bank of the Hudson up to Hudson
Heights, as well as Queens, Long Island City, Hunter's
Point and Williamsburg. The daytime working and resi-
dential population in this area amounts to at least 4 million. A mortality rate of 75 per cent would produce 3
million deaths, and the remainder would be so severely injured that they could survive only if hospitalized immediately. The 7-mile radius of heavy damage would include
Manhattan Island to just north of the George Washington
Bridge, a third of the Bronx, half of Queens and Brook-
lyn and all of Jersey City. A conservative estimate of cas-
ualities in this area would be 900,000 dead and at least
600,000 injured. To be sure, New York is more vulnerable
than most cities because of its great density of population.
On the other hand, it contains large unpopulated areas
such as Central Park, the rivers, the Upper Bay, and the
Jersey Meadows, which would be built-up areas elsewhere.
In any case, the attacker can always step up the power of
his weapon or utilize an additional bomb to cover the
desired area.

TABLE I

POPULATIONS OF THE TEN LARGEST CITIES IN THE
UNITED STATES AND THE SOVIET UNION

United States [a]		Soviet Union [b]	
1. New York	7,891,957	1. Moscow	4,389,000
2. Chicago	3,620,962	2. Leningrad	3,176,000
3. Philadelphia	2,071,605	3. Kiev	991,000
4. Los Angeles	1,970,358	4. Baku	901,000
5. Detroit	1,849,568	5. Kharkov	877,000
6. Baltimore	949,708	6. Gor'ky	876,000
7. Cleveland	914,808	7. Tashkent	778,000
8. St. Louis	856,796	8. Kuybyshev	760,000
9. Washington, D.C.	802,178	9. Novosibirsk	731,000
10. Boston	801,444	10. Sverdlovsk	707,000

[a] U.S. Bureau of the Census, *Statistical Abstract of the United States:
1956* (77th ed.; Washington: GPO, 1956), pp. 16-9.
[b] Russia, Central Statistical Administration, *National Economy of the
U.S.S.R.* (Moscow: State Statistical Publishing House, 1956), p. 8.

By the most conservative estimates, a successful attack on the 50 most important urban centers listed by the Air Defense Command, containing 50 per cent of the U.S. population, would produce 15 to 20 million dead and 20 to 25 million injured. Such a casualty rate would produce almost insuperable medical problems. Under normal conditions, a hospital requires five persons to care for one patient. It has been estimated that at Nagasaki, under the most primitive medical conditions, each survivor required two persons to care for him. The whole surviving population of an affected area would therefore either be injured or engaged in caring for the injured.

Even then, adequate medical assistance for the injured will be impossible, for most hospitals and most medical personnel are themselves within the target area. They will, therefore, suffer the same damage and casualties as the rest of the population. In the United States there are only 100 thousand medical doctors or 160 thousand medically trained personnel, if one adds veterinarians and trained nurses—a number which is barely sufficient even for peacetime conditions. Then, too, it will be impossible to stockpile blood plasma in the quantities which will be required for the casualties of a thermonuclear attack or to administer it could it be stockpiled. Since eight nurses working under favorable conditions can administer only 10 thousand blood transfusions a month, it is apparent that transfusions for casualties measured in the millions are out of the question. The medical situation is further complicated by the almost certain disappearance of hygienic conditions of life, leaving survivors of the attack open to a whole range of epidemic diseases caused by the destruction of water purification machinery, exhaustion of chlorine supplies, breakdowns of sanitary disposal systems, and putrification of normally refrigerated food.

A thermonuclear attack on an urban center, it is clear, differs fundamentally from anything previously known. In World War II the effects of bombing were cumulative, whereas today *one 10 megaton weapon represents five times the explosive power of all the bombs dropped on Germany during four years of war and one hundred times those dropped on Japan.*[4] In World War II, the population could get used to the gradually increasing tempo of bombardment, while a thermonuclear weapon would produce all the casualties at once. All the raids on Germany combined killed 330 thousand people. A single 10 megaton weapon exploded over any of the larger U.S. cities will kill several times that number. A World War II type of attack left no residual dangers except for land mines which could be identified fairly easily. An attack with modern weapons will contaminate the blast area with severe radiation and thus add to the psychological burdens of the survivors.

A disaster of such magnitude may prevent even trained persons from responding with efficiency and organization. Survivors of the raid on Nagasaki have reported the sense of shock which seized them after the attack. It was seven days before organized rescue operations began. And a 20 megaton thermonuclear bomb represents the same order of increase in explosive power over the atomic bomb exploded at Nagasaki as the Nagasaki bomb did over the largest blockbuster of World War II, that is, a thousandfold increase.

Moreover, in World War II even the largest raid affected only a limited area within a city; it never paralyzed the entire urban area. The parts of the city which were not under attack could come to the assistance of the stricken area and thus mitigate the worst effects of a raid, often while it was still in progress. Even within the section under attack essential services such as hospitals could frequently be maintained. World War II, therefore, represented the marginal case in which the highly elaborated

---

4 To be sure, the effects from blast and heat are not directly proportional to the explosive power, increasing only by the square of the cube root of the factor of stepped-up explosive power. Thus the 20 kiloton bomb exploded over Hiroshima which was one thousand times as powerful as a 20 ton TNT blockbuster produced blast effects only one hundred times greater. Therefore, the "real" increase in explosive power is only a factor of 2.2 over all the bombs dropped on Germany and of 4.7 over those dropped in Japan. On the other hand, conventional weapons caused no collateral effects such as fall-out.

structure which is a city could still profit from its specialized functions.

But confronted with a thermonuclear attack, the modern
city may carry the seeds of its own destruction within itself. Specialization of urban functions presupposes a
high order of managerial skill and the technical ability
to utilize the interlocking components of an organization.
Since most telephone exchanges, hospitals and institutions
of municipal government are located within the target
area, it may be weeks before any coordinated activity is
technically possible. In the meantime, the food and water
supplies will have been contaminated with radioactive
material and rescue operations will be hampered by the
fact that the zones of heaviest damage are also most heavily
radioactive.

What happens to a society in such circumstances is almost unpredictable. The specialization of functions which
in normal times serves as the condition of high productiv-
ity may create paralysis when the machinery for coordinated effort collapses. The elaboration of services may
become a burden when the energy on which it depends is
suddenly no longer available. A city without electricity,
without water supply, without communications, is a contradiction in terms—a concrete-and-steel jungle in which
nature does not offer even the barest means of survival. A
country as dependent as ours on the internal combustion
engine can be paralyzed by the destruction of its oil re-
fineries and distribution centers, most of which are located
in or near big cities. Even our agriculture is unthinkable
without tractors.

The effects of such a catastrophe cannot be measured
only in the loss of material wealth. The psychological impact on the country of the sudden disappearance of even
twenty-five population centers is incalculable. Since these
centers contain most of the technically skilled and professional cadres—the engineers, the doctors, the lawyers—a
society can lose most of its store of capital and accumulated
skills in one blow. And the psychological impact of the
loss will be compounded by the fact that the radiation
which produces many of the casualties cannot be seen or

felt while it is most pervasive and that the symptoms of radiation sickness may appear only after periods ranging from one to three weeks. A thermonuclear attack may thus become the symbol of the vanity of all human strivings. It may shake to the core the people's confidence in the economy, the government and the national purpose.

II

Even if the national morale should withstand the disappearance of its centers of control and the symbols of its power, it will be put to another test. For the cities which are attacked cannot count on drawing support from the surrounding countryside, as the Federal Civil Defense Administration seems to assume. While the city is subjected to heat and blast, the surrounding countryside will be subjected to a collateral effect of thermonuclear weapons— radioactive fall-out.[5]

When the first megaton hydrogen weapon was exploded over Eniwetok, the degree of fall-out had not been anticipated, although the phenomenon was well understood.[6] In retrospect, it appeared inevitable. In a sense this is the dilemma of the nuclear period: each technological breakthrough liberates forces which reach so far beyond all previous experience that most of the experts are at a loss to interpret the probable consequences. Indeed, the scale of experience on which their expertise is based often stands in the way of understanding the significance of new developments.

The fall-out of thermonuclear weapons is caused by a combination of two processes: fission, which in lay terms represents the force liberated by the break-up of atoms, and fusion, which is the process of combining atoms. Most

---

5 For excellent technical discussions of the fall-out problem, see Ralph E. Lapp, "Radioactive Fall-out," *Bulletin of the Atomic Scientists,* v. 11 (February 1955), p. 45 ff.; J. Rotblat, "The Hydrogen-Uranium Bomb," same (May 1955), p. 171 ff.; Willard F. Libby, "Radioactive Fall-out," same (September 1955), p. 256 ff.

6 U.S. Department of Defense and the U.S. Atomic Energy Commission, under direction of the Los Alamos Scientific Laboratory, *The Effects of Atomic Weapons* (Washington: GPO, 1950), p. 270.

of the fall-out problem is caused by the highly radioactive materials produced by fission. Unlike the atoms of familiar substances, such as gold or oxygen, the atoms of radioactive substances disintegrate spontaneously, that is, they change their composition. In the process they emit high-energy rays capable of penetrating the human tissue and producing chemical, biological and genetic changes in the cells they traverse. Radioactivity is measured in half-lives: the amount of time it takes for a given quantity of radioactive material to decay to half its initial value. The longer the half-life, the more dangerous the radioactive substance from the point of view of fall-out.

Were the thermonuclear weapon a "pure" hydrogen bomb, there would be little or no radioactivity, because the fusion of hydrogen atoms produces either stable substances or else radioactive particles of very short half-lives measured in seconds or minutes. But a thermonuclear device operates in three stages: fission, which is then used to produce fusion, which in turn is used to produce a much more powerful fission reaction. In colloquial terms, an atom bomb is used to trigger a hydrogen reaction, which in turn is used to trigger a superatom bomb reaction. Thus the radioactive material of a thermonuclear bomb stands in a direct relationship to its explosive power. The bomb exploded over Hiroshima, equivalent to 20 kilotons of TNT, yielded about 2 pounds of radioactive material. A 10 megaton weapon will produce about 1,000 pounds of radioactive products, and a 20 megaton bomb, 2,000 pounds.

Differences in explosive power account for different radiological effects. The fireball of a 20 kiloton weapon has a diameter of 1½ miles. The fireball of a 10 megaton thermonuclear weapon has a diameter of 6 miles. Unless exploded at very high altitudes (above 16 thousand feet), it will, therefore, come in contact with the ground below. As it does so, the blast of the explosion dislodges millions of tons of the surface. The rising fireball sucks up this debris and converts it into radioactive material which is then swept up into the stratosphere and deposited downwind. As a result, there takes place over a period of days a continual "fall-out" of radioactive material over an elliptically shaped area. The nature and distribution of the fall-out depends on meteorological conditions and on the constitution of the surface above which the bomb explodes. The material will fall out according to the weight of the debris, the heavier materials falling out first, the lighter drifting farther downwind, the very light material remaining in the stratosphere for some time, thereby affecting the background radiation of the universe. If the target is a city where brick is a common building material, fall-out is aggravated because the silicon in the brick and the lime in the mortar will themselves become highly radioactive.

The ellipse of the fall-out will vary with meteorological conditions. The United States test of March 1, 1954, dangerously contaminated an area of 7,000 square miles (or an area of the size of the state of New Jersey).[7] Dr. Libby, a member of the Atomic Energy Commission, has described a possible contamination of 100 thousand square miles (or an area of the size of the states of New York, New Jersey and Pennsylvania combined).[8]

The effect of fall-out is dependent on the amount of radiation to which an area is subjected. In general, the damage caused by radiation is twofold: direct damage leading to illness, death or reduced life expectancy, and genetic effects. The direct damage is caused generally by gamma rays which penetrate the skin and affect the molecules of the cell structure. Alpha and beta rays cause burns and lesions; they cannot do internal damage unless they enter the system by means of contaminated food or water supplies.[9] Because gamma rays damage the constituents of the blood, they will produce a greater susceptibility to infection. There is strong evidence that radiation may induce

---

[7] "The Effects of High-yield Nuclear Explosions," AEC release, February 15, 1955.

[8] Libby, cited, p. 257.

[9] This is a simplification for purposes of exposition. Beta rays *can* do direct damage, if of sufficiently high energy, though they are not the usual agents. The relevance of the contaminated food or water supplies is that they act as *sources* of alpha and beta rays.

leukemia and cataracts months after exposure. The following table gives some indication of the effects of exposure to radiation. The estimates are conservative and disregard genetic effects entirely. The measurements are in roentgen which is an arbitrary standard of measurement for radiation.

TABLE II

DAMAGE FROM ROENTGEN DOSAGE

Direct Effects of Whole Body Dose on Individual

Roentgen (r)	
0-25	No obvious injury
25-50	Possible blood damages, but no serious injury
50-100	Blood cell damages, some injury, no disability
100-200	Injury, possible disability
200-400	Injury and disability certain, death possible
400	Fatal to 50%
600	Fatal

Source: The Effects of Atomic Weapons, cited, p. 342.

What then will be the likely exposure to fall-out? Exposure varies, of course, with the degree of radioactivity, and this in turn depends on the area covered by fall-out. On the basis of the figures given by Libby, the 7,000 square miles contaminated by the United States test of March 1, 1954, would have received an average exposure during the first twenty-four hours of 938 r's.[10] This is twice the lethal dose and it will produce disability even at the outer edges of the ellipse. To be sure, after the first twenty-four hours radioactivity drops rapidly: it decreases roughly tenfold for every sevenfold increase in age. Thus at the end of a week the radioactivity assumed above would have dwindled to 93.8 r's. This is still a dangerous dosage, however, and exposure to it over any length of time would have serious consequences. Moreover, the

---

[10] Libby assumes an average dose of 69 r's over 100 thousand square miles. This is a conservative figure. After the March 1, 1954, explosion the dosage 100 miles away was 2,300 r's during the first thirty-six hours. See Bulletin of the Atomic Scientists, v. 11 (May 1955), p. 182. (Testimony of Dr. John C. Bugher at the Kefauver hearings.)

radioactivity is persistent: the residual dosage for the period from one week to one year would equal the dosage
received during the first week, or about 1,500 r's.

The casualty rate will depend to a considerable extent
on the awareness by the civilian population of the danger
facing it. If the phenomenon of fall-out is not understood,
or if there are no preparations to deal with it, the casualty
rate from fall-out will approach that produced by the
heat and blast of the explosion. If precautionary measures
are taken, the casualty rate will be reduced, but it will
still remain substantial. Precautionary measures include
shelter of any kind, particularly underground shelters with
very small openings. Basements will reduce exposure and
foxholes will be more effective still. As soon as radiation
has dropped to a relatively safe level, say below 100 r's, decontamination can be started by sweeping radioactive
ash from rooftops and streets, flushing them with water
or even raking the earth. If these decontamination measures are not taken, the area may be uninhabitable for
several months or even years.

The danger from fall-out has been treated rather cavalierly. During the Symington hearings General LeMay testified that a person covered by three feet of dirt would be
relatively safe.[11] But the question remains whether millions
of inhabitants of a 7,000-square-mile area (not to speak of
a 100 thousand-square-mile area under a different set of
meteorological conditions) can remain underground for
the first forty-eight hours of intense radioactivity and apply all necessary precautions afterwards. And the problem
will be even more complicated in case of a sustained attack, because the fall-out patterns of various explosions
may overlap and the explosions may not occur simultaneously. Since the fall-out pattern is so dependent on
meteorological conditions, its effects will be relatively unpredictable in any given attack. Thus fall-out will almost
inevitably catch a substantial proportion of the population
of the affected area above ground. Given the fact that
communications will probably have been impaired by the

---

11 U.S. Senate, *Study of Airpower*, cited, p. 165.

explosion, concerted action will be extremely difficult. Indeed, even informing the population of radiation levels or organizing effective measures for the simplest public health function will not be an easy matter.

Moreover, the fall-out will contaminate crops and water supply. And since animals will not take shelter, livestock will either be killed or contaminated by eating radioactive matter. Thus, even in the best circumstances, fall-out after an attack on the fifty most important metropolitan areas in the United States is likely to produce about 30 per cent of the casualties caused by the explosion, or five to ten million dead and seven to fifteen million injured. More importantly, very few undamaged areas would remain to give assistance to the stricken parts of the country. Indeed, an enemy could plan to detonate his weapons so as to blanket the greatest possible area. Thus all energies of every affected area would have to be directed toward the sheer problem of survival, preventing epidemics, caring for the injured and avoiding so far as possible exposure to radiation.

This will strain the recuperative powers of a country to the utmost. The cities will not be able to count on assistance from the surrounding countryside. Evacuation of cities, even when practicable, may not reduce casualties, for it may simply move the evacuees into a fall-out area. And the fall-out area would not be able to support a large influx of refugees in the face of the destruction of all food supplies. When the question of survival is posed in such elementary form, organized activity will tend to be reduced to the local level and directed to meeting immediate needs.

More refinements could be added, but, at this level of catastrophe, even minimum estimates suffice to make the basic point that a society which suffers a disaster of this magnitude would of necessity have to undergo a fundamental transformation. Europe has never recovered either from the bloodletting or from the shock of World War I. For World War I did more than destroy an elite, it undermined faith in a way of life. On the battlefields of France disappeared the hopes of the Golden Age, of inevitable progress, of triumphant reasonableness, that were as much cardinal principles of nineteenth-century Europe as they are of contemporary America. Since the shock of World War I, strong yet democratic government in Europe has been difficult, because confidence in the traditional leadership has been lacking and because the leaders had lost faith in their mission. The result, in many countries of Europe, was either dictatorship, which represents an abdication of responsibility by the people, or governmental instability, which represents an abdication of responsibility by the leadership.

Analogous, though more abrupt, reactions can be expected in a society which has undergone a sustained thermonuclear attack. Any society operates through confidence in an orderly succession of events, either natural or social. A catastrophe is an interruption in what has come to be considered natural. The panic it often produces is the reflection of an inability to react to an unexpected situation and the attempt to flee as rapidly as possible into a familiar and, therefore, predictable environment. If a familiar environment remains, some confidence can be restored. Most natural catastrophes can be dealt with, because they affect only a very small geographic area or a very small proportion of the population. The remainder of the society can utilize its machinery of cooperative effort to come to the assistance of the stricken area. Indeed, such action tends to reinforce the cohesiveness of a society, because it becomes a symbol of its value and efficiency. The essence of the catastrophe produced by an all-out thermonuclear war, however, is the depth of the dislocation it produces and the consequent impossibility of escaping into familiar relationships. When all relationships, or even most relationships, have to be reconstituted, society as we know it today will have been fundamentally transformed.

III

In addition to its drastic impact on the social structure and the material well-being of the warring nations, an all-out war with modern weapons would produce genetic effects and consequences from long-term fall-out, which might affect all humanity.[12]

The same gamma rays which in larger doses produce radiation sickness are at all levels of exposure capable of producing genetic effects. Any radiation which reaches the reproductive organs will cause changes in the units governing heredity, the genes. A gene which becomes permanently altered is said to mutate. Changes in the genes of the reproductive cells, though usually causing no detectable damage to the person concerned if the dosage is fairly low, may profoundly affect the following and subsequent generations.

Geneticists believe that mutations which are large enough to be measured are generally harmful. In the genetic sense, relatively minor mutations may have as severe consequences as more drastic ones. A serious dosage of radiation may produce sterility and thus work itself out in one generation. A less critical exposure may cause the offspring to be obviously handicapped and not likely to reproduce; it would, therefore, work itself out in two generations. Other dosages may produce handicaps which are transmitted for many generations and which become part of the biological inheritance of the race. Thus a mutation need not necessarily, or even usually, produce freaks. The most common mutations, in fact, are only slightly detrimental in any one generation.

Of course, there are so-called spontaneous mutations which are not induced by radiation. Others are induced by the radiation which is part of the natural background of the universe, as, for example, by cosmic rays. These two causes, in fact, produce most of the mutations which supply the mechanism of evolution. But any additional radiation produces mutations in direct proportion to the exposure. And the genetic effect of radiation is thought by most geneticists to be cumulative; 1 r received yearly over a

---

[12] The best study of the genetic effects is the Report of the Genetics Committee of the National Academy of Science, "Biological Effects of Atomic Radiation," *New York Times*, June 13, 1956. See also H. J. Muller, "How Radiation Changes the Genetic Constitution," and M. Westergaard, "Man's Responsibility to his Genetic Heritage," *Bulletin of the Atomic Scientists*, v. 11 (November 1955), pp. 329-38 and 318-28.

period of thirty years is genetically as significant as 30 r's received at one time.[13] According to the predominant view, there is no such thing as a genetically safe dose, although some dosages may not produce statistically noticeable short-term effects. Since half the United States children are born to parents below the age of thirty, the significant dosage from the genetic point of view is the accumulated exposure over a thirty-year period. At present the population of the United States is exposed to radiation from three sources: general background radiation from cosmic rays—the thirty-year dosage averages about 4.3 roentgens; x-rays and fluoroscopes—the thirty-year dosage amounts to about 3 roentgens; fall-out from weapons tests.

The effects from fall-out, in turn, are of three types: (1) close-in fall-out occurring over an area of several thousand square miles where the radioactive material descends within a period of ten to twenty hours; (2) intermediate fall-out where radioactive material descends within several weeks after the explosion, usually by providing a nucleus for the condensation of rain or snow; (3) delayed fall-out composed of material that remains in the air over a period of months or even years. The last category is composed of very tiny radioactive particles which are swept up into the stratosphere and dispersed by the prevailing winds. They become, in effect, part of the background radiation. If weapons tests were continued at the rate of the two most active years, 1953-55, they would produce an average thirty-year dose of about 0.2 roentgens in the Northern Hemisphere.[14] While *any* increase in radiation should be avoided, the indicated dosage from weapons tests is not of itself likely to produce statistically significant mutations.

It would be different, however, with an all-out thermo-

---

[13] Judgments of this kind are necessarily difficult to verify. The above is the view of the Genetics Committee of the National Academy of Science. While there is some dispute whether radiation exposure is strictly additive over time, all geneticists agree that radiation will induce mutations and that most mutations are harmful.

[14] The Genetics Committee of the National Academy of Science estimates that this figure may vary by a factor of five. That is, it may vary from .04 r's to 1 r.

nuclear war. If even present weapons tests raise the background radiation, it is clear that there must be a theoretical point at which thermonuclear war would produce a level of background radiation which would have serious genetic effects even in the short term. Indeed it is theoretically possible, although less likely, so to contaminate the atmosphere as to wipe out life in the Northern Hemisphere. The background radiation that is of immediate concern to geneticists is the "doubling dosage:" the radiation which would cause the present rate of genetic defects of about 2 per cent to be doubled. Of the 100 million children which are expected to be born to the presently alive population of the United States, 4 million would then have inherited genetic defects, of which 200 thousand would appear in tangible form in the first generation.

Geneticists have not agreed on the amount of radiation required to produce a doubling dosage, estimates varying from 5 r's to 150 r's. The report of the National Academy of Science placed the doubling dosage at between 30-80 r's over a thirty-year period. These levels of background radiation can be produced by a relatively small number of high-yield weapons, as is shown by the following table:

TABLE III

DEGREE OF BACKGROUND RADIATION
PRODUCED BY DIFFERENT TYPES OF NUCLEAR WEAPONS

R	50 MT	20 MT	10 MT	1 MT	50 KT	20 KT
0.2	2	5	10	100	2,000	5,000
3	30	75	150	1,500	30,000	75,000
10	100	250	500	5,000	100,000	250,000
30	300	750	1,500	15,000	300,000	750,000
80	800	2,000	4,000	40,000	800,000	2,000,000
400	4,000	10,000	20,000	200,000	4,000,000	10,000,000

Source: Computed from information given in an article by J. Rotblat, "The Hydrogen-Uranium Bomb," *Bulletin of the Atomic Scientists*, v. 11 (May 1955), p. 172.

Thus 750 20 megaton bombs exploded in the Northern Hemisphere over a thirty-year period would in all likelihood produce a doubling dosage. Even 250 such weapons —a figure well within the combined capabilities of the United States and the U.S.S.R.—would increase the background radiation by 10 r's. This does not take into account the radiation produced either by close-in or intermediate fall-out. Most individuals in these two zones would suffer severe genetic damage in addition to other radiological injuries. In the 7,000 mile fall-out pattern from a 20 megaton weapon, described in the Atomic Energy Commission release of February 12, 1955, the accumulated average dosage at the end of one week would have been in excess of 1,500 r's. With the best precautions, shelter program and decontamination, it is unlikely that the exposure can be reduced to much below 100 r's. This would avoid the worst symptoms of radiation illness; it would, however, almost certainly have very serious genetic effects. Even the 100 thousand-square-mile fall-out pattern described by Libby would have an accumulated average dosage by the end of one week of close to 200 r's. Since decontamination of so vast an area is next to impossible, it would be difficult even with a good shelter program to avoid a dosage which has serious genetic consequences.

Explosions of high-yield weapons produce another serious long-range peril: the fall-out of strontium-90. The danger from strontium is due to its extremely long half-life of nearly twenty years and the fact that it falls out over so wide an area that it may become a source of peril all over the Northern Hemisphere. Strontium-90 is thought to produce bone cancer if absorbed in sufficient quantities; at least it invariably does so in mice. Because it is concentrated in plants, its absorption by humans is almost unavoidable either directly or through the consumption of meat and other products, such as milk, from contaminated animals. Because of its extremely long half-life, the concentration of strontium-90 tends to be cumulative. Thus the current concentration of strontium-90 from weapons tests is on the average 1/10,000 of what is generally considered a dangerous dose; by 1970 the concentration produced by these same tests will have risen to 1/1,000 of the danger dose.[15] After 1970 the concentration will gradually decline, assuming that the testing of high-yield weapons is not carried out at the same scale as in the first years of their development. If even the relatively few test explosions could produce such a concentration of strontium-90, it is clear that an unrestricted thermonuclear war would probably lead to the decimation of the population of the Northern Hemisphere by strontium-90 alone.

Enough has been described to make clear that an all-out war with modern weapons will have consequences far transcending anything previously experienced. The blast and heat effects of thermonuclear and nuclear explosions can paralyze the intimate interrelationships of modern urban life. The immediate fall-out can reduce large areas to subsistence levels. The genetic effects and strontium-90 could threaten the whole human race.

In such a situation, it is futile to speak of "purely" military considerations. From a purely military point of view, nothing is more efficient for cratering airfields, destroying port facilities or eliminating transportation centers than a megaton weapon. But the crucial problem of strategy is the relationship between power and the willingness to use it, between the physical and the psychological components of national policy. Faced with the knowledge of the consequences of a thermonuclear war, policy-makers will be reluctant to engage in a strategy, the penalty for which may well be social disintegration.

The new technology thus increases our dangers at the precise moment when our commitments have never been greater. For the first time in our history we are vulnerable to a direct hostile attack. No remaining margin of industrial and technological superiority can remove the consciousness of our increasing vulnerability from the minds of policy-makers who have to make the decision of peace or war. But perhaps our dangers offer us at the same time a way out of our dilemmas. As long as the consequences of all-out thermonuclear war appear as stark to the other

---

[15] *New York Times,* February 8, 1957.

side as to us, they may avert disaster, not through a reconciliation of interests but through mutual terror. Perhaps our identification of deterrence with retaliatory power, however faulty its historical analogies, provides the basis for achieving a durable peace, after all?

4

THE ESOTERIC STRATEGY—
PRINCIPLES OF ALL-OUT WAR

OF COURSE, stalemates have occurred frequently in the history of warfare. Normally they have been brought about by the emergence of a balance between offense and defense on the battlefield. The distinguishing feature of the current use of the term is that it refers not to a balance on the battlefield, but to a calculus of risks. With each side possessing the capability of inflicting catastrophic blows on the other, war is said to be no longer a rational course of action. To be sure, even if a nuclear stalemate does exist, it would not make for stability in the present volatile state of technology, much less for a sense of harmony. The specter of a technological breakthrough by the other side would always loom large; it would give an apocalyptic quality to all internal relations.

It is important to be precise, however, about the meaning of nuclear stalemate. A great deal will depend on the correctness of our assessment of what the stalemate actually deters or does not deter, and of whether the kind of war to which the term stalemate can properly be applied exhausts the strategic options of either side. In one sense, nuclear stalemate can be taken to mean that victory in all-out war has become meaningless. It is to the implications of nuclear technology for all-out war that we must now turn.

The renunciation of total victory is repugnant to our military thought with its emphasis on breaking the enemy's will to resist and its reliance on the decisive role of

86

industrial potential. Because we have thought of war more in moral than in strategic terms, we have identified victory with the physical impotence of the enemy. But while it is true that a power can impose its will by depriving the opponent of the resources for continued resistance, such a course is very costly and not always necessary. The enemy's decision whether to continue the struggle reflects not only the relation of forces, but also the relationship between the cost of continued resistance and the objectives in dispute. Military strength decides the physical contest, but political goals determine the price to be paid and the intensity of the struggle.

Far from being the "normal" form of conflict, all-out war constitutes a special case. It comes about through the abdication of political leadership or when there exists so deep a schism between the contenders that the total destruction of the enemy appears as the only goal worth contending for. Thus war has been based on "purely" military considerations only during relatively brief periods: during the religious wars of the sixteenth and seventeenth centuries, when a religious schism induced both sides to seek to destroy their opponent; during the wars of the French Revolution, when an ideological schism caused the contenders to attempt to impose their notion of justice by force; and during the cycle of wars beginning with World War I, which started with an abdication of political leadership and has since turned into a revolutionary struggle.

In the intervals between these explosions of maximum violence, war was considered an extension of policy. Between the Congress of Vienna in 1815 and the outbreak of World War I, wars were limited by the political objectives of the opponents.[1] Because they were fought for specific goals which did not threaten the survival of any of the powers, there existed a rough commensurability between the force employed and the transformation sought to be achieved. But, with the outbreak of World War I, war suddenly seemed to become an end in itself. After the first few months of the war, none of the protagonists would

---

[1] The American Civil War was the only exception; it approached the status of a total war precisely because it was a revolutionary struggle.

have been able to name an objective other than the total defeat of the enemy, or at least they would have named objectives, such as the German demand for the annexation of Belgium, which amounted to unconditional surrender. This was all the more remarkable because none of the political leaders had prepared for anything but a war in the nineteenth-century style, with rapid movements and quick decisions, so that the stalemate of the first winter was due primarily to the exhaustion of munitions supplies.

During World War I a gap appeared between military and political planning, which has never been bridged. The military staffs had developed plans for total victory because in such plans no political limitations interfere with the full development of power and all factors are under the control of the military. But the political leadership proved incapable of giving these military objectives a political expression in terms of peace aims. It was forgotten that the rapid decisions of nineteenth-century warfare had been due, above all, to the willingness to acknowledge defeat. And defeat was acknowledged with relative ease because its consequences did not threaten the national survival. When the purpose of war became total victory, however, the result was a conflict of ever increasing violence which petrified its hatreds in a peace treaty which considered more the redressing of sacrifices than the stability of the international order.

It was overlooked, moreover, that total victory was made possible in both wars only through a fortuitous combination of circumstances. The strategy of both world wars rested on two related factors: national economies which yielded a substantial surplus above bare subsistence, and weapons of relatively small destructiveness so that any increase in the strength of one side could prove strategically significant. Until the industrial revolution, total war in the modern sense of fully mobilizing all national resources had been impossible. A subsistence economy simply could not spare the manpower or the resources for such large-scale operations. Armies were, therefore, largely composed of mercenaries, and they were small because the economy could not support a substantial standing force. A mercenary army did not possess the morale of modern citizen armies; the soldiers were not personally concerned with the fate of the country for which they fought and, in the crudest sense, their ability to carry on their profession depended on their survival. Typical battles of the eighteenth century involved complicated maneuvers, which determined the relative position of the two sides, but which caused relatively few casualties because both commanders were eager to conserve their resources and could not rely on the staying power of their troops. Citizen armies, on the other hand, which appeared during revolutionary periods when passions ran high, could not conduct uninterrupted operations; in the absence of a surplus of manpower, they frequently had to disband during the harvest season. This does not mean that wars fought by countries with subsistence economies did not produce great suffering. The very narrow margin of survival ensured that any disturbance of the economic balance was likely to produce cataclysmic effects on society. As a result, until the industrial revolution the collateral effects of war, the casualties caused by starvation or pestilence, were usually more severe than those of the battlefield.

It was the industrial revolution and the specialization of functions it brought about which made possible the total mobilization of modern war. Even then the quest for total victory would have been self-defeating but for the relatively small destructiveness of what is now called conventional technology. For total victory is meaningful only if at the end of the war the victor retains sufficient physical resources to impose his will. And the margin has to be great in proportion as the victory sought is total. The objective of nineteenth-century warfare was to create a calculus of risks according to which continued resistance would appear more costly than the peace terms sought to be imposed. The more moderate the peace terms, the smaller the required margin of superiority. The war ended when a sovereign government agreed to the victor's terms and thereby assumed responsibility for their execution. The victor's task in these circumstances was to supervise the fulfillment of his conditions by a government which in turn retained control over its own population.

With the coming of total war, war has ceased to be an effort to determine the actions of a government; its goal has become, almost invariably, to overthrow the enemy leadership. This has not only transformed every war into a variety of civil war, it has also increased the margin of superiority required to impose the victor's will. Success in overthrowing the enemy government in effect forces the victor to assume responsibility for the civil administration of the defeated. We could afford to do so at the end of World War II, because neither our social nor our material structure had been seriously impaired by the war; if anything, they had been strengthened.

At the scale of catastrophe produced by an all-out thermonuclear war, however, it is doubtful whether any society will retain either the physical or psychological resources to undertake the administration and rehabilitation of foreign countries. When energies are absorbed in an effort to assure bare survival, it is difficult to imagine a sustained effort to assume responsibility for governing the people of the recent enemy, whose social disintegration and physical destruction is likely far to exceed those of Germany and Japan after World War II. And, in the absence of physical occupation, victory may prove illusory. It may create a vacuum which can be exploited by powers whose position relative to the contenders has been improved by the devastation of all-out war. The decline of Europe started with the exhaustion produced by the first World War, for in it even the victors were weakened in relation to the non-European powers.

The destructiveness of modern weapons deprives victory in an all-out war of its historical meaning. Even the side which inflicts a greater devastation than its opponent may not retain sufficient resources to impose its will. And the same exorbitant destructiveness has altered the significance of the industrial potential on which we have traditionally relied for victory. Since World War I our strategic doctrine has always been built around the proposition that our forces-in-being at the beginning of a war need only be large enough to avoid disaster and that we could then crush the enemy by mobilizing our industrial potential after the outbreak of hostilities. The strategic significance of our industrial potential has presupposed a fortuitous combination of circumstances, however: our invulnerability to direct attack, the existence of allies to hold a line while we were mobilizing, and, above all, a certain stage of industrial and technological development.

Our industrial potential would have been unavailing if it could have been destroyed at the outset of a war. Our geographic remoteness would have become a liability if we had not had allies to hold a line while we mobilized. The same factors which made it difficult for an enemy to attack us would have militated against an attempt on our part to restore the situation if Eurasia had fallen under the domination of a single power. Thus, even at the stage of conventional technology, the emergence of the U.S.S.R. as the dominant power in Eurasia and the decline in strength of our traditional allies would have altered the significance of our forces-in-being and the relative importance of our industrial potential. Because resistance in major areas of the globe is now impossible unless the United States lends its support at the very outset or pledges it in advance, we require forces-in-being to carry out a large part of the task which has heretofore been performed by our allies: to hold a line while we bring our power to bear. And the importance of forces-in-being becomes all the greater because we are now subject to a devastating attack at the beginning of any war and because the increased power of modern weapons has demonstrated that the significance of industrial potential depends on a certain balance between the complexity of weapons and their destructiveness.

Until the middle of the nineteenth century, weapons were simple and easy to manufacture and their destructive power was very low. As a result, trained manpower was scarcer than military equipment; military superiority depended on human rather than on material resources. Even a backward nation could achieve eminence, provided it had sufficient human material, because simple weapons systems did not require an elaborate industrial plant.

Thus Russia became a major power despite an almost complete lack of industry. Until the middle of the nineteenth century, the limiting condition to the conduct of war was rarely the lack of equipment. Time and again powers rose from complete defeat by replenishing their military arsenals, often in a matter of a few months. Victory, almost invariably, was due to greater reserves of manpower or to a superior strategy, rarely to a superior industrial capacity.

In order to put a premium on industrial potential, weapons must be sufficiently complex to require a substantial production effort, but not so destructive as to drain the national substance before industrial mobilization can make itself felt. If the stockpiles of weapons available at the beginning of a war suffice to destroy the opponent's industrial potential, it is clear that industrial potential has lost a great deal of its significance and that the side whose forces-in-being are superior, whatever its industrial base, will gain a decisive advantage. As a result, our industrial potential proved strategically most significant when there existed a balance between the destructiveness of weapons and the complexity of the means of their delivery. Any increase either in the power of weapons or in their number could then be translated into a strategic advantage. But when weapons have become extremely powerful, there is an upper limit beyond which increased destructiveness pays diminishing returns. When both sides are capable of inflicting catastrophic losses on each other with their forces-in-being, an increment of destructive power may be strategically insignificant.

The greater the power of individual weapons, the less the importance of numbers or even of quality—the twin expressions of a superior industrial capacity. When one plane can carry a weapon capable of destroying a city, the side with the larger number of planes will derive little advantage from them if its opponent possesses a sufficient quantity to inflict a devasting counterblow. Even superior quality may be overcome to some extent by the power of modern weapons. A more sophisticated delivery system will be meaningless as long as both sides can reach their targets. Thus an all-out war fought with modern weapons will be decided by the forces-in-being. We can no longer afford to count on a more or less prolonged period of mobilization. The only way we can derive an advantage from our industrial capacity is by utilizing it *before* the outbreak of a war.

The importance of forces-in-being, coupled with the destructiveness of modern weapons, means that Douhet's classic description of air strategy, which has determined to a considerable extent our thinking about all-out war, is now obsolete: ". . . aerial warfare admits of no defense, only offense. *We must therefore resign ourselves to the offensives the enemy inflicts upon us, while striving to put all our resources to work to inflict even heavier ones upon him.*"[2] The identification of victory with a superior offensive effort—in effect, the air strategy of World War II—made sense so long as a superior load of explosives represented an absolute margin of effective power; it could be decisive to the degree that attrition of industrial potential was significant. In a war fought with modern weapons, however, the significant attrition is that which reduces not the industrial potential, but the forces-in-being. The industrial potential can be wiped out in the later stages of a war, almost at will, but if the enemy's forces-in-being are not destroyed at the very beginning, they will inflict a series of blows which may cause the social fabric to break down long before the enemy's stockpile of weapons is exhausted.

The importance of forces-in-being compared to industrial potential has a paradoxical consequence: that a war can continue long after victory has become meaningless. For example, it is possible for a surprise attack to destroy the fifty most important metropolitan centers in the United States, with the consequences described in the previous chapter. While this could produce social disintegration, it would probably not affect the ability of our

---

[2] Giulo Douhet, *The Command of the Air* (translated by Dino Ferrari; New York: Coward-McCann, 1942), p. 55, as quoted by Bernard Brodie in "Some Notes on the Evolution of Air Doctrine," *World Politics*, v. 7 (April 1955), p. 368. (The italics are Douhet's.)

Strategic Air Command to retaliate. The result of such an exchange of blows might well be the social collapse of *both* contenders. The fact that an all-out strategy can be implemented after the social basis for it has disappeared lends an esoteric quality to the strategy of all-out war. It has been compared to a situation where two hostile tribes armed with poison darts face each other across a canyon. The poison takes several hours to be effective, but is fatal afterwards. In these circumstances, landing the first blow will not be decisive. It will ruin the "economy," but the weapons are still useful and they can deliver an equally lethal counterblow.[3] Thus victory can be achieved only if one side succeeds in destroying the other's poison darts—its forces-in-being—*before* they can be launched.

In assessing the strategy appropriate for all-out war, it is important to distinguish two sets of circumstances: the strategy appropriate for the offensive and that for resisting attack. In the past, the strategy for avoiding defeat was roughly identical with that which aimed for victory. In an all-out thermonuclear war, on the other hand, the two strategies differ. Victory, in the sense of imposing one power's will, can be achieved only by eliminating the opponent's retaliatory force while retaining sufficient striking power to exact acquiescence through the threat of thermonuclear devastation.

The fact that victory in all-out war presupposes the destruction of the opponent's forces-in-being has given rise to the argument that such a war could be confined to destroying the installations of the opposing strategic striking forces. Because the outcome of the war depends on the issue of the air battle, it is argued, the bombing of cities would be unwise in the early stages of a war and unnecessary after air superiority has been achieved.[4]

This argument assumes that victory is the only rational objective in an all-out war and that both sides can aim for victory simultaneously. But the nature of modern

---

[3] C. R. Sherwin, "Securing Peace Through Military Technology," *Bulletin of the Atomic Scientists*, v. 12 (May 1956), p. 160.

[4] Paul H. Nitze, "Atoms, Strategy and Policy," *Foreign Affairs*, v. 34 (January 1956), p. 193.

war works counter to such assumptions. Victory, the destruction of the opponent's forces-in-being or the reduction of it to levels which can be contained by the defense system, is in practice unattainable except by surprise attack. For, with adequate warning, the victim of aggression can disperse or launch his forces-in-being and alert his defenses.

Once a surprise attack has been carried out, however, the strategic problem for the victim is transformed. Instead of aiming to wipe out the enemy's retaliatory force which, with the advantage of initiative is probably airborne, he must now strive to deprive the opponent of the fruits of his assault. The strategy for avoiding defeat would not seek to keep damage to a minimum, which is the reason for limiting a war initially to the destruction of air installations. On the contrary, the most effective reaction to surprise attack may well be to inflict maximum devastation on the opponent's society. An air battle would be the most rational strategy for the side which has the advantage of surprise, because it would place the enemy at its mercy at minimum cost. But for the side which stands to lose the air battle, the most rational strategy may well be to exact the highest price by inflicting the greatest possible devastation. Thus, there exists no "cheap" way for fighting an all-out war, for the losing side, whatever its initial strategy, may resort to the kind of bombing which will maximize the damage inflicted on its opponent. It must not be forgotten that fifty 10-megaton weapons, properly placed, could kill or injure at least 30 per cent of the population of the United States and approximately the same proportion in the Soviet Union.

It is against this background that the strategic problem of all-out thermonuclear war must be considered. An all-out war will be primarily an air war, or at least a war of strategic striking forces, and it will be decided by the forces-in-being. As for the United States, our strategic problem is complicated by the fact that we have explicitly rejected surprise attack as an instrument of our policy. This is demonstrated not only by repeated statements of policy, but above all by our entire past behavior. If we refrained from utilizing our atomic monopoly at a time when the Soviet capability to retaliate was almost nonexistent, it is against all probability that we would do so now.

But the side which concedes the first blow in all likelihood also concedes the margin required to impose its will. As a result, unless our air defense is capable of reducing the enemy blow below the level of catastrophe—an unlikely situation—the strategic problem of all-out war must be stated for us not in terms of a strategy to achieve victory, but of a strategy to avoid defeat. The purpose of our capability for all-out war will be to deter Soviet aggression against us by developing a retaliatory force of a size which can inflict an unacceptable amount of damage on the enemy, no matter what level of destruction he may accomplish by a surprise attack. "A deterrent force," General LeMay has said, "is one that is large enough and efficient enough that no matter what the enemy force does, either offensively or defensively, he still will receive a quantity of bombs or explosive force that is more than he is willing to accept. Therefore, he never starts a war." [5]

II

Deterrence is the attempt to keep an opponent from adopting a certain course of action by posing risks which will seem to him out of proportion to any gains to be achieved. The higher the stakes, the more absolute must be the threat of destruction which faces him. But the reverse is also true: the smaller the objective, the less should be the sanction. For the power of modern weapons deters not only aggression, but also resistance to it. An all-out strategy may, therefore, be highly effective in deterring all-out war. If it is the sole counter to enemy aggression, it may at the same time invite limited aggressions which by themselves do not seem "worth" a final showdown.

---

[5] U.S. Senate, *Study of Airpower,* Hearings before the Subcommittee on the Air Force of the Committee on Armed Services, 84th Cong., 2nd Sess. (Washington: GPO, 1956), p. 202.

The crucial problem for a strategy which seeks to deter all-out war is to prevent a situation from arising in which the U.S.S.R. can calculate that it possesses a sufficient margin of certainty to make a surprise attack on the United States seem a worthwhile risk. To be sure, such a strategy presupposes a certain amount of rationality in an enemy. But strategy can only count with a somewhat rational enemy; nothing can deter an opponent bent on self-destruction.

What is a sufficient degree of certainty, and how can it be achieved? Obviously, the mere ability to inflict a greater amount of damage than the enemy will be meaningless if at the end of the war the victor does not retain sufficient resources to impose his will. An aggressor, in trying to decide whether to launch an all-out war, must therefore be able to count on a combination of the following factors: he must be certain that his surprise attack will reduce our forces-in-being to a level at which his defense can contain them, or at least at which they are no longer able to inflict unacceptable damage; he must be confident that our air defense will not reduce his attacking force to a level at which it will no longer be able to inflict the amount of damage he calculates as necessary to impose his will. The degree of certainty, moreover, must be almost foolproof: a slight probability will not be sufficient, for the attacker is staking not his chances of victory, but his national survival.

An all-out attack by the U.S.S.R. could, therefore, be impelled only by a consciousness of overwhelming power, of great United States vulnerability, or the fear of an imminent United States attack. The last contingency is a special case and will be discussed separately. Can the U.S.S.R. then calculate with the possession of an overwhelming superiority? Many witnesses before the Symington Committee argued as if military superiority depended almost entirely on numbers of airplanes, particularly of long-range bombers. ". . . the only thing I can say," testified General LeMay, "is that from 1958 on, he [the U.S.S.R.] is stronger in long-range air power than we are, and it naturally follows that if he is stronger, he may feel that he should attack." [6]

But this does not follow naturally at all. Superiority cannot be measured in numbers of offensive planes alone; it depends also on the capability for defense. A country which staked everything on its offensive air power would be simplifying the strategic problem of its opponent. In planning his offensive, an aggressor could calculate precisely the number of planes required for maximum destructiveness. They could operate at optimum levels of performance and use the most efficient tactics. Except for mechanical failures, they would suffer no losses and their bombing accuracy would be high. Nor would the country which placed all its bets on its offensive air power gain a significant advantage by utilizing for its strategic striking force the resources which might otherwise have gone into air defense. With modern weapons, the point of diminishing returns in increased offensive power is reached fairly quickly.

The best strategic posture for an all-out war depends on the proper "mix" of offensive and defensive capabilities. If so many resources are devoted to defense that the offensive striking force can no longer inflict an unacceptable degree of damage on the aggressor, the enemy may be tempted to attack. Once freed of the danger of retaliation, the worst that could happen to him would be his inability to reach the target. If the defense is slighted, too great a demand is put on the powers of resistance of society. The ideal offense-defense relationship is one in which the defense can reduce the enemy attack to acceptable levels while the offense cannot be so contained by the enemy's defense.

Such a relationship is unattainable in practice, but the adequacy of the posture for all-out war depends on the degree to which it can be approximated. Since the ultimate outcome of an all-out war depends so importantly on the ability of the strategic striking forces to reach their

---

[6] Same, p. 213.

targets, any discussion of the strategy for all-out war must start with the problems of the offensive.

The Soviet Long-Range Air Force is a comparatively recent development, dating in effect from 1954. To be sure, ever since 1948 the U.S.S.R. has possessed a moderate number of TU-4's (for which the NATO code name is "Bull"). This was a copy of our B-29, one of which had fallen into Soviet hands during the war after making an emergency landing in Siberia. Since the range of the TU-4's was only 2,200 miles, they could reach only a very small portion of the United States mainland, and then only on one-way missions. The development by the U.S.S.R. of long-range planes capable of undertaking two-way missions, when coupled with the growth of the Soviet nuclear stockpile, therefore, represented a basic trans-formation in the postwar strategic balance. Henceforth, in every decision of peace or war we would have to weigh our risks in terms of the prospective destruction of our major cities.

The present Soviet Long-Range Air Force is composed of two basic types of planes: a turbo-propeller-driven plane of very long range, for which the NATO code name is "Bear," and a heavy jet bomber, for which the NATO code name is "Bison." The United States Air Force has no equivalent for the "Bear," whose major asset is its long radius of about 4,000 miles. Because of its relatively slow speed (450 miles per hour) compared to that of modern jet planes, its losses against high-performance fighters and missiles would be considerable. The "Bison" was first seen in some quantity during the May Day parade of 1955 when thirteen of them flew over Moscow. The "Bison" is estimated to have a radius of around 3,000 miles and a top speed of 610 miles per hour.[7] Thus the "Bison" is able to reach only a third of the United States without aerial refueling, even from Soviet advanced bases on the Kola and Chukchi peninsulas. The "Bear" can cover from

---

[7] This is an Air Force estimate, based on Air Force testimony before the Symington Committee, U.S. Senate, *Study of Airpower,* cited, p. 175. See also Richard E. Stockwell, *Soviet Air Power* (New York: Pageant Press, 1956), Illustrations.

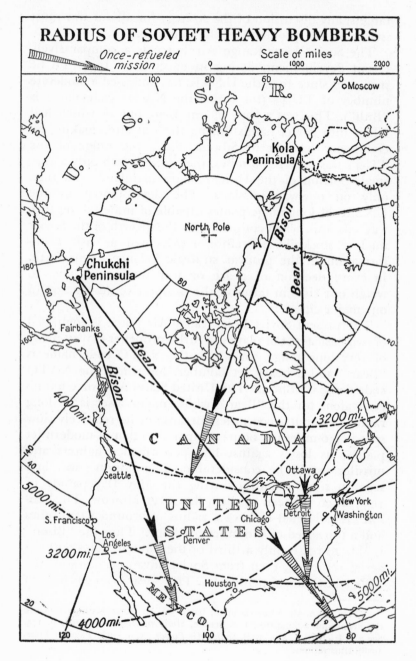

RADIUS OF SOVIET HEAVY BOMBERS

one-third to one-half of United States territory from advanced Soviet bases without aerial refueling. From the Chukchi peninsula the "Bison" can cover seven-eighths of the United States with one aerial refueling and all of the United States with two refuelings. From the Kola peninsula the "Bison" can cover one-fourth of the United States with one refueling and all except the southern tip of Texas on a twice-refueled mission. The "Bear," of course, will be able to cover all of the United States from Soviet advanced bases with one aerial refueling.[8] (See map, p. 100.)

The United States Strategic Air Force possesses three basic types of bombers: the medium-range B-47, which has a top speed in excess of 600 miles per hour and a range in excess of 3,000 miles; the obsolescent B-36, which has a top speed of 435 miles per hour and a range of 10,000 miles; and the new heavy bomber, the B-52, which has a range in excess of 6,000 miles and a top speed in excess of 650 miles per hour. The B-47, of course, is not an intercontinental bomber. It requires aerial refueling to reach Soviet targets from United States territory, although it can cover most of Soviet territory from overseas bases. The B-52 is an intercontinental bomber which can attack metropolitan Russia from the United States, but whose effectiveness will be increased by our overseas base structure. We now possess 33 wings of B-47's with 45 planes in a wing; 5 of these are reconnaissance wings with 30 planes in a wing, so that the effective force of B-47's is 1,410 planes.[9] Our B-36's are organized in 11 wings of 30 planes. As they are replaced by B-52's, the number of planes in a wing will increase to 45. By 1959, when our heavy bomber wings will be all jet, we will have about 500 B-52's.[10] The consensus of Air Force testimony at the Symington hearings was that by 1959 the Soviet Long-Range Air Force

8 U.S. Senate, *Study of Airpower*, cited, p. 175.

9 Same, p. 1,810. (These figures are not quite consistent, but they are the official ones given in the Air Force testimony before the Symington Committee.)

10 Same, p. 117.

would outnumber ours and that for this reason we would be in dire peril.[11]

Strategic superiority cannot be measured numerically, however, for it depends also on such factors as the quality and range of planes and the location of air bases. The prospective numerical superiority of the U.S.S.R. is confined, to begin with, to the category of heavy bombers. The B-52's will be fewer than the combined numbers of "Bisons" and "Bears." To be sure, the Soviet Air Force also has a substantial number of medium-range jet bombers, code-named "Badger," with a range of about 3,000 miles. They are unable, however, to reach the United States from present Soviet bases, except on one-way missions. Their role in an all-out war would be confined to attacking our overseas air bases. Our medium bombers, on the other hand, are capable of attacking Soviet targets either from our overseas bases or from the United States by using aerial refueling techniques which have become standard practice in our Strategic Air Command. As a result, even quantitatively the strategic equation is not as foreboding as a comparison of heavy bomber forces would make it appear.

Moreover, a Soviet attack on the United States is a technically more complex undertaking than performance figures of planes would indicate. In order to achieve maximum surprise and cut warning time to a minimum, an all-out attack should be launched from the airfields where planes are based for training. But neither the "Bison" nor the "Bear" can reach any part of the United States, except the tip of Maine, from the interior of the U.S.S.R., without aerial refueling.[12] To launch a massive blow they would have to be staged to advanced bases in Russia's Arctic regions. This in turn would give us some additional strategic warning. At the very least, it would cause the United States Strategic Air Force to be placed on the alert, thus reducing the possibility or the degree of surprise. Under certain conditions it might induce us to launch a preventive attack.

---

11 Same, p. 212 (General LeMay); p. 818 (General Twining).
12 Same, p. 175.

Even from advanced bases the Soviet heavy bombers cannot reach major United States targets and return without at least one aerial refueling. There is little evidence, however, that the Soviet Air Force has mastered the intricate technique of aerial refueling; it is not even certain that the Soviet Union possesses any substantial number of tankers. Even after the Soviet Air Force has developed aerial refueling, it may be prevented by geography from deriving full benefit from it. A plane which is refueling in the air is extremely vulnerable; it should therefore do so in an area relatively immune from hostile interference. This is all the more important because the meeting between tanker and bomber must be precisely calculated, so as to take place on schedule. Diversionary tactics forced on either plane can wreak havoc with refueling plans.

A look at the map (p. 100) demonstrates that in an attack on the United States, the Soviet Long-Range Air Force would possess no safe areas for refueling once it leaves its advanced bases. It would have to refuel over hostile territory exposed to constant attack. This would tend to increase the rate of attrition and minimize the possibility of surprise. Aerial refueling, in short, is not an efficient Soviet tactic, and one-way missions are uneconomical, given the cost and complexity of present planes and the difficulty of replacing them.

Unless the U.S.S.R. possessed a really staggering number of planes and unless its initial attack completely eliminated our retaliatory force, the reliance on one-way missions would shift the balance against the Soviet Long-Range Air Force with every raid. A strategy based on one-way missions would eliminate the aggressor's forces-in-being and thereby the instrument to impose his will. A country which has suffered a surprise attack by one-way missions would already have experienced the worst its opponent is capable of inflicting. Surrender is induced, however, not only as a reaction to past punishment but by the prospect of future danger. Even the maximum damage accomplished by one-way missions may not enable an aggressor to impose his will unless he retains resources to inflict *additional* devastation as the penalty for not complying with his wishes.

An aggressor who used up all or most of his delivery vehicles in a surprise attack would become totally vulnerable to retaliation if his opponent had any remaining offensive strength. One-way missions with present complicated planes are more suitable for a strategy of desperation than for a surprise attack. Thus a comparison of relative offensive capabilities does not indicate a sufficient Soviet margin to make it seem probable that the Kremlin will deliberately unleash all-out war, at least until its strategic striking forces become much larger and its planes develop longer range.

III

New Soviet planes with longer range may, of course, overcome the refueling problem and enable the Soviets to launch an attack from the interior of metropolitan Russia. Even then complete surprise will be difficult to achieve. The directions from which a Soviet attack by airplanes on the United States can take place are limited. Equivalent resources put into air defense by the United States and the Soviet Union will yield greater strategic returns for the United States with fewer approaches to guard than for the Soviet Union with a long periphery to defend.

To be sure, an effective air defense is complicated by the power and range of modern weapons. In World War II, a rate of losses of 10 per cent was considered unacceptable. With conventional weapons the cost of producing the plane and of training the crew was so high in relation to the damage which could be inflicted in a single raid that, unless a plane could perform several missions on a statistical average before being shot down, strategic bombing became a wasteful operation. But when one plane can carry a weapon capable of destroying a city, much heavier demands are placed on the air-defense system. To produce significant attrition, it must be able to hold the enemy offensive to a level which preserves the social fabric from destruction. Against a strategic air force armed with thermonuclear weapons, losses of as high as 90 per cent inflicted upon the attacking force may not prevent catastrophic devastation.

Although no air-defense system now foreseeable is capable of preventing widespread devastation, its mere existence imposes an additional strain on the enemy. It forces him to devote more resources to his offensive striking force without adding to its strategic impact. The very existence of an air defense throws off an attacker's calculations. He cannot be certain about the effectiveness of the defense until he has tested it, and he must, therefore, allow a wider margin for error than in the case of an unopposed attack.

In order to overcome a determined defense, it is necessary to increase the attacking force considerably. But the larger the striking force, the more obvious the preparations which have to be made before launching a blow and the greater will be the chances of obtaining warning. As the defense gains in effectiveness, the attacker must also divert resources to combat it directly, further decreasing his strategic effectiveness. To be sure, as Paul Nitze has shown in a brilliant paper, the attrition rate of defense will not remain fixed at the same percentage, regardless of the nature of the attack.[13] By exceeding a certain scale of attack, it is possible to overwhelm the opposing defense. A defense system may exact 80 per cent attrition of the first 2,000 planes, but only 20 per cent of the next 1,000. But the basic function of defense still holds: at best, to reduce the enemy attack to acceptable levels; at worst, to force the enemy to devote the greatest possible amount of resources to his offensive mission without improving its probable effectiveness.

Work on the United States air-defense system did not start seriously until 1952, when we first became concerned about the Soviet Long-Range Air Force. Its primary functions are detection, identification, interception and destruction of hostile aircraft. The magnitude of the problem is shown by the fact that on an average day there are

---

[13] Paul H. Nitze, "Impact of New Weapons on Political and Strategic Problems of the West," speech delivered before the Nobel Institute, Oslo, June 1955.

30 thousand domestic and 600 foreign flights which have to be monitored, at least as they approach sensitive areas.[14] Detection is crucial. Not only must it provide time for effective interception, but it must also give sufficient warning to prevent our retaliatory force from being caught on the ground. By 1959, the United States will possess a detection system against which surprise attack by manned bombers will be very difficult, and it will be supported by a defensive force that should impose a substantial rate of attrition on the attackers.

The United States air-defense system is based on four lines: two primarily for detection and two others for interception as well. The first detection apparatus is at the Distant Early Warning Line (DEW Line) which extends across the Arctic circle. This is a network of heavy radar stations supported by an elaborate communications system. When fully developed, it should be able to detect a Soviet attack soon after it leaves Soviet advanced bases on the Kola and Chukchi peninsulas. The DEW Line is backed up by another series of detection stations from the base of Hudson Bay across Canada. The mid-Canada Line, like the DEW Line, is designed for detection only, although, given the power of modern weapons and the effects of fall-out, it would be desirable to destroy hostile planes as far away from their targets as possible and over relatively uninhabited regions. It has been proposed for this reason to move the first fighting line into Canada, and this may be the case by 1961 when the detection system has been fully developed.

At present, the first sustained interception—except for Canadian efforts—will occur at a line along the United States-Canadian border. From their first contact with this line, enemy planes will be exposed to heavy interceptor attacks. As they approach sensitive areas, they will be subject to antiaircraft fire, which by 1959 will be almost entirely composed of guided missiles: either the Army Nike or the Air Force Talos and other missiles still under development. With a range of 60-100 miles, soon to be

---

14 For a very good description of our air-defense system, see U.S. Senate, *Study of Airpower*, cited p. 303 ff. (Testimony of General Partridge.)

extended, and with atomic warheads which can destroy anything within a cubic mile of air, the missile defenses are becoming increasingly formidable. Many experts estimate that they will be able to inflict losses of up to 80 per cent of an attacking force. Such losses might not discourage pilots in the first wave of attack, especially if they were unacquainted with the risks confronting them, but there is at least some doubt about their morale once the rate of attrition became known. Conceivably pilot morale may become the limiting condition of strategic air war conducted by manned bombers.

There exists, moreover, another factor which makes it difficult for the U.S.S.R. to achieve surprise or wipe out our forces-in-being—our system of overseas air bases. (See map, p. 108.) Since the aggressor cannot know the precise pattern of dispersal of our retaliatory force, he must, in order to have a calculable margin of success, seek to hit all the bases of our Strategic Air Command, preferably simultaneously. But their geographic location makes a simultaneous attack on all United States bases almost impossible. Since the SAC bases in the continental United States are located at a much greater distance in flying time from Soviet territory than our overseas bases, the Soviet Long-Range Air Force would have two options. It could launch its attacks simultaneously against our bases both in the United States and overseas, with the result that Soviet planes would be detected overseas before the planes destined to attack our domestic bases had reached the DEW Line, thus adding to the alert time available to SAC in the United States. Or the Soviet Air Force could arrange its flight plans so that planes would reach the two sets of targets simultaneously. In this case, our overseas bases would have the same warning time as those bases located within the territorial United States—the time it takes a jet bomber to cover the distance between our DEW Line and the target.

The first of these two contingencies—an attempt so to arrange flight plans that our overseas bases will be attacked about the time that the first Soviet long-range planes reach the DEW Line—is the more rational course

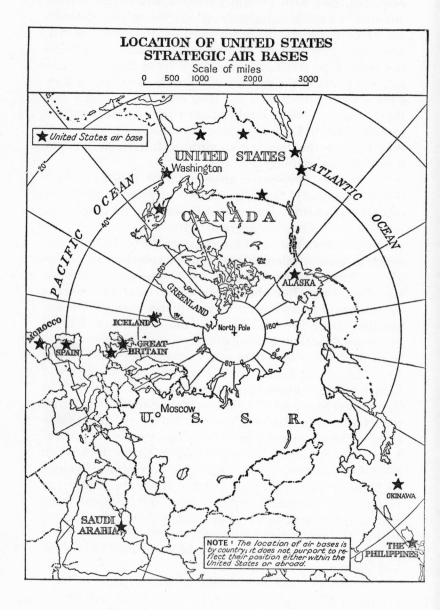

LOCATION OF UNITED STATES
STRATEGIC AIR BASES
Scale of miles
0   500 1000   2000   3000

★ United States air base

UNITED STATES
Washington
PACIFIC OCEAN
CANADA
ATLANTIC OCEAN
ALASKA
GREENLAND
North Pole
ICELAND
MOROCCO
GREAT BRITAIN
SPAIN
Moscow
U.   S.   S.   R.
OKINAWA
SAUDI ARABIA
THE PHILIPPINES

NOTE: The location of air bases is
by country; it does not purport to reflect their position either within the
United States or abroad.

of action. An effort to attack both sets of targets simultaneously would expose the Soviet Union to a counterblow launched from our overseas bases while Soviet planes were still crossing Canada.

But surprise even against our overseas air bases will not be easy to achieve. Because they are located along the periphery of Eurasia, any attack against them must cross intervening friendly territory, and this in turn should give them between one to two hours of warning time. And even a successful attack against our overseas bases would still leave the retaliatory force in the United States to be reckoned with, and it would be all the more formidable because of the additional warning time thus made available to it. Our overseas air bases therefore increase not only our offensive but also our defensive strength. They force the Soviet Air Force either to add to our warning time or to absorb a heavier United States offensive effort; they function either as a form of early warning or as an addition to our retaliatory power.

By contrast, the Soviet defensive problem is much more complicated than ours. While we have to defend a limited number of approaches, the Soviet Union must be prepared to repel raids from many directions, because our overseas bases ring the Soviet periphery. The existence of our carrier task forces, soon to be equipped with attack planes with a combat radius in excess of 1,500 miles, further adds to the Soviet problem. And our advantages in geographic position make aerial refueling a much more useful tactic for us than for the U.S.S.R. Even should a Soviet surprise blow against our overseas bases force us to launch our retaliatory attack from the United States, our planes could refuel over friendly areas and out of range of Soviet detection.

Finally, while the Soviet Air Force can reach its targets in the United States only across some 1,500 miles of hostile Canadian territory, many of the presumed targets of our Strategic Air Force in the U.S.S.R. lie much closer to the Soviet early warning line. While we can expect a warning time of about two hours, the minimum considered necessary for effective defense measures, the Soviet will have no such assurance. To be sure, if the Soviet Air Force launches a surprise attack, their defensive system will be previously alerted against our counterblow. Nevertheless, the need to disperse their defenses, due to our superior base system, makes it highly unlikely that the U.S.S.R. will be able to reduce our retaliatory blow to acceptable levels.

Two conclusions emerge from this brief sketch of the United States air defenses. (1) The strategic significance of the Soviet Long-Range Air Force resides not in its total numbers but in that part of it which can escape attrition. Estimates of the attrition rate run as high as 80 per cent by 1959, when the Soviet heavy bomber fleet is expected by some to exceed ours in numbers. (2) Whatever the attrition rate, the U.S.S.R. will find it almost impossible to achieve complete surprise. Against the present family of Soviet bombers, targets in the northern part of the United States should have at least two hours of warning, and targets in the southern part, where most of our SAC bases are located, would have three hours' warning. If we are reasonably effective, such a warning time should in turn enable us to launch a substantial proportion of our retaliatory force, and this, together with the portion of SAC which is constantly airborne at any given moment, should give us the opportunity to inflict a devastating counterblow.

In fact, in assessing the relative capabilities of both sides for winning an all-out war, it seems that for a limited period of time, until the Soviet Long-Range Air Force grows substantially stronger than it now is, we could probably impose our will on the U.S.S.R. through a surprise attack. A surprise attack launched simultaneously from our overseas bases and the continental United States might overwhelm the Soviet air defense and seriously cripple the Soviet Long-Range Air Force. Even then the U.S.S.R. could probably inflict serious losses on us.

This is not an argument for preventive war. It is simply an attempt to analyze the real nature of strategic relationships. In the face of our strategic superiority, there is no need to be panicked by Soviet atomic blackmail. The Soviet leadership, as will be seen below, has skillfully fostered the illusion that it is willing to run all risks and that resistance to its pressures or any attempts to exploit its embarrassments may unleash a cataclysm.[15] However useful this position may prove from the point of view of psychological warfare, it is belied by the strategic facts. The notion of nuclear stalemate under present conditions is more a testimony to the fears and conscience of the non-Soviet world than to actual Soviet power. In the short term the stalemate, if it exists, will be a balance between our unwillingness to use all-out war to achieve our goals and the Soviet inability to do so. With the growth of the Soviet Long-Range Air Force and thermonuclear stockpile, the stalemate in all-out war will be between the ability of each side to inflict catastrophic blows on the other but to do so only at the risk of national catastrophe.

IV

There is no reason for complacency, however. Even today there exist vulnerabilities which in time may cause serious changes in the strategic equation and expose us to unnecessary peril. Unless we reverse present attitudes, these vulnerabilities can be expected to increase. They are the dispersal of our Strategic Air Force, the neglect of civil defense, and the lag in antisubmarine warfare. All three vulnerabilities are produced by the same attitude: a preference for active to passive measures, a predilection for offense over defense. Few concepts have been more difficult for us to accept than that the outcome of an all-out war may be determined not only by offensive power, but by the relative vulnerability of the contenders.

Since our strategic doctrine concedes the first blow to the other side, dispersal of the Strategic Air Force becomes of cardinal importance. Dispersal is a form of defense, because it makes it more difficult to destroy our striking forces and their installations on the ground. Today our Strategic Air Force of some 2,000 planes is concentrated

---

[15] See below, Chapter 11, p. 392.

on about 30 bases. The danger of inadequate dispersal was demonstrated in 1952 when a tornado damaged 80 per cent of our strategic striking force then located on some 18 bases. Today equipment worth $300 million is frequently located on bases costing $40 million. This degree of concentration not only improves the economics of a Soviet attack; it is also a wasteful investment of our offensive resources. To be sure, our overseas bases afford a greater degree of dispersal than is indicated by mere numbers of installations. Nevertheless a moderate additional investment in base construction could halve our vulnerability.

Then, too, much of our present air-defense system was designed for use against subsonic planes. Increased speed and altitude, even of manned Soviet bombers, will greatly reduce its effectiveness. It is vulnerable, moreover, to electronic countermeasures, at which the Soviet Air Force is becoming increasingly adept, and to low-level attacks. Finally, the present concept of beginning interception close to the United States-Canadian border is no longer adequate to the power of the new weapons. If the attacking planes are equipped with "dead-man fuses" which detonate the bomb in case the plane is destroyed, fall-out casualties would approach catastrophic proportions, even if the target itself escaped the effects of heat and blast.

As the increasing power and speed of delivery vehicles multiply the difficulties of active defense, ever greater importance should be attached to civil defense. While active defense seeks to destroy the largest possible proportion of the enemy attacking force before it reaches its target, civil defense strives to blunt the enemy offensive by reducing as much as possible the damage which it can inflict. A dispersion of targets will reduce the value of enemy hits. Locating essential resources in deep shelters will deprive a successful attack of a great deal of its effectiveness. A country whose steel industry can be wiped out by one weapon is more vulnerable than an opponent whose steel industry is dispersed over 30 different locations. A power whose population is protected to some degree by a deep shelter program can run greater risks than an enemy whose people are totally exposed to attack.

Civil defense has the advantage, moreover, that it is relatively immune to advances on the part of the offensive. Any improvement in the speed or range of delivery vehicles alters their relationship to the active defense. It improves their chances of survival, but it does not affect their ability to destroy the target if they can reach it. Dispersal would be a form of insurance after the present air-defense system has become obsolescent. Deep shelters would offer a measure of protection even after ballistic missiles have replaced the manned bombers.

In the present state of our civil defense an attack against us with high-yield weapons would be devastating. An attempt to evacuate a city like New York would clog all traffic arteries and prevent effective assistance being rendered. In the absence of shelters the casualties from heat and blast would be enormous. Without foreknowledge of the effects of fall-out, people might behave in precisely the manner calculated to bring about the highest level of casualties. An attempt to flee the fall-out area during the first two days of maximum radioactivity would expose an individual to the largest dosage of radiation. An insufficient awareness of the nature of radioactive contamination would multiply casualties. The absence of a tested communications system would put the population at the mercy of rumor and prevent any concerted effort to alleviate suffering.

The psychological impact of a sudden thermonuclear blow against an unprepared population would prove even more pernicious. Since the physical effects of an all-out war waged with modern weapons will prove devastating, the individual will be confronted with the collapse of all the material objects and arrangements which he has associated with the ordered flow of life. To a considerable extent his reactions will depend on how well he has been prepared psychologically. A thermonuclear war which broke over a psychologically unprepared population might lead to a loss of faith in society and government. A comparable disaster which has been foreseen and provided against might actually serve to demonstrate the value of the existing network of social relationships. World War II produced a much smaller social dislocation than did World War I, although the devastation it caused was at least as great, because it was entered with fewer illusions. The psychological crisis after World War I was caused as much by the incongruity between performance and aspiration as by the casualty lists. It rose as much out of the undermining of faith in the ideal of a rational and harmonious world as out of the realities of trench warfare which made the previous expectations appear fatuous.

It is important, therefore, to prepare a "familiar environment" in advance of the catastrophe of all-out war, and to avert panic by discipline even when many of the physical objects which confer a feeling of security have disappeared. A major effort should be made to train the American population in the most effective behavior in order to reduce casualties from fall-out and blast to the minimum. Great emphasis should be placed on creating an emergency communications system as immune as possible to nuclear attack, so that organized activity can be resumed at the earliest possible moment.

Because the warning time available will become progressively shorter, falling to a maximum of twenty minutes in the missile age, and because of the perils of fall-out, protection for the civilian population can be achieved, if at all, only by a program of deep shelters. Others have described a shelter program in detail,[16] but a few salient characteristics may be outlined here. Because of the short warning time likely to be available in the missile age, shelters should be so located that they can be reached in fifteen minutes—the approximate time between the detection and the explosion of a missile. Because the high level of radio-activity immediately after an attack makes prolonged exposure highly dangerous, shelters should have supplies of food, water and medicine for several days. They should be connected with a central communications system, so that levels of radiation and instructions for cooperative behavior can be communicated. Even simple home-shelters,

---

16 See Edward Teller, "If an H-Bomb Hits—", *U.S. News and World Report*, v. 40 (March 2, 1956), pp. 42-3.

it has been estimated, should be able to reduce casualties by a significant percentage.[17]

Even with these precautions, the effect on society of a catastrophe on the scale of a thermonuclear attack must not be underrated. History suggests that suffering, if pressed beyond a certain point, inevitably leads to political or social transformations. Society can exact a measure of sacrifice as the price of maintaining itself, but excessive suffering tends to tear the social fabric apart. However just a war may appear at the beginning, it may be ascribed in retrospect to inadequate leadership if the losses it causes are thought exorbitant. Within limits, civil defense can contribute to the cohesiveness of society in the face of massive shock. While it cannot avert the traumatic effect of vast physical destruction, its efficient operation may make the difference between the survival of a society and its collapse.

Another source of grave peril is the growing Soviet submarine fleet. Germany entered World War II with 65 submarines, and even at the height of the war their number never exceeded 100. The German submarines were really submersible surface ships which could not cruise underwater for long periods. Yet even this fleet equipped only with conventional explosives nearly gained control of the Atlantic.

At the end of the war the Soviet Union captured a number of German "Schnorkel" submarines capable of cruising underwater for long periods, and it has since built up its fleet to a total of perhaps 450. After nuclear-powered submarines have been developed—and, given the state of Soviet nuclear technology, this is only a question of time—the Soviet Union will possess a "true" submarine craft which can remain submerged indefinitely and which can cruise underwater quietly and at high speed. By 1960 the Soviet Fleet may possess as many as 700 submarines of various types, including nuclear-powered submarines, most

---

17 See Willard Bascom, *Civil Defense Against Great Fires,* prepared for the National Academy of Sciences, Advisory Committee on Civil Defense (n.p.: June 1956); and also "Difference Between Victory and Defeat," *Life,* v. 42 (March 18, 1957), pp. 150-62.

of which will be able to fire missiles with nuclear and thermonuclear warheads.

A force of this magnitude will pose a tremendous threat both to our allies and to our command of the seas. Submarines with 1,500-mile missiles will in effect be able to place any island under siege and threaten portions of the globe which are now immune to Soviet attack, such as Australia. They will add considerably to the Soviet strategic striking power even against the continental United States. Over 50 per cent of the population of the United States lives within three hundred miles of the coastline. Submarines with 1,500-mile missiles lying 500 miles off-shore could cause fearful damage. To be sure, such an attack could not prevent our launching a devastating counterblow against the U.S.S.R. and would therefore not enable the Soviet Union to win an all-out war. But it will be an additional form of blackmail. It will increase the reluctance of the free world to run the risks of an all-out war and may thereby paralyze resistance to aggression short of a direct onslaught on the United States.

The large and growing Soviet submarine fleet will increasingly offer a threat to our command of the seas. Submarines of the World War II type were highly vulnerable to surface vessels because of their slow speed, inferior armament, and lack of armor. In a battle between a well-armed surface vessel and a submarine, the former was almost inevitably the victor. For the submarine could sink its opponent only by a direct hit below the waterline and could launch its torpedoes only when close to the surface and therefore most vulnerable. Modern weapons have, however, equalized the relationship between submarines and surface vessels to a considerable extent. A direct hit anywhere with a nuclear weapon will sink any ship, however heavy its armor. A miss of several miles with a thermonuclear weapon may put the largest ship out of action. Even if the ship remains afloat, casualties to its personnel may cause it to become useless as an instrument of war. Modern submarines can no longer be out-run by surface ships and they are able to fire missiles from the depths of the sea. When anything that can be detected can be sunk, protection is above all afforded by the superior ability to hide, and here the submarine seems to have a decided advantage over the surface ship. Moreover, whatever restrictions on methods of warfare the combatants may accept explicitly or tacitly because of the mutual fear of destroying each other's civil population, these will not apply in sea warfare. The largest weapon can be used at sea without fear of decimating populations.

Against a submarine fleet of the size of the Soviet one, surface ships will have a very difficult time, particularly when submarines have learned to overcome their difficulty in locating targets, perhaps by using guided missiles. The Soviet leadership will then be able to employ its submarine fleet in support of peripheral aggressions, to interdict communications and to confront us with the dilemma of whether Soviet submarine activity is "worth" an all-out war. Against large-scale Soviet submarine activity, the Seventh Fleet, charged with protecting Formosa may, for example, be so occupied with purely defensive operations that it will not be able to carry out its primary mission. And unless the Soviet submarine fleet can be hunted down and destroyed in the early stages of a war, supply by sea of foreign bases and allies may become impossible.

One of the most important tasks of United States strategy is, therefore, to develop an effective antisubmarine strategy. During the Symington hearings, the Navy argued that the best method for dealing with enemy submarines was to destroy their home ports by air attacks from carrier task forces. But such a strategy will probably not eliminate the submarine menace quickly enough and it may not prove possible to apply it in limited war.[18] As the Soviet fleet of nuclear-powered submarines grows, a large number of long-range submarines can be kept constantly at sea. It may even be possible to develop civilian uses for submarines, such as carrying freight, which would make the presence of Soviet undersea craft near United States or allied shores "legitimate" and thus overload our detection apparatus. Because of the ability of these submarines

---

[18] See below, Chapter 5, p. 165 ff., for a discussion of the role of the submarine in limited war.

to stay at sea for very long periods of time and the enormous damage which can be caused by even one submarine equipped with nuclear weapons, it is essential to develop methods for destroying enemy submarines at sea as rapidly as possible in the event of war. As in air strategy, the submarine forces-in-being must be eliminated *before* they have done their damage. Attrition through the destruction of port facilities is not likely to be effective quickly enough to avert widespread devastation by submarines at sea when the war breaks out.

The vulnerabilities of the United States to nuclear attack, while extremely serious, must be viewed in proper perspective. For the immediate future they are not likely to be so great as to tempt the Soviet leaders to undertake a surprise attack, either because the Soviet Long-Range Air Force is not yet sufficiently strong, or because some of our vulnerabilities, as in the field of civil defense, are matched by similar deficiencies in the U.S.S.R. Thus if we behave effectively we have time to make good our shortcomings. We should press more vigorously the dispersal of our Strategic Air Force. We must bring into being a really effective civil defense organization. And we must develop new antisubmarine capabilities. If we carry out these measures, all of which lie in our own control, all-out war should remain an unattractive course for the U.S.S.R.

v

How will new technological developments affect the strategic equation of all-out war? There has been a great deal of discussion about the possible consequences of technological breakthroughs which may be achieved by either side, and, given the current rate of technological change, this factor presents a real problem. Not every technological advance is a technological breakthrough, however. A considerable effort goes into simply keeping up in the technological race. An improved fighter plane may do no more than balance a new type of bomber without affecting the strategic equation. A technological breakthrough is an advance which either establishes a *new* capability or improves an existing one to a point at which it can overwhelm the opposition. Thus the strategically significant technological breakthroughs are likely to occur in the relation between offense and defense: either through the discovery of a means of defense that can contain the opposing offense, or through the development of an offense that can overwhelm the opposing defense and eliminate the retaliatory force before it has been launched.

Our thinking about technological breakthroughs may, in any case, have been too much affected by the memory of our atomic monopoly. Then, to be sure, an unparalleled increase in power was coupled with our exclusive possession of the new discovery. Both of these conditions were almost unique in history. In the past, new inventions generally brought about only a slight increase in destructive capability; gunpowder in its early stages was not significantly more destructive than the crossbow. And generally, the technological advance was available to several powers, even if for conceptual or political reasons they did not avail themselves of it.

It is likely that the future impact of technology on strategy will approximate the traditional pattern rather than the dramatic discovery of nuclear weapons. A significant breakthrough has become technically much more difficult, not because major advances are no longer possible, but because they may add little to a power's strategic effectiveness. Traditionally, a scientific breakthrough was strategically significant if it improved either the destructiveness of weapons or the speed and efficiency with which they could be delivered. In both of these categories the upper limit of what can be translated into strategic advantage has either been reached or is rapidly being approached. It is already the case that an increase in explosive power will pay hardly any strategic returns, for existing weapons are sufficiently powerful to encompass the destruction of even the largest area targets. And with the advent of intercontinental missiles, which can traverse a distance of 5,000 miles in less than half an hour, added speed may prove only marginally significant.

Henceforth, technology can assist strategy primarily by developing new applications for existing weapons, by combining them more efficiently and by developing subtler and more discriminating uses rather than by adding to their power and speed.

In assessing the significance of new technological developments, it is necessary to examine the advantage they may give to the side which discovers them first, as well as the implications for strategy if both sides come to possess them concurrently. A strategic gain is possible even if *both* sides develop a new weapon at the same time. The almost simultaneous invention of the thermonuclear bomb improved the Soviet strategic position more than ours. Whereas we were already able to inflict devastating damage with nuclear weapons, the tremendous power of the new bomb enabled the Soviet Air Force to redress the balance between the two strategic striking forces with fewer planes. Similarly, an atomic submarine developed by the U.S.S.R. will pose a greater threat to an ocean-going nation like ours than to a landlocked power like the U.S.S.R.

Are the technological developments which loom ahead likely to affect the strategic balance in an all-out war? On the offensive side, two basic advances are in prospect: the nuclear-powered airplane and ballistic missiles. The advantage of the nuclear-powered plane is its extraordinary range, which will in fact be limited only by crew fatigue. (The atom-powered submarine, "Nautilus," for example, traveled 50,000 miles on its original supply of fuel.) It will also probably be able to carry a heavier bomb load, although, given the power of modern weapons, this is strategically of marginal significance. Such a plane would make our overseas bases less important and it would eliminate the need for aerial refueling. It would also greatly complicate the enemy's problem of defense, for it could circle just outside the range of enemy detection and then attack at a moment's notice. Because nuclear planes can remain aloft for such long periods, the vulnerability of the retaliatory force will be reduced by its ability to keep a larger percentage of its planes in the air at any given time.

Because a nuclear-powered striking force can attack from its training bases, it has a greater opportunity to achieve surprise.

Nevertheless, the development of the nuclear airplane will not by itself upset the strategic balance. If we develop it first, it would simply enable us to do more efficiently and from the continental United States what we are already capable of achieving by aerial refueling and the use of overseas bases. It would not add a decisive increment to our strategic power. If the Soviet Union develops the nuclear plane first—which is unlikely—it would complicate our defensive problem. We would lose the warning time which is now conferred by the necessity for the Soviet forces to stage their planes to advanced bases. But the basic relationship described above would continue. The speed of the first family of nuclear planes is not likely to exceed that of the present family of jet planes. The Soviet Long-Range Air Force, therefore, would still have to negotiate a band of 1,500-3,000 miles exposed to our air defense before they reach their targets. Our present detection system would thus probably continue to give us two to four hours of warning. In the most likely contingency that both sides possess nuclear planes concurrently, the effect will be that the increase in the possibility of surprise will be made up by the decreased vulnerability of the forces-in-being. Hence the stalemate in an all-out war is not likely to be broken by the introduction of nuclear-powered airplanes.

This is all the more true because over the next ten years the defense is likely to be gaining relative to the manned bomber. The utilization of missiles for air defense, which is still in its infancy, is certain to be spurred by research into the offensive uses of guided missiles. The speed of missiles is enormously greater than that of any manned plane now in prospect, and they can be launched in such quantities as to make the survival of manned bombers exceedingly difficult. They will soon possess atomic warheads which can destroy any plane within a cubic mile of air and, as nuclear technology advances, they can be engineered to encompass an ever bigger radius of destruction. The attrition rate of the air defense against manned planes, however powered, is likely to continue to rise. That rate is already sufficiently high so that a strategic attack carried out with conventional explosives would be uneconomical. And even thermonuclear attacks with manned planes may in time become very difficult. Long before this point is reached, however, a new family of offensive weapons will have been developed, which will pose extraordinarily difficult problems for the defense: the ballistic missiles of varying ranges.

After it receives its initial impetus, a ballistic missile pursues a fixed trajectory, analogous to that of an artillery shell. The ballistic missiles which will be used for strategic bombing are propelled by rockets: the first such weapon was the German V-2 of 1944-45 which had a range of about 200 miles. The distinguishing features of ballistic missiles are their speed and the altitude at which they fly. The highest point of the trajectory of the German V-2 was 50 nautical miles and its speed approached five times the speed of sound. An Intercontinental Ballistic Missile will fly at a speed twenty times that of sound, and will have a range in excess of 5,000 miles. Its transit time between Soviet and United States territories will be only about thirty minutes. Against this weapon our present detection apparatus will not be powerful enough and our air-defense system will have neither adequate weapons nor a sufficiently rapid reaction time.

Do the ballistic missiles constitute a technological breakthrough, then? It is necessary to distinguish the kind of missile—whether of intercontinental or intermediary range (around 1,500 miles)—and the probable consequences of which side develops it first.

If the Soviet Union develops a 1,500-mile missile first, it will not fundamentally upset the strategic balance. A 1,500-mile missile would be useful primarily for blackmailing our allies or threatening our overseas air bases. Both tasks can now be accomplished by Soviet light and medium jet bombers (the "Beagle" and the "Badger"). To be sure, a 1,500-mile missile could carry out these missions more rapidly. It could reduce the warning time to practically nothing and, if its aim were sufficiently accurate, it might make overseas air bases untenable. On the other hand, it could do so only by provoking an all-out war, and it could not avert a retaliatory blow against Soviet territories from bases in the United States. A 1,500-mile missile could not, therefore, decide an all-out war, although if launched from submarines it could wreak considerable havoc. Indeed, the major utility of a 1,500-mile missile for Soviet strategy may lie in a twilight zone of naval warfare where missile-launching submarines are used for interdiction and siege operations just short of all-out war.

Possession by us and our allies of a 1,500-mile missile would add substantially to our strategic capabilities. From present United States bases or from ships, a 1,500-mile missile could reach all of Soviet territory except a small portion of Asiatic Russia. Even if both sides should achieve a 1,500-mile missile concurrently, it would add more to our effective strength than to that of the Soviet bloc. In the possession of our allies, it might improve their ability to withstand Soviet atomic blackmail by enabling them to pose a similar counterthreat. Nevertheless, possession of a 1,500-mile missile will not confer a decisive advantage. Unless we strike the first blow, and perhaps not even then, the U.S.S.R. would still be able to launch a devastating attack against us. Moreover, the intermediate-range missile will probably not be available in sufficient quantity or with adequate accuracy before the development of another weapon, the Intercontinental Ballistic Missile, which will make it almost impossible for either side to achieve total victory through all-out war.

It is expected that both sides will possess Intermediary-Range Ballistic Missiles by 1961 and Intercontinental Missiles by 1963. Even if one side develops one of these missiles a year or two before the other, the first prototypes will not have sufficient accuracy, and they will not exist in sufficient operational quantity to confer a decisive advantage. After 1963 both sides will possess increasing numbers of Intercontinental Ballistic Missiles armed with thermonuclear warheads. The consequences of this development will be paradoxical. While it will enable both sides to achieve complete surprise—or reduce the period of warning under optimum conditions to twenty minutes—it will also make it impossible to achieve any significant advantage through surprise.

In a strategy based on manned bombers, the purpose of a surprise attack is to destroy the enemy's bombers where they are most vulnerable—on the ground. The apparatus for launching a bomber—the airfield—is so costly relative to an airplane that it must house a certain minimum number of planes in order to operate efficiently, and an upper limit is thus placed on the ability to disperse the retaliatory force. Since there will always be far fewer air bases than airplanes, the most efficient strategy in a war fought with manned bombers is to seek out and destroy the enemy's forces-in-being on the ground by launching a surprise attack against them before they can take to the air.

With the advent of ballistic missiles, however, dispersal will be almost complete. The launching mechanism of an Intercontinental Missile is less elaborate than an airfield. It is more maneuverable and easier to conceal or camouflage. When Intercontinental Ballistic Missiles exist in quantity, many of their launching sites will undoubtedly be underground; others will be mobile. Under such conditions a surprise attack can have no purpose. It would be next to impossible to identify all launching sites or to destroy them, if identified. Even the maximum of surprise could at best destroy the opponent's national substance; it would not eliminate his ability to inflict a retaliatory blow of similar power. All-out war could still be devastating, but it could no longer achieve its purpose—the destruction of the opponent's retaliatory force.

As weapons grow more destructive, and forces-in-being more invulnerable to surprise attack and to defense systems, the real contest in an all-out war will be between the vulnerabilities and the resiliency of the opposing societies. If an aggressor became convinced that a sudden blow might dissolve the fabric of our society while his own society would remain intact, he might be willing to risk all-out war despite the severe damage he would suffer in return. As the strategy shifts from an attempt to eliminate forces-in-being to a conscious attempt to disrupt society, a great premium is placed on the civil defense measures outlined above. In the age of the ballistic missile the known ability of a society to withstand a severe attack will become an increasingly important deterrent. When no strategic advantage can be gained from additional offensive power, superiority can be achieved, if at all, only through an improved protection of the population. Nevertheless, while such a course is essential to conserve as much of the human resources as possible, it does not suffice to make all-out war a rational policy choice for either side, short of a naked struggle for survival. Little can be done to avoid widespread physical devastation, and even the best shelter program would not reduce civilian casualties below the point of major disaster.

VI

Whatever the calculation, then, whether it be based on the feasibility of a surprise attack with present weapons and delivery systems or on the impact of imminent technological trends, it is difficult to see how either side can count on achieving its objectives through all-out war. It is possible to calculate relative advantages in base structure or delivery capabilities, but they do not add up to a margin which would leave either side sufficient resources to impose its will. The essence of the nuclear stalemate is that it keeps the two superpowers from launching an all-out war because each can force the other to pay an exorbitant price for victory.

The speed and power of modern weapons has thus brought about a paradoxical consequence: henceforth the only outcome of an all-out war will be that *both* contenders must lose. Under almost any foreseeable circumstances, an upper limit of destruction will be reached before attrition of industrial potential can make itself felt and, long before that point is reached, the forces-in-being on

both sides will have inflicted losses completely disproportionate to any objective which is likely to be the original
purpose of the war. Nuclear stalemate should, therefore,
not be confused with nuclear parity. It comes about because, after a certain point, superiority in destructive
power no longer pays strategic returns.

In such a situation deterrence becomes a complex problem. From now on the decision between peace and war,
never an easy one, will be complicated by the consciousness
that all-out war entails the risk of national catastrophe.
Obviously no power will start a war it thinks it is going
to lose. But it will also be reluctant to start a war if the
price may be its national substance. All-out war is therefore
likely to turn into a last resort: an act of desperation to
be invoked only if national survival is unambiguously
threatened. And what constitutes an unambiguous threat
will be interpreted with increasing rigidity as the risks of
all-out war become better understood.

The capability for waging all-out war thus operates as
a protection against a sudden onslaught on the territorial
United States. It also poses risks which may make the decision to initiate war for any lesser objective increasingly
difficult. The nuclear stalemate may prevent all-out war.
It will not deter other forms of conflict; in fact it may
even encourage them. The side which can present its
challenges in less than an all-out form thereby gains a
psychological advantage. It can shift to its opponent the
agonizing choice of whether a challenge which explicitly
stops short of all-out war should be dealt with by total
retaliation.

If the decision to engage in all-out war is going to
be difficult for the United States, it will be next to impossible for most of our allies. We have, for a little while at
least, the protection of distance. While this cannot avert
a heavy attack, it can at least provide a measure of warning and it permits some degree of defense. Most of Europe, however, is only some forty minutes' flying time
from advanced Soviet bases, and the greatest Soviet air
strength is in light and medium jet bombers. Moreover,
while the size of the United States makes it at least con-

ceivable that our society could withstand a thermonuclear onslaught, both history and geography combine to cast doubt on Europe's ability to do so. Thermonuclear devastation, coming after the ravages of two world wars, might lead to the collapse of the European social structure. And the density of Europe's population would involve fearful casualties. A minister who knows that a small number of megaton weapons properly distributed could kill or injure over half the population of his country will not resort to all-out war except as a very last resort—and perhaps not even then.

Finally, the nuclear stalemate affects not only relations among the nuclear powers but their relations to powers which do not have a nuclear establishment. At a time when the relations between the two great powers are increasingly shaped by the awareness that their thermonuclear capability enables them to avoid defeat but not to achieve a meaningful victory, the role of the smaller nations is being strangely enhanced by the increased strength of the superpowers. This is true not only because the rivalry of the two blocs endows the uncommitted nations with an increased importance. It is equally due to the fact that vis-à-vis the underdeveloped countries the modern weapons confer no meaningful increase of strength. Because the underdeveloped areas are hopelessly inferior to the major powers, even in terms of conventional technology, they will not be impressed by the fact that nuclear weapons make it possible to encompass their destruction even more efficiently than before.

Although the margin of superiority of the industrialized over the underdeveloped nations has never been greater, it has also never been less effective. In every crisis from Korea to Suez, the nonnuclear powers have behaved as if nuclear technology did not exist. They could do so because they knew that two considerations would inhibit the major powers: the consciousness that the employment of nuclear weapons would bring about a feeling of moral revulsion in the rest of the world, and the fear that the employment of nuclear weapons anywhere might set off a chain of events ending in an all-out war. Thus, the

minor powers are in a sense insulated from the nuclear
age by the incommensurability between the power of
nuclear weapons and the objectives for which they might
be employed, as well as by the inhibitions which are generated by a major reliance on an all-out strategy.

All-out war has therefore ceased to be a meaningful instrument of policy. It cannot be used against the minor
powers for fear of the reaction of world opinion and also
because its intricate strategy is not appropriate to wars
of limited objectives. And it cannot be used against
a major power for anything except negative ends:
to prevent the opponent's victory. Thus an all-out war
which starts as an all-out war is the least likely contingency, although it is the only one for which we have an
adequate doctrine. To be sure, an all-out war could come
about as the result of an irrational decision or of a miscalculation or because a small war may gradually spread.
There is no protection against irrational decision except
to deprive the other side of the power to injure us with it—
a possibility which ended with our atomic monopoly. Miscalculation and the gradual spreading of little wars will be
considered in a later chapter, although, with national catastrophe the penalty for miscalculation, all the pressures
will operate on the side of caution. The fact remains that
under present or foreseeable conditions it is difficult to
think of a national purpose that could be advanced by
all-out war.

This is not to say that we can afford to be without a
capability for fighting an all-out war, or that it will be
easy to maintain the conditions which will make such a
war seem unattractive to an opponent. Obviously, if we do
not retain a well-protected capability for massive retaliation, the calculus of risks described in this chapter with
respect to all-out war would shift. An opponent might
then consider it worth the gamble to launch a surprise
attack against us. It does mean, however, that, if we behave effectively, we can always make the risks of all-out
war seem prohibitive to an adversary. The control over
the conditions which will determine whether there is going to be an all-out war will depend to a large ex-

tent on us. Whether we keep up in the technological race, whether our retaliatory force is well dispersed, whether our air defense exacts the maximum attrition and our civil defense is capable of preventing panics—all these decisions are within our exclusive control. But although these conditions are within our control they will not be easy to achieve. At the current rate of technological change the side which has conceded the first blow to its enemy will always live on the verge of catastrophe, for an adverse technological breakthrough is always possible. Thus the stalemate for all-out war is inherently precarious. It will impel a continuous race between offense and defense, and it will require a tremendous effort on our part simply to stay even.

It is the complexity of maintaining the nuclear stalemate which gives its esoteric quality to much of our military thought. The military must plan on the basis of the opponent's capabilities, and in a period of budgetary squeeze they must devote scarce resources in the first instance to guard against the worst contingency, which is an all-out war. This leads to the concern with surprise attack, with destroying the enemy's forces-in-being, with all the eventualities that are least likely to occur. As a result, high-powered detection apparatuses sweep the skies along thousands of miles of perimeter. Hundreds of planes are poised on airfields ready to hurtle into the sky. A fearful responsibility falls on an ever smaller group of men: the individuals who have to interpret the information gathered by the detection systems. Is an unidentified flight of planes a strayed training mission, a reconnaissance effort, or the precursor of a surprise attack? On the correct answer to this question depend the lives of tens of millions on both sides. And, given the speed of modern weapons, there is no margin for error. There will not even be the moral consolation that a Soviet surprise attack will appear unambiguous to world opinion. Given the distribution of the base system, our retaliatory blow is likely to reach Soviet territory before the first Soviet planes have reached their targets after crossing the Distant Early Warning Line.

Because all-out war is so intricate and so sophisticated, and because its risks are so fearful, the necessary concern with it leads to a psychological distortion: it tends to transform the modes of a war which can only be a last resort into a doctrine for the only feasible strategy; it leads our military and political leaders to identify each technological advance with strategically significant progress. In every crisis, short of direct Soviet attack, it furnishes arguments for a policy of minimum risk, not only because of the dangers of all-out war but also to reserve our all-out capability either for a principal enemy or to meet a less ambiguous challenge.

In the process, the relationship between policy and strategy tends to be lost. The more stark the consequences of all-out war, the more reluctant the responsible political leaders will be to employ force. They may invoke our all-out capability as a deterrent, but they will shrink from it as a strategy for conducting a war. The more military strategy emphasizes the resort to an all-out strategy, the more the responsible policy-makers will come to believe that no cause except a direct attack on the United States justifies the use or the threat of force and that the Soviet leadership is equally strongly motivated to avoid all-out war.

This dilemma is well illustrated by the Symington hearings. The military leaders, particularly of the Air Force, described Soviet power as if all options were equally open to the Kremlin and as if every increase in Soviet air strength were immediately translatable into a strategic advantage. Secretary Wilson, however, insisted that the growing Soviet nuclear stockpile and its expanding Long-Range Air Force were less significant than the transformation of Soviet society toward a more peaceful outlook.[19] Thus an exclusive concern with a war fought on the basis of "purely" military considerations stimulates, as its counterpart, an emphasis on "pure" diplomacy, or a reliance on historical trends. The counterpart to "massive retaliation" is a belief that diplomacy can settle disputes through the

---

[19] U.S. Senate, *Study of Airpower,* cited, p. 1,666. (Testimony of Secretary Wilson.)

processes of negotiation, detached from the pressures which otherwise shape international intercourse. As a consequence, the crucial problem of modern strategy is rarely considered explicitly: what kind of military superiority is strategically significant, and what strategy can give an impetus to policy rather than paralyze it.

The dilemma which has been pointed up by the Symington hearings has been defined as the choice between Armageddon and defeat without war. The enormity of modern weapons makes the thought of all-out war repugnant, but the refusal to run any risks would amount to handing the Soviet leaders a blank check. We can overcome the paralysis induced by such prospects only if our strategy can pose less absolute alternatives to our policymakers. To be sure, we require at all times a capability for all-out war so great that by no calculation could an aggressor hope to destroy us by a surprise attack. But we must also realize that a capability for all-out thermonuclear war can only avert disaster. It cannot be employed to achieve positive ends.

We thus return to the dilemma which has plagued all our postwar military thinking. Does the nuclear age permit the establishment of a relationship between force and diplomacy? Is it possible to imagine applications of power less catastrophic than all-out thermonuclear war?

5

WHAT PRICE DETERRENCE?
THE PROBLEMS OF LIMITED WAR

PERHAPS THE BASIC PROBLEM of strategy in the nuclear age is how to establish a relationship between a policy of deterrence and a strategy for fighting a war in case deterrence fails. From the point of view of its impact on the aggressor's actions, maximum deterrence can be equated with the threat of maximum destructiveness. From the point of view of a power's readiness to resist aggression, the optimum strategy is one which is able to achieve its goals at minimum cost. The temptation of strategic doctrine is to seek to combine the advantages of every course of action: to achieve maximum deterrence but also to do so at minimum risk.

Ever since the end of our atomic monopoly, however, this effort has been thwarted by the impossibility of combining maximum destructiveness with limited risk. The greater the horror of our destructive capabilities, the less certain has it become that they will in fact be used. In such circumstances deterrence is brought about not only by a physical but also by a psychological relationship: deterrence is greatest when military strength is coupled with the willingness to employ it. It is achieved when one side's readiness to run risks in relation to the other is high; it is least effective when the willingness to run risks is low, however powerful the military capability. It is, therefore, no longer possible to speak of military superiority in the abstract. What does "being ahead" in the nuclear race mean if each side can already destroy the other's national substance? What is the strategic significance of adding to the destructiveness of the nuclear arsenal when the enormity of present weapons systems already tends to paralyze the will?

It is the task of strategic doctrine to strike a balance between the physical and the psychological aspects of deterrence, between the desire to pose a maximum threat and the reality that no threat is stronger than the belief of the opponent that it will in fact be used. A strategy which poses alternatives that policy-makers are unwilling to confront will induce either inaction or improvisation. A strategy which establishes a superior balance between power and will may then gain a crucial advantage, because it permits initiative and shifts to the other side the risks inherent in making countermoves.

The reliance on all-out war as the chief deterrent inhibits the establishment of this balance. By identifying deterrence with maximum power it tends to paralyze the will. Its concern with the physical basis of deterrence neglects the psychological aspect. Given the power of modern weapons, a nation that relies on all-out war as its chief deterrent imposes a fearful psychological handicap on itself. The most agonizing decision a statesman can face is whether or not to unleash all-out war; all pressures will make for hesitation, short of a direct attack threatening the national existence. In any other situation he will be inhibited by the incommensurability between the cost of the war and the objective in dispute. And he will be confirmed in his hesitations by the conviction that, so long as his retaliatory force remains intact, no shift in the territorial balance is of decisive significance. Thus both the horror and the power of modern weapons tend to paralyze action: the former because it will make few issues seem worth contending for; the latter because it causes many disputes to seem irrelevant to the over-all strategic equation. The psychological equation, therefore, will almost inevitably operate against the side which can extricate itself from a situation *only* by the threat of all-out war. Who can be certain that, faced with the catastrophe of all-out war, even Europe, long the keystone of our security, will seem worth the price?

As the power of modern weapons grows, the threat of all-out war loses its credibility and therefore its political effectiveness. Our capacity for massive retaliation did not avert the Korean war, the loss of northern Indo-China, the Soviet-Egyptian arms deal, or the Suez crisis. A deterrent which one is afraid to implement when it is challenged ceases to be a deterrent. Moreover, whatever the credibility of our threat of all-out war, it is clear that all-out thermonuclear war does not represent a strategic option for our allies. Thus a psychological gap is created by the conviction of our allies that they have nothing to gain from massive retaliation and by the belief of the Soviet leaders that they have nothing to fear from our threat of it.

This gap may actually encourage the Soviet leaders to engage in aggression. The destructiveness of nuclear weapons having made it unlikely that any responsible statesman will lightly unleash a general war, one of the gravest dangers of all-out war lies in miscalculation. This is the only war which it is within our power to avoid, assuming we leave no doubt concerning our capabilities and our determination. But even this "avoidable" war may break out if the other side becomes convinced that we cannot interfere locally and that our threats of all-out war are bluff. If that should happen, the Soviet bloc may then decide, as its nuclear arsenal grows, to absorb the peripheral areas of Eurasia by means short of all-out war and to confront us with the choice of yielding or facing the destruction of American cities. And because the Sino-Soviet leaders may well be mistaken in their assessment of our reaction to such a contingency, the reliance on "massive retaliation" may bring about the total war it seeks to prevent.

To be sure, a threat to be effective need not be *absolutely* credible. An aggressor may be reluctant to stake his national existence for a marginal gain even if he should have some doubts about whether a threat will in fact be implemented. It has even been argued that a reduction of our forces around the Soviet periphery would multiply Soviet hesitations because it would make clear to the Soviet leaders, beyond doubt, that *any* aggression may involve all-out war.[1] And for purposes of deterrence, so the argument goes, what we *may* do will prove as effective as what we *will* do.

Such a strategy, however, would be highly risky and demoralizing. It would widen the gap between the psychological and physical components of policy even more. It is a strange doctrine which asserts that we can convey our determination to our opponent by reducing our overseas commitments, that, in effect, our words will be a more effective deterrent than our deeds. It overlooks that all Soviet and Chinese aggressive moves have occurred in areas where our commitment of resources was small or nonexistent: Korea, Indo-China and the Middle East. Above all, a strategy which sought to compensate for its lack of plausibility by posing ever more fearful threats would be demoralizing. It would place control over our survival entirely in the hands of another power, for any Soviet move, however trivial, would force us to respond, if at all, by what may amount to national suicide. It ignores the contemporary revolution which, as events in the Middle East and the satellite orbit have shown, may create its own tensions independent of the plans of the major powers and which may force the United States and the U.S.S.R. to contest certain areas despite themselves.

This is another way of saying that the threat of all-out war purchases deterrence at an exorbitant risk. It requires us in every crisis to stake our survival on the credibility of a threat which we will be increasingly reluctant to implement and which, if implemented, will force us into the kind of war our strategy should make every attempt to avoid. The costs of all-out war are too fearful for it to be our only response to a challenge. Even if it could be won, we should seek to achieve our objectives at smaller

---

[1] See, for example, Basil Henry Liddell Hart, "Military Strategy vs. Common Sense," *The Saturday Review*, v. 39 (March 3, 1956), pp. 7-8.

sacrifice. Strategy can assist policy only by developing a maximum number of stages between total peace (which may mean total surrender) and total war. It can increase the willingness of policy-makers to run risks only if it can demonstrate other means of preventing amputations than the threat of suicide.

The power of modern weapons has thus set our statesmanship a problem unique in our history: that absolute security is no longer possible. Whatever the validity of the identification of deterrence with maximum retaliatory power, we will have to sacrifice a measure of destructiveness to gain the possibility of fighting wars that will not amount to national catastrophe. Policy, it has been said, is the science of the relative. The same is true of strategy, and to understand this fact, so foreign to our national experience, is the task history has set our generation.

II

What strategic doctrine is most likely to enable us to avoid the dilemma of having to make a choice between all-out war and a gradual loss of positions, between Armageddon and defeat without war? Is limited war a conceivable instrument of policy in the nuclear period? Here we must analyze precisely what is meant by limited war.

It is a historical accident reflecting the nature of our foreign involvements that we should have come to consider limited war an aberration from the "pure" case and that we have paid little attention to its strategic opportunities. In a sense this is due, too, to the manner in which we have legitimized the limited wars which we *have* fought. Every war in which we have been engaged in the Western Hemisphere was a limited war, in the sense that it did not involve a mobilization of all our material resources. But since we generally justified them as expeditions, punitive or otherwise, they rarely entered our national consciousness as part of the phenomenon of limited war.

Our wars in the Western Hemisphere illustrate, however, that limited wars have been both more frequent and more productive than the disputes generated by the Korean war indicate. The debate which has since raged on the subject of limited war has tended to confuse the issues because it has not sufficiently distinguished between the various forms of limited war. Some wars are inherently limited because of the disparity in power between the protagonists. A war between the United States and Nicaragua would not require more than a fraction of our strength whatever the objectives we set ourselves. Such a war would be all-out in relation to Nicaragua, but limited with respect to us. Another variation of this form of limited war occurs when the stronger power is restrained from exerting its full potential by moral, political or strategic considerations. This was the case in the Korean war, in which the Chinese probably made the maximum military effort of which they were capable while we, for a variety of reasons, limited our commitment. Still another kind of limited war is one between major powers in which the difficulty of supply prevents one side from making a total effort. An example of this is the Russo-Japanese war of 1905 in which the Russian commitment was limited to the forces that could be supplied over a single-track railway. Finally there may occur limited wars between major powers which are kept from spreading by a tacit agreement between the contestants and not by difficulties of technology or of logistics.

If one inquires which of these types of limited war are possible in the present situation, four broad categories can be distinguished. The first includes wars between secondary powers, such as between Israel and Egypt or between India and Pakistan, whether or not they involve the danger of the major powers joining in. The second type consists of wars involving either the Western powers or the Soviet bloc against powers which are clearly outmatched and under circumstances in which outside intervention is not likely. Examples of this would be Soviet intervention in the satellites, or United States military action in the Western Hemisphere. A third category are conflicts which begin as struggles between a major and a minor power but which may involve the prospect of spreading as in the case of a Chinese move against South Vietnam or the Anglo-French "police action" against Egypt. Finally, there is the problem of limited war which begins explicitly as a war between the major powers. This is obviously the most explosive situation. If a war between major powers can be kept limited, it is clear that the first three situations would also stand a good chance of being kept from expanding.

In the history of warfare, limited wars between major powers have been a frequent occurrence. For a long time, however, they remained limited less by conscious choice than by considerations of domestic policy. In the seventeenth century Louis XIV employed almost his entire army for a period of close to twenty-five years. Still his military establishment utilized only a small proportion of the national resources because of a domestic structure which prevented him from conscripting his subjects, levying income taxes, or confiscating property. His military establishment was therefore limited by the availability of resources and so were the wars he fought. On the other hand, the wars of Prussia, without exceeding those of France in scope, required a far greater mobilization of the national resources. Because of Prussia's limited resources, it was able to survive as a major power only by organizing the entire state for war. But Prussia's exertions only gave it a precarious parity with the other powers; it did not force them to emulate it. Wars remained limited because the major powers were able to mobilize only a small proportion of their national resources for war and because Prussia, the one power which was not so restrained, did not thereby gain a decisive advantage.

Since the French Revolution the domestic restrictions on the capacity of governments to mobilize national resources have increasingly disappeared. And this has occurred simultaneously with an industrial revolution which has made it technically possible to devote a substantial proportion of the national product to war without imposing a degree of privation which would shake the social order. To be sure, there still exist differences in *the willingness* of governments to exact sacrifices. One of the sources of Soviet strength is the readiness to devote a much

larger proportion of the national income to military expenditures than the United States. But for purposes of
present strategy it is clear that no major power will be
forced to adopt a strategy of limited objectives because of
insufficient resources. With modern weapons, a limited
war becomes an act of policy, not of necessity.

What, under modern conditions, is a limited war? One
can think of many models. It may be a war confined to a
defined geographic area, or a war that does not utilize the
entire available weapons system (such as refraining from
the use of thermonuclear weapons). It may be a war which
utilizes the entire weapons system but limits its employment to specific targets. But none of these military definitions seems adequate. A war may be confined to a
geographic area and yet be total in the sense of draining
the national substance, as happened to France in World
War I. The fact that the most destructive weapons are not
employed, or that the destructiveness of weapons used is
small, is no guarantee against excessive suffering. In the
Thirty Years' War the power of weapons was negligible
compared to modern armaments and the number of men
in each army was small by present-day standards—the
Austrian Field Marshal Montecuccoli put at 15,000 the
absolute maximum that could be commanded efficiently
in one army.[2] Yet it is estimated that the population of
Germany was reduced by 30 percent during its course. A
new world war fought with what are now called conventional weapons would also produce appalling casualties
since the destructive power even of these weapons has increased between five- and tenfold since World War II.

In short, there exists no way to define a limited war in
purely military terms. The end result of relying on purely
military considerations is certain to be all-out war: the attempt to render the enemy defenseless. Such a strategy
is an attempt to resolve by force the frustration produced by the fact that foreign policy seems much
less tractable than domestic policy. Domestic policy
is limited only by technical feasibility and by the sense of

---

[2] Raimund Montecuccoli, *Ausgewaehlte Schriften* (Leipzig: Wilhelm
Braumüller, 1899), p. 74.

justice of the majority of the citizens, at least in a democracy. (Even totalitarian regimes are so limited to some extent. To gain acquiescence they institute elaborate propaganda machines to achieve a consensus and a secret police apparatus to liquidate dissenters.) Foreign policy, on the other hand, is limited not only by technical feasibility, but also by the sovereign wills of other states which may have different criteria of justice and incompatible conceptions of their interests. At home, foreign policy is justified by the same criteria as domestic policy, for a nation has no other. Internationally, what is defined domestically as justice becomes an object of negotiation. It is little wonder that a nation like ours, which has never experienced the limits of its domestic possibilities, rebels against this double standard which treats what is defined as absolute domestically as negotiable abroad. Our predilection for all-out war represents an effort, perhaps subconscious, to transform foreign policy into an aspect of domestic policy, to bring about a situation abroad in which the will of other nations, or at least that of the enemy, is no longer a significant factor.

A limited war, by contrast, is fought for specific political objectives which, by their very existence, tend to establish a relationship between the force employed and the goal to be attained. It reflects an attempt to *affect* the opponent's will, not to *crush* it, to make the conditions to be imposed seem more attractive than continued resistance, to strive for specific goals and not for complete annihilation.

Limited war presents the military with particular difficulties. An all-out war is relatively simple to plan because its limits are set by military considerations and even by military capacity. The targets for an all-out war are fixed, and the force requirements are determined by the need to assemble overwhelming power. The characteristic of a limited war, on the other hand, is the existence of ground rules which define the relationship of military to political objectives. Planning becomes much more conjectural, much more subtle, and much more indeterminate, if only because a war against a major enemy can be kept limited only if both parties so desire, and this desire in itself tends to introduce a factor which is outside the control of planning officers. Since the military can never be certain how many forces the opponent will in fact commit to the struggle and since they feel obliged to guard against every contingency, they will devise plans for limited war which insensibly approach the level of all-out conflict.

From a purely military point of view they are right, for limited war is essentially a political act. Its distinguishing feature is that it has no "purely" military solution. The political leadership must, for this reason, assume the responsibility for defining the framework within which the military are to develop their plans and capabilities. To demand of the military that they set their own limits is to set in motion a vicious circle. The more the military plan on the basis of crushing the enemy even in a limited area, the more the political leadership will recoil before the risks of taking *any* military action. The more limited war is conceived as a "small" all-out war, the more it will produce inhibitions similar to those generated by the concept of massive retaliation. The prerequisite for a policy of limited war is to reintroduce the political element into our concept of warfare and to discard the notion that policy ends when war begins or that war can have goals distinct from those of national policy.

III

To what extent can the nuclear age leave room for a policy of intermediate objectives? Do any of the factors apply today which in the past made possible a diplomacy of limited objectives and a military policy of limited wars?

In the great periods of European cabinet diplomacy, between the Treaty of Westphalia and the French Revolution and between the Congress of Vienna and the outbreak of the first World War, wars were limited because there existed a political framework which led to a general acceptance of a policy of limited risks. This political framework was based on several factors. There was, to begin with, a deliberate decision that the upheavals of the Thirty

Years' War and the Napoleonic wars should not be allowed to recur. While most effective in the period immediately following these conflicts, this decision gave the newly established international orders a breathing spell in which the major powers became convinced that none of the outstanding disputes involved their survival. More important was the fact that the international order did not contain a revolutionary power. No state was so dissatisfied with the peace settlement that it sought to gain its ends by overthrowing it, and no power considered that its domestic notion of justice was incompatible with that of the other states. Finally, in an era of stable weapons technology both the strength of the powers and the assessment of it were relatively fixed; the risks of surprise attack and of unforeseen technological developments were relatively small. All this did not make conflicts impossible, but it limited them to disputes within a given framework. Wars occurred, but they were fought in the name of the existing framework and the peace was justified as a better arrangement of a basically unchanged international order.[3]

If we inquire which of these factors—fear of war, the principle of legitimacy and a stable power relationship—is present today, little cause for optimism remains. The Soviet bloc refuses to accept either the framework of the international order or the domestic structure of the non-Soviet states. For over a generation the U.S.S.R. has proclaimed the incompatibility of its domestic notion of justice with that of other states and has built up its internal control system on the myth of a permanently hostile world. Every agreement with the Soviet bloc has proved temporary because it has been considered by it as a tactical maneuver to prepare positions for the inevitable showdown. The slogan of "peaceful coexistence" cannot obscure the fact that we are living in a revolutionary period. Peaceful coexistence has been justified by the Soviet leaders as the most efficient offensive tactic, as the best means

---

[3] For a fuller discussion of Europe after the settlement of 1815, see the author's forthcoming book, *A World Restored* (Boston: Houghton Mifflin, 1957).

to subvert the existing structure by means other than all-out war.[4]

Nor is the nature of power relationships more reassuring. Even with a less volatile technology, a two-power world would have an inherent element of instability because an increase in strength of one side is tantamount to an absolute, perhaps fatal, weakening of its opponent. But weapons technology is far from stable. Almost up to the outbreak of World War II, a weapons system would be good for a generation at least, while today it may be obsolescent when it has barely passed the blueprint stage. Yet the failure to plan on the basis of these "prematurely aged" weapons may at any given point of time create a fatal weakness. In the technological race, moreover, the side which has adopted the military doctrine that its opponent can always strike the first blow is at a distinct disadvantage. It must phase its planning and procurement over an indefinite period while its opponent, if he is determined on a showdown, can plan for a target date and need prepare only for the one war he is planning to fight.

But if neither an agreed legitimacy nor a stable power relationship exists today, they may be outweighed by a third factor, the fear of a thermonuclear war. Never have the consequences of all-out war been so unambiguous, never have the gains seemed so out of relation with the sacrifices. What statesman who declared war in 1914 would not have recoiled had he known the shape of the world in 1918? Today every weapons test augurs much worse horrors. The miscalculation of a short, inexpensive war which produced World War I is therefore no longer possible. And even a leader of Hitler's deranged frame of mind might have hesitated before the consequences of thermonuclear devastation.

It is often argued that since limited wars offer no inherent guarantee against their expansion, they may gradually merge into all-out war. On purely logical grounds, the argument is unassailable. But it assumes that the major

---

[4] For an expansion of these ideas, see below, Chapter 10, p. 350 ff.

protagonists will be looking for an excuse to expand the war whereas in reality both sides will probably grasp at every excuse, however illogical, to keep a thermonuclear holocaust from occurring. This, in fact, was what happened in the Korean war, at a time when the weapons technology was much less horrendous. We refused to retaliate against the Manchurian air bases from which enemy planes were attacking our forces. And the Chinese made no effort to interfere with our aircraft-carriers, or with our bases in Japan, or even to launch an attack against our only two big supply ports, Pusan and Inchon.

These limitations were not brought about by logic but by a mutual reluctance to expand the conflict. It is clear that war cannot be limited unless both sides wish to keep it limited. The argument in favor of the possibility of limited war is that both sides have a common and overwhelming interest in preventing it from spreading. The fear than an all-out thermonuclear war might lead to the disintegration of the social structure offers an opportunity to set limits to both war and diplomacy.

The key problem of present-day strategy is to devise a spectrum of capabilities with which to resist Soviet challenges. These capabilities should enable us to confront the opponent with contingencies from which he can extricate himself *only* by all-out war, while deterring him from this step by a superior retaliatory capacity. Since the most difficult decision for a statesman is whether to risk the national substance by unleashing an all-out war, the psychological advantage will always be on the side of the power which can shift to its opponent the decision to initiate all-out war. All Soviet moves in the postwar period have had this character. They have faced us with problems which by themselves did not seem worth an all-out war, but with which we could not deal by an alternative capability. We refused to defeat the Chinese in Korea because we were unwilling to risk an all-out conflict. We saw no military solution to the Indochinese crisis without accepting risks which we were reluctant to confront. We recoiled before the suggestion of intervening in Hungary lest it unleash a thermonuclear holocaust. A strategy of limited war might reverse or at least arrest this trend. Limited war is thus not an alternative to massive retaliation, but its complement. It is the capability for massive retaliation which provides the sanction against expanding the war.

IV

The conduct of limited war has two prerequisites: a doctrine and a capability. So long as we consider limited war as an aberration from the "pure" case of all-out war we will not be ready to grasp its opportunities, and we will conduct the wars we do fight hesitantly and ambiguously, oscillating between the twin temptations to expand them (that is, to bring them closer to our notion of what war should be like), or to end them at the first enemy overture.

A doctrine for limited war will have to discard any illusions about what can be achieved by means of it. Limited war is not a cheaper substitute for massive retaliation. On the contrary, it must be based on the awareness that with the end of our atomic monopoly it is no longer possible to impose unconditional surrender at an acceptable cost.

The purpose of limited war is to inflict losses or to pose risks for the enemy out of proportion to the objectives under dispute. The more moderate the objective, the less violent the war is likely to be. This does not mean that military operations cannot go beyond the territory or the objective in dispute; indeed, one way of increasing the enemy's willingness to settle is to deprive him of something he can regain only by making peace. But the result of a limited war cannot depend on military considerations alone; it reflects an ability to harmonize political and military objectives. An attempt to reduce the enemy to impotence would remove the psychological balance which makes it profitable for both sides to keep the war limited. Faced with the ultimate threat of complete defeat, the losing side may seek to deprive its opponent of the margin to impose his will by unleashing a thermonuclear holocaust.

Nevertheless, a strategic doctrine which renounces the imposition of unconditional surrender should not be confused with the acceptance of a stalemate. The notion that there is no middle ground between unconditional surrender and the *status quo ante* is much too mechanical. To be sure, a restoration of the *status quo ante* is often the simplest solution, but it is not the only possible one. The argument that neither side will accept a defeat, however limited, without utilizing every weapon in its arsenal is contradicted both by psychology and by experience. There would seem to be no sense in seeking to escape a limited defeat through bringing on the cataclysm of an all-out war, particularly if all-out war threatens a calamity far transcending the penalties of losing a limited war. It simply does not follow that because one side stands to lose from a limited war, it could gain from an all-out war. On the contrary, both sides face the same dilemma: that the power of modern weapons has made all-out war useless as an instrument of policy, except for acts of desperation.

The West has accepted several contractions of its sphere without resorting to all-out war. If the military position of the Soviet leadership became untenable and it were offered face-saving alternatives short of surrender, it too might accept local withdrawals without resorting to all-out war. Even if limited war offered no more than the possibility of local stalemates, it would represent a strategic improvement, for our current problem is our inability to defend major areas except by the threat of a thermonuclear holocaust which we should make every effort to avoid.

The development of a wide spectrum of capabilities would be of crucial importance even should it be assumed that any war between us and the U.S.S.R. or China will inevitably be all-out. For, unless the exchange of nuclear and thermonuclear blows leads to the social collapse of both contenders—a distinct possibility—the side which has in being superior forces for other forms of conflict may win out in the end. If the Red Army, for example, should succeed in overrunning Eurasia during or after an exchange of all-out blows, we would probably not have sufficient resources remaining to undertake a reconquest.

As stockpiles of the largest modern weapons are exhausted or delivery vehicles are used up, an increasing premium is placed on a diversified military capability and not only vis-à-vis the enemy but toward hitherto secondary powers as well. In the absence of forces for other forms of conflict, all-out war may merely pave the way for the dominance of the world by states whose social structure and forces-in-being have remained more or less intact during the struggle-to-death of the superstates.

There exist three reasons, then, for developing a strategy of limited war. First, limited war represents the only means for preventing the Soviet bloc, at an acceptable cost, from overrunning the peripheral areas of Eurasia. Second, a wide range of military capabilities may spell the difference between defeat and victory even in an all-out war. Finally, intermediate applications of our power offer the best chance to bring about strategic changes favorable to our side. For while a balance can be maintained along existing lines on the Eurasian continent, it will aways be tenuous. So long as Soviet armies are poised on the Elbe, Western Europe will be insecure. So long as Chinese might presses upon free Asia, the uncommitted powers will seek safety in neutralism. To the outside world the Soviet bloc presents a picture of ruthless strength allied with artful cunning, of constant readiness to utilize force coupled with the diplomatic skill to secure the fruits of its use. The United States, therefore, faces the task not only of stemming the Soviet pressures, but also of reducing the Soviet sphere and demonstrating the limitations of Soviet power and skills. The last is almost as important as the reduction of the Soviet sphere. For the resolution of the free world, now assailed by a sense of its impotence, will improve to the extent that it realizes that the Soviet bloc, behind its façade of monolithic power, also shrinks from certain consequences.

A strategy of limited war is more likely to achieve this objective than the threat of a total nuclear war. Either the threat of an all-out war will be considered a bluff or it will turn every dispute into a question of prestige, inhibiting any concessions. Actions short of total war, on the other hand, may help restore fluidity to the diplomatic situation, particularly if we analyze precisely what is meant by the concept of reducing the Soviet sphere. The Sino-Soviet bloc can be turned back short of general war in one of two ways: by a voluntary withdrawal or by an internal split. The former is unlikely and depends on many factors beyond our control, but the latter deserves careful study.

While it is impossible to predict the precise circumstances of a possible split within the Soviet orbit, its general framework can be discerned. The U.S.S.R. may be forced to loosen its hold on its European satellites if it finds that the effort to hold them in line absorbs ever more of its strength. And relations between China and the Soviet Union may become cooler if the alliance forces either partner to shoulder risks for objectives which are of no benefit to it. Tito's break with Moscow was caused at least in part by his disenchantment over the Soviet Union's lukewarm support on the Trieste issue, and that in turn was due to the unwillingness of the Kremlin to risk an all-out war for the sake of a peripheral objective. Similarly, it is not clear how much China would risk to rescue the U.S.S.R. from embarrassments in Europe or in the Middle East, or to what lengths the U.S.S.R. is prepared to go to increase the power of China in Asia. A test of our strategy is, therefore, its ability to bring about situations which accentuate potential differences within the Soviet bloc. In these terms, one of the basic indictments of an excessive emphasis on a strategy of all-out war is that its inability to differentiate and graduate its pressures may actually contribute to the consolidation and the unity of the Soviet bloc.

It is therefore misleading to reject a strategy of limited war on the ground that it does not offer a military solution to our strategic problem. Its merit is precisely that it may open the way to a political solution. Had we defeated the Chinese Army in Korea in 1951, the U.S.S.R. would have faced the problem of whether the risk of expanding the war was worth keeping China from suffering a limited defeat. Had we followed up our victory with a conciliatory political proposal to Peiping, we could have caused it to reconsider the wisdom of being too closely tied to the U.S.S.R. Even if we had failed in our primary task of dividing the U.S.S.R. and China, we would have greatly improved our position toward our allies and even more toward the uncommitted nations in Asia. The best counterargument to the charge of colonialism is political moderation after a military victory. A military stalemate, on the other hand, always leaves open the question whether what is advanced as a proof of moderation is not in reality a sign of weakness or at least of irresolution. Thus, if limited actions are implemented as part of a policy which offers the other side a way out short of unconditional surrender, they may bring about local reversals. These in turn may set off chain reactions which will be difficult to control and which may magnify the tensions within the Soviet bloc. A strategy of limited war, then, would use our retaliatory power as a means to permit us to fight local actions on our own terms and to shift to the other side the risk of initiating all-out war.

V

Whatever the theoretical advantages of limited war, is it practical? Does not a policy of limited war run up against the geographic reality that the Soviet bloc possesses interior lines of communication and may therefore be able to assemble a superior force at any given point along its periphery? Can we afford a policy of limited war or will it not overstrain our resources just as surely as would all-out war? Does not the concern with local resistance mistake the real security problem which, in major areas, is political instability and a standard of living considered oppressively low by the majority of the population?

Admittedly, we alone cannot possibly defend the Soviet periphery by local actions and the present period of revolutionary change will not be managed solely by reliance on a military doctrine. Our task also includes strengthening the will to resist among the peoples threatened by Communist expansionism. In the underdeveloped third of the world this means pursuing a variety of measures, on whose need there is a substantial consensus: a political program to gain the confidence of local populations and to remove the stigma of colonialism from us, together with a degree of economic assistance which will help bring about political stability.[5] But such programs, although essential, will in the end be ineffective unless we improve our capacity for local defense. We have a weakness for considering problems as "primarily" economic or "primarily" military rather than as total situations in which political, economic and military considerations merge, which is the way the Soviet leadership regards policy.

As a result, we often seem in danger of focusing so much attention on whatever is the Soviet threat of the moment that we are taken unawares by the frequent changes in Soviet tactics. Until Stalin's death we were so preoccupied with building defensive barriers that we neglected the supporting political and psychological framework. After the Soviet leaders have launched an effort at economic and political penetration, we stand in danger of overlooking that economic development cannot go forward without a modicum of security against foreign invasion. The actions of statesmen are not determined merely by their moral preferences, but also by their assessment of the risks confronting them. Economic progress alone, or even genuine sympathy for our principles, will not serve to stabilize a situation which is overshadowed by the threat of Soviet intervention, direct or indirect.

Thus one of the conditions of political stability is our capacity to react to local aggression at the place of its occurrence. Few leaders of threatened countries will wish to rely for protection on our strategic superiority in an all-out war. Victory in a general war will mean little to a country which meanwhile has undergone the moral and physical ravages of Soviet occupation. This attitude was well expressed in an editorial in a leading German newspaper: "We must oppose any strategy, the basic postulate of which involves giving up our territory. Our partnership in the Atlantic alliance means more to us than that our 12 divi-

---

[5] See below, Chapter 8, p. 255 ff., for an expansion of these ideas.

sions represent a strategic asset for the West; it includes a demand for the protection of the German people. . . . A substantial retreat is equivalent to our moral and physical destruction." [6]

The argument thus runs in a circle. Can the non-Soviet countries of Eurasia be defended, assuming the willingness of the threatened countries to resist and an ability on our part to help them? In support of a negative answer such factors are cited as the "unlimited" Soviet manpower and the vast distances of the threatened areas from the centers of our strength. But while underestimating an adversary can be disastrous, overestimating his resources may lead to a dangerous paralysis of policy. Absolute numbers are important, but only the part of them that can be utilized effectively is strategically significant. The value of Sino-Soviet manpower is limited by the capacity of the Soviet bloc to equip and train it, and its effectiveness is reduced by the power of modern weapons and by difficulties of communications and supply.

The vision of hordes of Chinese or Soviet soldiers streaming into what has come to be known as the "Gray Areas," stretching from Turkey to Malaya, is unrealistic. The Soviet bloc cannot increase at will its commitments in areas far from its own centers of production and possessing only elementary communications. If we examine the potential danger zone in which limited wars are most probable, we find that it coincides either with regions where we can count on a measure of indigenous support or where the Chinese and Soviet investment of resources will be limited both by the nature of the new weapons and by the difficulties of supply.

The particular danger zone for limited wars is the arc which stretches from the eastern border of Turkey around the periphery of Eurasia. Within that area the Indian subcontinent is protected by mountain barriers and by extremely difficult communications. Aggression against the Middle East would have to count on the flanking position of Turkey and, despite the Suez fiasco, Great Britain

---

6 *Frankfurter Allgemeine Zeitung*, December 2, 1954.

would probably join in resistance. An attack on Burma would antagonize India and would be difficult to supply, and the same would be true of the remainder of Southeast Asia. An attack in the Far East would have to take place either across water or against indigenous forces, as in Korea. Moreover, if we utilize nuclear weapons there will be an inherent upper limit to the number of troops that can be profitably employed in threatened areas.[7] Thus if we could develop forces capable of conducting limited war and of getting into position rapidly, we should be able to defeat the Soviet Union or China in local engagements despite their interior position.

This is the case despite the seemingly contrary lessons of the war in Korea. It must not be forgotten that after the beginning of the armistice negotiations, in June 1951, that war was fought under conditions which were nearly ideal for an army, such as that of Communist China, with inferior technology and firepower. Actions were always confined to small segments of the front. They could be delayed until there had been an adequate build-up and broken off when stocks had been depleted. The risks were always tactical, never strategic, and the penalty for failure was limited by our self-imposed restrictions arising out of our effort to negotiate an armistice. "Operation Strangle," the attempt of our Air Force to interdict Chinese communications, did not represent a fair test of the ability of the Soviet bloc to sustain a major effort over a considerable period of time and in the face of an enemy possessing superior firepower. The only continuous drain on Chinese supplies occurred after the front was stabilized in March 1951, and from then until the beginning of the armistice negotiations in June the Chinese were much closer to a decisive defeat than we. Had we committed even four more divisions, indeed, even if we had put a time limit on the truce negotiations, we could have achieved a substantial military victory.

To be sure, the limitations which were imposed on the Chinese freedom of maneuver by the narrow peninsula

---

[7] For a discussion of limited nuclear war, see below, Chapter 6, p. 174 ff.

and by the proximity of our bases in Japan gave us an advantage in Korea which probably could not be duplicated in other areas. On the other hand, certain circumstances were propitious for the Chinese Communists. Korea was close to their main production centers and to Russian supply lines, and communications between Korea and China were good. Neither of these conditions would be duplicated in, for example, Southeast Asia. Moreover, the Korean war was conducted with conventional weapons, which permit the substitution of manpower for technology, at least to a degree. But in a war fought with nuclear weapons, or under their shadow, there is an upper limit beyond which massed manpower becomes a liability. Even if nuclear weapons are not utilized initially, the concentration of troops on the model of World War II and the Korean war might supply the incentive to resort to them. And since neither side can be certain that its opponent will not resort to nuclear weapons, it will have to deploy *as if* nuclear weapons might be used. In the nuclear period a limited war would be fought by much smaller, more self-contained units, whether or not nuclear weapons are actually employed. In such circumstances, firepower and mobility will be of greater importance than manpower.[8]

If we commit ourselves to a strategy of local defense, do we not run the risk of having our forces always at the wrong place? Cannot the Soviet bloc utilize its interior position to keep us constantly off balance? To be sure, the Soviet bloc is able to pick the initial point of attack, but the greater mobility of its interior position is illusory because of the difficulties of communication. Once the Soviet armies are committed in one area, they cannot be shifted at will against our air power or with greater speed than we can shift ours by sea or air. The Chinese Communists, for example, cannot draw us into Indo-China and then attack in Burma with the same army. They can, of course, build up two armies, but we should be able to learn of this in time and then decide to defend one or the other area, or both, depending on the strategic

---

8 For an expansion of these ideas, see below, Chapter 6, p. 176 ff.

situation. In any case, the two armies cannot support each other (the classic advantage of interior lines), and the power of modern weapons places an upper limit on the numbers of troops that can be profitably employed in any given area.

The objection has been raised that even if limited war is feasible, it would be unwise to permit ourselves to be drawn into a war of attrition with the Soviet bloc. "If it is preferable to engage in a war of attrition," said Secretary of the Air Symington in 1949, "one American life for one enemy life, then we are wrong. That is not our way. That is not the way in which the mass slaughter of American youth in an invasion of Japan was avoided. To whatever extent we can bring it about that weapons fashioned in Los Alamos and carried in aircraft fashioned at Fort Worth can destroy or diminish the power of an enemy to kill American soldiers, sailors, and airmen, we are for pursuing that method." [9] It is an expression of our reliance on industrial potential and of the persistence of a belief in our invulnerability that a war of attrition should be identified with land warfare and that massive retaliation should appear as the cheapest way of achieving our objectives. "A B-36, with an A-bomb," said Secretary Symington on another occasion, "can take off from this continent and destroy distant objectives which might require ground armies years to take—and then only at the expense of heavy casualties. The B-36 could do the job within 16 hours . . .—all this at the risk of only 16 American lives." [10]

However valid this view may have been during the period of our atomic monopoly, the growth of the Soviet nuclear stockpile has transformed massive retaliation from the least costly into the most costly strategy. With the end of our traditional invulnerability, the risk of all-out war has become much higher than sixteen American lives. All-out war has turned into a strategy which in-

9 U.S. House, *The National Defense Program—Unification and Strategy,* Hearings before the Committee on Armed Services, 81st Cong., 1st Sess. (Washington: GPO, 1949), pp. 402-3. (Hereafter to be referred to as B-36 hearings.)

10 Same, p. 315.

evitably involves trading a life for a life; it has become the war of attrition par excellence. Moreover,
the formulation of the alternative as between a war
of attrition and all-out war is misleading. By its very nature war is a process of attrition. The problem for strategy
is not to avoid attrition, but to determine which kind of
attrition is strategically most significant. We have seen in
the previous chapter that the power of modern weapons
reduces the importance of our industrial potential in an
all-out war because each side can destroy the industrial
plant of its opponent with its forces-in-being at the very
outset. With modern weapons, industrial potential can be
significant only in a war in which it is not itself the target.

As a result, limited war has become the form of conflict
which enables us to derive the greatest strategic advantage
from our industrial potential. It is the best means for
achieving a continuous drain of our opponent's resources
without exhausting both sides. The prerequisite for deriving a strategic advantage from industrial potential is a
weapons system sufficiently complex to require a substantial production effort, but not so destructive as to deprive
the victor of any effective margin of superiority.[11] Thus
the argument that limited war may turn into a contest of
attrition is in fact an argument in favor of a strategy of
limited war. A war of attrition is the one war the Soviet
bloc could not win.

VI

One of the most urgent tasks of American military policy
is to create a military capability which can redress the
balance in limited wars and which can translate our technological advantage into local superiority. It is often maintained that the call for forces capable of fighting local
actions is a misreading of the nature of our military establishment. By building up forces for deterring all-out
war, it is argued, we are also creating the capability to
fight limited war.

Such an argument misunderstands the nature of our

---

11 See below, Chapter 6, p. 195 ff., for an expansion of these ideas.

strategic problem. The strategic striking force is the prime
deterrent against all-out war; it must therefore be reserved
for this contingency. This is particularly important during
a limited war, because to the extent that our retaliatory
force suffers attrition in such conflict, the enemy would
lose his incentive for keeping the war limited. An aggressor who could tempt us to utilize our strategic striking
force in a limited war would gain a strategic advantage,
however military operations ended. To the extent that
our retaliatory force declined in strength, our ability to
deter all-out war would decline and therewith the sanction
for keeping the war limited. To use our strategic striking
force as a dual-purpose force would weaken the deterrent
to all-out war at the precise time when it should be strongest. Or else it will, in every crisis, furnish arguments for
conserving our strength for a "clearer" provocation or a
principal enemy—as was demonstrated by General Hoyt S.
Vandenberg's reluctance during the Korean war to commit our Strategic Air Force against Communist China.

Moreover, the nature of the weapons, the planning and
the concept of operations, differ radically between forces
useful for all-out war and those for limited war. The
weapons system for all-out war is designed to inflict maximum destruction in the shortest time. The weapons system for a limited war, on the other hand, must be flexible
and discriminating. In an all-out war the targets are known
in advance, in fact each crew of the Strategic Air Command is training for a specific Soviet target all the time.[12]
Everything depends therefore on the efficiency with which
the plan for all-out war can be implemented. In a limited
war neither the locale of the conflict nor the targets can be
determined in advance. Everything here depends on the
rapidity with which planning can be adjusted to a developing situation. In an all-out war the chief problem is to
eliminate the enemy's retaliatory force before it has done
too much damage. In a limited war the problem is to
apply graduated amounts of destruction for limited ob-

jectives and also to permit the necessary breathing spaces for political contacts.[13]

A weapons system for limited war is therefore basically different from a retaliatory force. Limited wars require units of high mobility and considerable firepower which can be quickly moved to trouble spots and which can bring their power to bear with discrimination. The capability for rapid deployment is crucial. Given the power of modern weapons and the speed of movement of military units, it will be very difficult to dislodge an enemy once he has become established. Since aggression is unlikely to occur unless the aggressor doubts either the capability or the willingness of his opponent to intervene, the ability to get into position rapidly even with relatively small forces can serve as a gauge of the determination to resist and contribute to the re-establishment of an equilibrium before either side becomes too heavily committed.

The biggest gap in our defense establishment is the lack of units capable of fighting local actions and specifically designed for this purpose. At present the Air Force is preoccupied with a doctrine of all-out war and of complete air superiority. The Army is small and its organization cumbersome. Only the Navy possesses a force capable of discriminating offensive operations, but it may be handicapped in a limited war by its doctrine of antisubmarine warfare.

In view of the fact that the Strategic Air Command is for all practical purposes the central core of the Air Force, the priority given to all-out war by air doctrine is understandable. It is only natural for the best crews, the best equipment and the choicest bases to be assigned to our retaliatory force. The penalty for our preoccupation with the strategic striking force is that it turns the mode of operation which is necessary for all-out war into the pattern for the conduct of limited war as well. The "pure" air doctrine, the basis of the strategy of the Strategic Air Command, maintains that the air is indivisible, that wars

---

[13] See below, Chapter 7, pp. 225-6, for the concept of "operations in phases."

can be won only by dominating the skies completely.[14] Because this goal can be achieved only in all-out war, air doctrine has never felt comfortable with a strategy of limited war and has sought to treat it as much like a "small" all-out war by stressing the goal of complete domination of the air over a combat zone.[15]

But with the growing speed and range of modern weapons such a course becomes increasingly difficult to reconcile with a policy of limited war. To achieve complete air domination over a combat zone, which under modern conditions will itself be several hundred miles in width, there will be a growing temptation to attack installations deep in enemy territory. The deeper the penetration, however, the greater the danger that it will unleash an all-out war. The enemy observing a flight of planes on his radar screen cannot know whether it is intended as the support for tactical operations or as the prelude to an all-out surprise attack. He may, therefore, react as if he were faced with the worst contingency and launch his own retaliatory force while there is still time.[16]

The preoccupation with all-out war determines not only the doctrine of the tactical air forces, but also their priorities for equipment and personnel and for mobility in case of conflict. Under present procedures many of the planes which have become obsolescent for strategic missions are assigned to the Tactical Air Command. Thus the Tactical Air Command took over the B-29 Superfortress when it was replaced by the B-47 medium jet bomber in the Strategic Air Command, and it will receive the B-47 as it is replaced by the B-58. Some of the planes of the Tactical Air Command are therefore always at one stage of development behind those of the Strategic Air Command. The practice of assigning the obsolescent planes of our retalia-

---

[14] Sir John Slessor, *Strategy for the West* (New York: Morrow, 1954), p. 105.

[15] U.S. Senate, *Study of Airpower*, Hearings before the Subcommittee on the Air Force of the Committee on Armed Services, 84th Cong., 2nd Sess. (Washington: GPO, 1956), p. 472. (Presentation of the Tactical Air Command.)

[16] For a further discussion of air strategy in limited war, see below, Chapter 6, p. 183 ff.

tory force to the Tactical Air Command (TAC) is a symptom of the tendency to consider the doctrines for limited and all-out war as essentially identical. This reduces the effectiveness of TAC against the latest types of enemy planes, and affects its utility for tactical operations. The very characteristics which make planes of value for strategic air war may limit their usefulness for tactical operations. The B-47 is a high-altitude bomber of medium range. It was designed to deliver high-yield weapons over an area target, not to outmaneuver enemy fighters over a combat zone. It is therefore not the ideal plane for the flexible operations and relatively discriminating attacks required in limited warfare.

The same priorities which determine the assignment of weapons will also determine the availability of support from other commands within the Air Force. In case of a limited war, a considerable proportion of the tactical air forces will have to be moved from the United States to the theater of operations. Since most of the planes of the Tactical Air Command are of medium and short range, such an operation requires tankers for aerial refueling as well as an airlift to move supplies. But the tanker fleet of the Tactical Air Command is composed of obsolescent B-29's, dangerous for the refueling of high-performance jet fighters and usable only in good weather.[17] And the Strategic Air Command properly has first call on the available airlift. In case of limited war, competition between the requirements of the Strategic and the Tactical Air Commands is therefore inevitable. Since a war can be kept limited only through the maximum readiness of our retaliatory force, there will be a very understandable temptation to reserve the available airlift for its use. But since the tactical air forces will be ineffective unless they get into position quickly, existing priorities will hamper our Air Force in its deployment for a limited war.

This is not put forward as a criticism of Air Force policy. Given the present assignment of missions and budgetary levels, the current system of priorities is inescapable. It

17 For a discussion of the refueling problem, see U.S. Senate, *Study of Airpower*, cited, p. 489.

does suggest the importance of creating distinct forces for both all-out and limited wars, forces which will be as self-contained as possible, with their own training, supply and equipment. Any other course will lead to a gradual merging of the forces designed for limited war into a reserve for the retaliatory force. It will either produce attrition of the retaliatory force in a limited war or will create pressures for inaction when the challenge does not seem to involve the national existence directly.

As for the Army's role in a limited war, it is handicapped by a split over doctrine with the Air Force, paralleling the difficulties already noted within the Air Force over the relative priorities for the Strategic and Tactical Air Commands. The strategic effectiveness of the Army is reduced further by the twin facts that its organization is in a state of transition and its force levels are too low. For the fiscal year 1958, the Army will consist of seventeen divisions and a number of combat teams; since some of these units are training cadres, only fourteen divisions can be said to be ready for combat. It may be argued that a force of this size does not absolutely preclude our fighting limited wars. Valid as this contention may be from a purely military point of view, it is unrealistic psychologically. A limited war of any size would absorb so large a part of our strategic reserve that we would lose a great deal of flexibility for dealing with any other threat. The likelihood that any Chief of Staff would be unwilling to commit an army of the present size to a local war is shown by the hesitations of the then Chief of Staff General Matthew B. Ridgway with regard to both Indo-China and the Chinese offshore islands. And the doubts of the military will reinforce the inhibitions of the political leadership.

Thus a vicious circle is set up. The civilian leadership will tend to make its participation in a limited war dependent on military advice, but the pressure of the military will in all good conscience have to be exerted against involvement, either because they do not possess adequate forces or because they lack an adequate doctrine, or both. The circle is broken in practice only if a strong President assumes the responsibility for defining the limits of the conflict and the nature of our commitment, as happened in the Korean war.

The increasing power of modern weapons affects the Army's need for forces in two ways. On the one hand, it sets a limit to the number of troops which can be concentrated in a combat zone, since an equilibrium of power can be established with much smaller forces than heretofore. On the other hand, the intricacy of the new tactics and the speed with which they must be executed place a very high premium on the readiness and mobility of the forces-in-being. It is no longer possible to count on a substantial mobilization of reserve forces to help redress the balance in case of local aggression, as was still the case in the Korean war, because mobilization may well unleash a retaliatory blow. In any case, the training of reserve forces is not likely to be adequate for using the complicated weapons and applying the intricate tactics of modern war. Limited war, like all-out war, will have to be fought by the forces-in-being; it requires a highly professional force at instant readiness of training, doctrine and equipment.

The introduction of modern weapons and the reorganization of its cumbersome units makes it possible to envisage a level of forces which would enable the Army to intervene effectively in threatened areas, particularly where there is a measure of local resistance. While these forces must be larger than the present Army strength, they are not so large as to be beyond the possibility of the economy to support them. The Chief of Staff of the Army, Maxwell D. Taylor, has estimated that twenty-eight modern divisions would be sufficient to meet all foreseeable dangers. And even an addition of four divisions to the present forces would greatly improve our posture for a limited war.[18]

But an increase in Army strength by itself will avail little, if our strategic reserve does not possess the necessary mobility to intervene rapidly in case of aggression. We reacted to the frustrations of the Korean war with a

18 New York Times, February 13, 1956.

determination never to be caught again in a predicament in which most of our strategic reserve was tied down in an exposed peninsula. Accordingly, we set about reducing the deployment of our troops overseas and concentrating most of our strategic reserve in the United States.

As a concept this is reasonable. A strategic reserve is useless, however, unless it is able to bolster local resistance quickly. Otherwise it will be either too small or too irrelevant for a general war, or too immobile to redress the strategic balance locally. The importance of forces ready to intervene rapidly was surely one of the lessons of the Korean war. Whatever the state of our readiness, militarily or psychologically, the attack occurred in a fortuitous area, close to our only concentration of troops in Asia. And even these untrained troops, hastily assembled and understrength, managed to hold a line and restore the situation within a few months. Had we required even one more week to bring troops into Korea, it would have been too late, and Korea could probably not have been recaptured without an effort that would have materially increased the risk of a general war.

To be strategically significant, a strategic reserve must have mobility. In the past this mobility was assured by our command of the seas. But in modern warfare so leisurely a deployment is no longer possible and in any case we have available sea transport for barely two divisions, either Army or Marine. We therefore have two choices: we can station ready forces in likely trouble spots or close to them, or we can keep the major portion of our strategic reserve in the United States, but give it the mobility to move quickly to threatened areas. The first of these alternatives is politically difficult and strategically risky. The second presupposes two conditions: an Army organization less cumbersome than the present division, and an airlift which will enable us to intervene in threatened areas within a strategically effective time span.

Our Army organization has been based on a doctrine of a war of position, and it has been geared to the speed of the internal combustion engine and the availability of roads. Because the traditional division has been designed to cover a segment of a front conceived as essentially uninterrupted, it may prove too large and too cumbersome to fight an effective action in a situation which is not likely to provide a stabilized front in the usual sense. Above all, it is too complicated to be moved efficiently by air. The current infantry division weighs approximately 28,000 short tons. It would require the entire available United States airlift, including the civil reserve fleet, over thirty days to move one division from the United States to the Middle East, provided all air-transport units were in position when the crisis occurred and provided they were not required for any other mission—two most unlikely contingencies.

One important means for improving the Army's mobility is to reduce the weight of its units, and substantial progress in this direction is taking place. The Army has given up its traditional divisional organization based on three regiments and is substituting a division composed of five combat teams. This change will increase the number of self-supporting commands and thereby enhance the flexibility of maneuver. It will permit the application of smaller and therefore more discriminating amounts of force. In addition, a new type of airborne division has been created designed for rapid air transport. It weighs 14,300 short tons and its combat element weighs 5,000 short tons. This would halve the time required to move one division to the Middle East from the United States even with existing airlift.

But the existing airlift places us in a precarious situation if we are called upon to wage a limited war. Unless the complete combat element of a division can be moved to a threatened area almost simultaneously, it may get there too late to affect events, or it may arrive in driblets so small that it can be defeated in detail. It would take the entire available airlift fifteen days to move even a streamlined Army division to the Middle East, and at least ten days to move a regimental combat team of 7,000 men to Laos.[19] But the entire airlift is unlikely to be available.

---

[19] U.S. Senate, *Study of Airpower*, cited, p. 520 ff. (Testimony of General Weyland.)

In fact, no part of the airlift is presently earmarked for Army use and its availability will depend on whatever priorities are in force upon the outbreak of a war.

Thus Army planning must of necessity take place in a vacuum or on the assumption of only a minimum availability of airlift. Indeed, any situation serious enough to require airlifting a division to the Middle East or to Laos is likely to be so serious as to cause the Strategic Air Command to exercise its first priority. Thus the Army faces exactly the same problem as the Tactical Air Command: it will have the greatest difficulty in utilizing the existing airlift at the very time when it is most needed.

To remedy this situation, it will be necessary to create additional airlift capacity and to separate the airlift designated for all-out war from that part of it which is to be utilized for limited war. The same considerations which make an all-purpose military force inadvisable also counsel against creating an all-purpose airlift. The wisest course would, therefore, be to earmark most of the existing airlift for the Strategic Air Command and to create additional airlift reserved specifically for deployment in a limited war. Any other course will have the practical consequence that the first priority of the Strategic Air Command will withdraw the available air transport from tactical use in case of a local aggression of any consequence.

The minimum requirement would seem to be a capability for moving the combat element of one new-type division simultaneously. To move the combat element of one such division to the Middle East simultaneously would require 200 C-133's at a cost of $1.9 billion for procurement. To airlift the entire division within ten days would require 272 C-133's at a cost of $2.6 billion. After the division is in place it would require 9,438 short tons of supplies over a thirty-day period, almost all of which can be moved by the original airlift. Moreover, an airlift capable of moving one division simultaneously will be able to move several divisions over a period of fifteen days. To be sure, if the Navy develops the high-speed nuclear-powered ships which are now being discussed, the requirements for airlift may decline. But until that time an adequate airlift remains our only means for attaining strategic mobility for a limited war.[20] Surely one of the lessons of the fiasco of the British and French invasion of Suez was that the slowness of their moves, based on traditional concepts of logistics and sea transport, forfeited any chance for success. In the nuclear age the capability for rapid and limited action may prove as important a deterrent as the capability for a powerful and all-out response.

The objection may be raised that airlift, to be effective, must rely on our ability to use bases close to the combat zone. But for the foreseeable future we should be able to count on Okinawa or perhaps the Philippines as a staging area for the Far East, on Cyprus or Libya as staging areas for the Middle East, and on Great Britain as a staging area for Europe. And if our policy is at all farsighted we should be able to create other friendly areas close to likely danger zones.

If the Army and Air Force are handicapped by the doctrinal problem of distinguishing between all-out and limited war capabilities, the Navy faces a different challenge. The Navy task forces, built around fast aircraft-carriers, are in some respects ideal supporting units for waging a limited war. They can provide air support in any area of the world, and they supply us with a floating base structure immune to the political upheavals which may affect our ability to use our overseas bases. To be sure, in the face of the power of modern weapons the Navy task forces will not be able to operate very close to the shores of an enemy possessing substantial air power and modern weapons. And a carrier of the Forrestal class costing $189 million represents a heavy investment compared to the ninety-five planes it can carry, half of which are purely defensive. Nevertheless, in offensive operations in support of a limited war the Navy carrier task forces could play a major role. This is obviously their most important function in our current doctrine because our plans for all-out war do not take into consideration the support which

---

20 For a discussion of the impact of the Key West agreement on the airlift dispute, see below, Chapter 12, p. 408.

might be given to the Strategic Air Command by naval air.[21]

But the effectiveness of the carrier task forces in a limited war is likely to be reduced by the growing Soviet submarine menace and by the fact that our strategy for dealing with that threat is essentially inconsistent with a policy of limited war. Based on the doctrine of the psychological ascendancy of the offensive, our naval strategy seeks to defeat the submarine menace by destroying the opponent's port facilities and base installations. "I do not know who said this a long time ago, but somebody has said that the best defense is a strong offense," testified Vice Admiral Thomas S. Combs before the Symington Committee. ". . . if we . . . concentrated on defensive antisubmarine forces, we would inevitably go from an offensive directly to a defensive force. This we cannot tolerate. That, I think, no red-blooded American would ever want anybody to do." [22] It is for this reason that the Chief of Naval Operations defined an attack on enemy bases as the primary task of antisubmarine warfare.[23]

This strategy raises serious problems, however. Quite apart from the fact that atomic-powered submarines at sea can wreak considerable havoc before they must return to port, an attack with nuclear weapons on metropolitan Russia is not consistent with a policy of limited war. A nuclear or thermonuclear attack on the port cities of the U.S.S.R. is almost certain to unleash a retaliatory blow, if only because the Soviet staff will not know what our target is when they detect our planes on their radar screen. Thus at a time when Soviet submarine forces are likely to be most active, our own antisubmarine strategy of destroying their home bases is likely to be most inhibited. Or else our retaliation against those bases will bring on an all-out war despite our intentions.

Like air doctrine, naval doctrine must distinguish between the strategy appropriate for an all-out war and that suitable for a limited war. It must not attempt to use the

---

21 See above, p. 58.
22 U.S. Senate, *Study of Airpower*, cited, p. 968.
23 Same, p. 1,355.

two concepts interchangeably. More emphasis will have to be placed on defeating submarines at sea by creating additional antisubmarine forces, both surface and submarine-killer types. Thus the naval contribution to limited war requires a clarification of Navy doctrine and the development of a distinctive strategy for waging limited war. Each of the services, in short, will have to create a spectrum of capabilities for the intermediate applications of its power, and within each service the forces required for limited war should have their own training, equipment and organization.[24]

VII

Limited war is not simply a question of appropriate military forces and doctrines. It also places heavy demands on the discipline and subtlety of the political leadership and on the confidence of the society in it. For limited war is psychologically a much more complex problem than all-out war. In an all-out war the alternatives will be either surrender or resistance against a threat to the national existence. In it the physical correlation of strength between the protagonists is likely to be more important than the psychological, for against the threat of national catastrophe implicit in the demand for unconditional surrender, the motivation to resist is likely to be high. To be sure, psychological factors will largely determine the relative willingness to engage in an all-out war, and the side more willing to run risks may gain an important advantage in the conduct of diplomacy. However, once the decision to fight is taken, the speed and power of modern weapons places a premium on a nation's physical ability to conduct war. Even a blow highly disruptive to society may not affect the ability of the strategic striking forces to retaliate. An all-out war will in all likelihood be decided so rapidly —if it is possible to speak of decision in such a war—and the suffering it entails will be so vast as to obscure disputes over the nuances of policy.

In a limited war, on the other hand, the psychological

---

24 See below, Chapter 12, p. 419 ff., for further discussion.

equation will be of crucial importance not only with respect to the decision to enter the war but throughout
the course of military operations. A limited war among
major powers is kept limited by the conscious choice of
the protagonists. Either side has the physical power to
expand it, and, to the extent that each side is willing to
increase its commitment in preference either to a stalemate or to a defeat, the war will gradually become an all-
out one. The restraint which keeps a war limited is a
psychological one: the consequences of a limited victory
or a limited defeat or a stalemate—the three possible out-
comes of a limited war—must seem preferable to the consequences of an all-out war.

In a limited war the choices are more varied than in an
all-out conflict and their nature is more ambiguous. Victory offers no final solution and defeat does not carry with
it the penalty of national catastrophe. As a result, the
psychological correlation of forces in a limited war is not
stable; it depends on a series of intangibles. The side
which is more willing to risk an all-out war or can convince
its opponent of its greater readiness to run that risk is in
the stronger position. Even when the willingness of both
sides to run risks is equal at the beginning of the war, the
psychological equation will constantly be shifting, depending on the course of military operations. Because the
limitation of war is brought about by the fear of unleashing a thermonuclear holocaust, the psychological equation
is, paradoxically, constantly shifting *against* the side which
seems to be winning. The greater the transformation it
seeks, the more plausible will become the threat by its
opponent of launching an all-out war. The closer defeat
in the limited war brings the losing side to the consequences which it would suffer by defeat in an all-out war,
the less it will feel restrained from resorting to extreme
measures.

At the same time, the winning side may become increasingly reluctant to test the opponent's willingness to
resort to all-out war. For while the winning side is staking
its chance for obtaining a favorable transformation, the losing side is risking an adverse change of position. The

better the position of the winning side, the more secure it will feel and the less it will be willing to take the risks of an all-out war. The more precarious the position of the losing side becomes, the more insecure it will feel and the more likely it is to raise its commitment toward the level of an all-out war. The prerequisite of victory in a limited war is therefore to determine under what circumstances one side may be willing to run greater risks for winning than its opponent will accept to avoid losing. A calculation of this character must pay special attention to the importance of diplomatic overtures which make clear that national survival is not at stake and that a settlement is possible on reasonable terms. Otherwise the result is almost certain to be either stalemate or all-out war.

Limited war, therefore, involves as many psychological complexities as a policy of deterrence. In some areas a power will have a considerable psychological potential for limited war because the region matters to it a great deal or is thought by its opponent to matter to it a great deal. This was the case with China's role in Korea. Some areas may be thought so important to one of the contenders that they will be protected by the belief of the opponent that any attack on them will lead to a general war. Protection for these areas will be achieved less by local defense than by the over-all strategic balance. This has been the case up to now with Western Europe with respect to the United States, or with the satellite regions with respect to the U.S.S.R. As total war poses increasingly ominous prospects, however, the over-all strategic balance will be a less and less adequate protection to threatened areas, for ever fewer regions will seem worth this price. As the implications of all-out war with modern weapons become better understood, security for many areas will increasingly depend on the capability for local action. Limited war would thereby become a test of the determination of the contenders, a gauge of the importance they attach to disputed issues. If one side attaches greater importance to an area or an issue and is willing to pay a higher price, and if it possesses a capability for waging a limited war, it may well achieve a favorable shift in the strategic equation.

The key to a successful policy of limited war is to keep the challenge to the opponent, whether diplomatic or military, below the threshold which would unleash an all-out war. The greater the risk in relation to the challenge, the less total the response is likely to be. The more the challenge approximates the risks posed by all-out war, the more difficult it will be to limit the conflict. A policy of limited war therefore presupposes three conditions: the ability to generate pressures other than the threat of all-out war; the ability to create a climate in which survival is not thought to be at stake in each issue; and the ability to keep control of public opinion in case a disagreement arises over whether national survival is at stake. The first condition depends to a considerable extent on the flexibility of our military policy; the second on the subtlety of our diplomacy; the third will reflect the courage of our leadership.

The problems posed by our military policy have been discussed earlier. But assuming that it will be possible to create a spectrum of military capabilities to meet the widest range of Soviet challenges, will our diplomacy be able to bring about a framework in which national survival is thought not to be at stake? Pressures severe enough to cause withdrawal or stalemate may, after all, seem severe enough to threaten survival, especially to a regime like that of Soviet Russia. It must be admitted that the challenge to our diplomacy is formidable. It would be hopeless except against the background of a retaliatory capability which can make the Soviet leadership recoil from the prospect of an all-out war. As long as we maintain a powerful strategic striking force, an all-out conflict is likely in only two contingencies: if the Soviets see an opportunity to achieve hegemony in Eurasia by peripheral actions which we would be unable to counter except by all-out war; or if the U.S.S.R. should misunderstand our intentions and interpret each military move on our part as a prelude to a thermonuclear holocaust.

Provided our military policy equips us with a wide spectrum of capabilities, the task of our diplomacy will be to convey to the Soviet bloc what we understand by limited war, at least to some extent. This becomes all the more important because Soviet reactions to our measures will depend less on what we intend than on what we are thought by the Soviet leaders to intend. The power and speed of modern weapons make too much obscurity dangerous. Unless there has been at least some degree of comprehension of the nature of limited war on both sides, it may be impossible to improvise it in the confusion of battle. Diplomacy should therefore strive to insure that the opponent obtains the information he requires to make the correct decisions.[25] To be sure, such a course will not restrain an enemy determined on a showdown. It may, however, prevent him from stumbling into an all-out war based on miscalculation or on the misinterpretation of our intentions.

The same program which may reduce the danger of miscalculation by the enemy would also go a long way toward educating public opinion in the realities of the nuclear age. This is, of course, less of a problem in the Soviet bloc where dictatorship confers a much greater freedom of action. In the Western world, however, and particularly in the United States, a considerable change in the concept of war is required. It is important for our leadership to understand that total victory is no longer possible and for the public to become aware of the dangers of pressing for such a course.

A long history of invulnerability has accustomed our public opinion to look at war more in terms of the damage we can inflict than of the losses we might suffer and to react to frustrations abroad by a demand for absolute solutions. The American people must be made aware that, with the end of our atomic monopoly all-out war has ceased to be an instrument of policy, except as a last resort, and that for most of the issues likely to be in dispute our only choice is between a strategy of limited war or inaction. It would be tragic if our Government were deprived of its freedom of maneuver by the ignorance of the public regarding the consequences of a course before which

---

25 See below, Chapter 7, p. 203 ff., for details of such a program.

it would recoil if aware of all its implications. This is all the more true since the same ignorance which underlies the demand for all-or-nothing solutions might well produce panic if our people were unexpectedly brought face-to-face with consequences of an all-out war. Conversely, a public fully aware of the dangers confronting it and forearmed psychologically by an adequate civil defense program will be better prepared to support a more flexible national policy.

VIII

Whatever aspect of our strategic problem we consider—mitigating the horrors of war, creating a spectrum of capabilities to resist likely Soviet challenges—we are brought to recognize the importance of developing a strategy which makes room for the possibility of limited war. Creating a readiness for limited war should not be considered a problem of choice but of necessity. It results from the impossibility of combining both maximum force and the maximum willingness to act. This may be hard to accept for nations which have heretofore fought their wars in outbursts of righteousness and have identified strategy with the greatest possible application of power. "If the effectiveness of the deterrent," wrote a leading British weekly, "resides precisely in its certainty and its horror, then any attempt to reduce either the certainty or the horror will reduce the power to deter." [26]

The dilemma of the nuclear age resides, however, in the impossibility of combining both maximum horror and maximum certainty. The greater the power, the greater the inhibitions against using it except in the most dire emergencies, and the more likely that no objective will seem important enough to justify resort to all-out war. On the other hand, the smaller the risks, the more likely they are to be accepted. A strategy of limited war would seek to escape the inconsistency of relying on a policy of deterrence whose major sanction involves national catastrophe. To be sure, from the point of view of power, a

---

[26] "Graduated Deterrence," *The Economist,* v. 177 (November 5, 1955), p. 458.

policy of limited war may reduce the effectiveness of the deterrent because it does not pose the ultimate sanction of total war. But from the aspect of political psychology, it may reduce the probability of war by enhancing the credibility of the threat and by increasing the willingness of our leaders to act. A strategy of limited war represents a realization that it is no longer possible to combine a deterrent based on the threat of maximum destructiveness with a strategy of minimum risk.

A strategy which makes room for the possibility of fighting limited wars will not eliminate the precariousness of our situation. In the nuclear age the best strategy can provide only a relative security, for the threat of all-out war will always loom in the background as a last resort for either side. Moreover, as nuclear technology becomes more widely diffused, other and perhaps less responsible powers will enter the nuclear race. The fear of mutual destruction, today the chief deterrent to all-out war for the major powers, may prove less effective with nations who have less to lose and whose negotiating position might even be improved by a threat to commit suicide.

Even among the major powers the strategy outlined in this chapter will not be easy to implement. It presupposes a military capability which is truly graduated. It assumes a diplomacy which can keep each conflict from being considered the prelude to a final showdown. Above all, it requires strong nerves. We can make a strategy of limited war stick only if we leave no doubt about our readiness and our ability to face a final showdown. Its effectiveness will depend on our willingness to face up to the risks of Armageddon.

6

THE PROBLEMS OF
LIMITED NUCLEAR WAR

IN SEEKING TO STRIKE a balance between a policy of deterrence and the strategy for fighting a war should deterrence fail, nothing is more important than to determine the significance of nuclear technology for the conduct of limited war. Is the dividing line between limited and all-out war identical with the difference between conventional and nuclear weapons? If limited nuclear war is, as some say, a contradiction in terms, then the whole thrust of our military policy toward developing a diversified nuclear establishment is meaningless and dangerous. We should then place our reliance on the most fearful application of our power to deter all-out war and on preparing conventional forces for limited wars. If, on the other hand, limited nuclear war is possible, it becomes important to determine whether it represents an advantageous strategy for us.

The arguments against limited nuclear war are persuasive. They call attention to the fact that nuclear weapons can now be made of all sizes from less than one kiloton of TNT equivalent up to almost any desired explosive force. In the absence of a natural cut-off point, it is argued, the employment of any nuclear weapon may start a cycle of gradually expanding commitments ending in all-out war. Even if the war should be fought initially with so-called low-yield nuclear weapons, the losing side will always be tempted to redress the balance by resorting to weapons of greater power, thus inviting counterretaliation. Moreover, so the argument goes, limitations on the size of weapons to be employed cannot be enforced in practice, and each side will, therefore, seek to anticipate its opponent by using the largest practicable weapon. All-out war could thus occur in circumstances under which it would never be clear which side had taken the crucial step that caused the struggle to become total. A conventional war, on the other hand, has a clearly defined cutoff point; it can have a self-enforcing limit. If nuclear weapons of whatever power were employed, it would be clear which side had committed "atomic aggression."

Limited nuclear war is not only impossible, according to this line of reasoning, but also undesirable. For one thing, it would cause devastation in the combat zone approaching that of thermonuclear war in severity. We would, therefore, be destroying the very people we were seeking to protect. Moreover, the belief that nuclear weapons would permit economies of manpower is said to be an illusion. On the contrary, the technical complexity of modern weapons requires a heavy investment of manpower in all supporting services, and their destructiveness necessitates preparing a large pool of trained replacements. Finally, it is argued, a limited war fought with nuclear weapons would reduce the importance of our industrial potential. It would enable the Soviet bloc to concentrate its resources in a limited area of production and to bring about an equilibrium with a smaller investment of resources.[1]

These arguments have great force. No one even generally familiar with the destructiveness of modern weapons can regard the prospect of any kind of nuclear war with equanimity. Yet the dilemma of nuclear war is with us not by choice, but because of the facts of modern technology. One of the difficulties with discussing the problem of limited nuclear war is that its nature is so rarely understood. It is not sufficiently realized that it must be based on a different order of tactics than conventional warfare. The argument of this chapter that limited nuclear war is

---

[1] James E. King, Jr., "Nuclear Plenty and Limited War," *Foreign Affairs*, v. 35 (January 1957), pp. 238-56.

in fact a strategy which will utilize our special skills to best advantage, and that it may be less likely to become all-out than conventional war, must, therefore, begin with a discussion of the tactics appropriate to the new technology.

II

Such an analysis is all the more important because the entire planning, procurement, research and development of our defense establishment is built around nuclear weapons. A decision to refrain from using them would, therefore, place Eurasia at the mercy of the Soviet bloc, at least in an interim period while we were readjusting the planning of our military establishment and redirecting the equipping of our forces. Then, too, there are some applications of nuclear weapons that it will be very difficult to discard, for example, the employment of atomic warheads for antiaircraft missiles. Should this defensive employment of nuclear weapons be admitted, however, it will set in motion pressures for their offensive use. As attacking planes become more vulnerable, they must carry larger bomb loads, and the most efficient explosives are nuclear weapons. Thus conventional war will soon become the most "unnatural" war and the most difficult to plan. A decision to rely on conventional forces in resisting local aggressions committed by a major power would represent a drastic break with present trends in the United States and among our allies.

Moreover, in a war against a nuclear power the decision between conventional and nuclear weapons is not entirely up to us. An aggressor will always be able to shift to nuclear weapons even in a war which starts out as a conventional war, perhaps by using initially weapons of very low yield. To be sure, such an action would make the identification of the "atomic aggressor" unambiguous, but the consequences which would follow are far from obvious. If the Soviet Union or Communist China is prepared to accept the onus of military aggression, it may also be willing to accept the onus of "atomic aggression." It is not the onus attached to atomic aggression which would deter resort to nuclear weapons, but the consequences which would flow from using them.

What then would be our possible rejoinders to the introduction of nuclear weapons into a limited conventional war, particularly if it were accompanied by a Soviet announcement that they would be used only against "tactical" targets or that only weapons of a certain size would be utilized? Two reactions are possible. We can either seek to deter the use of nuclear weapons by the threat of "massive retaliation," by reacting to *any* employment of nuclear weapons by all-out war. Or we can respond by using nuclear weapons in turn, but within a framework designed to keep their employment limited.

Either course is subject to serious objections. The resort to all-out war would expose us to all the inhibitions of massive retaliation. Since an all-out war stakes the national substance, the decision to engage in it will depend less on the nature of the weapons employed by the enemy than on whether the provocation is considered "worth" a national catastrophe. And the judgment about whether the provocation warrants a final showdown will depend to a considerable degree on the importance which is attached to the area or the objective in dispute. Thus a Soviet attack on Western Europe with conventional forces may unleash an all-out war, while Soviet repression of satellite revolts with nuclear weapons may not. Even if nuclear weapons were employed against United States forces, say, in the Middle East or Southeast Asia, a resort to all-out war by us would not be a foregone conclusion. It is difficult to believe that we would rush into the cataclysm of a thermonuclear war to prevent the defeat of a few conventional divisions, particularly if the Soviet leaders showed their usual skill in presenting their challenge ambiguously. Thus, at the precise moment that decisive action would be most necessary, we might recoil before the implications of so absolutist a strategy. At the very least we would be tempted, and rightly so, to ascertain whether all alternatives to an all-out struggle had been exhausted. And one of these alternatives is an effort to conduct a limited nuclear war.

A limited nuclear war which had to be improvised in the midst of military operations would be undertaken under the worst possible conditions, both psychological and military. A prerequisite for keeping a war limited is for both sides to have correct intelligence about each other's intentions. Because of the need for rapid reaction which is imposed by the speed and power of modern weapons, a misinterpretation of the opponent's intentions is always possible and may well produce a cataclysm. The sudden introduction of nuclear weapons while military operations are taking place would force the powers to confront the problems of a limited nuclear war in the confusion of battle, at a time when correct intelligence is most difficult to come by. And their difficulties would be compounded by the fact that they would have had no previous experience to serve as a guide.

Moreover, if we concede the first nuclear blow, we can be certain that nuclear weapons will always be used against us at a moment when we are most vulnerable, either physically or psychologically. In fact, the sudden introduction of nuclear weapons against a conventional force almost guarantees military success. Conventional forces must concentrate to be effective. The power of individual conventional weapons is so small, relatively, that they can hold a line or achieve a breakthrough only by massed firepower. But if troops are concentrated, they may supply the very incentive needed to tempt the opponent to use nuclear weapons. Thus, in a conventional war against a nuclear power, the choice is between accepting military ineffectiveness by employing formations which have been dispersed *as if* nuclear weapons might be used, or courting disaster by concentrating forces. It may be argued that both sides will face the same problem and will labor under the same handicap. But the aggressor has the advantage of initiative whether he uses conventional or nuclear weapons. Against a widely dispersed conventional defense, the task of even a dispersed conventional offensive is simplified, because the force required to overwhelm any given point is relatively small. And, if the aggressor suddenly resorts to nuclear weapons, he may sweep all before him before effective retaliation can take place.

Any attempt to define the role of limited nuclear war will therefore have to start with the realization that a revolution in technology carries with it a revolution in tactics. With each new technological discovery the temptation is strong to integrate it into what is familiar. Thus the first automobiles were built as much as possible like horse-drawn carriages. The first electric light was made to approximate the gas lamp it replaced. In each case, progress was impossible until a break was made with traditional patterns of thought and until the new discovery developed the forms appropriate for it.

It is no different with the impact of nuclear technology on strategy. As long as nuclear war is considered by analogy to conventional war, strategy will be stymied by the incommensurability between the power of the new weapons and the rigidity of traditional tactics. One of the most important tasks confronting strategic doctrine is to devise tactics appropriate to the new technology.

The tactics of conventional warfare were based on the same principle of specialization of functions which has given such a strong impetus to industrial technology. The fighting units were designed to inflict the greatest amount of destruction at the lowest possible loss to themselves, but they were completely dependent on service organizations for their supply, maintenance and equipment. Since the combat units had only a limited staying power when deprived of their logistic support, encirclement was the most efficient offensive tactic.

These tactics assumed that each side was in substantial control of the territory behind its battle zone and that the front was in effect a line without flanks. To be sure, in World War II deep thrusts by armored units were common. But they were in the nature of advancing the front-line as far as the supply of fuel would carry the attacker. A tank force which lost contact with its supporting units or whose supporting units could not catch up with it sufficiently rapidly was totally vulnerable, as Germany learned during its Russian campaign. Because the supplies and ammunition for conventional war were too bulky to be stored in the immediate combat zone, conventional warfare placed a premium on interdiction campaigns against cities, communication centers and industrial installations.

But such tactics would produce appalling casualties in a nuclear war. Whatever the degree of dispersion, a linear concept of defense would invite the aggressor to step up the power of his weapons to achieve a breakthrough. Limited nuclear war is unthinkable as long as the reliance on traditional tactics causes the most profitable targets to be identical with the largest centers of population.

The tactics for limited nuclear war should be based on small, highly mobile, self-contained units, relying largely on air transport even within the combat zone. The units should be small, because with nuclear weapons firepower does not depend on numbers and because a reduction in the size of the target will place an upper limit on the power of the weapons it is profitable to employ against it. The units must be mobile, because when anything that can be detected can be destroyed, the ability to hide by constantly shifting position is an essential means of defense. The units should be self-contained, because the cumbersome supply system of World War II is far too vulnerable to interdiction. The proper analogy to limited nuclear war is not traditional land warfare, but naval strategy, in which self-contained units with great firepower gradually gain the upper hand by destroying their enemy counterparts without physically occupying territory or establishing a front-line.

While it is impossible to hold any given line with such tactics, they offer an excellent tool for depriving aggression of one of its objectives: to control territory. Small, mobile units with nuclear weapons are extremely useful for defeating their enemy counterparts or for the swift destruction of important objectives. They are not an efficient means for establishing political control. The Hungarian revolution of October and November 1956 demonstrated the difficulty faced even by a vastly superior army in attempting to dominate hostile territory. The Red Army finally had to concentrate twenty-two divisions in order to crush a practically unarmed population. No such concentration is feasible in a nuclear war. Nuclear units of high mobility should, therefore, be used to make the countryside untenable for the invader. They should be supplemented by stationary defensive positions in deep shelters, immune to any but direct hits by the largest weapons to discourage sudden coups against cities.

A defense structure of this type would pose a very difficult problem for an aggressor. To defeat the opposing mobile units he would require highly mobile detachments of his own. To control hostile territory and reduce nuclear hedgehogs, he would have to utilize massive forces. Against determined opposition, it will prove very difficult to combine these two kinds of warfare. Stationary, well-protected hedgehogs should force the aggressor to concentrate his forces and to present a target for nuclear attack. Mobile nuclear units should be able to keep the enemy constantly off balance by never permitting him to consolidate any territorial gains and by destroying any concentration of his forces. If these tactics were coupled with rapid offensive thrusts by units of the defensive force deep into the aggressor's territory, which in Europe at least can be assumed to be hostile to the U.S.S.R., the Soviet Union might soon confront an untenable situation.

These tactics will require a radical break with our traditional notions of warfare and military organization. The Army has already made a start by reorganizing some of its divisions, each into five self-contained combat teams. It stresses the development of troop-carrying helicopters, and even the individual soldier in some units has been given a rudimentary ability to transport himself through the air by means of the "flying platform."

These measures, while useful, are only a beginning. The ultimate aim should be units which carry to its conclusion the analogy between limited nuclear war and naval strategy. Since the mobile units will not be able to rely on a logistics system of the traditional type, they should be able to carry all their supplies and maintain their own equipment. A great deal of thought will have to be given to measures for reducing the bulkiness of equipment, par-

ticularly to developing a substitute for the internal combustion engine, whose demands for fuel and maintenance
severely limit the range and staying power of mobile units.
Since mobile nuclear units will often be operating deep
within enemy territory, they will also have to acquire an
understanding of political relationships, particularly of
methods for organizing and supporting partisan activities.
In short, the units for nuclear war should be conceived to
approximate a naval vessel as a self-contained tactical for-
mation, but also to act as a political and military spear-
head for disorganizing the enemy rear.

It is clear that units of this type cannot both remain
mobile and capable of fighting conventional war. Without
nuclear weapons they would not have the firepower to
defend themselves, and the amount of ammunition required for conventional weapons would present almost
insuperable logistic problems for mobile warfare. To be
sure, it is possible to create dual-purpose forces, trained
for both conventional and nuclear war. But whatever the
training and weapons of such forces, they will find it very
difficult to shift from conventional war to nuclear war on
the opponent's initiative. While conducting "conventional" operations, even dual-purpose forces will have to
establish an approximation to a continuous line and a
specialized supply system. They would, therefore, be highly
vulnerable to the sudden introduction of nuclear weapons
by the enemy. The side which cedes the first nuclear blow
to its opponent compounds the traditional disadvantage
of the defensive with a deployment disastrous in nuclear
war. The side which has the initiative, on the other hand,
can disperse its formations *before* resorting to nuclear
weapons. It will therefore be much less vulnerable to retaliation by its opponent. The only safe way for conducting a conventional war against a nuclear power is to have
a reserve in the combat zone deployed for nuclear operations. But this, in turn, would transform conventional
war among nuclear powers into the most unstable kind of
warfare, because each side will constantly be tempted to
anticipate its opponent in the first use of nuclear weapons.

III

With proper tactics, nuclear war need not be as destructive as it appears when we think of it in terms of
traditional warfare. The high casualty estimates for nuclear war are based on the assumption that the most
suitable targets are those of conventional warfare: cities
to interdict communications and airfields (most of which
are located close to cities) to dominate the sky. In conventional war, the interdiction of communications is important because the large numbers of troops involved, the
relatively small destructiveness of individual weapons, and
the specialization of functions combine to place a premium
on the denial of transportation by road and rail. When
armies are becoming both mobile and self-contained, however, the elimination of communication centers may lose
its former significance.

Moreover, in nuclear war industrial potential will play
a smaller role than heretofore. With conventional technology a decisive victory on the battlefield could be
achieved only by using quantities of arms too large to
stockpile. Munitions and weapons had to be supplied out
of current production. Under these circumstances, it made
sense to attempt to achieve attrition by bombing industrial facilities. Under conditions of nuclear plenty,
however, weapons may be more decisively employed
against opposing military forces than against production
centers. With cities no longer serving as key elements in
the communications system of the military forces, the risks
of initiating city bombing may outweigh the gains which
can be achieved.

The same applies to the traditional doctrine of the need
of control of the air. The concept that air supremacy is the
prerequisite of victory and that it is achieved by bombing
enemy airfields will soon be outstripped by technological
developments. So long as planes had to be concentrated on
a relatively few bases for efficient operation, it was more
economical to destroy them on the ground than in the air.
But the concurrent development of missiles and of vertical
take-off aircraft, which require little or no runway, are al-

tering this relationship. Within ten years most tactical air support will be accomplished by these two weapons. It will then become meaningless to speak of air supremacy in the traditional sense. Against vertical take-off aircraft there will be no airfield left to crater, and launching sites, especially for short and medium-range missiles, can be so dispersed and concealed that they will be hard to locate and even more difficult to destroy.

Even before the advent of missiles and of vertical take-off aircraft, the concept of complete air supremacy will have become inconsistent with a policy of limited war. As the range of planes increases, complete air superiority can be achieved only by deep penetrations into enemy territory. But a deep penetration of the territory of a major nuclear power may unleash a retaliatory blow. The enemy, observing a flight of planes on his radar screen, cannot know whether they intend to attack a "tactical" or a "strategic" target and, faced with the risk of having his strategic striking power caught on the ground, he may launch his retaliatory attack. In a limited war between major powers, sanctuary areas immune to attack are almost essential, because any threat to the opponent's strategic striking force will invite a thermonuclear holocaust.[2] Even in a limited conventional war, deep penetration into the air space of a major nuclear power will have to be avoided. For, when the enemy's early warning line is crossed, he cannot know whether the attacking planes are carrying nuclear or conventional weapons. He may, therefore, act on the assumption of the worst contingency and start his counterblow.

The corollary of these propositions is that for destroying targets deep within enemy territory, it is necessary to develop forms of attack as distinguishable as possible from an all-out strategic blow. Mobile units may be able to attack selected enemy targets at a considerable distance from the combat zone without unleashing all-out war, so

---

[2] This is true at least as long as the strategic striking force is composed of airplanes. When missiles take over the functions heretofore performed by the strategic air forces, the dispersal of launching sites will make the destruction of the retaliatory force almost impossible. Deep penetrations of enemy territory may then paradoxically be less risky but also less fruitful.

long as their intentions are sufficiently clear: they should, therefore, be transported to their target by means which are least likely to be mistaken for the precursor of total war. A great premium will be placed on small, low-flying aircraft, on mobile tactical units and even on unorthodox forms of attack such as sabotage and partisan activity. After missiles exist in quantity, the possibilities for this kind of warfare will increase rather than diminish. Since strategic striking forces composed of missiles will be better dispersed and less vulnerable than those based on manned bombers, powers may become less sensitive to a penetration of their air space. With their retaliatory forces almost impossible to wipe out and in the face of the horror of all-out war, the opposing sides may be more prepared to wait to determine the *actual* intentions of the enemy and to graduate the response to the extent of the challenge.

In these circumstances, it is possible to conceive of a pattern of limited nuclear war with its own appropriate tactics and with limitations as to targets, areas and the size of weapons used. Such a mode of conflict cannot be improvised in the confusion of battle, however. The limitation of war is established not only by our intentions but also by the manner in which the other side interprets them. It, therefore, becomes the task of our diplomacy to convey to our opponent what we understand by limited nuclear war, or at least what limitations we are willing to observe. Unless some concept of limitation of warfare is established in advance, miscalculation and misinterpretation of the opponent's intentions may cause the war to become all-out even should both sides intend to limit it. If the Soviet leadership is clear about our intentions, on the other hand, a framework of war limitation may be established by the operation of self-interest—by the fear of all-out thermonuclear war and by the fact that new tactics make many of the targets of traditional warfare less profitable. The distinction should not be between "tactical" and "strategic" weapons, but between weapons suitable for the targets appropriate for limited nuclear war.[3]

---

3 A concept of war limitation is discussed in Chapter 7, p. 224 ff.

There remains the objection that, whatever the theoretical feasibility of limiting nuclear war, it will be thwarted in practice by the new tactics themselves and by the tendency of the losing side to redress the balance by expanding the area of conflict or by resorting to bigger weapons. The new tactics, it may be argued, will inhibit a program of war limitation. The very mobility of units and the uncertainty about their location may tempt one side or the other to saturate an area with the highest-yield weapons. It is important, however, to distinguish between difficulties of limiting war in general and those peculiar to nuclear war. If it is true that the losing side will invariably resort to every weapon in its arsenal and will disregard all restrictions as to targets and depth of the combat zone, then the only possible outcome of limited war is either stalemate or all-out war. Nor would these alternatives be avoided by a strategy of conventional war. A power which is prepared to unleash an all-out holocaust in order to escape defeat in a limited nuclear war would hardly be more restrained by an initial distinction between conventional and nuclear weapons. The argument that neither side will accept defeat amounts to a denial of the possibility of limited war, nuclear or other, an argument which is valid only if nations in fact prefer suicide to a limited withdrawal.

As to the contention that limited nuclear war would spread by slow stages into an all-out war, it is necessary to examine what these stages might be. One of the most persuasive opponents of limited nuclear war has admitted that even a conventional war is unthinkable without some limitations and that unrestricted conventional war in the age of nuclear plenty is a contradiction in terms.[4] These limitations, presumably defined in terms of targets and the depth of the combat zone, are essentially independent of the nature of weapons used. If they can be made to stick in a conventional war they can be made to stick in a nuclear war as well. The distinguishing feature of nuclear war, which is said to make any effort at

---

[4] King, cited, p. 244.

limitation illusory, is the variety of available weapons which would invite the losing side to resort to weapons of ever greater explosive power.

It must be admitted that the wide spectrum of nuclear explosives makes restrictions as to the size of weapons impossible to control, at least below the level which would produce significant fall-out or about 1 megaton. Assuming, however, that both sides are eager to avoid all-out war —the prerequisite for *any* kind of war limitation—there exist some "built-in" restrictions which can form the basis of self-restraint. As long as both sides retain a retaliatory force capable of devastating the opponent, they will not look for an excuse to expand the war; rather, they will have a powerful incentive to work out some set of limitations, however tenuous its logic. This at least was the experience of the Korean war, even at a time when nuclear stockpiles and delivery systems were still in a relatively elementary state.

The "built-in" restrictions rest on the assumption that high-yield weapons are not employed for their own sake, but to achieve a military advantage. Much of the argument about the indiscriminate use of high-yield weapons in limited nuclear war supposes that there will be a stabilized front with both sides pulverizing everything behind the enemy lines. But, given the fluidity of nuclear war, such a situation is most unlikely. When small mobile detachments are operating deep in each other's territory, there will be greater rewards for weapons with relative discrimination than for those which may destroy friendly troops and friendly populations together with a small number of the enemy.

Thus, in a nuclear war it is difficult to conceive of very many suitable targets for really high-yield weapons or of an advantage to be gained by using them which cannot be offset by retaliation. High-yield weapons cannot be used in proximity to friendly troops, or on territory expected soon to be occupied by friendly troops, or against friendly populations. Because of the unpredictability of fall-out, they cannot be exploded near the ground within any reasonable definition of a combat zone. In Europe, at least, the prevailing westerly winds would make fall-out a much greater hazard for Soviet-controlled territory than for that of the free world. To be sure, high-yield weapons could be exploded at an altitude which does not produce fall-out, but the problem of sparing friendly populations would still remain. Moreover, if each destruction of an area target by one side leads to the destruction of an area target in retaliation, the risks involved in stepping up the power of weapons may outweigh the gains to be achieved. It would seem much more effective to utilize weapons suitable for destroying the enemy mobile units whose success or failure will ultimately decide the control of territory.

Are high-yield weapons useful in order to stave off defeat? Here we must analyze what is meant by "defeat" in a limited nuclear war. If proper tactics are utilized, defeat will involve a gradual disintegration of control by one side over part of its territories. Like the weaker side in a naval war, the loser in nuclear war may find itself reduced to fixed positions and to hit-and-run tactics. It will, therefore, be more vulnerable to high-yield weapons than its opponent, psychologically and physically: psychologically, because the most suitable targets are at that stage likely to be in its own territory, and physically, because a measure of its defeat will be a loss of mobility. If the side which has the upper hand utilizes its advantage to offer peace on moderate terms—an indispensable condition for limited war, nuclear or otherwise—its opponent may prefer local adjustments to total devastation.

This is not to say that every limited war should necessarily be fought as a nuclear war. It does indicate that, as long as we are confronted by an opponent capable of initiating nuclear war against us, we require a continuous spectrum of nuclear and nonnuclear capabilities. Nor should we be defeatist about the possibility of limiting nuclear war or about the casualties it might involve. It is far from certain that a conventional war involving fixed positions would produce less devastation than a nuclear war, and in certain circumstances it may produce more. To be sure, conventional weapons are by and large more discriminating than nuclear weapons. On the other hand, the target systems of nuclear war may lend themselves more easily to an effort at limiting war. And among combat units the absolute number of casualties in nuclear war will almost certainly be smaller than those of conventional war, although they may be higher in proportion to the number of troops involved.

It is impossible to be certain about contingencies which have not yet arisen. Even the most careful analysis may be belied by events. But this is no more than a restatement of the dilemma and the challenge of the nuclear age: the side which believes more in itself than its opponent, which has more faith in its assessment of its opportunities, may gain a crucial advantage. In the nuclear age the quest for certainty is a prescription for inaction.

IV

Is limited nuclear war an advantageous strategy for us? It is important to define what is meant by an advantageous strategy in the nuclear age. It emphatically does not mean that limited nuclear war should be our *only* strategy. We must maintain at all times an adequate retaliatory force and not shrink from using it if our survival is threatened. Even against less than all-out challenges, limited nuclear war may not always be the wisest course. In a police action against a nonnuclear minor power, in a civil war in which the population must be won over, the use of nuclear weapons may be unnecessary or unwise for either political or psychological reasons. As a general rule, in a limited war the smallest amount of force consistent with achieving the objective should be used. The problem of limited nuclear war arises primarily in actions against nuclear powers or against powers with vast resources of manpower which are difficult to overcome with conventional technology.

The decision of whether it is to our strategic advantage to fight nuclear or nonnuclear wars must be made well in advance of hostilities. We cannot utilize the threat of nuclear war for purposes of deterrence and at the same time keep open the option of waging a conventional war should deterrence fail; at least we cannot do so against a nuclear power. For an aggressor may not guess our intentions correctly. In the absence of an unmistakable indication on our part, he may assume the worst contingency and conduct nuclear operations.

In a war against a nuclear power, the decision to rely on conventional war will be ineffective by itself unless it is understood in advance by the opponent. It, therefore, implies a different diplomacy from that which would be appropriate for creating the framework for a limited nuclear war. The decision to resist aggression by nuclear war requires a diplomacy which seeks to break down the atmosphere of special horror which now surrounds the use of nuclear weapons, an atmosphere which has been created in part by skillful Soviet "ban-the-bomb" propaganda.[5] It should treat the utilization of nuclear weapons as nonnegotiable, but should put great emphasis on measures to mitigate their effect. The focus of disarmament negotiations, for example, should be shifted from eliminating the use of nuclear weapons to reducing the impact of their employment.[6]

If, on the other hand, we decide to rely on conventional warfare as the chief deterrent to local aggression, it would be to our interest to emphasize the horror of nuclear weapons, to seek to restrain the Soviets from taking us by surprise in a limited war, not only by the threat of our reaction to the utilization of nuclear weapons, but also by the opinion of the rest of the world. To elaborate a distinction between limited and all-out war based on the difference between nuclear and conventional weapons would, therefore, play into the hands of Soviet "ban-the-bomb" propaganda. This would be a serious though not a fatal objection if limited conventional war were thought in fact to be to our best interest. But we must be clear that whatever strategy we adopt must have a diplomacy appropriate to it and whatever course we propose to follow cannot be improvised under the pressure of events.

Everything depends, therefore, on our assessment of

[5] See below, Chapter 11, pp. 373-8.
[6] See below, Chapter 7, p. 222.

whether limited nuclear war represents an advantageous strategy from our point of view. Advantageous, as here used, should not be confused with desirable: the nuclear age permits only a choice among evils. It is important also to distinguish among the various senses in which a strategy may be deemed advantageous. It can apply to a strategy under which our relative superiority over our opponent is greatest. It can refer to a strategy which is most likely to avoid general war. It can mean the strategy which is least costly. It can imply the strategy which is most suitable for purposes of deterrence.

The four meanings of strategic advantage do not always coincide and are sometimes incompatible. Throughout the period of our atomic monopoly, our relative superiority was greatest in the field of all-out nuclear war. Yet, since we were eager to avoid a final showdown and because the cost of an all-out war seemed out of proportion to the objectives in dispute, we recoiled from using it as an instrument of policy. A strategy which is most likely to avoid general war may not be the least costly strategy; it may be advantageous only by comparison with the horrors of thermonuclear war. Finally, a strategy which concentrates entirely on achieving minimum cost may weaken the deterrent to the point at which its inadequacy invites aggression.

We thus return to the basic problem of limited war in the nuclear age: where to strike the balance between the desire for posing the maximum threat and the need for a strategy which does not paralyze the will. The quest for the greatest physical threat may create a psychological vulnerability, for the risks may always seem greater than the goals to be achieved. An overemphasis on a strategy which maximizes the readiness to act may reduce the physical sanctions of deterrence below the level of safety. In this task of posing the maximum *credible* threat, limited nuclear war seems a more suitable deterrent than conventional war. From the point of view of deterrence, the availability of a wide spectrum of nuclear weapons increases the aggressor's risks. It puts him on notice that any additional increment of power which he commits to the war can be matched by a similar increase in the power of the other side. And, limited nuclear war greatly complicates the problem of controlling territory, which is one of the purposes of aggression.

As compared to conventional war, does limited nuclear war reduce the credibility of the threat? Will it lower our willingness to resist? To be sure, limited nuclear war poses greater risks for both sides than conventional war. But it is a mistake to assume that the risks of nuclear war can be avoided by a decision to resist aggression with conventional weapons. Against a nuclear power, conventional war carries with it almost the same risks as nuclear war, for the side which engages in a conventional war against a nuclear power, without being willing to accept the risks of nuclear war, is at a hopeless disadvantage. Such an effort to hedge the risks would enable the opponent to gain his ends either by the threat or by the reality of nuclear war. Against a nuclear power, the decision to fight a conventional war can be justified only on the grounds that it represents an advantageous strategy; the over-all risks are not substantially less.

Does a strategy of limited nuclear war increase or decrease the risks of all-out war? The previous discussion has shown that there is no inevitable progression from limited nuclear war to all-out thermonuclear conflict. It remains to demonstrate that under most circumstances limited nuclear war may actually be less likely than conventional war to produce an all-out showdown.

Whether a limited war, nuclear or otherwise, may remain limited will depend on the working out of a subtle equation between the willingness of the contenders to assume risks and their ability to increase their commitments. By definition, a limited war between major powers involves the *technical* possibility that either side will be able to raise its commitment. If both sides are willing to do so in preference to accepting a limited defeat, a limited victory or a stalemate, the result will be all-out war. If one side is willing to run greater risks, or, what amounts to the same thing, is less reluctant to engage in an all-out war, it will have a decisive advantage. If both sides are willing to run the same risks and are able to make the same commitments short of all-out war, the result will be a stalemate or a victory for the side which develops the superior strategy.

Assuming that our determination is equal to that of our opponent—and no strategy can be productive without this—the crucial question is whether, from the point of view of the desirability of avoiding all-out war, a conventional war will be "safer" than a nuclear war. Obviously, a nuclear war involves a larger initial commitment than a conventional war. Is it safer then to begin a limited war with an initial commitment so large that any addition involves the danger of merging into all-out war or is it wiser to begin it with a commitment which it is possible to raise at smaller risk?

Paradoxically, in a war which begins with a smaller investment it may prove much more difficult to establish an equilibrium. The consciousness that the opponent is able at any moment to increase his commitment will insert an element of instability into the psychological equation of limited war. The temptation to anticipate the other side may lead to an increasingly explosive situation and to a cycle of gradually expanding commitments. Moreover, if reliance is placed on conventional war, it follows almost inevitably that the nature of limited nuclear conflict will not be fully explored either in staff planning or in diplomacy. Because the two sides will be less clear about each other's contentions, the detonation of any nuclear device could then set off an all-out holocaust. The fact that there exists a clear cut-off point between conventional and nuclear war may turn into a double-edged sword: the existence of two families of weapons may serve to limit the war as long as the limitation holds. Once breached, however, it may set off a vicious spiral, difficult to control. At best it will force the contenders to confront the problem of limited nuclear war under the most difficult circumstances; at worst it might unleash a thermonuclear holocaust.

A war which began as a limited nuclear war would have the advantage that its limitations could have been established—and, what is more important, understood—well in advance of hostilities. In such a conflict, moreover, the options of the aggressor are reduced in range. Whereas in a conventional war the choice is between continuing the war with its existing restrictions or risking an expanded *limited* war, in a nuclear war the choice is the much more difficult one between the existing war and all-out conflict. To be sure, even in a nuclear war it is possible to step up the commitment by resorting to higher-yield weapons. But, given the proper tactics, such a course may not drastically alter the outcome and, if carried beyond a certain point, it will unleash all-out war. As long as both sides are eager to avoid a final showdown, a nuclear war which breaks out after diplomacy has established a degree of understanding of the possibilities of the new technology would probably stand a better chance of remaining limited than would a conflict that began as a limited conventional war in an international environment which was unsure about the significance of nuclear weapons and which has come to identify any explosion of a nuclear device with total war.

The choice between conventional and nuclear war then becomes an essentially practical one: which side is likely to gain from adopting limited nuclear war? Here our superior industrial potential, the broader range of our technology and the adaptability of our social institutions should give us the advantage. When the destructiveness of individual weapons is too small, manpower can substitute for technology, as was the case with Communist China in Korea. If weapons are too destructive, the importance of industrial potential is reduced because a very few weapons suffice to establish an equilibrium. For a nation with a superior industrial potential and a broader base of technology, the strategically most productive form of war is to utilize weapons of an intermediary range of destructiveness, sufficiently complex to require a substantial productive effort, sufficiently destructive so that manpower cannot be substituted for technology, yet discriminating enough to permit the establishment of a significant margin of superiority.

It would seem that the weapons systems appropriate for limited nuclear war meet these requirements. The Soviet Union has shown an extraordinary ability to produce results by concentrating its effort on one strategic category, as it did in developing its nuclear weapons and its Long-Range Air Force. It is much less certain that with its inferior industrial plant it could compete with us in developing the diversified capability for a limited nuclear war—the wide spectrum of weapons, means of transportation and elaborate systems of communication. In this respect the difficulties of the Soviet Union would be compounded by the backwardness of Communist China. While it is possible for China to develop a rudimentary nuclear technology within a decade, it would remain completely dependent on the U.S.S.R. for the sophisticated equipment needed for a limited nuclear war. And mere possession of complicated equipment by a backward nation offers no guarantee that it can be used effectively, as was demonstrated by Egypt's incapacity to use Soviet arms. When manpower can no longer be substituted for materiel, the strategic significance of Communist China may be much reduced, and in certain circumstances it may even constitute a drain on the resources of the U.S.S.R.

Even should the Soviet Union overcome its difficulties in producing the required spectrum of weapons—and over a period of time it undoubtedly can do so—it will still be handicapped by the nature of its institutions and by its historical experience. For just as the growth of the Soviet Long-Range Air Force and nuclear stockpile should force us to reassess our traditional reliance on all-out war, the introduction of nuclear weapons on the battlefield will shake the very basis of Soviet tactical doctrine. No longer will the Soviet bloc be able to rely on massed manpower as in World War II and in Korea. In a limited nuclear war dispersal is the key to survival and mobility the prerequisite to success. Everything depends on leadership of a high order, personal initiative and mechanical aptitude, qualities more prevalent in our society than in the regimented system of the U.S.S.R. To be sure, the Soviet forces can train and equip units for nuclear war. But self-reliance, spontaneity and initiative cannot be acquired by training; they grow naturally out of social institutions or they do not come into being. And a society like that of the Soviet Union, in which everything is done according to plan and by government direction, will have extraordinary difficulty inculcating these qualities.[7]

While it may be true, as many advocates of the conventional war thesis maintain, that nuclear weapons do not permit economies of manpower, the significant point is how that manpower is used and on what qualities it places a premium. In conventional war, manpower is required to establish an equilibrium on the battlefield; its training is in the handling of a few relatively simple weapons; it can substitute discipline for conception. To conduct a nuclear war, manpower must be trained in a wide spectrum of abilities; here rewards go to initiative and technical competence at all levels. Such a utilization of manpower would seem to take advantage of the special qualities of our society. It is not for nothing that Soviet propaganda has been insistent on two themes: there is "no such thing" as limited nuclear war, and "ban the bomb." Both themes, if accepted, deprive us of flexibility and undermine the basis of the most effective United States strategy.

It may be objected that if a strategy of limited nuclear war is to our advantage it must be to the Soviet disadvantage, and the Kremlin will therefore seek to escape it by resorting to all-out war. But the fact that the Soviet leadership may stand to lose from a limited nuclear war does not mean that it could profit from all-out war. On the contrary, if our retaliatory force is kept at a proper level and our diplomacy shows ways out of a military impasse short of unconditional surrender, we should always be able to make all-out war seem an unattractive course.

v

What about the impact on strategy of the possession of nuclear weapons by many now secondary powers? Will

---

[7] For an elaboration of these ideas see below, Chapter 11, pp. 398-400.

they not be able to redress the strategic balance much more easily by means of nuclear war? Within a decade the diffusion of nuclear technology through its peaceful uses will give many powers the wherewithal to manufacture nuclear weapons. And to the extent that nuclear weapons are thought to confer an advantage, they may be used regardless of what strategy we propose to follow. We, therefore, have no choice but to base our strategy on the assumption that a war between nuclear powers, even of the second rank, *may* involve the use of nuclear weapons.

It is important to distinguish, however, between the possession of nuclear weapons and their strategic effectiveness. By themselves, nuclear weapons have a considerable nuisance value. But, unless they are coupled with sophisticated delivery means, highly complex communication systems and appropriate tactics, it will be difficult to utilize them effectively. Unless the whole military establishment is geared to nuclear tactics, nuclear war becomes a highly dangerous adventure. What has been said above about Communist China would be even more true in many other underdeveloped regions.

In these terms, the only area where nuclear weapons would represent an increase in real strength is Western Europe because there the technical skill is coupled with the industrial resources to maintain, with United States assistance, a diversified capability.[8] In the rest of the world it will be difficult for the foreseeable future to bring about either the equipment or the training required for sustained nuclear war. Moreover, limited nuclear war is possible only if there exists a substantial stockpile of fissionable material. As long as fissionable material is scarce—as it will remain in the underdeveloped regions at least in relation to the requirements of limited nuclear war—it is impossible to create a wide spectrum of weapons. Emphasis will then have to be placed on a few bombs of maximum power, which in turn require complicated and costly delivery means.

---

8 For the impact of nuclear weapons on NATO strategy see below, Chapter 9, p. 269 ff.

Thus, the presently underdeveloped regions will, for the foreseeable future, lack the fissionable material and the industrial base to bring about a capability for limited nuclear war and they will be even less able to create a meaningful capability for all-out war. A few nuclear weapons will not be strategically significant against a well-equipped enemy trained for nuclear war. They may merely serve to emphasize further the imbalance between weapons, training and industrial potential, which already besets the military establishments of so many countries.

The possession by our European allies of nuclear weapons, on the other hand, will improve the over-all position of the free world. It will make an attack by the Soviet Union on Western Europe an increasingly hazardous undertaking and it may improve the ability of the free world to hold other areas around the Soviet periphery. On balance, therefore, the diffusion of nuclear weapons technology will be to our net strategic advantage.

This is not to say that we should be complacent about the prospect of a world armed with nuclear weapons. Even if the secondary powers will not be able to create a capability for fighting on equal terms against an opponent with a diversified military establishment, the possession by them of nuclear weapons will make tense situations in their relations with each other even more explosive. And powers whose major negotiating weapon is the threat to commit suicide will be little restrained by the horrors of the new technology from engaging in acts, even toward stronger states which, while militarily inconclusive, may set off a cycle of violence difficult to control. It is, therefore, imperative that in the time remaining before this eventuality, the United States demonstrate its ability to intervene rapidly and with discrimination and that it establish an understanding of the significance of the new technology, lest irresponsibility set off a holocaust.[9]

---

[9] For an expansion of these ideas see below, Chapter 7, pp. 231-2, and Chapter 8, p. 261 ff.

VI

The discussion in this chapter has led to these conclusions: War between nuclear powers has to be planned
on the assumption that it is likely to be a nuclear war.
Nuclear war should be fought as something less than an
all-out war. Limited nuclear war represents our most effective strategy against nuclear powers or against a major
power which is capable of substituting manpower for technology.

Such a strategy is not simple or easy to contemplate. It
requires an ability to harmonize political, psychological
and military factors and to do so rapidly enough so that
the speed of war waged with modern weapons does not
outstrip the ability of our diplomacy to integrate them
into a framework of limited objectives. It presupposes a
careful consideration of the objectives appropriate for a
limited war and of the weapons systems which have a sufficient degree of discrimination so that limited war does
not merge insensibly into an all-out holocaust. More than
ever the test of strategy will be its ability to relate military
capability to psychological readiness. It cannot strive to
combine the advantages of every course of action, of deterrence based on a maximum threat and of a strategy of
minimum risk. It must decide on the price to be paid
for deterrence, but then make certain that this price will
be paid if deterrence should fail. It is a paradoxical consequence of a period when technology has never been more
complicated that its effectiveness depends to such an extent on intangibles: on the subtlety of the leadership and
on its conception of alternatives.

Nor should a policy of limited nuclear war be conceived
as a means to enable us to reduce our readiness for all-out
war. None of the measures described in this chapter is
possible without a substantial retaliatory force; it is the
fear of thermonuclear devastation which sets the bounds of
limited war. It may be argued that a strategy, based on
what Sir Winston Churchill called a balance of terror, is
inherently tenuous and that one side or the other will find
the temptation to resort to all-out war irresistible. In the

past, so this argument goes, new discoveries often have been greeted with prophecies of impending doom or assertions that they made war impossible, and in every case they were nevertheless used to the limit of their effectiveness.

It cannot be denied, of course, that many new discoveries have been taken to augur the end of war and have ended up by adding to the horror of war. Yet it is equally true that no new discovery has ever added to armaments the increment of destructive power that is represented by nuclear weapons, or has ever come into existence so suddenly. Gunpowder, for example, was introduced gradually over a period of centuries. In the early sixteenth century—over a hundred years after it became widely known—Machiavelli could still argue that it was less efficient than the then "traditional" armaments. As late as 1825, the British War Office could still seriously discuss a proposal to reintroduce the crossbow to replace the musket. Nuclear weapons, on the other hand, have brought with them an increase in the scale of destructiveness which leaves no margin for misinterpretation.

When shrapnel or dum-dum bullets were employed, despite international prohibitions against their use, these actions demonstrated that treaties will not restrain antagonists engaged in a mortal struggle unless the international agreements are reinforced by considerations of self-interest. These weapons were used because one side or the other promised itself a net advantage. The essence of the nuclear stalemate, on the other hand, is that neither side can gain from all-out war. Each can use it only to escape unconditional surrender. To be sure, should one side ever achieve a clear superiority in its capacity to conduct an all-out war, the balance of self-interest would no longer hold, and all efforts must be made to prevent this contingency from arising. The purpose of a policy of limited nuclear war is not to provide a substitute for all-out war, but to create a range of options within which the response can be brought into balance with the provocation and where military capability and the will to use it will be in greater harmony than in the stark case when all-out war remains our only response to a challenge.

The strategy described in this and the preceding chapters must be considered not against the background of nostalgia for a more tranquil past, but against the perils of an all-out thermonuclear catastrophe. To be sure, this strategy offers no final solutions, and stalemates are more likely than complete victory. But in many areas now overshadowed by the Soviet threat, the possibility of a stalemate represents a strategic advance. Moreover, both the risks and the frustrations of limited nuclear war are the penalties we pay for living in the nuclear period, penalties which we consciously accepted when we permitted our atomic monopoly to be broken without having first achieved a workable system of international control.

The American strategic problem can, therefore, be summed up in these propositions:

1. Thermonuclear war must be avoided, except as a last resort.

2. A power possessing thermonuclear weapons is not likely to accept unconditional surrender without employing them, and no nation is likely to risk thermonuclear destruction except to the extent that it believes its survival to be directly threatened.

3. It is the task of our diplomacy to make clear that we do not aim for unconditional surrender, to create a framework within which the question of national survival is not involved in every issue. But equally, we must leave no doubt about our determination to achieve intermediary objectives and to resist by force any Soviet military move.

4. Since diplomacy which is not related to a plausible employment of force is sterile, it must be the task of our military policy to develop a doctrine and a capability for the graduated employment of force.

5. Since a policy of limited war cannot be implemented except behind the shield of a capability for all-out war, we must retain a retaliatory force sufficiently powerful and well protected so that by no calculation can an aggressor discern any benefit in resorting to all-out war.

Nevertheless, it would be risky to rely too much on the

self-evidence of the horrors of nuclear war. Limited nuclear war is impossible unless our diplomacy succeeds in
giving an indication of our intentions to the other side.
It may even have to make up for any lack of imagination
on the part of the Soviet leaders by conveying to them
our understanding of the nature and the limits of nuclear
war. To be sure, such a program will not deter an opponent determined on a final showdown. No diplomatic
program can be a substitute for an adequate retaliatory
power. But to the extent that it is possible to prevent a war
from becoming all-out because of miscalculation of our
intentions or because of a misunderstanding of the nature
of nuclear warfare, our diplomacy should seek to bring
about a better comprehension of the range of strategic options of the nuclear period. This is all the more important
because whatever the possibilities of limited nuclear war,
it cannot be improvised under the pressure of events.
In seeking to avoid the horrors of all-out war by
outlining an alternative, in developing a concept of limitation that combines firmness with moderation, diplomacy can once more establish a relationship with force
even in the nuclear age.

7

DIPLOMACY, DISARMAMENT
AND THE LIMITATION OF WAR

IT MAY SEEM LIKE a paradox to ask diplomacy that it rescue mankind from the horrors of a thermonuclear holocaust by devising a framework of war limitation. How can there be an agreement on the limitation of war when all negotiations with the Kremlin have proved that the two sides have rarely been able to agree even on what constitutes a reasonable demand?

Diplomacy has never faced a more fearful challenge. For almost everything conspires against the subtle negotiation, the artful compromise, of classical diplomacy. Diplomacy, the art of settling disputes by negotiation, presupposes that all the major powers accept a framework which recognizes the necessity of both change and continued harmony. Negotiations are made necessary by the dissatisfaction of some power with the *status quo,* for were all powers perfectly satisfied there would be nothing to negotiate about. But negotiations can be successful only if all parties accept some common standard transcending their disputes. They must agree either that the maintenance of the international system is more important than their disagreements or that the consequences of not making concessions will be more serious than those of doing so, or both. In the past, settlements have come about because the realization of the advantage of harmony was combined with the fear of the consequences of proving obdurate. The smaller the interest in harmony, the greater has been the requirement of fear produced by force or the

threat of force. The greater the interest of the major powers in maintaining good relations, the less necessary it has
been to resort to force.

The result has been that diplomacy has proved most effective when disagreements did not concern issues considered vital by the contenders. Diplomacy has been least
able to settle disputes when disagreements were produced
by clashing notions of "vital" interests. For no nation can
negotiate about its survival and no nation will give up
conditions which it considers essential to its survival for
the sake of harmony. An international order that does not
protect the vital interests of a particular power, as it con-
ceives them, will not seem worth preserving to that power,
and its relations with the remainder of the international
community will become revolutionary. And whenever
there appears a revolutionary power or group of powers
the emphasis of diplomacy changes. The need for harmony will no longer seem a sufficient motive for the settlement of disputes. Vital interests will constantly seem in
conflict and negotiations will turn increasingly futile. Disagreements tend to be pushed to their logical extreme and
relations come to be based on force or the threat of force.

Contemporary diplomacy is taking place in unprece-
dented circumstances. Rarely has there been less common ground among the major powers, but never has
recourse to force been more inhibited. This brings about
a dual frustration: with respect to power and with respect
to diplomacy. Were weapons technology stable, the fear of
war might be counted on to counterbalance the antagonisms of a revolutionary period. But weapons systems
are changing at an ever accelerating rate, and every major
power is aware that its survival is at the mercy of a technological breakthrough by its opponent. The inhibitions
with respect to the use of force, therefore, do not end the
revolutionary contest between us and the Soviet bloc;
they transform it into an armaments race.

At the same time the more absolute the sanctions of
modern war, the more extreme have been the demands
made on diplomacy. The fear of total war has had as its
counterpart the call for total diplomacy. Diplomacy is

asked to solve two major concurrent revolutions, that of the Soviet bloc and that of the newly independent states, at a moment when many of the pressures traditionally available to it have lost their potency. In a situation which has never been more tense, diplomacy has never had fewer tools at its disposal. The imbalance between the tensions produced by the contemporary revolution and the pressures available to diplomacy may be inherent to the present state of weapons technology. If so, it will not make for stability; rather it will depreciate the seriousness of diplomatic intercourse. It is said that, force having abdicated, diplomacy must take over. But diplomacy may be handicapped in taking over precisely because force has abdicated.

It is, therefore, asking too much of diplomacy that it should *resolve* present-day conflicts. Diplomacy can provide a forum for the settlement of disputes which have become unprofitable for both sides. It can keep open channels for information. Most importantly, it can enable each side to convey its intentions to the other.

For the primary bridge between the two sides is a common fear. The Soviet bloc and the free world may not agree on any positive goals, but they have at least one interest in common: given the horror of thermonuclear weapons, neither side can be interested in an all-out war. In these circumstances, all-out war is likely in only three contingencies: it can be caused by a consciousness of overpowering strength, for example, by the belief of the Soviet leaders that a surprise attack could eliminate our retaliatory force. Or all-out war could result from a miscalculation by the Soviet bloc that we are unwilling or unable to resist local aggression while we treated it as the prelude to a final showdown. Finally, all-out war may be produced by a Soviet misinterpretation of our intentions. The Soviet leaders may, for example, consider the use by us of nuclear weapons in a local engagement as the beginning of a strategic attack and react by launching a retaliatory blow.

The first contingency can be avoided only by a military policy which brings about a strong strategic striking force at a maximum degree of invulnerability. But to prevent miscalculation and a misinterpretation of our intentions is the task of our diplomacy. It must see to it that the other side obtains the information it requires to make correct decisions; it must convey what we understand by limited war and to some extent how we propose to conduct it.

To state the task is easier than to accomplish it. The same suspicions which cause our arguments to lack persuasion in diplomatic conferences may lead the Soviets to mistrust an effort to convey our intentions with respect to military strategy. Nevertheless, the catastrophe of all-out war is so frightful that it should provide a strong incentive for the Soviet leaders at least to test the sincerity of American professions. If diplomacy cannot give effect to the one interest both sides have overwhelmingly in common—the avoidance of an all-out holocaust—it is futile to ask of it to settle the more fundamental issues of ideological conflict and revolutionary upheaval.

II

Unfortunately, the diplomacy concerned with the new technology has addressed itself to the problem of eliminating the use of nuclear weapons almost to the exclusion of measures to mitigate their consequences. It is unfortunate, not because the goal is undesirable but because disarmament negotiations as heretofore conceived may address themselves to the most insoluble problem. The corollary of the preoccupation of our military policy with all-out war has been, almost inevitably, the predominant concern of our diplomacy with all-out peace, with intermediate solutions rejected by both. In their quest for total remedies, both our diplomacy and our military policy have inhibited the consideration of more attainable goals: an understanding of some principles of war limitation which may not prevent war, but which could keep any conflict that does break out from assuming the most catastrophic form.

The notion that armaments are the cause and not the

reflection of conflict is not new. It has been the basis of schemes of disarmament throughout history; it was the rationale for all the disarmament conferences in the Twenties and Thirties. Nevertheless it is open to serious doubt. The level of armament of a power reflects the extent to which it believes its vital interests to be in danger. If the contested issues seem peripheral to the question of survival, the need for vigilance will decline. If the major powers constantly feel on the brink of catastrophe, a rising level of armaments is inevitable. Between the Congress of Vienna and the unification of Germany, the standing armies were very small, because the outstanding disputes did not involve, or were not thought to involve, matters of life and death. After 1871 there started an armaments race which has not ended to this day. Between the unification of Germany and World War I, Europe was torn by two schisms which to the powers concerned seemed to involve "vital" interests: that between France and Germany over Alsace-Lorraine and that between the Austro-Hungarian Empire and Russia over the fate of the Balkans. After the first World War the rebellion of Germany and the U.S.S.R. against the Treaty of Versailles and the rise of the dictatorships created a climate of insecurity which doomed all disarmament efforts to futility. And after the second World War the intransigence of the Soviet bloc forced the free world to restore a measure of its strength even after it had disarmed unilaterally almost to the point of impotence.

There is little indication that the level of armaments itself produces tension. Great Britain has a strategic air force and a nuclear stockpile capable of inflicting serious, although perhaps not fatal, damage on the United States. But this fact has caused no uneasiness in the United States and no increase in our defense effort. Conversely, Great Britain did not seek to forestall the development by the United States of a navy superior to its own—something it had fought innumerable wars to prevent. This was because the "vital interests" of both powers are in sufficient harmony so that they can have a large measure of confidence in each other's intentions. Each can afford to permit the other to develop a weapons system capable of imperiling its security and perhaps even its survival because it knows that this capability will not be so used.

To be sure, the degree of confidence between the United States and Great Britain is exceptional. More usually, powers are conscious of some clashing "vital interests." As a result, a rise in the level of armaments of one major power may set in motion a vicious circle. Increased military preparedness serves as a warning of an increased willingness to run risks. The other powers can escape the pressure implicit in a stepped-up defense effort only by making concessions (a dangerous course for it may whet appetites and establish a method for settling future disputes), or by entering the armaments race themselves. But while the vicious circle of an armaments race is plain, it is not nearly so obvious that it can be ended by an international convention. If disagreements on specific issues had been tractable, the armaments race would never have started. Since negotiations on outstanding disputes have proved unavailing, it is improbable that a disarmament scheme acceptable to all parties can be negotiated.

A general disarmament scheme to be successful must deprive each party of the ability to inflict a catastrophic blow on the other; at the very least it must not give an advantage to either side. A meaningful agreement is, therefore, almost impossible. For the same mistrust which produced the armaments race will reduce confidence in any agreement that may be negotiated, and it will color the proposals which may be advanced. Each side will seek to deprive the other of the capability it fears most as a *prelude* to negotiations, while keeping its most effective weapon under its control until the last moment. Thus, the phasing of disarmament has proved almost as difficult a matter to negotiate as the manner of it. During our atomic monopoly, the Soviet Union insisted that the outlawing of nuclear weapons precede any negotiations on disarmament, while we in turn refused to discuss surrendering our atomic stockpile until an air-tight control machinery had first been put into operation. With the growth of the Soviet nuclear stockpile, both sides have continued to

strive to neutralize the other's strongest weapon. The Soviet Union has attempted to expel our troops and particularly our air bases from Eurasia. We have striven for means
to neutralize the Soviet ground strength. Each side wishes
to protect itself against the consequences of the other's
bad faith; each side, in short, brings to the disarmament
negotiations the precise attitude which caused the armaments race in the first place.

A reduction of forces is all the more difficult to negotiate because it seeks to compare incommensurables. What
is the relation between the Soviet ability to overrun Eurasia and American air and sea power? If the United States
weakens its Strategic Air Command, it would take years
before it could be reconstituted. If the Soviet Union reduces its ground forces, the strategic impact would be much
smaller and, given the structure of Soviet society, the
troops could be reassembled in a matter of weeks. A substantial reduction of Soviet forces would not deprive the
Kremlin of its large reserves of trained and rapidly-
mobilizable manpower. That such thoughts were not far
from Soviet minds is shown by Marshal Georgi Zhukov's
speech to the Twentieth Party Congress in February 1956,
explaining the Soviet arms reduction: "As a result of the
reduction of the armed forces, a certain proportion of the
draft group will not enter the forces. We must take steps
to see that the young people who are released from the
draft can receive, even outside the army, the military
training necessary to fulfill their duty to defend the homeland." [1]

In such circumstances, a reduction in forces would not
contribute a great deal to a lessening of tensions. Even
should a scale of comparison of different weapons systems
be negotiable among powers which have been unable to
agree on much less complicated issues, it would still not
remove the real security problem: the increasingly rapid
rate of technological change.

Disarmament plans of the past were based on the assumption of a reasonably stable weapons technology. Once the

---

[1] *Current Digest of the Soviet Press*, v. 8 (April 18, 1956), p. 37.

proposed reduction of forces was implemented, strategic relationships would remain constant. But under present conditions, the real armaments race is in the laboratories. No reduction of forces, however scrupulously carried out, could protect the powers against a technological breakthrough. Even were strategic striking forces kept at fixed levels and rigidly controlled, an advance in air defense sufficient to contain the opposing retaliatory force would upset the strategic balance completely. The knowledge by each side that the other is working on ever more fearful means of destruction or on means of attacking with impunity would cause current international relations to be carried on in an atmosphere of tenseness and imminent catastrophe, whatever agreements may be concluded about reduction of forces.

In addition to the technological problems, the structure of international relations will prevent a reduction of forces from going beyond a certain point. None of the major powers, certainly not the U.S.S.R., will accept a disarmament scheme which impairs its relative position vis-à-vis secondary states. Nothing will induce the U.S.S.R. to accept a level of armaments which reduces its ability to control the satellites or to play a major role in contiguous areas such as the Middle East. But forces sufficient to accomplish this task are also sufficient to imperil all the peripheral powers of Eurasia. A reduction of forces which does not affect the relative Soviet position vis-à-vis the secondary powers will not diminish the basic security problem of the non-Soviet world.

Nor is it a foregone conclusion that a reduction of forces, even could it be negotiated, would inevitably be beneficial. A reduction of nuclear stockpiles might well increase the tenseness of international relationships and cause any war that does break out to assume the most catastrophic form. Given the diffusion of nuclear technology, a reduction of stockpiles would be almost impossible to verify. Thus each power would probably seek to keep back part of its stockpile to protect itself against the possibility that its opponent might do so. An attempt to reduce nuclear stockpiles far from removing existing insecurity may, therefore, merely serve to feed suspicions.

Moreover, to the extent that nuclear stockpiles are in fact reduced, any war that does break out is likely to assume the most catastrophic form. The technical possibility of limiting nuclear war resides in the plentifulness of nuclear materials. This makes it possible to conceive of a strategy which emphasizes a discriminating use of modern weapons and to utilize explosives of lesser power which, from a technical point of view, are really "inefficient" high-yield weapons. But if the quantity of weapons decreases, a premium will be placed on engineering them to achieve maximum destructiveness and to use them on the largest targets. The horrors of nuclear war are not likely to be avoided by a reduction of nuclear armaments.

III

Because a reduction of forces has proved so nearly impossible to negotiate and because its rewards would be so questionable even if achieved, the major emphasis of disarmament efforts has turned to the problems of inspection and control and to the prevention of surprise attack. However, since the Soviet domestic apparatus is difficult to maintain in the face of any control system which would reassure the West, every inspection scheme that has proved acceptable to the free world has been objectionable to the U.S.S.R. As a result, the negotiations about control and inspection have produced the same vicious circle as the efforts to bring about a reduction in armaments: were it possible to agree on an inspection and control machinery, it would also be possible to settle some of the disputes which have given rise to existing tensions. As long as specific issues prove obdurate, there is little hope in an over-all control plan.

In addition to the psychological and political problems, the technological race makes it difficult to negotiate a control plan. For the rate of change of technology has outstripped the pace of diplomatic negotiations, so that control plans change their meaning while they are being debated. The control scheme of the first United States disarmament proposal (the Baruch plan) assumed that an international authority with powers of inspection and in control of mining, processing and producing fissionable materials would be able to eliminate nuclear weapons from the arsenals of the powers. The United States contribution was to be the destruction of our nuclear stockpile as the last stage of the process of disarmament. Even this scheme would not have been "foolproof." Within the United States atomic energy program, with every incentive to achieve an accurate accounting and no motive for evasion, the normal "slippage" in the handling of fissionable materials due to error and mechanical problems of handling is several per cent. A nation determined on evasion could easily multiply this percentage without being in obvious violation of international agreements and utilize the "saved" slippage slowly to build up a nuclear stockpile of its own. Their awareness of this possibility would in turn give other powers a motive for evasion.

Nevertheless, at the early stages of the atomic energy program the stockpiles were still so small and the possibility of building them up to substantial proportions through evasion was so slight that an inspection program would have contributed materially to reducing the danger of nuclear war. Any power determined to produce nuclear weapons would have had to break existing agreements flagrantly and thereby bring down on itself either the international enforcement machinery or war with the United States. But in the age of nuclear plenty, the control machinery envisaged by the Baruch plan will prove futile as a means to eliminate stockpiles. So many nuclear weapons have been produced of so many different sizes and they are so easy to conceal that not even the most elaborate inspection machinery could account for all of them. Control machinery cannot effectively prevent the accumulation of nuclear weapons at this stage of their development, even assuming the desirability of doing so.

And so it is with each new technological discovery. In the very early stages of development, a scrupulous control system may forestall its being added to the weapons arsenal. But by the time disarmament negotiations have run their tortuous course, the weapon will have become so sophisticated and the production of it will have reached such proportions that control machinery may magnify rather than reduce the existing insecurity: it may compound the fear of surprise attack with fear of the violation of the agreement by the other side.

The inconclusiveness of negotiations about inspection machinery reflects also the difficulty of controlling the development of new weapons. And without such control, disarmament schemes will be at the mercy of a technological breakthrough. Since each scientific discovery opens the way to innumerable other advances, it is next to impossible to define a meaningful point to "cut off" weapons development. At the beginning of the atomic age, a strict inspection system might have succeeded in stopping the elaboration of nuclear weapons. By 1952 it might still have been possible to "control" the development of thermonuclear weapons, albeit with great difficulty. For the hydrogen bomb developed so naturally out of research on nuclear weapons that the definition of a meaningful dividing-line would have been exceedingly complicated. By 1957 the production of thermonuclear devices had so far outstripped any possible control machinery that the emphasis of disarmament negotiations has turned from eliminating stockpiles to methods of restraining their use. And with the diffusion of nuclear technology among other powers, effective control of the development of nuclear weapons even by smaller states will be almost out of the question.

Moreover, once a weapon is developed its applications are elaborated until ever wider realms of strategy become dependent on it. A nation may be willing to forego the offensive uses of nuclear weapons, but it will be most reluctant to give up its defensive applications, for example, in the form of antiaircraft or antimissile devices. But in advanced stages of their elaboration, weapons find a dual purpose: the launching site for antiaircraft missiles can be used as well for attacking ground targets; a nuclear weapon launched from a plane against enemy bombers will be equally effective against enemy supply centers.

Thus, weapons can be kept from being added to stockpiles only at their inception when their implications are least understood. By the time their potential is realized, the possibility of preventing their addition to existing arsenals by means of inspection or control has usually disappeared. Hence the only time to control the missiles which are now being developed would be within the next two years, before they go into mass production.

IV

The difficulty of devising effective machinery to control the development of ever more destructive weapons has caused most disarmament negotiations since 1955 to concern themselves with means to prevent surprise attack. Since, so the argument goes, one of the causes for present tensions is the insecurity caused by the fear of imminent catastrophe, an inspection system which would reduce the danger of surprise attack would also remove some of the urgency from international relationships. This reasoning produced President Eisenhower's proposal at the Geneva summit conference in July 1955 to exchange military blueprints with the Soviet Union and to permit aerial reconnaissance of each other's territories. The principle of inspection to prevent surprise attack has been accepted in the Soviet counterproposal for stationing ground observers at strategic points in the territory of the other nation.

It cannot be denied that the danger of surprise attack contributes to the tensions of the nuclear age even if it does not cause them. It is less clear, however, that inspection schemes so far proposed would add a great deal to existing warning methods and intelligence information, or that they would significantly reduce the element of surprise.

The relative ineffectiveness of inspection in preventing surprise in an all-out war is due to the nature of strategic striking forces. Because it cannot afford to be caught on the ground, a strategic striking force must be prepared to attack from its training bases at a moment's notice. If properly prepared, it should require no noticeable mobilization

to launch its blow. Since "normal" peacetime maneuvers of a strategic striking force should approximate as
much as possible its behavior in case of emergency, an enemy should not be able to tell whether a given flight is a
training mission or a surprise attack until his early warning line is crossed. To be sure, the Soviet Long-Range Air
Force has not yet reached this stage of readiness. Because
it probably does not possess a capability for aerial refueling, it would have to transfer its planes to advanced bases
on the Kola or Chukchi peninsulas before it could attack.[2]
A system of inspection would inform us of this move
and it might, therefore, increase our warning time.
Nevertheless, the gain would only be a relative one,
because any substantial movement of the Soviet Long-
Range Air Force to advanced bases can hardly escape high-
altitude detection or general intelligence surveillance even
in the absence of inspection. And the next family of Soviet
planes will be able to launch an attack on the United
States from their training bases.

Because of the greater range of our planes and the nature of our base system, the Soviet Union would gain very
little either from ground inspection or from aerial surveillance. They know the location of most of our air bases,
and, since they will presumably strike the first blow in an
all-out war, they are assured of maximum warning in any
case. It can be argued, of course, that the U.S.S.R. may not
evaluate the danger of a United States surprise attack so
low and that it would, therefore, obtain added security
from an inspection system. But it is not clear what added
assurance would be so achieved. Unless most planes are
grounded all the time and both sides are certain that no
substantial air installations are hidden, there is no guarantee that planes on so-called training missions will not be
used for a surprise attack.

Even filing flight plans in advance will not eliminate
this danger. Given the speed of modern planes, by the
time inspectors realize a violation of a flight plan and can
communicate this information to their government, the

---

2 See map, p. 100.

planes will probably have reached the opposing early warning lines. If flight plans are cleverly arranged—and every incentive would seem to exist for doing this—it will be very difficult to discover whether a given flight is a move to advanced bases or a prelude to an all-out attack.

Inspection could, of course, be coupled with the grounding of all planes, except perhaps a very small number insufficient to inflict a catastrophic blow. Such a course would be highly dangerous, however. Without constant training, it is difficult to maintain the readiness or the morale of the retaliatory force. Since our strategy is more dependent on its strategic striking forces than that of the Soviet Union, the grounding of all planes will work to the advantage of the other side. Even should we develop a capability for limited war equal to that of the Soviet Union, the grounding of our Strategic Air Force would stand to benefit our opponent. It would tell him our precise deployment and enable him to concentrate his attack and his defenses against it. To be sure, we would have the same information about the Soviet Long-Range Air Force. But, since we concede the first blow, it would be much less useful to us: the Soviet planes presumably will have left their bases by the time we become aware that an attack is imminent.

Even when all planes are grounded, the maximum warning achievable by inspection is the interval between the time when planes leave their bases and the time when they would have been detected by existing warning systems. With the present family of airplanes, an inspection system at best would add perhaps three hours' warning to the side which is being attacked. The aggressor would gain no additional warning time from an inspection system because he would, in any case, alert his defenses before mounting his blow. To be sure, three hours' additional warning is not negligible; it may indeed spell the difference between survival and catastrophe. But, since the victim of aggression cannot be certain what the apparent violation of inspection signifies, he may have difficulty in utilizing the additional warning effectively. And if inspection is coupled with the grounding of the strategic striking force, the gain in warning time may be outweighed by the aggressor's knowledge of the opponent's deployment.

As the speed of planes is increased, the warning time afforded by even a perfect inspection system, correctly interpreted, is progressively reduced. In the age of the Intercontinental Ballistic Missile—in less than ten years—the maximum warning time possible, assuming perfect communication between the inspector and his government, would be thirty minutes, the period of time the missile would be in transit. In the age of the missile and the supersonic bomber, even a foolproof inspection system will tell the powers only what they already know: that the opponent possesses the capability of launching a devastating attack at a moment's notice and with a minimum of warning.

The proposals for inspection as a bar to surprise attack in fact reflect the thinking of a period when forces-in-being could not be decisive and when their power and speed were of a much lower order. As long as the forces-in-being were relatively cumbersome and had to be concentrated before an attack could be launched, the warning afforded by an inspection system might have been strategically significant. As late as 1946, had the Baruch plan been accepted, a nation determined on nuclear war would have had to wait several months or even years after a violation until its stockpiles had been built up to respectable levels. The existence of a control system in such conditions afforded a breathing spell to all powers. With the power and speed of current weapons, however, even an airtight inspection system would not supply such guarantees. When wars can be fought by the forces-in-being and when striking forces are designed to be able to attack with no overt preparation, warning can be attained under optimum conditions only for the time the delivery vehicles, whether planes or missiles, are in transit. At present this is a maximum of ten hours, a substantial proportion of which is already under surveillance by existing warning methods.

The extreme readiness of the forces-in-being also reduces the value of aerial reconnaissance. Since flying time from the interior of Russia to our Early Warning Line is less than five hours with the present family of airplanes, air bases of the Soviet Long-Range Air Force would have to be photographed at least every five hours. If the reconnaissance occurred at longer intervals, the Early Warning Line would provide a better indication of a surprise attack because an attack launched immediately after an aerial inspection would reach our Early Warning Line before the next reconnaissance sortie discovered that the opposing force had left its base. As the speed of planes increases, the frequency of reconnaissance missions will also have to be increased, so that in practice reconnaissance planes would probably have to hover over enemy airfields almost constantly. And in the missile age aerial reconnaissance would be fortunate if it could discover launching sites: it would not be able to furnish an indication of impending attack.

It is, therefore, difficult to imagine that present vigilance could be reduced or that insecurity would be removed by any inspection system now in prospect. The machinery required would be so formidable and the benefits relatively so trivial that an inspection system may actually have pernicious consequences. It may give a misleading impression of security and, therefore, tempt us into relaxing our preparedness. More likely, given the prevailing distrust, it will induce both sides to place their striking forces into an even greater state of readiness in order to compensate for the loss of secrecy by a demonstration of power.

Indeed, unless designed with extraordinary care, a system of inspection may well make a tense situation even more explosive. The value of an inspection system depends not only on the collection, but also on the interpretation, of facts. But the information produced by inspection is of necessity fragmentary, and it is likely to be most difficult to obtain when it is most needed, when international tensions are at their height. On the other hand, the only meaningful reaction to an apparent violation of the inspection system is to launch an immediate retaliatory attack, because negotiations or protests could not begin to be effective before the enemy force has reached its targets.

The knowledge that all-out war is the sanction for seeming violations may well add to the tenseness of relationships. Instead of reducing the danger of all-out war, inspection systems may make more likely a showdown caused by a misunderstanding of the opponent's intentions.

V

The technical complexity of inspection and its futility in the present climate of distrust has induced some thoughtful individuals, appalled at the prospect of nuclear war, to advocate an international disarmament authority as the only solution. As long as both sides possess thermonuclear weapons and the means to deliver them, it is argued, a vicious spiral of constantly growing insecurity is inevitable. The only solution, this school of thought maintains, is the surrender of all strategic weapons to a world authority which would be the sole agency to possess heavy armaments and the means for delivering them. The disarmament executive should be composed of minor powers which are not part of the East-West struggle. With a preponderance of force, it could play the role of a world policeman and enforce peace if necessary.[3] The United Nations Emergency Force for Egypt was greeted in some quarters as the forerunner of such an international agency.

The idea of escaping the tensions of international relations by an analogy to domestic police powers has come up repeatedly in the past, and usually at periods when international schisms made it least realizable. It is true, as the advocates of the plan of world government contend, that the system of sovereign states produces international tensions because a sovereign will can be ultimately controlled only by superior force. But it is hardly realistic to expect sovereign nations, whose failure to agree on issues of much less importance has brought about the armaments race, to be able to agree on giving up their sovereignty. History offers few examples of sovereign states surrendering their

---

3 See Thomas K. Finletter, *Power and Policy* (New York: Harcourt, Brace, 1954), p. 392 ff.; and also Charles Bolté, *The Price of Peace* (Boston: The Beacon Press, 1956), p. 68 ff.

sovereignty except to outside compulsion. To be sure, the lessons of history are no more conclusive than the unparalleled destructiveness of modern weapons. Still it is difficult to imagine any motive which could induce the Soviet Union to give up its thermonuclear stockpile to an international body. And the reaction of the United States Congress will hardly be more hospitable.

The various proposals for a world authority would, therefore, scarcely warrant extensive consideration were they not such an excellent illustration of the prevailing notion that the United Nations somehow has a reality beyond that of the powers comprising it. It is a symptom of our legalistic bias that so many consider a legal entity, the United Nations, as somehow transcending the collective will of its members. For as long as the United Nations is composed of sovereign states, it will reflect the precise rivalries that animate these powers outside that organization. To be sure, the United Nations offers a convenient forum for the settlement of disputes, and it can give symbolic expression to the consensus of world opinion on particular issues. But the gap between the symbolic acts of the United Nations and its willingness to run substantive risks is inherent in its structure.[4] The delegates represent not a popular constituency but sovereign governments, and they vote not according to their convictions but in pursuance of the instructions they receive. The effectiveness of the United Nations can be no greater than the willingness of its component governments to run risks. The United Nations Emergency Force would never have entered Egypt had not both parties to the dispute accepted it and had not both parties sought a device to liquidate military operations. The United Nations Emergency Force did not cause the cessation of the war; rather it ratified a decision already made. For this reason it does not offer a particularly hopeful model for what will be the real security problem of our period: the growing Soviet power coupled with a refusal to yield to anything except superior force.

---

4 See below, p. 248 ff.

The argument that a supranational authority composed of neutral minor powers will be able to resolve tensions which have proved intractable to direct negotiations, and that it can be entrusted with the exclusive custody of weapons capable of encompassing the destruction of humanity, reflects two related beliefs: that the nature of aggression is always unambiguous and that weakness somehow guarantees responsibility and perhaps even superior morality. But in the nuclear age recognizing aggression has proved as complicated as resisting it. Were a supranational disarmament executive charged with enforcing the peace, it is predictable that its major problem would be to define a meaningful concept of aggression. It is significant that in 1957 the United Nations has had to give up a prolonged effort to achieve such a definition.

Moreover, it would be difficult to find powers clearly recognized as neutral to act as custodians of the thermonuclear stockpile or with sufficient technical competence to administer it were they so recognized. And the very quality which would make powers acceptable as members of a disarmament authority—their neutrality—will reduce their willingness to run risks. In the face of a dispute between the United States and the U.S.S.R., these states will lack the power to impose their will or the will to use their power.

Nor is it clear why a monopoly of power in the hands of states dependent for equipment, training and facilities on the two superpowers should bring about stability. It is not at all obvious that weakness guarantees responsibility or that powers which have difficulty playing a role in their own regions will be able to judge global problems with subtlety and discrimination. And this still overlooks the dilemmas of where to store the international stockpile of bombs, where to locate the bases of the international air force—all of which will become matters of life and death to the nations of the world. In short, there is no escaping from the responsibilities of the thermonuclear age into a supranational authority, for, if all its complicated problems could be negotiated, the substantive issues now dividing the world would be soluble too.

VI

Our disarmament efforts have been directed to the most intractable element of the problems posed by nuclear weapons. By leaving no middle ground between total peace and total war, they require the major atomic powers to stake their survival on the observance of an international agreement in an international order where the breach of agreements has become commonplace and where one of the great power blocs explicitly rejects the observance of agreements if they do not reflect a relation of forces.

The attempt to eliminate war through disarmament is the obverse of the effort to deter aggression through maximum retaliatory power and to defeat the enemy through the widest system of collective security. Each of these measures is highly useful and desirable as long as it succeeds; the objection concerns not the goal, but the consequences of failure. For in each case the exclusive concern with the avoidance of war carries with it a fearful sanction. The more total the peace sought, the more absolute the consequences of violating an agreement. The policy of deterrence through maximum retaliatory power involves the sanction of all-out thermonuclear war; a doctrine of world-wide collective security involves the sanction of global war; and a system of general disarmament has as a sanction a combination of these. By posing total war as the only alternative to total peace, disarmament negotiations, as heretofore conceived, may cause war, if it does come, to take the most absolute form: in their quest for final solutions they may prevent the achievement of intermediate goals which are attainable.

A diplomatic program looking toward eventual disarmament should, therefore, have as one of its cardinal points a program to mitigate the horrors of war. There has been a shrinking away from advancing such plans, as if the admission that war may occur could itself be a factor in bringing it on, or perhaps because of lack of clarity about the nature of war limitation in the nuclear age. But a disarmament plan based entirely on an attempt to avoid war is hopelessly one-sided: it will put a premium on the conservatism of military staffs because, in the absence of an alternative framework, they will have to base their plans on the worst contingency, which is all-out war. Since present disarmament schemes give no indication of intentions in case a war does break out, they increase the likelihood that *any* war will spread to become all-out either because of miscalculation or because of a misinterpretation of the other side's intentions.

And the possibility of war does not even have to assume bad faith on the part of the major protagonists. The revolution taking place in so many parts of the globe will provide its own impetus; it will create its own tensions, not necessarily sought by any of the major powers. The conflict over the Suez Canal was hardly foreseen by the Western powers and perhaps not even by the Soviet Union. And the Hungarian revolution came as a rude shock to the Kremlin. Both situations resulted in military actions which, with the prevailing strategic doctrines, might easily have turned into all-out war. Similar Soviet moves in East Germany or Poland would be fraught with even more serious danger. In turn, the absence of any generally understood limits to war undermines the willingness to resist Soviet pressures. A gap is thus opened between the quest for total peace and the military doctrine of total war, a gap within which the Soviet Union can operate with relative impunity.

A program to mitigate the horrors of war would have the advantage of focusing thinking on things to accomplish rather than on those which should not be done. It would relate disarmament to strategy and thus help to bridge the gap between force and diplomacy. It would overcome a situation in which the Soviet leaders can conduct atomic blackmail in the guise of disarmament negotiations and transform conferences into a fertile ground for paralyzing the will to resist by evoking the most fearful consequences of such a course. Above all, a program to mitigate the horrors of war could be used to clarify, insofar as diplomacy is able, the intentions of the opposing sides, and it may therefore prevent the catastrophe of an all-out war caused by miscalculation. Even a unilateral declaration of what we understand by limited war would accomplish a great deal, because it would provide a strong incentive to the other side to test its feasibility.

It has been argued that the deliberate ambiguity of our present position, which refuses to define what we understand by limited war or under what circumstances we might fight it, is in itself a deterrent because the enemy can never be certain that military action on his part may not unleash all-out war. But, if we wish to pose the maximum deterrent, an explicit declaration of massive retaliation would seem by far more advantageous. The purpose of our ambiguity is to combine the advantage of two incompatible courses: to pose the threat of all-out war for purposes of deterrence, but to keep open the possibility of a less catastrophic strategy should deterrence fail. If the ambiguity is to serve any purpose, however, it may have precisely the contrary effect; it may give rise to the notion that we do not intend to resist at all and thus encourage aggression. Or it may cause an aggressor to interpret resistance which we intend to localize as a prelude to all-out war. Instead of strengthening the deterrent and giving scope for a noncatastrophic strategy, the deliberate ambiguity of our position may weaken the deterrent and bring on the most catastrophic kind of war.

Moreover, a diplomatic program designed to convey our understanding of the nature of limited war to the other side may be important because it is not certain that the Soviet leadership has fully analyzed all the options of the nuclear period.[5] Insofar as the repeated Soviet denials of the possibility of limited nuclear war represent a real conviction and not simply a form of psychological warfare, an energetic diplomacy addressed to the problem of war limitation can serve as a substitute for lack of imagination on the part of the Soviet General Staff.

Before we can convey our notion of war limitation to the other side, however, we have to admit its possibility to ourselves and we have to be clear in our own mind about

_____

[5] For the Soviet reactions to nuclear war see below, Chapter 11, p. 362.

its nature. And at present, as we have seen, no such clarity exists either among the military or the political leaders. Our services are operating on the basis of partially over-lapping, partly inconsistent doctrines, some of which deny the possibility of limited war while others define it so vari-ously that we can hardly be said to possess the capability for limited war, either conceptually or physically. The separation of our strategic doctrine from diplomacy, its notion that victory is an end in itself achieved by render-ing the enemy defenseless, approach to what Clausewitz considered the most abstract notion of war: a war char-acterized by an uninterrupted series of blows of ever in-creasing intensity, until the will of the enemy is broken.

Such a doctrine is inconsistent with a policy of limited war. It is not only that limited war must find means to prevent the most extreme of violence; it must also seek to slow down the tempo of modern war lest the rapidity with which operations succeed each other prevent the establish-ment of a relation between political and military objec-tives. If this relationship is lost, any war is likely to grow by imperceptible stages into an all-out effort. The goal of war can no longer be military victory, strictly speaking, but the attainment of certain specific political con-ditions which are fully understood by the opponent. A limited war between major powers can remain limited only if at some point one of the protagonists prefers a limited defeat to an additional investment of resources, or if both sides are willing to settle for a stalemate in preference to an assumption of continued risk. Since in either case the protagonists retain the *physical* resources to increase their commitment, the ability to conduct a limited war presupposes an understanding of the psychol-ogy by which the opponent calculates his risks and the ability to present him with an opportunity for settlement that appears more favorable than continuation of the war.

For this reason, limited war cannot be conceived as a small all-out war with a series of uninterrupted blows pre-pared in secrecy until the opponent's will is broken. On the contrary, it is important to develop a concept of mili-tary operations conducted in phases which permit an assessment of the risks and possibilities for settlement at each stage before recourse is had to the next phase of operations. Paradoxical as it may seem in the jet age, strategic doctrine should address itself to the problem of slowing down, if not the pace of military operations, at least the rapidity with which they succeed each other. Strategic doctrine must never lose sight of the fact that its purpose is to affect the will of the enemy, not to destroy him, and that war can be limited only by presenting the enemy with an unfavorable calculus of risks.

This requires pause for calculation. A strategic concept for limited war should, therefore, seek to devise a measured pace in the sequence of military operations, lest the speed of modern weapons outstrip the capacity of the human mind to comprehend the significance of unfolding events. Every campaign should be conceived in a series of self-contained phases, each of which implies a political objective and with a sufficient interval between them to permit the application of political and psychological pressures.

Therefore, too, it will be necessary to give up the notion that direct diplomatic contact ceases when military operations begin. Rather, direct contact is never more necessary to ensure that both sides possess the correct information about the consequences of expanding a war and to be able to present formulas for a political settlement. To the extent that diplomacy presents alternatives to expanding a conflict, it will inhibit the decision to run greater risks. To the extent that military operations can be conducted in stages so that a sequence of events is approximately concluded before the next commitment is made, it will give an opportunity for the evaluation of the circumstances which make a settlement advisable. Not the least of the paradoxes of the nuclear age may be that lack of secrecy may actually assist in the achievement of military objectives and that in a period of the most advanced technology, battles will approach the stylized contests of the feudal period which served as much as a test of will as a trial of strength.

If our military staffs could become clear about a doctrine of limited war, we could then use the disarmament negotiations to seek a measure of acceptance of it by the other side. It would not be necessary that such a concept be embodied in an international treaty or even that the Soviet Government formally adhere to it. There should be no illusions, in fact, about the ease with which the Soviets might be induced to forego the advantages of atomic blackmail. The primary purpose of such a program would be to convey our intentions to the Soviet bloc and to encourage it likewise to consider a limitation of war in its own military planning. The incentive for Soviet cooperation in substance, if not in form, would be self-interest. Limited war is possible only to the extent that our military policy leaves no doubt that all-out war would mean disaster for the Soviet bloc. A program of war limitation would presuppose an adequate retaliatory capability. It would not prevent every kind of all-out war, only those which develop from miscalculations or a misunderstanding of the opponent's intentions.

The previous analysis has shown that with a doctrine of limited war many of the long-cherished notions of traditional warfare have to be modified. They include the principle that wars can be won only by dominating the air space completely. Since an attempt to deprive an enemy of his retaliatory force would inevitably bring on all-out war, the minimum condition of war limitation will be the immunity of the opposing strategic striking forces. Another concept which, as we have seen, will have to be modified is the elimination of enemy communication and industrial centers, a goal which was meaningful only so long as the major movement of armies was effected by road or rail. Finally, in a war which will be largely fought by the forces-in-being, the destruction of industrial potential will play a much smaller role than in the past.[6]

Thus it is possible to visualize limitations at least as to targets and the size of weapons used. We might propose that neither bases of the opposing strategic air forces nor

---

6 See above, p. 90 ff. Also Rear Admiral Sir Anthony Buzzard and others, *On Limiting Atomic War* (London: Royal Institute of International Affairs, 1956).

towns above a certain size would be attacked, provided these bases would not be used to support tactical operations and that the towns would not contain military installations useful against armed forces. Such a proposal could be combined with the control schemes of the general disarmament proposals. For example, each side could be required to list its strategic air bases which would then be immune from attack. It would be helpful, although not essential, that inspectors be admitted to all these bases. No air base within a stated distance of the initial demarcation line, say five hundred miles, could purchase immunity by being declared strategic save by admitting inspectors who would verify that it was not being used for tactical purposes.

Again, all cities within five hundred miles of the battle zone would be immune from nuclear attack if they were declared "open" and if their status were certified by inspectors (although the latter condition is not absolutely essential). An open city would be one which did not contain within a radius of thirty miles from the center any installations that could be used against military forces, such as air bases or missile-launching sites. The term "military installation" should be defined literally and not extended to include industrial plants. Cities located at a greater distance than five hundred miles from the battle zone would be immune altogether, whatever installations they contained. The inspectors might consist of a commission of neutrals; it would be preferable if they were experts of the other side because this would give their reports a much higher credibility. The inspectors would have their own communications system and would operate even during hostilities.

The elimination of area targets will place an upper limit on the size of weapons it will be profitable to use. Since fall-out becomes a serious problem only in the range of explosive power of 500 kilotons and above, it could be proposed that no weapon larger than 500 kilotons will be employed unless the enemy uses it first. Concurrently, the United States could take advantage of a new development which significantly reduces fall-out by eliminating the last stage of the fission-fusion-fission process.[7] We could propose that all weapons above 500-kiloton explosive power should be "clean" bombs.

Such a program would have several advantages over disarmament schemes designed only to prevent surprise attack. It would accomplish most of the goals sought by the general inspection scheme. It would afford warning, insofar as an inspection system is able to do so. In addition it would also serve as an instrument of war limitation. Moreover, it would be self-policing. Within a relatively small combat zone, it will be much more difficult to hide installations against modern means of detection than in the vastness of a continent. And any significant amount of fall-out would indicate a violation of the agreement to limit the size of weapons employed.

Because it is self-policing, such a system would work even without inspection. Nevertheless, it would be desirable to couple it with an inspection scheme. The objection to inspection as a bar to all-out surprise attack is not that inspection is incapable of producing the required information, but that the information it produces does not address itself to the basic security problem. Given the high state of readiness of strategic striking forces, their increasing speed and constantly growing dispersion as the missile age approaches, even a perfect inspection system will not add significantly to the existing warning time. With respect to all-out war, inspection either tells the opposing powers what they already know or it produces information too late to be helpful. In limited war, by contrast, inspection supplies the precise information required to determine whether the opponent is carrying out his side of the bargain. The information will be useful because at best the enemy will gain a tactical advantage which can be overcome by retaliation.

Moreover, in all-out war the aggressor, having already staked his national existence on his decision to launch an all-out surprise attack, will lose every incentive to make

---

[7] See above, Chapter 3, p. 74. Since fusion produces very little radioactivity, the fall-out is confined to the radioactivity of the trigger mechanism and this does not present a serious problem.

the inspection system work. In a limited war, on the other hand, the aggressor will probably continue to be anxious to avoid all-out war; otherwise he would not be fighting a limited war in the first place. He will, therefore, have a strong motive to keep the opponent correctly informed of his adherence to the rules. Given this attitude, both sides will probably be eager, not reluctant, to overlook occasional violations, or at least to hold off from drawing the most drastic consequences until they have tried other measures.

Another advantage of a system of inspection is that the inspectors could serve also as points of political contact. Thus the mechanics of arms limitation might also bring about the possibility of a rapid settlement should the contenders so desire.

It may be objected that a program of war limitation would in effect neutralize cities and seriously interfere with military operations. But the neutralization of cities is inherent in modern technology quite apart from any arms limitation schemes. It would seem to make little difference whether a city is neutralized by the self-restraint of the protagonists, the presence of inspection teams, or the explosion of megaton weapons. As for impairing military operations, the handicap would be the same for both sides, and the military will have to accept the fact that, short of a thermonuclear holocaust, purely military decisions are no longer possible.

Other criticisms assert that a program of war limitation assumes a degree of human rationality for which history offers no warranty. But history offers no example for the extraordinary destructiveness of modern weapons either. A program which sought to establish some principles of war limitation in advance of hostilities would seem to make fewer demands on rationality than one which attempted to improvise the rules of war in the confusion of battle.

Still others argue that an attempt to convey our understanding of limited war to our opponent would tell him the exact price of each piece of real estate and, therefore, weaken the deterrent. If this is true, however, the deliberate ambiguity of our present position is almost equally dangerous, for it makes sense only if we mean to imply that in certain circumstances we *might* resist locally. Ambiguity has certain advantages in making the calculations of an aggressor more difficult. But it should encompass only the range of alternatives one is willing to carry out. Ambiguity which implies courses of action which are not intended to be adopted approaches a strategy of bluff.

Moreover, the notion that deterrence is achieved only by the threat of maximum destruction deserves close scrutiny. It is an understandable outgrowth of our desire to enjoy our existence without interference from the outside world. As a result, aggression has, for us, always had the quality of an immoral act undertaken for its own sake, and we have come to think of resistance to it more in terms of punishment than in terms of balancing risks.

But usually aggression is caused by the desire to achieve a specific objective. It is not necessary to threaten destruction of the home base of the enemy to inhibit him; it is sufficient to prevent the aggressor from attaining his goal. An aggressor would seem to have no motive for an attack if he cannot count on a reasonable chance of success. To be sure, it is unwise to inform an aggressor of the precise price he will have to pay for aggression. But we should make certain that we will be prepared to pay whatever price we either express or imply. A wise policy will not depend on a threat it is afraid to implement.

The United States should, therefore, shift the emphasis of disarmament negotiations from the technically almost impossible problem of preventing surprise attack to an effort to mitigate the horror of war. Such a course would have the additional advantage of enabling us to make a distinction between Soviet "ban-the-bomb" propaganda and disarmament, and to appeal to the rest of the world with a show of moderation. We should leave no doubt that any aggression by the Communist bloc may be resisted with nuclear weapons, but we should make every effort to limit their effect and to spare the civilian population as much as possible. Without damage to our interest, we could announce that Soviet aggression would be resisted with nuclear weapons if necessary; that in resisting we would not use more than 500 kilotons explosive power unless the enemy used them first; that we would use "clean" bombs with minimal fall-out effects for any larger explosive equivalent unless the enemy violated the understanding; that we would not attack the enemy retaliatory force or enemy cities located more than a certain distance behind the battle zone or the initial line of demarcation (say five hundred miles); that within this zone we would not use nuclear weapons against cities declared open and so verified by inspection, the inspectors to remain in the battle zone even during the course of military operations.

We would lose nothing even if we made such an announcement unilaterally, since our strategy for an all-out war is based in any event on permitting the other side to strike the first blow. In case of a local Soviet attack, limited war could be fought according to rules established well in advance. If the war begins with an all-out surprise attack on us, the same relation obtains as heretofore, and we could react by using every weapon in our arsenal. The same would be true if the Soviet leadership sought to threaten our national existence directly even if by means less than all-out.

To be sure, it is not likely that the Soviet Government will formally accept such a proposal, because the belief of the non-Soviet world in the inevitable horror of nuclear war is the prerequisite of Soviet atomic blackmail. In order to undermine the will to resist, the Soviet leaders have every interest in painting the consequences of war in the most drastic terms. But whatever the utility of the pronouncements of impending doom for paralyzing resistance, the Soviet leaders would face a considerable dilemma if we maintained our position in the face of a Soviet rejection and if we reinforced it by periodically publicizing those aspects of our weapons development which stress the more discriminating uses of our power. The horrors of all-out war would provide a powerful incentive to test our sincerity.

The limitation of war described here is impossible, however, without a strategic doctrine adapted to the new role of nuclear weapons. It presupposes an ability to use force with discrimination and to establish political goals in which the question of national survival is not involved in every issue. It also requires a public opinion which has been educated to the realities of the nuclear age. A strategy of limited war, in short, cannot be used as a cheaper means of imposing unconditional surrender. The relationship of force to diplomacy cannot be established as a variation of all-out war. The possibility of total security has ended with the disappearance of our atomic monopoly. Limited war and the diplomacy appropriate to it provide a means to escape from the sterility of the quest for absolute peace which paralyzes by the vagueness of its hopes, and of the search for absolute victory which paralyzes by the vastness of its consequences.

PART THREE

STRATEGY AND POLICY

8

THE IMPACT OF STRATEGY
ON ALLIES AND THE
UNCOMMITTED

Nowhere are the dilemmas of the nuclear age more apparent than in the attempt to construct a system of alliances against Soviet aggression. It reveals once more the problem of establishing a relationship between a policy of deterrence and the strategy we are prepared to implement, between the temptation to pose a maximum threat and the tendency to recoil before it. In our alliance policy, these problems are compounded by the vulnerability of our allies and the sense of impotence produced because they are either junior partners in the atomic race or excluded from it altogether. Moreover, we have never been clear about the strategy behind our alliance policy—whether we mean to defend our allies against invasion or whether we rely on an over-all strategy superiority vis-à-vis the Soviet bloc to defeat aggression. To us this choice may represent a strategic option; to our allies it appears as a matter of life and death, for they have been convinced that a Soviet occupation would mean the collapse of their social structure.

In the past, coalitions have generally been held together by a combination of three purposes: (1) To discourage aggression by assembling superior power and to leave no doubt about the alignment of forces—this, in effect, is the doctrine of collective security. (2) To provide an obligation for assistance. Were the national interest unambiguous and unchangeable, each power would know its

237

obligations and the alignment of its potential opponents without any formal pact. But the national interest fluctuates within limits; it must be adapted to changing circumstances. An alliance is a form of insurance against contingencies, an additional weight when considering whether to go to war. (3) To legitimize the assistance of foreign troops or intervention in a foreign country.

An alliance is effective, however, only to the extent that it reflects a common purpose and that it represents an accretion of strength to its members. The mere assembling of overwhelming power is meaningless if it cannot be brought to bear on the issues actually in dispute. The strongest purpose will prove ineffective if it cannot find a military expression in terms of an agreed strategic doctrine. Thus the French system of alliances in the interwar period broke down when put to the test, because its political purpose and the military doctrine on which it was based were inconsistent with each other. The political purpose of the French system of alliances was to assure the integrity of the small states of Central and Eastern Europe. Militarily, this implied an offensive strategy on the part of France, because only by forcing Germany into a two-front war could the latter's pressure on the Central European powers be eased. But, with the building of the Maginot line, the condition of military cooperation between France and its allies disappeared. For when France adopted the strategic defensive, Germany was enabled to defeat its opponents in detail. In every crisis France was torn between its political and military commitments, and its allies were forced to choose between suicidal resistance or surrender. In the event, whatever course they chose—whether surrender, as Czechoslovakia, or resistance, as Poland—proved equally disastrous. The French system of alliances, so imposing on paper, could not survive any of the tests for which it was designed. It did not discourage aggression because its strategic doctrine made it impossible to assemble superior power, and its calls for assistance went unheeded because a legal obligation by itself will not impel common action if the requirements of national survival seem to counsel a different course. In short, it is not the fact of alliance which deters aggression, but the application it can be given in any concrete case.

Since the end of World War II, the United States has created a vast and complicated system of alliances which includes forty-four sovereign states. We have multilateral pacts in the Western Hemisphere expressed in the Inter-American Treaty of Reciprocal Assistance. We have been instrumental in creating the North Atlantic Treaty for the defense of Western Europe. We were the chief force behind the Southeast Asia Collective Defense Treaty which unites us with Australia, France, New Zealand, Pakistan, the Philippines, Thailand and the United Kingdom. Then there is the ANZUS Pact signed by us together with New Zealand and Australia. Finally, we have entered into bilateral defense treaties with Japan, Nationalist China, South Korea and the Philippines. Moreover, we are indirectly connected with the Baghdad Pact which unites Iraq with two of our allies in NATO, Britain and Turkey, and one of our partners in SEATO, Pakistan.

The chief purpose of this intricate structure is to surround the Soviet periphery with a system of alliances so that an attack on any part of it will always confront an aggressor with an alignment of powers which would make him hesitate. A world-wide system of collective security hides great complexities, however. For if we examine the alliances on which United States policy is based in terms of the criteria outlined above, we find that some of them do not share a common purpose, others add little to our effective strength, or both. To us the Soviet threat overshadows all else; but Pakistan is more concerned with India than with the U.S.S.R. and China; the Baghdad Pact is of greater significance for relationships within the Middle East than for defense against Soviet aggression. And in neither SEATO nor the Baghdad Pact are we associated with partners with whom we share the degree of common purpose conferred by the cultural heritage which unites us with our European allies. In such circumstances, a system of collective security runs the danger of leading to a dilution of purpose and to an air of unreality in which the existence of an alliance, and not the resolution behind it, is considered a guarantee of security.

These problems are magnified, moreover, by the tendency of our strategic doctrine to transform every war into an all-out war. For, while it is true that all our security arrangements are regional in nature, they are given a world-wide application by our increasing reliance on all-out war, both doctrinally and technically. Thus the outbreak of any war anywhere becomes of immediate concern to all our allies and causes them in every crisis to exert pressure for a policy of minimum risk. Nor will these pressures be avoided by declarations that the United States reserves the right of unilateral action, such as Secretary Dulles' statement to the NATO Council in December 1956. As long as our military doctrine threatens to transform every war into an all-out war, it becomes of inevitable concern to our allies, whether by right or by self-interest, and they will do their best to prevent *any* action on our part which threatens to involve them.

The inconsistency between a reliance on all-out war and the political commitment of regional defense has been the bane of our coalition policy. Our strategic doctrine has never been able to decide how to protect threatened areas: whether to defend them locally or whether to treat an attack on them as *the cause* of war. The former strategy would require resisting aggression where it occurred, at least in areas we wished to deny to the Soviets. The second strategy would treat aggression as a cause of war, but it would involve no commitment about the area where we proposed to fight—it is in effect the doctrine of massive retaliation "at places of our own choosing." In such a strategy, security against Soviet aggression is achieved, if at all, by the over-all strategic balance between us and the Soviet bloc. But, whatever the deterrent effect of massive retaliation, it removes the incentive for a military effort by our allies. They realize that in an all-out war they will add to our effective strength only by supplying facilities or by serving as bases; they see no significance in a military contribution of their own. A reliance on all-out war as the chief deterrent will sap our system of alliances in two ways: either our allies will feel that any military effort on their part is unnecessary, or they may be led to the conviction that peace is preferable to war even on terms almost akin to surrender.

Our attempt to take account of this feeling has led to a further strategic distortion. In order to reassure our allies, it has caused us and Great Britain to build up forces in Western Europe too small to resist an all-out attack and too large for police actions. Thus Great Britain has four divisions in Germany and the United States five of its combat-ready fourteen. Our European allies, in turn, have made just enough of a defense effort to induce us to keep our forces on the Continent, but not enough of one to constitute an effective barrier to Soviet aggression. The result of all these half-measures and mutual pretenses has been the stationing of substantial ground forces in an area where our strategic doctrine explicitly rejects the possibility of local war.[1] While in the peripheral areas of Asia and the Middle East, where the possibility of local war is admitted, we have neither forces on the spot nor the mobility to get our strategic reserve into position quickly enough.

It is difficult to relate our present deployment to an all-out strategy, although various explanations have been attempted. It is said, for example, that one reason for stationing nearly half of the strategic reserve of the Western alliance so close to the sources of Soviet strength is to prevent a Soviet attack with the garrison troops in East Germany, which vary between twenty-five and thirty divisions. According to this argument, a Soviet offensive against our forces in Western Europe would require substantial reinforcements, and this in turn would enable us to undertake diplomatic steps to avert the conflict or to issue the most solemn and unambiguous warning to the U.S.S.R.[2] But nine divisions seem a heavy price to pay for an opportunity to repeat a threat that we have made often and

---

1 See, for example, General Alfred M. Gruenther's final statement on leaving NATO, *New York Times*, November 14, 1956.

2 See Chester Wilmot, "If NATO Had to Fight," *Foreign Affairs*, v. 31 (January 1953), p. 203.

presumably ineffectually if the U.S.S.R. is reinforcing for an attack.

Another argument maintains that the troops in Western Europe do not have any strategic significance by themselves. Their function is to serve as a token of our determination, as a trip-wire or a plate glass window the smashing of which would unleash all-out thermonuclear retaliation.[3] In many respects this is a most remarkable argument, though it has rarely been challenged. For it says nothing less than that our repeated assertions that we will defend Western Europe by all-out war will not be believed by themselves: that it requires an additional proof of our determination besides the most solemnly repeated declarations. This in itself is a symptom of the low credibility of a threat of all-out war even for the defense of Europe, and it was reflected also in the insistent demand of our European allies in 1950 to increase our ground commitments in Europe.

Moreover, the very term "trip-wire" removes the incentive for a military effort by our allies and, therefore, the possibility of local defense. The organizations to be unleashed by the trip-wire are the United States Strategic Air Force and the British Bomber Command. The best guarantee that they will in fact be employed is to make sure that the trip-wire is predominantly American and British, which is exactly the direction of the pressures of our Continental allies. By the same token, once an all-out war is under way, the significance of substantial indigenous ground forces is problematical—or so it seems, at least, to economy-minded governments on the Continent.

This is not to say that it is a mistake to attempt a local defense of Europe; it is simply to indicate the inconsistency between our deployment and the strategy we propose to pursue in case of war, between the desire of our allies for protection against occupation by the Red Army and the military effort they are willing to make. If the protection of threatened areas resides in our retaliatory capability, we should be able to devise less elaborate means for

---

[3] Sir John Slessor, "The Great Deterrent and Its Limitations," *Bulletin of the Atomic Scientists*, v. 12 (May 1956), p. 143.

demonstrating our determination than stationing one-third of our strategic reserve where it is totally vulnerable and where it is not expected to be able to hold. If a local defense of Europe is illusory, the stationing of more than a screen of token forces is a diversion of resources.

The implications of the growing Soviet nuclear capability would seem to impose a measure of harmony, however, between the interest of the United States in an over-all strategy and the concern of our allies with local defense. For the end of our invulnerability has altered our strategic options: until the development of the Soviet Long-Range Air Force and thermonuclear stockpile, we had a theoretical choice between a strategy of massive retaliation and a strategy of local defense. The only inhibition to our action was then produced by the range of our heavy bombers. To the extent that these required overseas air bases, we had to provide the degree of security against foreign invasion which alone could induce allies to furnish facilities.[4] In all other areas we had the option of defense by local or by all-out war. But in the face of the horrors of thermonuclear war, it is in our interest, as much as in that of our allies, to seek to defend Eurasia by means other than all-out war: to devise a strategy which will enable us to achieve our objectives at less fearful cost than a thermonuclear exchange.

This applies even to the defense of Europe. We have insisted for so long that an attack on Europe would be the signal for an all-out war, that we may well find ourselves engaged in the most wasteful kind of struggle because other alternatives have never been considered. It may be true that Europe is the chief strategic prize, but it does not follow that we must inevitably adopt a strategy in its defense which is certain to drain our national substance. As the awareness of the destructiveness of modern weapons becomes more diffused, it is not reasonable to assume that the United States, and even more the United Kingdom, would be prepared to commit suicide to deny an area, however important, to an enemy, all the more so if the Soviet

---

4 See Denis Healey, "The Atom Bomb and the Alliance," *Confluence*, v. 5 (April 1956), pp. 70-8.

Union shows its customary skill in presenting its challenge ambiguously. What if the Red Army attacks in Europe explicitly to disarm West Germany and offers to the United States and the United Kingdom immunity from strategic bombing and a withdrawal to the Oder after achieving its limited objective? Is it clear that France would fight under such circumstances? Or that the United Kingdom would initiate an all-out war which, however it ended, might mean the end of British civilization? Or that an American President would trade fifty American cities for Western Europe? And, even if he should be prepared to do so, it would still be the task of our strategy to develop less fearful options than national catastrophe or surrender.[5]

It may be argued that the U.S.S.R. faces the same problem that it too may not be prepared to risk total devastation for a marginal gain. But the psychological bloc against *initiating* all-out war cannot be emphasized often enough. If the Soviets can force us to shoulder the risk of initiating all-out war, there is great danger that soon no areas outside the Western Hemisphere will seem "worth" contending for. And even should the assessment prove mistaken, it would still not be in our interest to resort immediately to all-out war. It is not simply that there are inherent limitations to the credibility of the threat of suicide; it is above all that the most wasteful and cataclysmic strategy should not be our only possible riposte. There is a contradiction in conducting a war fought presumably to maintain the historical experience and tradition of a people with a strategy which is almost certain to destroy its national substance.

Thus our alliances should not be considered from the aspect of an all-out strategy, but as a means to escape its horrors. In an all-out war few of our allies will add to our striking power, and they will have no incentive to furnish the trip-wire to unleash it. But our capability for all-out war can be used as a shield to organize local defense, and our assistance should be conceived as a means to make local defense possible. In this resides our only chance to avoid the impasse which has been the bane of our coali-

---

[5] See below, Chapter 9, p. 269 ff., for an elaboration of NATO strategy.

tion policy: the gap between the belief of our allies that they are already protected by our thermonuclear capability to which they do not feel they have a contribution to make, and their terror of its consequences which makes them reluctant to invoke it as a strategy for fighting a war. Only by developing a strategy which admits the possibility of local defense can we escape the never-never land where our military contributions to the ground defense of our allies is greater than their own, and where current investment in local defense cannot have any strategic return because our strategic doctrine does not feel comfortable with limited war and neither we nor our allies have yet considered an alternative strategy.

The sense of common purpose which has been lacking in our coalition policy can be conferred by the interest we now share with our allies in avoiding all-out thermonuclear war. Thus our policy of coalitions should not be justified as an addition to our strategic striking power, but as a means to enable all allies to pursue the least costly strategy. The incentive for our allies would not be to furnish a trip-wire, but their conviction that the best means of avoiding thermonuclear war resides in our joint ability to make local aggression too costly. Our task is to convey to them that they cannot avoid their dilemmas by neutrality or surrender, for either will bring on what they fear most: confined to the Western Hemisphere, we would have no choice but to fight an all-out war. And all-out war, as has been seen above, will have almost as fearful consequences for neutrals as for the chief protagonists.[6] To be sure, the Soviets have skillfully fomented neutralism by giving the impression that local resistance must inevitably lead to all-out war. But the Soviets can be no more interested than we in all-out war—at least if we behave effectively and maintain adequate retaliatory forces. The fear of thermonuclear extinction would provide a powerful sanction against expanding a conflict.

Far from being inconsistent with a strategy of limited war, our policy of alliances should represent a special

---

6 See above, Chapter 3, p. 65 ff.

application of it. As in a strategy of limited war, it is less a question of physical resources than of understanding the strategic implications of the new technology. For neither the necessity of a strategy of limited war nor the conduct of it has been clarified by us or by our partners. This has been compounded by the fact that, among our allies, only the United Kingdom is a nuclear power and that as a result neither technology nor training nor doctrine exists among our other partners to deal with the problems of a nuclear war. No progress can be made in our policy of alliances until there has been an agreement on strategic doctrine.

II

A strategic doctrine which poses less absolute sanctions than all-out war would go far toward overcoming another difficulty of our coalition policy: the tendency of our system of alliances to merge into a world-wide system of collective security. For all-out war is of direct concern not only to every ally, but also to every neutral. As long as our strategic doctrine threatens to transform every war into an all-out war, our allies will not only be reluctant to make a military effort of their own; they will also seek, in most issues likely to be in dispute, to keep us from running major risks ourselves. By the same token, as long as our strategic doctrine relies on all-out war as the chief deterrent, our policy-makers will be tempted to give our coalition policy the same global scope as to our strategy. As a result, in every crisis from Korea, to Indo-China, to the Middle East, we have left the impression that, unless all allies (and sometimes even all powers) resist aggression jointly, no effective action is possible at all. Thus whatever our formal commitments, our coalition policy has in practice encountered many of the difficulties of a system of general collective security.

And a world-wide system of collective security is extremely difficult to implement. The acid test of an alliance is its ability to achieve agreement on two related problems: whether a given challenge represents aggression and, if so, what form resistance should take. But differences in geographic position, history, power and domestic structure ensure that a world-wide consensus is difficult to attain except against a threat so overpowering that it obliterates all differences, both about its nature or about the strategy for dealing with it. Against any other danger, united action is almost inevitably reduced to the lowest common denominator, for the essence of sovereignty is that powers have, or at least *may* have, different conceptions of their interest and, therefore, also about what constitutes a threat. Even if there should be agreement that a given act constitutes aggression, the willingness of the powers to run risks to vindicate their view will differ. A state will not easily risk its national existence to defeat an aggression not explicitly directed against its national existence. A North Vietnamese troop movement may be a mortal danger to Laos, but it can be of only marginal interest to Italy. A domestic upheaval in Syria may disquiet Turkey; it will seem much less dangerous to Portugal.

Against an aggressor skilled in presenting ambiguous challenges, there will occur endless wrangling over whether a specific challenge in fact constitutes aggression and about the measures to deal with it should it be considered a threat. If the aggression is explicitly less than all-out or if it is justified as the expression of a "legitimate" grievance, at least some of the members of an alliance will be tempted to evade the problem by denying the reality of the threat. They will prefer waiting with the most drastic sanctions until the aggressor has "demonstrated" he is intent on world domination, and he will not have demonstrated it until the balance of power is already overturned.

As long as the challenge is not overwhelming, an aggressor may, therefore, actually be aided by a world-wide system of collective security, or by a system of alliances which is given world-wide application. It is the essence of limited aggression that it affects the interests of various powers differently. The wider the collective action sought, the more various the purposes which have to be harmonized and the more difficult it will be to apply it in resisting local aggression. To be sure, all states have a *symbolic* interest in every dispute, however far removed from their primary sphere of concern. They will oppose the development of a set of rules of international conduct which, when applied to them, might work to their disadvantage. They will, therefore, be prepared to assist in elaborating a concept of aggression which they may invoke for their own protection. But the *substantive* interests of states in most disputes vary, a difference which expresses itself in the risks they are willing to run to implement their definition of aggression or their interpretation of the merits of a dispute. There is an inevitable disparity in a world-wide system of collective security between the readiness to pass resolutions and the willingness to back them up.

The result of this inevitable difference in emphasis is that the wider the system of alliances the more difficult it will be to apply it to concrete cases. In a world-wide system of collective security, it is easier to obtain agreement on inaction than on commitment; indeed, inaction may represent the only consensus attainable. Even where there is agreement on the symbolic aspect of collective security, on the nature of aggression, or on what constitutes a just claim, it will still be exceedingly difficult to achieve a common stand on the consequences that should flow from this agreement. The difference in effectiveness between the United Nations in Egypt and in Hungary illustrates this point. In both cases the United Nations, which exhibits the difficulties of a general system of collective security in their most extreme form, expressed its disapproval. This symbolic act was effective toward Britain and France, primarily because it involved no assumption of substantive risk. It worked because Britain and France recoiled before the fact and not the consequences of united world opinion.

By contrast, United Nations resolutions have so far proved ineffective in bringing about the evacuation of Hungary or the unification of Korea. For in these cases a pronouncement as to the merits of the dispute was unavailing against a power prepared to defy the system of collective security. Compliance could be achieved only by a willingness to employ more drastic measures. But the majority which was prepared to go on record condemning Soviet actions was not ready to face perils to have its view prevail. The gap between the symbolic and the substantive aspect of collective security may, therefore, actually demoralize resistance. The statesman of a threatened country faced with the decision of whether to resist aggression will not draw too much comfort from the fact that an attack on his state may be condemned. Unless he can be assured of more tangible guarantees, he may make the best terms he can.

A world-wide system of collective security, in its quest for assembling maximum power, may bring about a threshold below which common action is impossible and unilateral action is inhibited by the doctrine of collective security. As with the doctrine of massive retaliation, the greater the force assembled the less may be the willingness to use it and the smaller may be its credibility. It leads to an inconsistency between the attempt to leave no doubt about the alignment of forces and providing an added incentive for common action. In every crisis the magnitude and complexity of a world-wide system of collective security will supply a powerful incentive for inaction. It is not that the value of common action will be denied; it is simply that many actions will not seem to warrant calling into action the machinery of collective security or of drawing drastic consequences once it has been set into motion.

To seek to give too generalized an application to a system of alliances may, therefore, have the paradoxical result of paralyzing the power or powers capable of resisting alone. The theoretical gain in strength may be more than outweighed by the dilution of a common purpose. At the same time, in every crisis short of an overriding attack, such a system of collective security gives a veto to the ally with least interest in the issue at dispute and often with least power to make his views prevail. From Korea, to the Chinese offshore islands, to Indo-China, to Suez, some powerful members of our system of coalitions have found that they disagreed with their allies about the extent of the danger, or else they took positions which made unity attainable only by foregoing any risks. And the reaction to the disunity on issues actually in dispute was a heightened determination to "strengthen" the alliance, to seek to compensate for the inability to apply the alliance concretely by escaping into a formal unity. Thus Korea led to the ANZUS Pact, Indo-China to SEATO, and the Suez crisis to an effort to "tighten" the bonds of NATO.

The attempt to apply what are in effect regional alliances on a world-wide basis has tended to inhibit the action of the powers with most at stake in a given dispute. It has turned our alliances into targets of many national frustrations and therewith confronted many governments with the following dilemma: if they have acted outside the sphere of their primary interest, it has undermined their domestic support and, if they did not, it has strained the alliance. A vacuum has thereby been created in which formal unity becomes a substitute for common action, or the alliance is blamed for the failure to take measures which the government concerned was most reluctant to undertake in the first place. Thus Secretary Dulles implied that only lack of British support prevented our intervention in Indo-China, and the British Cabinet has given the impression that American vacillation was solely responsible for the failure of its policy in the Middle East.

The prerequisite of an effective system of alliances, then, is to harmonize our political and our military commitments by a strategy of local defense and a diplomacy of regional cooperation. Within the region covered by alliances we should concert our efforts militarily and politically. Outside that region we must be free to act alone or with a different grouping of powers if our interest so dictates. Such a course would take account of the fact that the United States alone of the powers of the non-Soviet world is strong enough physically and psychologically to play a global role.

Fortunately, the imbalance in our system of alliances has been caused less by our diplomacy than by our military policy. In fact, from a legal point of view, all our alliances are explicitly regional, although, in practice, we have often sought to give them world-wide application. If we can develop a strategic doctrine which makes regional cooperation meaningful militarily, it should not be too difficult to create a pattern of political and economic cooperation on a regional basis.

The corollary to a regional system of alliances, however, is the willingness of the United States to exercise its leadership in defining the transformations the alliance is prepared to resist. For the factors that counsel a regional system of alliances also ensure that we cannot rely on the consensus of humanity to define the issues for which to contend. It is not only that our allies, with the possible exception of Great Britain, are too weak to act outside the area of their primary concern. It is also that *within* this area or on the issues most directly affecting it, they will be at a serious disadvantage without United States support.

For none of our allies, not even Great Britain, can be considered major powers any longer. In the nuclear age, a major power is a state which can afford a retaliatory capability sufficient to destroy any possible opponent. In this sense, only the United States and the U.S.S.R. are major powers. This imbalance inhibits action by our allies not only vis-à-vis the Soviet Union, but also toward other states. It goes without saying that none of our allies is capable of conducting a war against the U.S.S.R. without our assistance. But the change in the position of the European powers goes further. Since they are unable to deter all-out war by themselves, they cannot even conduct limited war against smaller powers except under our protection or with the acquiescence of the U.S.S.R. Whatever the remaining margin of superiority of the European powers over the underdeveloped part of the world—and in some respects it is larger than in the heyday of colonial rule—they can no longer impose their will if the United States does not provide the shield of its retaliatory force. Surely one of the lessons of the fiasco of the invasion of Egypt by Britain and France was that none of our allies can fight a limited war and keep it limited by its own effort.

The result of this demonstration of impotence is that

the responsibility for defining the issues for which to
contend has explicitly fallen on us. Any possibility for
independent action by our European allies disappeared,
for better or worse, with the Suez fiasco. Henceforth as
much importance attaches to the subtlety of our comprehension of the strategic balance as on our physical strength.
We are projected into this role, moreover, when an understanding of the nature of security has become infinitely
complicated. The traditional concept of aggression, as military attack by organized units across a sovereign boundary,
presupposed a society of nations in which domination of
one power by another was possible only by military victory
or by annexation. But in the age of "volunteers" and "arms
bases," of guerrilla warfare and economic penetration, the
strategic balance may be upset without a clear-cut issue
ever being presented. Does Soviet repression of satellite
revolts warrant United States intervention? Is a Soviet
base in the Middle East aggression when it is stocked
with weapons or only when Soviet troops appear against
the will of the indigenous government?

It is impossible to answer these questions in the abstract. They demonstrate, however, that we may have as
much difficulty identifying the transformations we will
resist by force as in assembling the force to resist them.
Moreover, while the precise circumstances that might
justify recourse to force cannot be laid down in advance,
our ultimate decision to resist and, therefore, that of some
of our allies as well, will depend to a considerable extent
on the concepts regarding the nature of our strategic interest which we have developed well in advance of crisis
situations. Are we opposed to the forcible expansion of
communism, or is the existence of a Communist regime in
some areas a threat to our security, however the regime is
established? Do we resist Communist domination of an
area only when it is "illegal," or because the domination
of Eurasia by communism would upset the strategic balance against us? If the former, we would resist only the
manner of Communist expansion; if the latter, we would
resist the *fact* of Communist expansion. It may happen,
of course, that in neither case will we be able to arrest

developments, as was the case in China, for example. If we are clear about our strategic interest, however, the form of resistance, and indeed the decision whether to resist, will be technical questions. Without such concepts our actions will be haphazard and our alliances uncertain.

In the task of defining principles of resistance equal to the challenges confronting us, great demands will be made on our wisdom and sense of proportion. We must avoid the temptation of identifying our alliances with the consensus of their members, because in practice this reduces common action to the willingness to run risks of the most timid or the weakest ally. But we must also refrain from attempting to prescribe to our allies what their interests should be in every situation, because this is dissolving of any coalition. The former danger has already been discussed, but the latter deserves serious consideration. While it is true that our strategic interests transcend those of our allies, our allies may well be more sensitive than we within the region of their primary concern or on matters that affect this region, as for example Middle Eastern oil for Europe. Because their margin of safety is so much narrower, our allies may well feel threatened by transformations which do not seem to affect our security directly. In such a situation, we must be prepared to make some concessions to what our allies consider their essential interests. If we reserve the right to judge each issue on its "merits," we shall remove the psychological basis of a coalition policy. If other powers are assured of our support without formal commitment whenever we agree with them, or if they can suffer our opposition regardless of past association when we differ, no special significance attaches to alliances any longer. The insistence on complete freedom of action blurs the line between allies and the uncommitted.

This is not to say we must support our allies however arbitrary their behavior. It does imply that a coalition is meaningless unless it takes into account one of the traditional purposes of alliances mentioned at the beginning of this chapter: to provide an obligation for assistance beyond the immediate considerations of national interest or the particular interpretation of the merits of a dispute. To be sure, if the disparity between the national interest and the obligations of the alliance becomes too great, the alliance ceases to be effective, for no nation will give up its vital interests simply for the sake of allied unity, But by the same token, if the existence of an alliance does not furnish an added motive for support, there is no purpose in entering into it. It is the art of statesmanship to harmonize these considerations. Our coalition policy must strike a balance between identifying an alliance with the consensus of its members and the desire for freedom of action in situations where our views and those of our allies diverge. To conduct an alliance on the principle of unanimity will cause the alliance to be geared either to the willingness to run risks of the ally with least interest in a given dispute, or it will enable the most irresponsible partner to force all other allies to underwrite its actions. But to insist on complete freedom of action in case of disagreement with our allies will wreck our system of alliances.

In short, our system of alliances can thrive only if we curb our penchant for pushing principles to their ultimate conclusion. It must be built on an understanding by all partners that our interests and those of our allies cannot be of the same order, because the disparity of power and responsibility is too great. We can cooperate on matters of mutual concern, which in almost every case means regional cooperation. But our allies must understand that we have an obligation to maintain not only a regional equilibrium, but the world balance of power as well. Provided our military doctrine does not threaten to transform every war into all-out war, our allies must, therefore, be prepared to let us act alone or with a different grouping of powers outside the area of regional cooperation. We, in turn, should show understanding and compassion for the problems of states whose margin of survival—military, political and economic—is far smaller than ours. Any other course will make for paralysis: it will cause our allies to hamstring us *outside* the area of mutual concern, and it will cause us to frustrate our allies *within* it.

III

What of the relationship of the uncommitted part of the world to our coalition policy? It is often said that our policy of military alliances is one of the causes of our difficulties with the newly independent nations, and to a certain extent this is correct. We must be careful, however, not to confuse the symptom with the cause of our difficulties or to identify the policy toward the newly independent states with a quest for popularity.

The importance of the newly independent nations cannot be doubted. It is equally beyond question that it is to the American interest that we identify ourselves with their hopes and aspirations and that we seek to prevent an alignment of the white against the colored races of the world. The consequences that flow from this realization are much less obvious, however. Any discussion of policy toward the uncommitted third of the world must, therefore, begin with an examination of the tendencies they represent, even at the risk of some digression.

The revolution that is taking place in the newly independent and still dependent states can only be narrowly understood as a revolution against colonialism. In a real sense, it is a continuation of a revolution *started* by the colonial powers and carried on under their aegis. Moreover, not all the protest movements of formerly subjugated people are either of the same order, nor do they all represent the same phenomenon: there is a basic difference between areas in which colonialism ruled directly and those in which it governed indirectly.

The remarkable aspect of colonialism from its beginning was the imposition of rule by a very small group of Europeans over vast populations. This was due not so much to the military superiority of the West—in many respects it is greater today than it was in the nineteenth century—as to the fact that the European powers displaced an existing ruling group in a society where the vast majority of the population neither enjoyed nor expected direct participation in government. The structure of government in what is now the uncommitted third of the world had been feudal for centuries, and in their first appearance the Europeans appeared as a new governing group substituting itself for the existing one according to a pattern which had characterized these areas for many generations. The domination of vast territories by small groups of Europeans was possible precisely because they were not considered as "foreign;" the notion of their foreignness was introduced in the first instance not by the governed but by their rulers.

For the Europeans were not content with displacing a feudal upper class. They brought with them the twin doctrines of rational administration and popular participation in government, which in time had inevitably to prove inconsistent with their continued domination. The rationalizing of administration led to the consolidation of many areas into viable units for the first time in their history: Indonesia, for example, was nothing but a geographic expression until the Dutch found it more efficient to unite the islands of the Indies under a single administration. At the same time the colonial powers trained a group of indigenous leaders in European universities where they absorbed the doctrines of the right to self-government, human dignity and economic advancement which had been the rallying points for European revolutionary and progressive movements throughout the nineteenth century.

The result was two sets of paradoxes: in its revolutionary aspect colonialism represents one of the greatest conversions of history. Almost without exception the leaders of the newly independent states, as well as the heads of anti-colonial uprisings in still dependent countries, are opposing their present or former masters in terms of values they have learned from them. Their challenge to the West is not in terms of a different set of beliefs; on the contrary, they are demanding that the West live up to its own principles. The leaders in the uncommitted third of the world are playing a role drawn from a Western script. As the ideals of the British, French and American revolutions became diffused, partly through the very spread of colonialism, the seeds were sown for the destruction of colonialism itself. The more successful the teachings of the colonial powers, the more untenable their positions became. Thus the greater the participation of the indigenous population in their own government, the more insistent grew their demands for independence, as is demonstrated by the difference between the British and the Portuguese colonies. What is taking place in the areas once under direct colonial rule is the second stage of the revolution started by the colonial powers. It is an attempt by the leaders of the newly independent states to spread among the masses of their people the values which they themselves acquired from the colonial power and which furnished the original impetus of the revolution.

This leads to the second paradox of the uncommitted third of the world: that the situation of areas which had been under direct colonial rule is more advantageous than that of countries where the colonial powers exercised their influence only indirectly. The territories governed directly, such as India, benefited through administrative consolidation and the overthrow of the old feudal order by an outside force. The countries controlled indirectly, such as most of those in the Middle East, suffered the demoralizing influence of foreign rule without a corresponding gain in the training of leadership groups or of administrative cohesion. On the contrary, while in areas governed directly boundaries were drawn with an eye to what constituted a viable unit, in other territories they were often drawn to ensure that the countries would *not* be viable. Thus the only reason for the existence of what is now the Kingdom of Jordan was its need of a British subsidy over an indefinite period of time. For the most part, boundaries in the Middle East reflected neither a common history nor an economic or administrative necessity. They were drawn to guarantee weakness and rivalry.

In the areas once ruled indirectly, several revolutions are, therefore, going on concurrently: there is, to begin with, the revolt by a small Western-educated elite against feudal rule; there is the quest for administrative, political and economic cohesiveness; there is, finally, the attempt to raise the level of economic welfare and of education of the masses. The revolutionary urgency is much greater and the problems more nearly insoluble in areas which had been governed indirectly than in the countries which had been under direct rule, because in the latter many of these upheavals were accomplished by the fiat of the colonial power and over a long period of time. Therefore, while a legalistic concept of sovereignty and aggression may be a stabilizing element in Southeast Asia, it invites explosions in areas like the Middle East because it works counter to the consolidation of inherently volatile and economically unviable units.

These paradoxes make the quest for popularity such a treacherous course with respect to the newly independent states. For, while the leadership groups have been trained in Western universities and have on the whole accepted Western thinking, this very fact may limit the degree to which they can identify themselves with the Western powers politically. It is not so much that these leaders would be suspected by their countrymen of collaboration with the former colonial rulers; the motivation is more complex and more subtle. To sustain the dedication and the suffering of the rebellion against the colonial powers, the leaders of independence movements had to elaborate a distinction between themselves and their rulers which they derived from a claim to superior morality or at least superior spirituality. But, when the battle was won and independence finally achieved, many leaders of newly independent countries have had to realize, at least subconsciously, that they were inwardly a good deal closer to their former rulers than to their own countrymen. It may be too much to say that they resent the West for having taught them patterns of thinking which make them strangers to their own people; it is clear that they require anti-colonialism as a means of achieving a sense of personal identity. Precisely because they are inwardly so close to the West, many of the leaders of the newly independent states cannot afford to align themselves with it politically. If they must think in the categories of their former colonial masters, they can at least refuse too close political association.

In these terms, neutralism and anti-colonialism are not

so much a policy as a spiritual necessity. The constant reiteration of nonalignment may be the means by which the leaders of newly independent nations reassure themselves; they can be certain of their independence only by acting it out every day and on every issue. This explains why the most strident advocates of neutrality are often the very people who in dress, bearing, and manner of thinking are closest to the West—indeed who often have spent very little of their lives in their own countries. Individuals with firm roots in their own tradition, on the other hand, such as the Burmese leadership, seem to feel less compulsive about proclaiming their independence daily and seem more prepared to act jointly with the Western powers when their interests coincide.

Therefore, too, the extent of anti-colonialism reflects less past suffering, than the difficulty of achieving a national consciousness. For, contrary to the nations of Western Europe from which they drew their ideal of nationhood, many of the newly independent states are based neither on a common language nor on a common culture. Their only common experience is the former colonial rule. Their leaders require anti-colonialism to achieve not only a sense of personal but also of national identity. The collection of islands called Indonesia is meaningful only in terms of the history of Dutch rule; its frontiers follow precisely the frontiers of empire and so does its national consciousness. Because West New Guinea was part of the Dutch East Indies, Indonesia has laid claim to it although it is inhabited by people as different from the Polynesian stock of Indonesia as the Dutch themselves. Indonesia does not covet Malaya, although racially and linguistically it is much closer, because no common experience connects it to Malaya. Conversely, Malaya has no desire to join its cultural brethren in Indonesia, but will become a state within the boundaries of former British colonial rule.

The close identification of nationalism with the memory of colonial rule also accounts for the seeming blind spot of so many newly independent states with respect to Soviet colonialism. The leaders of the uncommitted nations may condemn such Soviet actions as the repression of the

Hungarian revolt. They may dislike Soviet control of the satellite orbit. But they will not be prepared to consider it as the same phenomenon which causes their own frustrations. Until they develop a stronger sense of personal identity and until their nations can develop purposes not drawn from the struggle for independence, they will require anti-colonialism, and it must have an anti-Western connotation. For beyond anti-colonialism lies psychological chaos.

In the uncommitted areas, popularity is an unattainable goal. To seek to gear our policy to an inquiry into what people desire may merely force the newly independent states to dissociate themselves from us in order to demonstrate their independence. It would not be the least paradox of the contemporary situation if we drove the newly independent states toward the Soviet bloc by a too ardent embrace. On the other hand, we should be able to utilize the combination of spiritual kinship and political nonalignment for acts of leadership. For, whatever their protestations, the leaders of almost every newly independent state, particularly in areas which had been under direct colonial rule, are spiritual heirs of the West at least to some extent. The very fact that India considered it a great achievement to obtain Soviet acquiescence to its five principles of coexistence indicates that its assessment of the real threat to peace is not so very different from ours. For no attempt was made to ask for the agreement of the former colonial powers or of the United States, so often depicted in Asian folklore as imperialist and eager to restore colonial rule. It was obviously self-evident to India that relations between it and the United States were so firmly based on the principle of peaceful coexistence that no explicit reiteration was necessary.

If, then, we are prepared to exercise leadership, we may be able to induce many of the newly independent nations to travel in a direction to which they incline, if always a few steps behind us. They will not surrender their nonalignment, but they may be willing to act in the pursuance of common interests provided we are prepared to chart the road and provided we tolerate a measure of dissociation.

In the uncommitted nations popularity may be less important than respect.

IV

The importance of United States leadership is all the greater because of the unfamiliarity of many of the leaders of the newly independent nations with the elements of international stability and with the nature of modern power relationships. The leaders of the newly independent states achieved their positions by distinguishing themselves in the struggle with the former colonial powers. But the independence movements, almost without exception, provided a poor preparation for an understanding of the element of power in international relations. Based on the dogmas of late nineteenth-century liberalism, especially its pacifism, the independence movements relied more on ideological agreement than on an evaluation of power factors, and to this day the claim to superior spirituality remains the battle cry of Asian nationalism. Moreover, the bad conscience of the colonial powers and their preoccupation with European problems gave the struggle for independence more the character of a domestic debate than of a power dispute. To be sure, many of the leaders of the newly independent powers spent years in jail and suffered heroically for their cause. It is not to deny the measure of their dedication to assert that the results achieved were out of proportion to their suffering. Empires which had held vast dominions for hundreds of years disappeared without a battle being fought.

And if it is difficult for the leaders to retain a sense of proportion, it is next to impossible for the mass of the population. On the whole, they were involved in the struggle for independence only with their sympathies; to them the disappearance of the colonial powers must seem nothing short of miraculous. Moreover, most of the people of the newly independent states live in preindustrial societies. It would be difficult enough for them to grasp the full impact of industrialism; it is too much to expect them to understand the meaning of nuclear technology. It is therefore understandable that in most former colonial areas there is an overestimation of what can be accomplished by words alone. Nor is this tendency diminished by the rewards that fall to the uncommitted in the struggle for allegiance by the two big power centers.

But however understandable, it is a dangerous trend. If this were a tranquil period, nothing would be involved but minor irritations. In the present revolutionary situation, however, the dogmatism of the newly independent states makes them susceptible to Soviet "peace offensives" and their lack of appreciation of power relationships causes them to overestimate the protection afforded by moral precepts. Indeed, their very insistence on principle contributes to the demoralization of international politics, for it tempts them to accept at face value the protestations of peaceful intentions with which the Soviets inevitably accompany their aggressive moves. It reinforces the quest for a "pure" case of aggression which almost insures that the actual aggressions which may take place will not be dealt with and in many instances not even be recognized as aggression.

Moreover, such understanding of power as the newly independent states do possess does not favor the United States. The power chiefly visible to the newly independent states are the Chinese or Soviet armies on their borders. This is a category of military force which is both concrete and in keeping with their historical experience. By contrast the power of the United States is highly abstract and nearly invisible. Two hundred Chinese divisions represent a familiar element of power; by comparison the destructive capability of a B-52 or the strategic impact of a ballistic missile is esoteric and difficult to grasp. Thus considerations of both power and principle combine to inspire the newly independent nations with caution. In every crisis they exercise a pressure for solutions which combine abstractness with minimum risk, and in many situations they may provoke a crisis by their attempt to sublimate domestic policy in the international field.

In this situation the United States has particular responsibilities. It is imperative that the uncommitted powers understand not only the benefits but also the duties of independence. Many of the leaders of the newly independent states have found the temptation to play a major role in international affairs almost overwhelming. Domestically, their problems are intractable; even a major economic advance would still fall short of the aspirations of their people, and many countries will have a serious problem to maintain their standard of living in the face of their rising birth rate. In domestic policy each action has a price and sometimes a high one. Even so well-established a leader as Jawaharlal Nehru found that reshaping the boundaries of the Indian states could provoke major communal riots. But in the international field the division of the world into two contending camps exalts the role of the uncommitted, and the collapse of the structure of the old international system creates a fertile field of manipulation for ambitious men. This produces an overwhelming temptation to defer the solution of difficult domestic problems by entering the international arena, to solidify a complicated domestic position by triumphs in the international field. Unless the newly independent powers learn that every action has a price not only domestically but also internationally, they will increasingly seek to play a global role not commensurate with either their strength or the risks they are willing to assume. To the extent that foreign adventures are foreclosed, ambitious leaders will have to find an outlet for their energies in the domestic field.

Condescending as it may seem to say so, the United States has for this reason an important educational task to perform in the uncommitted third of the world. By word and deed we must demonstrate that the inexorable element of international relations resides in the necessity to combine principle with power, that an exclusive reliance on moral pronouncements may be as irresponsible as the attempt to conduct policy on the basis of considerations of power alone. To be sure we should, wherever possible, seek to identify ourselves with the aspirations of the newly independent states. But we must also be prepared to protect the framework in which these aspirations can be accomplished. We should never give up our principles nor ask other nations to surrender theirs. But we must also realize that neither we nor our allies nor the uncommitted can realize any principles unless they survive. We cannot permit the balance of power to be overturned for the sake of allied unity or the approbation of the uncommitted, for the condition of any future cooperation with them is the maintenance of a strategic balance between us and the Soviet bloc.

The challenge to our leadership is all the greater if it is considered against the background of the spread of nuclear technology. Within a generation, and probably in less time than that, most countries will possess installations for the peaceful uses of nuclear energy and, therefore, the where-withal to manufacture nuclear weapons. And even if this should not prove to be the case, the Soviets may find it advantageous to increase international tensions by making available nuclear weapons to other powers, on the model of their arms sale to Egypt and Syria. But nuclear weapons in the hands of weak, irresponsible or merely ignorant governments present grave dangers. Unless the United States has demonstrated a military capability meaningful in relation to the special conditions of the newly inde-pendent areas, many parts of the world will play the role of the Balkans in European politics: the fuse which will set off a holocaust. The United States, therefore, requires a twentieth-century equivalent of "showing the flag," an ability and a readiness to make our power felt quickly and decisively, not only to deter Soviet aggression but also to impress the uncommitted with our capacity for decisive action.

It is thus misleading to assert that strategic considera-tions play no role in our relations with the uncommitted powers. On the contrary, much as in our policy of alli-ances, the capability for local action is the prerequisite for an effective policy in the uncommitted areas of the world. But, while strategy can help to establish a framework within which to build our relations with the newly inde-pendent states, the main thrust of our policy with respect to them must be in fields other than military. In fact, our insistence that security is achieved primarily by a military grouping of powers has been one of the chief difficulties in our relations with many of the newly independent states. For, whatever the temptations for the uncommitted in the international field, their hopes for economic development and stability depend on a long period of peace. It may not be logical that they should seek to escape their dilemmas by denying the reality of the Soviet threat—but it is a fact of political life. The creation by us of military alliances in the former colonial areas is, therefore, considered by many of the newly independent states as an irritating interruption of their primary concern and lends color to Soviet peace offensives. Moreover, the military contribution of SEATO and the Baghdad Pact (to which we belong in all but in name) does not compensate for the decision of India and Egypt to stand apart and for the domestic pressures these instruments generated in some of the signatory countries.

The primary function of these pacts is to draw a line across which the U.S.S.R. cannot move without the risk of war, and to legitimize intervention by the United States should war break out. But the line could have been better drawn by a unilateral declaration, as in the Truman doctrine for Greece and Turkey and the Middle East doctrine of President Eisenhower. Behind this shield we could then have concentrated on the primary problem of creating a sense of common purpose by emphasizing shared objectives, for example by striving for a grouping of powers to assist in economic development. Had we emphasized these nonmilitary functions of SEATO, it would have been much more difficult for India or Indonesia to stay aloof. As these political groupings gain in economic strength, their own interest would dictate a more active concern for common defense; at the least it would provide the economic base for a meaningful defense. A powerful grouping of states on the Russian borders is against the interests of the Soviet Union whether or not the purpose of this grouping is fundamentally military. And by the same token, such a grouping is desirable from the American point of view even if it does not go along with our every policy.

The problem of the uncommitted states cannot be solved, however, merely by an economic grouping of powers. It is related to the whole United States posture. Anti-Americanism is fashionable today in many parts of the globe. As the richest and most powerful nation, we are the natural target for all frustrations. As the power which bears the primary responsibility for the defense of the free world, we are unpopular with all who are so preoccupied with the development of their own countries that they are unwilling to pay sufficient attention to foreign threats. We should, of course, seek to allay legitimate grievances, but we would be wrong to take every criticism at face value. A great deal of anti-Americanism hides a feeling of insecurity, both material and spiritual. Many of our most voluble critics in Southeast Asia would be terrified were our military protection suddenly withdrawn. The neutrality of the uncommitted is possible, after all, only so long as the United States remains strong spiritually and physically.

In its relations with the uncommitted, the United States must, therefore, develop not only a greater compassion but also a greater majesty. The picture of high American officials scurrying to all quarters of the globe to inform themselves on each crisis as it develops cannot but make an impression of uncertainty. The nervousness exhibited in our reactions to Soviet moves must contrast unfavorably with what appears to be the deliberate, even ruthless, purposefulness of the Soviets. Our attempt after every crisis to restore the situation to as close an approximation of the *status quo ante* as possible, may well convey the lack of a sense of direction. To gear our policy to what the uncommitted powers will accept may merely increase their feeling of insecurity or force them to move away from us to demonstrate their independence. Soviet rigidity can, therefore, profit from the pressures of the uncommitted to drive us back step by step. Conversely, firm United States positions might induce the uncommitted powers to develop formulas which meet us at least part way. The bargaining position of such countries as India depends, after all, on their skill in finding a position *between* the two major powers.

A firm United States posture is made all the more necessary by the desire of many of the uncommitted nations for peace almost at any price. Because they consider us the more malleable of the two superpowers, they choose in every crisis to direct their pressures against us as a means to preserve the peace or to resolve an issue. To the degree that we can project a greater sense of purpose, some of these pressures may be diverted against the Soviet bloc. A revolution like Egypt's or even India's cannot be managed by understanding alone; it also requires a readiness on our part to bear the psychological and military burden of difficult decisions.

v

The problem of American relations both with our allies and the uncommitted, therefore, depends on a close relationship of power and policy. Without a military policy which poses less fearful risks than all-out war, our alliances will be in jeopardy, and the uncommitted areas will vacillate between protestations of principle and a consciousness of their impotence. But even the wisest military policy will prove sterile, if our diplomacy cannot elaborate a concept of aggression which is directed to the most likely dangers. In our relation to both our allies and the uncommitted, we must realize that common action depends on a combination of common purpose and effective power. It is the task of our diplomacy to bring about common purpose but it can do so only if our military policy is able to develop a strategy equally meaningful to all partners.

Nevertheless, we must beware not to subordinate the requirements of the over-all strategic balance to our policy of alliances or to our effort to win over the uncommitted. In some situations, the best means of bringing about a common purpose is by an act of leadership which overcomes fears and permits no further equivocation. The price of our power is leadership. For what else is leadership except the willingness to stand alone if the situation requires? The failure to assume these responsibilities will not result in a consensus of humanity; it will lead to the creation of a vacuum.

9

AMERICAN STRATEGY AND NATO—
A TEST CASE

THE ACID TEST of our system of alliances is the North Atlantic Treaty Organization. It unites us with powers with whom we share both a common history and a similar culture. Of all our alliances it represents the greatest accretion to our strength. Western Europe contains the second largest concentration of industry and skills outside the United States. In a very real sense, the world balance of power depends on our ability to deny the resources and manpower of Western Europe to an aggressor.

This is why the argument usually advanced for our system of alliances, and particularly for NATO, is inadequate. It is generally said that we must maintain Western Europe in friendly hands because of the air bases NATO affords to our Strategic Air Force. But we have a strategic interest in Western Europe independent of the range of our heavy bombers, which will in time be made obsolescent by missiles: the geopolitical fact that in relation to Eurasia the United States is an island power, inferior at present only in human resources though eventually even in industrial capacity. Thus we are confronted by the traditional problem of an "island" power—of Carthage with respect to Rome, of Britain with respect to the Continent—that its survival depends on preventing the opposite land mass from falling under hostile control.

If Eurasia were to be dominated by a hostile power or group of powers, we would confront an overpowering threat. And the key to Eurasia is Western Europe because its loss would bring with it the loss of the Middle East and the upheaval of Africa. Were this to happen, the strategic advantage in all-out war would shift to the U.S.S.R. If the United States were ever confined to "Fortress America," or even if Soviet expansion went far enough to sap our allies' will to resist, the Western Hemisphere would be confronted by three-quarters of mankind and hardly less of its resources and our continued existence would be precarious. At best we would be forced into a military effort incompatible with what is now considered the American way of life. At worst we would cease to be masters of our policy.

From a military point of view, there is no need for this to occur. It should not be forgotten that in 1941 Germany alone nearly defeated the Soviet Union and today the combination of the United States and Western Europe should be able to contain it. The combined industrial resources and pool of skilled manpower of NATO still exceed those of the U.S.S.R. by a considerable margin. The task of creating a counter to the Soviet threat would, therefore, be far from hopeless if only the available resources were considered. Nevertheless, since its inception NATO has been beset by difficulties. It has not found it possible to organize its power effectively or to create a military force which can undertake a meaningful defense. Unsure about the implications of nuclear war, uncomfortable with a World War II type of strategy, NATO has attempted to combine elements of both at the price of lessened self-confidence and diminished ability to take decisive action in a time of crisis. It has not resolved the question of the significance of a military contribution by our allies to a strategy which relies on all-out war. It has not clarified to our partners the purpose of conventional forces in a war in which even the local defense of Western Europe will, as has been announced, involve the use of nuclear weapons.

The difficulties of NATO are, therefore, analogous to the dilemma posed by our own strategic doctrine. Without a clear concept of the nature of the war it proposes to fight and of the forces appropriate to it, even an alliance composed of members with a great degree of common purpose has lacked a sense of direction. In the absence of a strategic doctrine meaningful to all partners, pronouncements of formal unity have proved empty. None of the force levels of NATO, which have been announced periodically with much fanfare, has ever been achieved. Almost a decade after its creation, NATO is still without a force sufficient to prevent its members from being overrun by the Soviet Army. Nor has the significance of nuclear technology been fully understood, at least by our Continental allies. A NATO Council decision has declared nuclear weapons an integral part of the defense of Western Europe. But the public opinion of most of our allies and, judging from official statements, many of the leaders as well, tend to identify any explosion of a nuclear weapon with the outbreak of an all-out war. Heretofore a power threatened with attack would generally resist because the potential destruction was insignificant compared to the consequences of surrender. But when the outbreak of war has come increasingly to be considered equivalent to national catastrophe, a lagging defense effort is almost inevitable. It is doubly unfortunate that this should have happened at a time when the advent of tactical nuclear weapons in quantity has for the first time brought an adequate ground defense of Western Europe within reach.

There are many causes for the inadequacies of NATO. For one thing, the United States, by its strategic doctrine and its refusal to share atomic information, has inhibited the growth of a sense of common purpose. For another, our European allies have been unwilling to make the economic sacrifices required for a meaningful defense effort and some of them have tended to escape harsh realities by denying their existence.

So long as United States strategic doctrine identifies the defense of Europe with all-out war, a substantial military contribution by our allies is unlikely. They do not have the resources to create a retaliatory force and their small size and geographic proximity to the U.S.S.R. would make it impossible to protect such a force could it be created. They, therefore, see no sense in making a military contribution of their own except by furnishing facilities or contributing to a trip-wire for our Strategic Air Force. Since the purpose of a trip-wire is not to hold a line but to define a cause of war, it does not supply an incentive for a major effort.

Moreover, our Strategic Air Command has never been a part of the NATO structure. Since the alliance has no control over the instrument around which its whole strategy is built, there has inevitably been an air of unreality about NATO planning. The force levels of NATO almost necessarily have seemed less important than the determination of the United States to unleash its retaliatory power, if necessary.

On the other hand, to the extent that our allies have accepted the emphasis placed by our strategy on retaliatory power, they have been forced into a military effort which duplicates the strategic category in which we are already strongest. At considerable sacrifice, Great Britain has developed a strategic air force and a nuclear stockpile too small to fight an all-out war against the Soviet bloc, but sufficiently large to drain resources from the British capability for limited war, which, as events in the Middle East showed in 1956, is a much greater need for Britain. And our policy of withholding atomic information has caused the British effort in the field of strategic striking power to absorb a maximum amount of resources. Since Great Britain was prevented by our Atomic Energy Act from profiting from our research and development, it has had to duplicate much of our own effort, and to do so at great expense and with no substantial benefit to the overall strategic striking power of the free world.

Our Continental allies, deprived of access to our information about nuclear matters, and without the benefit of the British wartime experience in nuclear development, have, in turn, had no choice except to build up the conventional forces whose utility has constantly been called in question by the tactical nuclear weapons in the NATO arsenal which have remained under our exclusive control. Their exclusion from the nuclear field has made it very difficult for the Continental powers to assess the meaning of the new technology. It has contributed to the widespread confusion over the distinction between conventional and nuclear war, over the significance of tactical nuclear weapons, and over the feasibility of the local defense of Europe, which has beset NATO planning at every step.

Our reliance on an all-out strategy, therefore, has had two consequences. Either our NATO partners believe they are already protected by our assumed strategic superiority, as witnessed by the slow pace of rearmament on the Continent. Or else they strive to develop a nuclear establishment under their own control in order to reduce their dependence on the United States, as demonstrated by the course which Great Britain is pursuing. Both attitudes diminish the effectiveness of NATO: the former because it treats NATO merely as an instrument to elaborate a cause of war; the latter because it leads to a wasteful duplication of effort among the allies.

While the United States has been responsible for many of NATO's inconsistencies, our allies, with the exception of Great Britain, have not helped matters by the eagerness with which they seized upon the ambiguities of our doctrine as a justification for deferring difficult choices. Their self-confidence shaken by two World Wars, their economies strained by the recovery effort, they have recoiled before the prospect of fresh conflict. Instead of adopting the austere measures required for a major defense effort, they have tended to deny the reality of the danger or they have asserted that they were already protected by our retaliatory capability. Our Continental allies have been torn between a strategy of minimum risk and the desire for economy, between the wish for protection against Soviet occupation and the reluctance to face harsh realities. Each economy measure has been justified, much as in the United States, by the argument that the new weapons permit a reduction of forces. Yet the more fearful the resulting strategy, the more it has emphasized the sense of impotence among our allies.

These trends, however understandable, have placed the defense of Europe, and with it the strategic balance of the world, in great peril. The threat of an all-out war may have been effective in forestalling a Soviet onslaught on Europe in 1950-51; its risks have been radically altered by the growing Soviet nuclear stockpile and Long-Range Air Force. A strategy which requires us to maintain the strategic balance by the threat of suicide places a disproportionate psychological burden on us. An alliance which relies completely on the protection promised by only one of its members amounts to a unilateral guarantee.

NATO is, therefore, the key test for the possibility of an effective alliance policy in the nuclear age. If it is possible to devise a concept of defense equally meaningful to all its partners, the world may yet be spared the worst horrors of the new technology. If NATO insists on maintaining a doctrine developed to meet a different strategic equation, its efforts will become increasingly sterile. As a political organization it may retain a measure of validity, but as a military grouping it will prove ineffective. In every crisis it will force us either to resort to a suicidal nuclear war which would not save Europe from being overrun or to violate our solemn pledge. And over time, the sense of impotence among our European allies may turn into neutralism.

In order to assess the trends in NATO it will be helpful to analyze the defense policies and the attitudes taken toward nuclear matters by our strongest allies, Great Britain, Germany and France. Each is attempting to come to grips with one of the dilemmas of the nuclear period: Great Britain, through pursuing a policy of deterrence based on retaliatory power essentially similar to that of the United States; Germany, through grappling with the complexities of a local defense; France, through attempting to draw a distinction between nuclear and conventional technology.

II

Nowhere have the dilemmas posed by relying on an all-out strategy become more evident than in Great Britain. For its increasing vulnerability has not been coupled with a corresponding gain in relative strength. Britain can never hope by its own efforts to win an all-out war against the U.S.S.R. Yet in no country has the "pure" doctrine of air warfare taken a deeper hold. The notion that wars are won by destroying the enemy's industrial plant and undermining civilian morale has been as cardinal a tenet in British as in American strategic thought. As a result the predominant strategic view in Great Britain is almost identical with the United States doctrine of massive retaliation. Both place their chief reliance on the deterrent effect of the strategic air forces; both seek to inhibit aggression at its source by bombing production facilities.

In Britain, even more explicitly than in the United States, a distinction has been drawn in military doctrine between deterrent forces, identified with strategic striking power and other military forces. ". . . the strength of our forces and those of our Allies must be developed and sustained against the possibility of a major war," said the British *Statement on Defence* for 1955. "To this end increasing emphasis must be placed on the deterrent." [1] "The increased power of the deterrent," said the British *Statement on Defence* for 1956, "that is, the nuclear weapon and the means of delivering it, has made global war more frightening and less likely. Our first and chief objective must be to prevent war by maintenance of the Allied deterrent, to which we have begun to make our own substantial contribution." [2] And the British White Paper of April 1957 carried this trend to its logical conclusion by placing almost exclusive reliance on strategic striking power, particularly on intermediate-range missiles.[3]

The identification of deterrence with nuclear striking power emphasizes the basic problem of British defense policy. Nuclear weapons have revolutionized Britain's strategic position even more than that of the United States. The size of the United States and its geographic position offer at least some measure of protection in an all-out war.

[1] Great Britain, Ministry of Defence, *Statement on Defence, 1955,* Cmd. 9391 (London: HMSO, 1955), p. 6.

[2] Great Britain, Ministry of Defence, *Statement on Defence, 1956,* Cmd. 9691 (London: HMSO, 1956), p. 4.

[3] Great Britain, Ministry of Defence, *Defence: Outline of Future Policy,* Cmnd. 124 (London: HMSO, 1957).

While they cannot confer immunity, our early warning system, the geographic necessity for a Soviet attack to traverse great distances, and the dispersal of our air bases should enable us, even under the worst circumstances, to launch a part of our retaliatory force.

Great Britain enjoys no such fortunate position. In a crowded island dispersal of bases is very difficult and in any case a very few bombs—perhaps twenty of megaton size—can destroy or disable one-half of the population of Great Britain. Even under the best circumstances—assuming all British planes had been launched before the first Soviet bombs fell—the British bombing force is not powerful enough to inflict a mortal blow on the U.S.S.R., while Great Britain itself would probably be eliminated as a major power and perhaps even as a political entity by an all-out war. Given Britain's vulnerability, all-out war would seem to be the last strategy which it can afford to invoke. Why then the emphasis on strategic striking power? Why the reliance on a threat which, if implemented, must lead to the collapse of Great Britain?

The decision by Britain to develop a retaliatory force of its own reflects a problem common to all our European allies: a desire to remain world powers despite the losses suffered in the two World Wars. Heretofore a major power has been one which could conduct a war on a basis of relative equality with other major powers. With the advent of thermonuclear weapons an imbalance has been created, however, between the vulnerability of states and their ability to pose a corresponding threat. All states have become equally vulnerable, but only the United States and the U.S.S.R. possess the resources for the combination of warning systems, delivery means and weapons which provide the sinews of strategic striking power. Understandably powers which have long been the center of world affairs find it difficult to realize that even their maximum strategic effort cannot be decisive in an all-out war. But this is the basic fact of the nuclear period. Given their resources and the complexity of modern weapons, even the most powerful of our European allies must make a choice about which category of power they propose to emphasize. The attempt to be protected against every contingency leads inevitably to a dilution of their defense effort.

Its conception of its obligations as a world power has induced Great Britain to seek to duplicate the entire range of the United States military establishment with a defense budget a little more than one-tenth of ours. Such a course can only magnify the dilemmas already noted in the United States strategic doctrine. If our defense budget makes it difficult to maintain forces adequate both for limited and all-out war, Great Britain's effort to develop a dual-purpose capability must clearly lead to inadequacies in each strategic category. For a power with limited resources the wisest course is to define the most likely dangers and concentrate on meeting them. The fiasco of the British invasion of the Suez Canal Zone demonstrates that British defense planning has fallen between two stools. Its strategic striking force was not sufficient to deter a Soviet threat of rocket attacks, while its capability for limited war was not overpowering enough to gain control before pressures from other powers forced a halt in military operations.

The British White Paper on defense of 1957 indicates that Great Britain has realized the necessity of making a choice between a capability for all-out and for limited war. Unfortunately the decision to rely on an all-out strategy is not a happy solution either from the point of view of the over-all strategic balance or from that of Great Britain's immediate security interests. Regardless of the size of its retaliatory force, Great Britain cannot hope to win or even to conduct an all-out war without United States assistance. It would therefore seem to have been wiser for Britain to concentrate on developing forces for limited war and for the local defense of Europe.

To be sure, such a division of functions between us and the European ally most willing to make a substantial military effort has not been encouraged either by the United States Atomic Energy Act or by our strategic doctrine. Unable to obtain either atomic information or nuclear weapons from the United States, Britain has been forced into an atomic program of its own on a scale which has drained resources which might have been used better for other purposes. Moreover, Britain's decision to build up a strategic striking force has been due at least in part to a basic inconsistency within the NATO strategic concept: that the weapon on which NATO relies both for deterrence and for waging war—the United States Strategic Air Command—has remained under exclusive American control. In case of a crisis Great Britain could not be certain that our view of what constitutes an essential target would accord with its own. As a result, one of the chief justifications advanced for the British strategic striking force has been to give Britain control over selecting some of the targets which must be attacked in the early stages of any war. "There are . . . big administrative and industrial targets behind the Iron Curtain," said Sir Winston Churchill in 1955, foreshadowing every subsequent British *Statement on Defence,* "and any effective deterrent policy must have the power to paralyse them all at the outset, or shortly after. . . . Unless we make a contribution of our own . . . we cannot be sure that in an emergency the resources of other Powers would be planned exactly as we would wish, or that the targets which would threaten us most would be given what we consider the necessary priority. . . ." [4]

What has happened between us and our strongest ally has been the same duplication of functions which has already been produced within the United States military establishment through the absence of an agreed strategic doctrine. Because no one of our military services can be certain that a sister service's interpretation of what constitutes an essential target will be the same as its own, it strives to bring under its control every weapon which can have any bearing on the performance of its mission. Similarly, Britain, in order to be able to attack targets it considers vital, has created a strategic striking force which is incapable of fighting an all-out war by itself and useful only to ensure a measure of control over the common

[4] House of Commons *Debates,* v. 315 (March 1, 1955), col. 1901. (Hereafter referred to as *Hansard.*)

target system in a war which cannot be fought without United States assistance.

There must be some more imaginative means of coordinating target selection within an alliance than through a duplication of effort which is, in effect, an attempt to get along without allies. Instead of withholding atomic information, we should have made available nuclear weapons in quantity, and we could have coordinated our war plans much more closely with Britain's. Another possibility would have been to place a number of wings of our Strategic Air Command under British control, on the model of the Soviet specialist "volunteer" units in Korea and the Middle East. Behind this shield Great Britain could then have concentrated on developing its capability for limited war. In terms of the dangers confronting it, its vulnerability and the over-all interest of the alliance, an emphasis by Britain on forces for limited war would have made a major contribution toward restoring the strategic balance. To be sure, such a course would have met obstacles both in the United States and Great Britain, but they would have been more than outweighed by the strengthening of common purpose and the increase in common strength.

The argument that Great Britain would have been better served by emphasizing a strategy of limited war does not mean that it should not have entered the nuclear race. British statesmen were wise in insisting that without nuclear weapons of its own, Britain would be relegated to the position of a third-class power. But the possession of nuclear weapons was unnecessarily identified with an all-out strategy and with an emphasis on strategic striking power as the chief deterrent. A strategic striking force may deter an attack on Great Britain, although even this is doubtful so long as it cannot be a decisive factor. In any other situation it confronts Britain with the dilemma of whether an attack which is explicitly less than all-out shall be resisted by a strategy which involves national suicide. Moreover, a strategy which regards NATO as the trigger for the United States and British Air Forces comes up against the fact that the Continental powers have no particular incentive for providing more than the minimum forces required for a trip-wire.

The effort to overcome the reluctance to rearm of the Continental powers has created another imbalance in British military policy: the British Army of the Rhine, with its four divisions, the counterpart to the five American divisions in Germany. The difficulty with these forces is not that they represent a strategic diversion, although in terms of all-out strategy they are one, but that they constitute less the expression of a strategic doctrine than a concession to Continental fears. They are stationed in Europe as a warning to the U.S.S.R. and as an encouragement for our European allies to increase their defense contributions. The American and British forces in Western Europe thus have a dual and partly contradictory role: to convince the U.S.S.R. that an attack on Western Europe would bring on an all-out war and to persuade the Continental powers that Soviet aggression can be contained on the ground.

Both positions are to be found in British statements arguing the need for substantial ground forces. The *Statements on Defence* for 1954, 1955 and 1956 maintained that Great Britain required an army for the conduct of limited wars, identified with wars on the periphery of Eurasia. The *Statement* for 1954 spoke of the necessity of maintaining an army on the Continent for the "broken-backed" warfare which would follow the initial nuclear exchange.[5] Subsequent *Statements* have dropped the reference to "broken-backed" warfare, but this only emphasizes the dilemma of the British forces in Germany. For, if the distinction between a limited war and an all-out war is based on the difference between a war in Asia and a war in Europe, it is difficult to justify pinning down so large a British contingent on the Continent. What is to be the purpose of ground forces in an all-out war that, according to every *Statement on Defence,* would be largely fought as an air battle?

The answers have been as ambivalent as the strategic

---

[5] Great Britain, Ministry of Defence, *Statement on Defence, 1954,* Cmd. 9075 (London: HMSO, 1954), pp. 4-5.

doctrine from which they derive. It has been argued that ground forces stationed on the Continent permit the holding of a line until the nuclear counteroffensive has broken the enemy's back; [6] that the use of tactical nuclear weapons makes possible a forward strategy which may assure the defense of Europe on the ground,[7] that a defense of Europe is essential to keep Great Britain from again having to undertake the grim business of liberation and to prevent the U.S.S.R. from using Europe "as a shameful pawn" in negotiations.[8]

Each of these arguments raises as many questions as it answers. On the scale of devastation produced by an all-out thermonuclear war, it will be difficult to sustain any substantial ground action once the troops become aware of the devastation at home. If, on the other hand, the employment of tactical nuclear weapons permits a ground defense of Europe, there would seem to be no sense in accompanying it with a thermonuclear exchange which may well lead to the social collapse of both sides and which would in any case inflict catastrophic losses on Great Britain. The most convincing argument in favor of stationing British troops on the Continent is the proposition that, since neither the United States nor the United Kingdom would have sufficient resources left for a major effort to liberate Europe, the net result of all-out war might be Soviet domination of Eurasia unless the forces on the spot are sufficiently strong to hold a line. Thus the outcome of an all-out war would, according to this view, still be determined by the ability to hold or seize territory. If this is true, however, reliance on all-out war becomes not only costly but irrelevant. If the issue even of an all-out war depends ultimately on the outcome of the ground battle, it would seem to be the task of strategy to contest the possession of territory initially by means less drastic than all-out war.

To be sure, the White Paper for 1957 has sought to achieve consistency by reducing the British ground com-

---

6 *Statement on Defence, 1955,* cited, p. 4.

7 Same, p. 7.

8 Same, p. 8.

mitment on the Continent. But this course has merely accentuated the imbalance between Great Britain's strategic doctrine and its coalition policy, between its policy of deterrence and the strategy it is prepared to implement. The British *Statements on Defence* imply that *any* aggression in Europe will be deterred by the threat of all-out war. But the thermonuclear capability is primarily effective in deterring an all-out surprise attack against the home territory. Against other provocations—those of most concern to our Continental allies—the thermonuclear deterrent will either magnify the inhibitions against decisive action or will produce an all-out war without having exhausted all intermediate alternatives.

Given Britain's vulnerability, it is not surprising that this realization should have been more explicitly formulated in Great Britain than in the United States, although the basic argument of the advocates of "graduated deterrence" applies equally to the United States. The main thrust of the advocates of graduated deterrence is directed against the deliberate ambiguity of British defense policy. In NATO, this policy combines tactical atomic weapons with conventional ground forces supplemented by the threat of massive retaliation, but without making it clear under what contingencies these forces would be employed and for what kind of war they are designed. These were the arguments advanced by Denis Healey, an able Labour M.P.:

> If we are relying, as the Prime Minister suggested, on the deterrent of mutual terror, the greater the terror the greater the deterrent. The appalling ambiguity of the White Paper in this respect is that it does not make clear whether full-scale thermo-nuclear war must be the inevitable consequence of aggression in Europe. . . . The question we must ask ourselves . . . is: Does the White Paper mean that we must be prepared to use thermo-nuclear weapons from the word "go" against a strategic target, such as a centre of population inside the Soviet Union—or does it simply mean that we must use whatever weight of nuclear power is required in a tactical area, that is to say, an area where land fighting is going on upon the Continent? . . . If the Russians even think

that it is our intention to drop thermonuclear weapons upon their cities the moment fighting begins in Europe, then certainly the moment anything approaching a state of war develops in Europe Russia will start by dropping these weapons upon us. . . . It seems to me that the appalling ambiguity of the White Paper immensely increases the danger of a completely unnecessary thermonuclear war which might lead to the destruction of mankind. . . . The second great danger, if the Government really mean that any aggression in Europe will result in full-scale thermonuclear war, is that any local incident in Europe will leave us with no alternative between self-destruction . . . and appeasement.[9]

The difference between the advocates of graduated deterrence and the Government position thus resolved itself into a debate about a familiar problem: where to strike the balance between a policy of deterrence and the strategy for fighting a war should deterrence fail. The advocates of graduated deterrence, concerned with the strategy for conducting a war, have sought to insure that it would be fought in a noncatastrophic manner. A strategy, they argue, that inevitably involves destruction of the national substance is self-defeating. As a result, the advocates of graduated deterrence have proposed a strategy which would return war to a battlefield, however defined, and which would be directed against hostile military forces, not against civilian morale or industrial facilities. Graduated deterrence amounts to a strategy of limited war even for the defense of Europe.[10]

By contrast, the British Government, concerned with achieving maximum deterrence, has identified its strategic problem with the threat of maximum destruction. The proponents of the predominant strategic school in Britain, like their counterparts in the United States, reject the concept of graduated deterrence for two contradictory

9 *Hansard*, cited, col. 1935 ff. See also Denis Healey, "The Atom Bomb and the Alliance," *Confluence*, v. 5 (April 1956), pp. 70-8; and "The Bomb that Didn't Go Off," *Encounter* (July 1955), pp. 5-9.

10 See Sir Anthony W. Buzzard, "Graduated Deterrence," *World Politics*, v. 8 (January 1956), p. 230; for an American view, see Richard S. Leghorn, "No Need to Bomb Cities to Win Wars," *U.S. News and World Report*, v. 38 (January 28, 1955), p. 84 ff.; see above, Chapters 5 and 6, for a fuller development of these points.

reasons: that a distinction between the tactical and strategic uses of weapons is difficult to make and impossible to enforce; and that an intermediate course, by reducing the dangers faced by the Soviet Union, would increase its willingness to run risks. Sir Walter Monckton, while Minister of Defence, said:

> I am far from saying that any aggressive move against the West would inevitably be countered by the use of the hydrogen bomb. One cannot be specific in a matter of this kind, but one can imagine circumstances in which local aggression might be dealt with quite effectively by local retaliation. One cannot say that retaliation would not involve the tactical use of atomic weapons. . . . Nevertheless, I do not think . . . that it would be a practicable policy for any Government to define precisely in advance the circumstances in which it would use some weapons and not others. Any attempt to make a definition of that kind in advance . . . . might help others, who may be pondering on the question of whether they could take risks, to see how far they might go without bringing down upon them the ultimate deterrent. . . . Moreover, there is the further consideration that even if it were assumed that the adoption of the policy of graduated deterrence was right in itself, would there be any reasonable ground for believing that its adoption would ensure the adoption of a similar policy by the other parties to the argument? I think there are solid grounds for taking the other view.[11]

Graduated deterrence has, therefore, been rejected as both impractical and unwise, as making aggression more likely by reducing the threat to the aggressor, and as inadequate to prevent all-out war because of the impossibility of making distinctions between various types of nuclear warfare. These arguments are, in fact, inconsistent with each other and with British defense policy. If it is impractical to make distinctions between different types of nuclear warfare, it will be impossible to use nuclear weapons for local defense even on the periphery of Eurasia where every *Statement on Defence* has assumed their employment as a matter of course. And if it is unwise to make distinc-

---

[11] *Hansard,* v. 345 (February 28, 1956), col. 1,041.

tions, then the issue is only one of practicality. If a distinction between tactical and strategic weapons is workable in peripheral wars, it would seem only logical that the same distinction could be applied in a European war.

Thus British strategic doctrine suffers from the same inconsistencies as ours. Even more incongruously than in our case, it reflects nostalgia for a time when security was absolute and control over a great power's survival rested entirely in its own hands. When Britain reduced its defense budget, it did so significantly, in the category of its limited war capability, by reducing its ground forces with the argument that missiles had increased the power of the deterrent.[12] But the emphasis on a strategy which stakes the national substance on every dispute deprives the British defense effort of political effectiveness and causes NATO increasingly to lack a sense of direction. Vis-à-vis the United States, the British strategic striking force does not give the United Kingdom a stronger negotiating position, for it represents only a marginal increment to the capability in which we are strongest. The primary use of its strategic striking force is that it frees Britain to some small degree from its dependence on the selection of targets by the United States Strategic Air Force in case of an all-out war. But it achieves this only to a small degree because Britain could not hope to win an all-out war by itself. The bases made available to us by Britain are more important for our strategy and more useful to British diplomacy than the British strategic air force. And with respect to Europe the British reliance on an all-out strategy helps to undermine the willingness of our Continental allies to undertake a substantial military effort. The British defense effort reflects the absence of an agreed strategy, either with the United States or with our Continental allies. By adopting our theory of deterrence as its own, Britain has thrown into sharp relief the urgent necessity, if NATO is to be maintained, of developing a new approach to the defense of Europe.

---

12 See, for example, Duncan Sandys' conversation with Charles E. Wilson, *New York Times*, February 14, 1957.

III

With these uncertainties over doctrine among the two strongest powers of the Western alliance, it is little wonder that the other NATO powers should be torn between a desire for security and a wish to escape the consequences of an all-out war. The strategy developed by the dominant NATO powers has been based on the assumption that the United States and the United Kingdom have the option of local defense *or* of all-out war and that the choice between them depended on a balancing of the risks of a policy of deterrence against those of a strategy for fighting a war in the event deterrence should fail. However correct this conception of alternatives may be for us and for Britain, it has no meaning for our Continental allies. They lack the resources for developing a retaliatory capability and they believe that in an all-out war the fate of Europe will be decided by the contest between the United States and Soviet Air Forces. Thus decisions on nuclear strategy have been taken in an atmosphere that could only emphasize the feeling of impotence already prevalent among our Continental allies. Not without justice a leading German newspaper commented editorially on the NATO decision of December 17, 1954, to base the defense of Europe on nuclear weapons: "Allied atomic strategy already exerts an influence on our political destiny such as the Prussian General Staff never dared contemplate." [13] There are many reasons for the lag in the build-up of NATO, not all of them connected with United States strategy. But the difficulty of assigning a strategic significance to the Continental defense contributions has been the most important single factor.

The inconsistencies of NATO strategy have reacted perhaps most strongly on Germany, the ally which will have to bear the first impact of a Soviet attack and whose defense contribution has been considered the keystone of NATO. The impact of nuclear strategy upon German opinion has been all the greater because very little discus-

---

[13] *Frankfurter Allgemeine Zeitung*, June 23, 1955.

sion of military problems had taken place during the first
eight years after the war. This apathy had been due in
part to the shock of defeat, in part to the conviction that
Germany was protected by the United States atomic monopoly. Furthermore, the loss of the war and the discredit-
ing of the officer corps led most of Germany's military
experts to ignore the new weapons technology in favor of
studying the past or of defending their own actions. Except for reprints of Western studies, only a dozen or so
articles on nuclear weapons appeared in Germany between
1950 and 1954.[14] Most of them were restatements of the
Anglo-American theory of deterrence and therefore tended
to confirm the prevalent view that the defense of Germany
depended on United States readiness for all-out war. A few
articles gave overt or disguised support to the Communist
view, emphasizing the horror of atomic weapons, while
deprecating their impact on strategy.[15]

When the United States began to press for German
membership in NATO, however, and rearmament loomed
above the horizon, Germany was confronted directly with
the question of defining the purpose of its military contribution and its place in the over-all Western strategy. From
the beginning it was apparent that rearmament could be
justified within Germany, not in terms of its contribution
to a global strategy, but only as a means to defend German
territory. German newspapers commented critically on
the early efforts of NATO to turn the Rhine into a defensive bastion and on the construction of fortifications,
depots and airfields on its west bank.[16] A former German
military attaché in London, Geye von Schweppenburg,
who had commanded an armored division in World War
II, doubtless expressed the predominant feeling in Ger-

---

14 J. Robert Oppenheimer's article, "Atomic Weapons and American
Policy," *Foreign Affairs*, v. 31 (July 1953), pp. 525-35, was reprinted in
Aussenpolitik, v. 4 (November 1953).

15 Axel von dem Bussche, "Moderne Waffen-Atomare Strategie," *Die
Zeit*, v. 8 (November 5, 1953), represents the first of these categories. "Der
Kampf der Völker um das Verbot der Atomwaffe und die friedliche An-
wendung der Atomenergie," *Berichte des deutschen Wirtschaftsinstituts*
(Berlin), v. 5, no. 11 (1954), p. 20, is typical of the second category.

16 *Nürnberger Nachrichten*, October 22, 1955.

many: "The Germans are not interested in winning the last battle. They want to be defended, not liberated." [17]

As a result, within Germany the Western allies advocated German rearmament in terms differing from the strategic doctrine which prevailed at home. There the allies avoided talking of the "trip-wire" or the "plate glass window." On the contrary, General Eisenhower commented to a *New York Times* correspondent that the most striking result of adding twelve German divisions would be "the extension of the field of practical operations eastward from the Rhine." [18] General McAuliffe asserted that the addition of German troops would permit NATO to give up its earlier strategic concept of a withdrawal behind the Rhine and to defend Western Germany. [19] And the same theme was reiterated by General Gruenther.

But Germany's geographic position is so precarious that even a strategy that sought to defend the Federal Republic was not sufficient to overcome German hesitations. The next concern was to define a tactical doctrine which would stop a Soviet attack at the zonal boundary along the Elbe. The attack on the concept of a fluid defense of Germany was led by Adelbert Weinstein, the military commentator of the highly respected and generally pro-Western *Frankfurter Allgemeine Zeitung*. It gained impetus from Colonel Bogislav von Bonin, head of the planning section of the embryonic Defense Ministry, who resigned over the issue of how Germany could best be defended. In a brochure entitled "No One Can Win the War" Weinstein asserted that the NATO forces could not hold the line of the Elbe against the preponderance of Soviet armor and artillery. Western planners had therefore developed a strategy which envisaged using German troops as a screen while the main allied force withdrew to fortified positions on both sides of the Rhine, from which it would then attempt to cut Soviet communications and trap Soviet troops through a

---

[17] *Sueddeutsche Zeitung* (Munich), October 22, 1955.

[18] Drew Middleton, "NATO Changes Direction," *Foreign Affairs*, v. 31 (April 1953), p. 438.

[19] *Sueddeutsche Zeitung*, April 13, 1955.

series of encircling maneuvers.[20] The strategy of elastic defense, according to Weinstein, would transform West Germany into a battlefield: "Must not every German be deeply shocked by such considerations? We must ask ourselves whether we are the remainder of a nation fighting for its existence or whether we want to become the testing ground for unrealistic strategists determined to apply dogmatically in our territory a kind of warfare that can lead only to chaos, and not to victory. The idea of a bridgehead in the Frankfurt area shows a strangely abstract form of strategic thinking and a surprising lack of political instinct."[21] Weinstein accordingly proposed the creation of a static defense belt, thirty miles wide, along the Soviet boundary, to be heavily equipped with antitank weapons and backed by a highly mobile reserve designed to seal off Soviet breakthroughs.

Weinstein's plan was almost identical with a program developed by Colonel von Bonin. Bonin's program, first presented in July 1954, was rejected by the other planners in the German Defense Ministry. When Bonin continued to advocate his program through unofficial media, he was dismissed from the ministry. Subsequently published in the press, Bonin's plan stirred up much controversy. Its salient features reflected the same concern as Weinstein's with preventing both the occupation of West Germany and its transformation into a battlefield:

> Rearmament cannot have the purpose of turning Germany into the forward area of an elastic defense of Western Europe. Nor can its purpose merely be to deter the Soviets from aggression. . . . We view rearmament as a means to defend our country on its borders and to spare it, as far as possible, the horrors of a land war. . . . We see the only solution of this problem in a program under which, aside from a few armored divisions, the overwhelming mass of the new army is organized as blocking formations (*Sperrverbaende*) of

---

20 Adelbert Weinstein, *Keiner kann den Krieg gewinnen* (Bonn: Schimmelbusch, 1955), pp. 7-10. Although no authoritative pronouncements regarding allied strategy exist, there is little doubt that Weinstein's version is substantially correct.

21 Same, p. 12.

the most modern kind. Equipped with large quantities of antitank guns and automatic weapons, provided with strong engineer forces . . . fully motorized and hence highly mobile in any kind of terrain . . . and adequately supported by atomic artillery and antitank units . . . these blocking units should cover a defensive zone about thirty miles deep along the border of the Red Army and its armored masses. In other words, it is necessary to view the future German forces not . . . from the aspect of a defense of Western Europe but from that of a tactical defense close to the border.[22]

The remarkable thing about these plans is not their revolutionary quality, in which Bonin and Weinstein took such pride, but their conventionality. What was proposed was in effect a World War II type of defense to which atomic weapons had been added literally as an afterthought, for Bonin's first draft had contained no reference to atomic artillery.[23] It was a symptom of the barrenness of German strategic thought that one of the chief planners of the new Defense Ministry could propose a defensive zone of only thirty miles' width in a nuclear war and a tactical organization even more cumbersome than the World War II type of division. Indeed, the chief advantage claimed by Bonin for his plan was the rigidity it would impose on military maneuvers.

Although militarily obsolescent, Bonin's plan reflected the realities of the psychological situation within Germany. German rearmament could be made acceptable domestically only if it assured the defense of German territory. In discussions about German rearmament, the deterrent power of strategic bombing was rarely mentioned, partly because of ignorance about the nature of all-out war, but above all because all-out war is not an acceptable strategic option for Germany. Even Bonin's critics accepted his premise that any defense of Europe must start at the border of West Germany; they rejected his plan either on technical grounds or because current allied strategy already included this objective. "Once Germany is included in NATO," wrote the official

22 *Der Spiegel*, v. 9 (March 30, 1955), pp. 8-9.
23 Parlementarisch-Politische Pressedienst, April 1955.

organ of the Association for Military Science, an organization of former officers, "no military commander could do other than attempt a defense as far forward as possible, that is to say, at the zonal borders. Even if it did not coincide with German interests, as happens to be the case, he would have to do so because of the insufficient depth of the free Western European area. On the issue of forward defense, allied and German strategic interests are in harmony. . . ." [24]

It is against this background that the full impact of the nuclear age burst upon Germany. Until the end of 1954 all strategic discussions had assumed that an atomic war would be fought as a strategic air battle between the United States and the U.S.S.R. and that atomic weapons were so costly and difficult to manufacture that they would be employed only against strategic targets.[25] But when the NATO Council decided on December 17, 1954, that tactical atomic weapons would be used in the defense of Europe, the nature of nuclear war became of cardinal importance for German strategic thought. Even then most German military men continued to insist that atomic weapons had not affected the basic principles of strategy or tactics, as they had been applied in the two World Wars.[26] German strategic thought had thus occurred in a vacuum. It was motivated more by anxiety to avoid Soviet occupation than by an understanding of the implications of allied strategy, and it was further handicapped by a lack of comprehension of nuclear matters.

The first exposure to the real NATO strategy inevitably came as a severe shock to German opinion. The occasion for the awakening to the nature of allied strategy was a tactical exercise conducted by the allied air forces in Central Europe between June 20-28, 1955, under the somewhat inappropriate code name of "Carte Blanche."

---

24 Joachim Rogge, "Strategie des Wunschtraums," *Wehrkunde*, v. 4 (May 1955), p. 177 ff. See also Georg von Sodenstern, "Strategie oder Sicherheit," *Wehrwissenshaftliche Rundschau*, v. 5 (July 1955), p. 289 ff.

25 Otto Wien, "Gedanken über den strategischen Luftkrieg," *Wehrkunde*, v. 3 (1954), p. 352.

26 Eberhard Schmidt-Krusemarck, "Zur Anwendung der Atomwaffen im Felde," *Wehrkunde*, v. 3 (1954), p. 355.

Based on accepted air doctrine that the key to success was the elimination of the hostile air force through bombing enemy airfields, "Carte Blanche" for the first time involved the simulated mass dropping of atomic bombs over western Germany, the Lowlands and eastern France. The exercise was conducted in a north-south direction, partly because of political considerations but mainly to afford sufficient space for maneuver by high-speed jet aircraft. True to the British and American doctrine, the exercise began with a surprise attack by "Northland" (northwest Germany, Holland and Belgium) on air bases and other installations in "Southland" (southern Germany and eastern France). In the first attack 25 nuclear weapons were dropped. On the following day "Southland" forces dropped 55 bombs on "Northland" targets, half of them on airfields. Altogether 335 bombs were dropped within forty-eight hours, 171 on southern and 164 on northern targets.

Germany was thus exposed for the first time to a demonstration of what had heretofore been an abstract doctrine for it, however well developed it may have been in Great Britain and the United States. The impact of "Carte Blanche" was all the greater because it was witnessed by a large number of German journalists who, as observers, had been flown throughout the exercise area in allied military aircraft. By this arrangement, the full realization of the meaning of nuclear war was brought home to a psychologically unprepared population. In their extensive accounts the journalists combined praise for the realistic execution of the exercise with warnings about the grim prospects posed by atomic warfare for Europe and its peoples. All accounts stressed that in a nuclear war it would make little or no difference whether it was fought with tactical or strategic weapons. What could victory mean in a conflict that would bring total devastation to the area between Helgoland, Salzburg, Dunkirk and Dijon? [27]

German strategic thinking, which had only recently

---

[27] *Sueddeutsche Zeitung*, July 2, 1955.

been striving for an adaptation of World War II doctrine to assure a ground defense at the zonal border, now came up against the realities of the nuclear period. Because the exposure had been so sudden, the conclusions went from the extreme of stationary defense to the opposite extreme of all-out war. What emerged in Germany, at first crudely and then in more sophisticated formulations, was the assertion that any employment of nuclear weapons would inevitably lead to all-out war, thus undermining the entire basis of German rearmament. "Against the background of the air war test, the defense debate in Parliament strikes us as somewhat stale," wrote a leading German newspaper. ". . . if it is true that the NATO maneuvers have revealed a strategic revolution, the effect will be to blur the line between atomic and conventional weapons which so far has furnished the rationale of the twelve German divisions. The benefits supposedly derived from rearmament would become meaningless and obsolete while it was still in progress." [28]

"Carte Blanche" had been designed as a warning to the Soviet leaders and as a means to reassure Germany that NATO, by using tactical nuclear weapons, would be able to protect its territory. In fact, it became a demonstration that the power of nuclear weapons inhibits their use unless there exists a doctrine which poses alternatives less stark than total devastation. "From the point of view of psychological warfare," wrote the Bonn correspondent of a leading Swiss newspaper, "the outcome of the air battle was indecisive so far as the German public was concerned. The element of alarm that 'Carte Blanche' produced has been systematically kept alive by some publicists. Their aim obviously was to interpret 'Carte Blanche' in a way that would make the twelve German divisions appear hopelessly outmoded. . . . Now the political aim of 'Carte Blanche' was undoubtedly to give the enemy a convincing demonstration that the West possessed enough tactical atomic weapons to destroy his air bases and assembly areas. . . . However, the danger that the strategic content of

[28] Same, June 29, 1955.

NATO is being undermined in the public consciousness of the Federal Republic by fears of atomic war is not to be taken lightly. It will have to be dealt with sooner or later." [29]

Unfortunately the Government of the Federal Republic has not been able to deal with this problem because it is beset by the same ambivalence toward nuclear weapons which characterizes strategic thought in Britain and the United States. The German Government has not been able to achieve any greater clarity on the question of whether limited nuclear war in Europe is practicable or of the purpose of conventional forces if an attack on Western Europe will inevitably unleash all-out war. In a reply to the critics of "Carte Blanche," the then Defense Minister, Dr. Theodor Blank, asserted that tests in Nevada had demonstrated that ground troops, if properly dispersed, could survive an atomic attack; that in a period of nuclear plenty, both sides might abstain from using nuclear weapons, thereby making conventional war more likely; that in any case, ground troops were required to defend air bases and occupy territory.[30] In the debate over conscription the same arguments were repeated by an official spokesman for the Government.[31]

These arguments showed that Germany, again like its Western allies, sought to be prepared for every contingency while evading the real issues of a nuclear strategy. It is true that ground forces can survive an atomic attack but only if they have been properly trained and if they use tactics appropriate to nuclear war. The German Defense Minister may have been correct in his contention that it is possible to turn the nuclear stalemate into a shield behind which to fight a conventional war. But the nature of a war depends not only on one's own intentions but also on the assessment of these intentions by the other side. And the presence of nuclear weapons in NATO, the "Carte Blanche" exercise and the frequent pronouncements of allied military leaders seem to insure that, if the Soviet

---

[29] *Neue Zuercher Zeitung,* July 13, 1955.
[30] *Bulletin des Bundespresseamtes,* July 19, 1955, p. 113; see also p. 42.
[31] *Das Parlament* (Bonn), July 11, 1956.

Government launches its army into Europe, it is likely to do so in the expectation of a nuclear war. The protection of allied air bases is undoubtedly of crucial importance. It is more than doubtful, however, whether German public opinion would consider the protection of allied air bases a sufficient justification for a German defense effort.

The problem in Germany, as in the other countries of the alliance, therefore, resolves itself into two questions: Is a local defense of Europe possible? Is limited nuclear war a meaningful strategy? Chancellor Konrad Adenauer obviously believes in the possibility of a local war in Europe, for he used it as an argument in favor of conscription. "It is unrealistic always to imagine that a future war will be fought on the largest scale. I am of the opinion that it is essential to confine any potential conflict to one of local character . . . so as to prevent the outbreak of an intercontinental war with rockets." [32] But if Dr. Adenauer believes in the theoretical possibility of a local war in Europe, neither his policy, nor that of his chief allies, has prepared the necessary political or psychological framework. As long as German public opinion is ignorant of the nature of limited nuclear war and identifies the explosion of any nuclear device with the prelude to all-out war, the NATO decision to use nuclear weapons in the defense of Europe will confirm a feeling of futility and inhibit a substantial German defense effort. No formal announcements of a forward strategy are likely to shake the German conviction that in an all-out war local defense is largely irrelevant. "As conventional weapons are losing their importance, the West will be less dependent on German soldiers," wrote Erich Dethleffsen, a former general, now head of an influential group of industrialists and scientists (Wirtschaftspolitische Vereinigung von 1947). "West Germany will become less significant for the Americans . . . as the center of gravity of warfare shifts to atomic weapons. . . . The radar warning net stretching from North Africa over Spain and France to England and including Germany could provide adequate

32 *Bulletin des Bundespresseamtes*, August 21, 1956.

protection of the American continent against atomic attack." [33]

"Carte Blanche" and the NATO decision to use nuclear weapons can be reassuring for Germany only if they are coupled with a doctrine that is relevant to Germany's primary concern, which is to prevent Soviet occupation should deterrence fail. "Carte Blanche" demonstrated that the allied air forces in Europe can in effect fight only with atomic weapons, or at least it was so interpreted by responsible Germans.[34] But "Carte Blanche" did not make clear the relationship of the reliance on nuclear weapons to the strategic problems of Germany. In the face of the generally held notion that the employment of nuclear weapons would inevitably lead to all-out war, the military purpose of the alliance has shown signs of disintegrating. Fritz Erler, a Social Democratic leader, has expressed his disquiet over an alliance in which Germany seems to have no military function: "We are about to become an ally which is no longer acceptable, as the belated echo of a policy about to be discarded. We should heed the warning furnished by such examples as Syngman Rhee, Chiang Kai-shek or Bao Dai. The damage which would result from such a development would have to be borne by the entire German nation." [35]

Thus at the precise moment when the legal obstacles to German rearmament had been removed through Germany's joining NATO and passage of the conscription law, all the strategic premises for a German defense effort have been called in question because of the failure to develop a strategic doctrine which will be equally meaningful for all the partners. Nothing illustrates better the plethora of proposed solutions than the motley military establishment that has grown up on German soil: tactical air forces based on the use of nuclear weapons and wedded to a doctrine of air superiority which bids fair to transform any war into

---

[33] Erich Dethleffsen, "Apathie des Grauens," *Offene Welt*, no. 38 (July-August 1955), pp. 5-9.

[34] See an assessment in the professional *Wehrkunde*, v. 4 (May 1955), p. 351.

[35] *Das Parlament*, July 7, 1956.

an all-out holocaust; American and British divisions essentially of World War II type but with nuclear weapons added; a logistic structure dependent on a very small number of supply centers which can be eliminated by a few well-placed nuclear weapons. And all this is backed up by the United States and British strategic air forces, which are capable of fighting a war without any reference to NATO and are outside its direct control.

Against this background, what is surprising is not the German criticism of NATO strategy but its moderation. Nevertheless, the psychological basis of a common effort is disintegrating even while the physical power of the alliance is growing. There seems to be little sense in Germany's developing conventional divisions when the doctrine of its chief allies is based on a nuclear strategy. Even a German army equipped with the most modern weapons and trained in the most up-to-date tactics will lack a sense of direction unless it can find a place in a coherent strategy. NATO has become an alliance in search of a purpose.

IV

If in Great Britain and the United States the impact of nuclear weapons has produced a debate between the advocates of massive retaliation and of graduated deterrence, and if in Germany it resolved itself into an inquiry into the feasibility of local defense, in France the problems of the nuclear age have turned into a discussion of whether it is possible to escape the dilemmas of nuclear strategy by refusing to participate in it. France has refused to acquire an atomic stockpile, at least in the short run, but this decision has served only to postpone France's dilemma. For the decision to concentrate on the peaceful applications of nuclear energy has raised as many problems as it has solved: the distinction between military and civilian uses, the role of France in a world of nuclear powers, and the nature of security. And towering over it all is the end-product of the peaceful atomic energy program. The ever growing stockpile of plutonium, a constant temptation to enter the military field, is a standing reminder that the nuclear age cannot be evaded. The more France has sought to escape the dilemmas of the new technology, the more they have obtruded themselves.

While the French decision not to produce nuclear weapons has not solved the strategic or the political problem, it has caused the debate over nuclear policy to be pressed on two incommensurable planes: of strategy and of abstract moral principles. "It is necessary to speak frankly," wrote Paul Gérardot, an advocate of nuclear armament. "Do we want France to possess, as is possible, the modern and effective arm which can guarantee the defense of its independence and its sovereignty? Or do we really want to resign ourselves to France's having only outdated and worthless arms, worthy at best of a colonized nation which France incidentally is beginning to become? If we do not want to produce the indispensable nuclear arms, it is a waste of time to speak about French independence, for economic and political independence do not exist without a minimum of military independence. . . ." [36]

The reply to this challenge was in terms not of strategy but of prestige: "So far as the diplomatic aspect of the problem is concerned the response is clear," said a spokesman of the Socialist party, whose comments found an echo in all except the Gaullist party. "We would instantly lose the incontestable prestige which we have acquired as the sole great power which has opted for the peaceful uses of nuclear energy. We would be classified immediately as protagonists of the armaments race, alas, without even possessing the bomb." [37]

It was a remarkable argument that France could escape the dilemmas of the nuclear age by refusing to participate in its military applications, and it was also a symptom of a large measure of ignorance about atomic matters. It was the almost instinctive reaction of a power which had seen its influence decline after centuries of playing the premier role and which sought to substitute prestige for its lack of

---

[36] General Paul Gérardot, "Pour des armements atomiques," *Le Monde,* February 2, 1955.

[37] Marcel Roubault, "Socialisme et énergie nucléaire," *Revue Socialiste* (May 1955), p. 456.

power. Yet the decision against producing nuclear weapons left a vague feeling of uneasiness. How could France play a mediating role, as was advocated by the proponents of renouncing the production of nuclear weapons, if it did not possess sufficient strength to lend weight to its opinion? "If France and Western Europe wish to be respected and to play an important role in the world," wrote a French Deputy, "they must possess nuclear arms which cost less than the useless conventional arms with which we are equipped at present. . . . How can Western Europe play the role of a peaceful third force to which it aspires if its defensive organization remains at the mercy of a simple atomic threat?" [38]

French ambivalence was best demonstrated by an editorial in the influential *Le Monde*, supporting the decision against producing nuclear weapons, but warning France's allies against interpreting this as a renunciation of French influence:

> The statements [by Edgar Faure announcing the French decision to conc trate on peaceful uses of atomic energy] constitute an important political act. . . . France's position, far from undermining her prestige will be able to command respect. . . . Certain commentators in Great Britain have interpreted this renunciation as evidence of "harmonious cooperation" among the NATO powers. If by the latter phrase it is to be understood that France is resigned to being the tail-end of the alliance, it is necessary to demonstrate that . . . we intend to place ourselves at the head of those who wish to eliminate the terrifying menace which weighs upon the destiny of humanity. [39]

Thus France wanted to have the best of both worlds: it wished to play a principal role in allied councils, but without assuming the responsibility for effective defense. It desired to remain a great power, while following a policy of minimum risk. It is little wonder that a French officer replied with exasperation to these efforts to avoid a problem by denying that it existed:

---

[38] André Philip, Letter to the Editor, *Le Monde*, July 8, 1954.
[39] *Le Monde*, April 15, 1955.

It is . . . normal that the voices of military men in France are calling for atomic armament. What is surprising is that certain circles have been irritated by such an appeal. These are no doubt the same circles which criticized the military men after June 1940 for preparing for the last war and who sought to explain the causes of our defeat by the lack of imagination of our higher officers and by a serious backwardness in our armaments. Today it appears that the military are alone in drawing the lessons of our defeat.[40]

While the French military may have been more realistic than their political colleagues in pressing for the production of nuclear weapons, the strategy they propose for utilizing them helps produce inhibitions against going ahead with an arms program. For the French military, awakening late to the possibilities of nuclear weapons, have integrated them into the only strategic doctrine at hand: the Anglo-American theory of deterrence. Like their American and British colleagues, they assert that the classical doctrine of the primacy of ground troops is no longer valid. On the contrary, an air force equipped with nuclear weapons "destroys infallibly and totally the power of the enemy and thus lends an entirely new aspect to the problem of occupying terrain." [41] In future wars, they argue, there will be no need to occupy territory, for the defeated population can be made to obey by the threat of nuclear bombing. As a result, many French officers are highly critical of the French Defense Ministry for continuing to plan France's defense around the ground forces. "It is in the air that victory must be won," wrote General Gérardot. "It is around the air force that our national defense must be built. It is in the realm of air power that our military and technical effort must be made." [42]

It is not surprising that this school of thought considers the defense of Europe largely in terms of the ability to effect an immediate retaliatory attack. In the past, it ar-

---

[40] General Paul Gérardot, "La guerre atomique et l'occupation du terrain," Revue de Défense Nationale (April 1955), p. 391.

[41] Colonel E. J. Debeau, "Les armes atomiques et la défense nationale," Revue de Défense Nationale (July 1955), p. 4.

[42] Gérardot, "La guerre atomique et l'occupation du terrain." cited, p. 396.

gues, France could usually absorb the first shock of a hostile attack and mobilize its forces for a counteroffensive after the front had been stabilized. But nuclear war will have to be fought with the forces-in-being, and it requires above all a powerful, well-dispersed air force. "The aero-nuclear arms have neutralized the power of recovery. It follows that from now on the defensive coalition must pre-serve its retaliatory forces from an initial assault, the im-pact of which cannot be entirely warded off." [43]

This restatement of the Anglo-American doctrine of deterrence does not clarify what contribution France with its limited resources and cramped space can make to a strategy of retaliation. Nor does it explain why France should expose itself to the most catastrophic strategy so long as the United States Strategic Air Force possesses a striking power far overshadowing any possible French contribution. Thus French military doctrine has offered additional arguments for French neutralism. The strategy developed by the military men has provided the rationale for French reluctance to enter the nuclear race. In this France is only being true to its genius for pressing argu-ments to their most logical conclusions. The same inhibi-tions, implicit in our theory of deterrence, have been kept from reaching the surface in the United States only by the persistence of well-established doctrine, the conscious-ness of greater strength, and a social tradition which can live with paradox.

The most eloquent advocate of the position of the French Government has been Jules Moch, a Socialist Dep-uty, who has represented France in the United Nations disarmament negotiations throughout many changes of Government since 1952. However controversial his views, Moch is not simply a lay politician. As a graduate of the famous École Polytechnique and a naval reserve officer, his views command wide respect in official and scientific circles in France. In his book *Human Folly: To Disarm or Perish?* Moch summed up his view, which is that of the

---

[43] Colonel Gallois, "Défense aero-nucléaire," *Revue de Défense Nation-ale* (May 1955), p. 608 ff.

dominant current of French opinion.[44] He agreed with the prevailing strategic doctrine that thermonuclear weapons had effected a strategic revolution. In the past every technological advance by the offense had been followed by a corresponding gain by the defense. Against a determined thermonuclear attack, however, even the most effective defense could not avert devastating damage. As a result thermonuclear war was certain to produce social catastrophe. Peace, Moch argued, was unattainable by a "balance of terror." Only complete disarmament and the abolition of nuclear weapons could provide a remedy. "How are we to avoid this tragic possibility [nuclear war]?" he asked, adding that the choice seems evident. Either nations will continue to run the risk of perishing in a sudden attack or they will demonstrate sufficient composure, courage and reason to disarm under international control, prohibiting under such control the production for military purposes of fissionable matter. There is no intermediate solution.[45]

Whatever the validity of Moch's arguments, they expressed the predominant trend of French opinion. All political parties except the Gaullists united in opposition to the military applications of nuclear energy. Their arguments ranged from the great economic benefits of the peaceful uses of nuclear energy,[46] to the proposition that France could promote the relaxation of tensions by not entering the nuclear race; [47] to an appeal to the inconsistency of a nuclear military program with the principles of Christianity.[48] And the near unanimity of the political parties was reflected in popular opinion. In a public

---

[44] Jules Moch, *Human Folly: To Disarm or Perish?* (translated by Edward Hyams; London: Gallancz, 1955).

[45] Same, p. 131.

[46] This was more or less the position of the Radical-Socialist party. See Félix Gaillard, *La France et l'énergie atomique dans la paix et dans la guerre* (Paris: Parti Républicain Radical et Radical Social, 1954), p. 15.

[47] This is the position of the Socialist party; see *Franc-Tireur*, April 14, 1955.

[48] This is the position of the Catholic MRP. See André Piettre, "Armes nucléaires et conscience chrétienne," *Le Monde*, April 16, 1955; also G. Morel, "Options atomiques," *Revue de l'Action Populaire* (May 1955), pp. 540-8.

opinion poll conducted in February 1955 by the Institut Français d'Opinion Publique, only 33 per cent of those polled favored the production of atomic weapons by France; 49 per cent opposed their production; 18 per cent did not indicate a preference. Seventy-nine per cent of those who opposed a French nuclear military effort did so because they believed that the possession of nuclear weapons would not strengthen France's hand in international affairs. Significantly, 76 per cent of those who supported a French nuclear arms program were more interested in the effects of possessing nuclear weapons on France's friends than on the U.S.S.R. They favored a military program because it "would assure France more independence vis-à-vis its allies." [49] The result of this combination of public and political attitudes was the decision of the French Government of April 13, 1955, in which France renounced the military applications of nuclear energy, subject to re-examination in the light of later developments.

The problems of the nuclear age cannot be solved by administrative decree, however. The decision not to proceed with a military program raised almost immediately the question of the difference between military and civilian uses of nuclear technology. Was a ship's engine for example, a military or a civilian instrument? To press the predominant views to their ultimate conclusion would have reduced the incipient program for the peaceful applications of nuclear energy to absurdity. Thus the French Government was at once obliged to make a distinction between nuclear energy for propulsion and for explosives. Even prior to the Government's declaration, the Chief of Staff of the French Navy, Admiral Henry M. Nomy, had revealed that the construction of a nuclear-powered submarine was under study.[50] Less than nine months after the decision renouncing the military applications of nuclear energy, the Government announced plans for building a

49 "La France et les questions internationales," *Sondages,* no. 1 (February 1955), p. 20.
50 Speech by Admiral Nomy, *Le Monde,* March 24, 1955.

submarine of this type, whose engine could serve as a prototype for surface vessels as well.[51]

Moreover, the choice between peaceful and military uses cannot be made irrevocably. The final product of any peaceful program is plutonium, which is also the key component in nuclear weapons. The more extensive the peaceful energy program, the greater will be the opportunity to enter the military field. In 1957, France's peaceful atomic energy program will be producing over 15 kilograms of plutonium annually, and its stockpile will approach 100 kilograms, sufficient to produce several nuclear weapons.

The French decision therefore has only deferred the issue of the production of nuclear weapons to a time when it will be practical to make them. For a nation seeking to enter the nuclear field the most difficult step is to master the technology and develop a cadre of scientists capable of supporting a diversified program. It does not make a great deal of difference whether this knowledge is acquired by means of peaceful or military applications. In fact, the peaceful applications of nuclear energy may enable public opinion to become familiar with nuclear energy by stages and thereby bring about a psychological climate to support an eventual arms program. That such considerations have been present in French minds is shown in an article by a distinguished French physicist. "Let us take advantage of the years ahead to improve our general situation, to catch up on our backwardness by training engineers and scientists, by increasing our mining, technical and industrial potential . . . and by carrying through the experimental industrial projects which are indispensable in a program which is ambitious and reasonable. . . . The decisions we may have to take later can then be carried out very rapidly." [52]

France, for all its protestations of high principle, has not been able to escape any of the dilemmas of the nuclear age. As French nuclear technology developed and its na-

[51] Same, November 12, 1955.
[52] Louis Le Prince-Ringuet, "Prestige de la France et armements atomiques," *Le Monde*, March 19, 1955.

ture came to be more generally understood, the problem of its military applications has been reopened almost inevitably. Little more than a year after the decision to refrain from the building of nuclear weapons, the parliamentary correspondent of *Le Monde* reported: "With the exception of the Communists . . . all the speakers have shown themselves to be in accord that the choice is between possessing a nuclear armament and abandoning the national defense." [53]

French thought had come full cycle. France has been forced to realize that in the nuclear age national defense must begin with nuclear weapons. Under their protection other forms of conflict, even of the "conventional" kind, may be possible though, in a war between nuclear powers, unlikely. Without nuclear weapons, a country is at the mercy of any power that possesses them. As Prime Minister Guy Mollet told the National Assembly:

> The Government's position is as follows: France commits itself not to explode a bomb of the atomic type before January 1, 1961. Taking into account the delays for research and for construction . . . this moratorium will not occasion any delay in France's nuclear program. At its termination we will be at liberty to pursue independent policies. . . . During the period of the moratorium it can pursue research with respect to military applications. Nothing prevents it from orienting its efforts toward military purposes. . . .[54]

Mollet thus left no doubt that France was already engaged in research on the military applications of nuclear weapons. What had been announced hardly a year previously as a French effort to set the example for a reconciled humanity had become an essentially technical problem of priorities, a question of whether it is wiser to build up a nuclear technology by stressing the peaceful or the military applications of the atom.

If France has learned that it will have to face up to the nuclear age and that its only choice lies between a nuclear strategy and impotence, the question of the nature of nu-

---

[53] *Le Monde,* July 12, 1956.
[54] Same, July 13, 1955.

clear strategy has remained unresolved. France's attempt to sidestep the problem by refusing to enter the nuclear race was certain to fail. The choice depended not only on the will of France but also on that of other powers, and economic necessity impelled France into the very peaceful pursuits which ultimately make a military technology unavoidable. However, the adoption of nuclear strategy will not by itself overcome the problem of French vulnerability. For France, as for its allies, the task of strategy is to find a course somewhere between Armageddon and surrender.

v

From a military point of view, NATO's difficulties are due to its inability to resolve two issues in terms which are meaningful to all partners: the purpose of a military establishment on the Continent, and the implications of nuclear weapons for allied strategy. So long as the United States and Britain base their strategy on the assumption that any war in Europe will inevitably lead to all-out war and that all-out war will necessarily be fought as an intercontinental thermonuclear exchange, there is an inherent imbalance between their interest in the alliance and that of the other NATO powers. No soothing statements can bridge the gulf between our allies' concern with local defense and the requirements of an all-out strategy. The very location of our air bases along the periphery of Eurasia and beyond, in Spain, Morocco and Saudi Arabia, testifies to the dispensability of the Continental powers. This imbalance has caused NATO's military strategy to be built on a series of compromises, on concessions by us to European fears and reluctant concessions by the European members to our insistence on a military contribution by them. The result has been a proliferation of military establishments on the Continent, too strong to serve as a trip-wire, too weak to resist a Soviet onslaught, and in any case, not really designed for that purpose. NATO has evolved in a never-never land, where our strategic doctrine has undermined the European incentive to make a substantial military effort, while the Europeans have been

reluctant to make their hesitations explicit lest we withdraw the guarantee of their frontiers which, in terms of
an all-out strategy, has been NATO's only really meaningful function.

Nothing is more important, therefore, than to be clear
about the role we wish NATO to perform. Is it a device
to serve warning on the Soviet bloc that an attack on
Western Europe will inevitably unleash an all-out war?
Or is it designed to assure the integrity of Europe against
attack? In the former case there is little point in maintaining large British, American and Canadian forces on
the Continent, and the European military build-up in
turn is bound to be ambivalent, hesitant and essentially
meaningless. In the latter case, a radical adjustment is
required in our strategic doctrine and in supporting
policies.

Ever since the end of World War II, one notion has
been repeated so often that it has virtually acquired the
status of a dogma: that only the atom bomb and our retaliatory power stand between the Red Army and the occupation of Europe, and that any attack on Europe must
inevitably unleash all-out war. On behalf of this proposition several reasons are advanced: Europe is a "vital"
interest and, therefore, must receive the protection of our
massive deterrent, whereas local wars are appropriate only
for objectives of peripheral importance. Strategic air war
is our only possible riposte to a Soviet attack on Europe,
because we cannot afford to match Soviet manpower or
engage the Red Army in a war of attrition. We have no
choice, so the argument usually concludes, but to fight
an all-out war because our NATO partners will look
askance at any defense of their territories which involves
the local use of nuclear weapons.

The most unchallenged arguments often inhibit clear
thought most severely. It is a strange doctrine which asserts that vital interests can be defended only by the most
catastrophic strategy. To be sure, we must be prepared to
defend our vital interests by all-out war, if necessary.
But this is a far cry from asserting that we must *begin*
that defense with a thermonuclear holocaust or that it

is not to our interest to develop alternative strategies. Less cataclysmic strategic options are all the more important because of the very reason formerly advanced for an all-out strategy: that it would prevent a long drawn-out con test of attrition. Given the power of modern weapons, all-out war now makes inevitable the very result which our reliance on an all-out strategy immediately after World War II sought to prevent: whatever the outcome of an all-out war, it will drain, perhaps destroy, the national sub-stance. And if during a thermonuclear exchange the Red Army takes over Europe, we will not have sufficient re-sources left to liberate our allies. All-out war may fore-stall neither attrition nor Soviet occupation of Europe.

Nor is the argument based on our inadequate manpower conclusive. The combined manpower of the United States and its European allies has always exceeded that of the Soviet bloc in Europe. The disparity has not been the availability of manpower, but the willingness to mobilize it. Moreover, the advent of tactical nuclear weapons in quantity makes the difference in mobilized manpower strategically less significant, provided we and our allies are prepared to draw the consequences from the strategic revolution that has occurred and are willing to face up to the problem of limited nuclear war. On a nuclear bat-tlefield there is an inherent upper limit to the number of troops that can be strategically significant. While this number is larger than the present NATO force, it is not so large as to be beyond the realm of possibility. It pre-supposes, however, a diplomacy which establishes a clear understanding of the nature of limited nuclear war on the part of our allies and, perhaps more importantly, by our opponent.

Will not a limited nuclear war in Europe cause such widespread devastation as to defeat its purpose? Is not the lesson of "Carte Blanche" that a limited nuclear war would mean the end of European civilization just as surely as an all-out war? An all-out strategy is advocated by many in the belief that a limited nuclear war would reduce the battle zone to "radioactive rubble" and that this prospect will inhibit our allies' will to resist.[55] It is contradictory, however, to argue that our allies will be reluctant to undertake a limited war in defense of their territories but that we will remain prepared to implement an all-out strategy which would be infinitely more destructive. Why should Britain and the United States be ready to accept complete devastation when the countries most directly concerned shrink from much less drastic measures? Nor is it clear what reassurance allies which are to be saved from being turned into radioactive rubble can derive from the fact that as the consequence of an all-out war we share their fate.

Moreover, the argument in favor of a strategy of limited nuclear war is that it would keep the world from being turned into radioactive rubble. As we have seen, a limited nuclear war would approach all-out war in destructiveness only if it should be conducted with the tactics of World War II, with fixed lines, massive attacks on communication centers and an attempt to wipe out the enemy industrial potential. The lessons of "Carte Blanche" are therefore deceptive. In the near future—as strategic doctrine goes, within ten years—the massive attack on opposing air installations will become strategically unproductive or unnecessary. With the advent of missiles and vertical take-off aircraft there will be no need to drop some three hundred atomic devices within forty-eight hours.[56] The key goal in a limited nuclear war should not be to eliminate enemy communication centers but to prevent an enemy from controlling territory by keeping him from concentrating large bodies of troops in the contested area. A limited nuclear war should not be compared to a ground war in the traditional sense. Its units ideally should approximate the mobility of an air force but they should be capable of forcing the enemy either to concentrate his forces and thus to present a target, or so to disperse his

---

55 See Sir John Slessor, "The H-Bomb: Massive Retaliation or Graduated Deterrence," *International Affairs*, v. 32 (April 1956), pp. 158-62; and also "The Great Deterrent and Its Limitations," *Bulletin of the Atomic Scientists*, v. 12 (May 1956), pp. 140-6.

56 See above, p. 292.

forces that he will not be able to impose his political domination.

Other proponents of an all-out strategy have argued that an attempt to undertake local defense would serve Soviet interests because it would deliver the great prize of Western Europe into its hands undestroyed. "If we say that atomic weapons may be used only in the area of the front line . . . ," writes Sir John Slessor, "it will not ring a very cordial bell with our new NATO allies, and Russia herself would be immune except possibly for towns in the immediate neighbourhood of airfields. That seems to be a good bargain for the Russians who would surely rather capture places like Paris and the Channel ports intact than as masses of radio-active rubble." [57] It is contradictory to maintain that it may be to our interest to bring about a widespread devastation of the areas we seek to protect by a deliberately chosen strategy. It is not apparent why the adoption by the West of a strategy of massive retaliation would force the U.S.S.R. into destroying Paris or the Channel ports. On the contrary, in an all-out war the important targets would seem to be the United States and perhaps the British strategic air bases. This does not mean that a strategy of all-out war would be to the advantage of our European allies. Even if our allies should escape the direct effect of bombing, the problems of fall-out, of strontium-90, and of genetic effects would remain. The danger that unrestricted thermonuclear war might make life unsupportable and the fear of the ravages of Soviet occupation should be a powerful incentive for them to undertake local defense.

A strategy looking to the local defense of Europe should not be considered as a device for holding our alliance together. On the contrary, the alliance should be conceived as a means to bring about the common defense by means which do not involve national catastrophe for all partners. Such a strategy is impossible, however, until our allies have a better understanding of the nature of nuclear technology and, therefore, of the nature of limited nuclear

---

[57] Slessor, "The H-Bomb: Massive Retaliation or Graduated Deterrence," cited, p. 160.

war. One of the banes of our alliance policy has been the exclusion of the Continental powers from the nuclear race, in part because of the restrictions imposed on the exchange of information by the United States Atomic Energy Act. But it will not prove possible in the long run to maintain a strategy whose chief weapon is in the exclusive control of the two allies geographically most remote from the first line of Soviet advance. Since our allies possess neither a substantial nuclear technology, nor an arsenal of nuclear weapons, they are assailed by a sense of impotence and can fall easy prey to Soviet propaganda, which seeks to picture nuclear weapons as a category of special horror. If the United States retains exclusive control of nuclear weapons our allies will become increasingly vulnerable to Soviet atomic blackmail, which implies that they can escape their dilemmas by refusing to adopt a nuclear strategy.[58] The success of this tactic in an area outside NATO is illustrated by the announcement of the Japanese Government that none of the United States atomic support commands would be permitted to be stationed on Japanese soil.[59]

One of the chief tasks of United States policy in NATO, therefore, is to overcome the trauma which attaches to the use of nuclear weapons and to decentralize the possession of nuclear weapons as rapidly as possible. Nothing would so much dispel the air of mystery that surrounds nuclear weapons as their possession by the Continental powers. Nothing would do more to help restore a measure of consistency to allied military planning. The rationale for the secrecy imposed by the Atomic Energy Act has long since disappeared. It made sense only so long as we possessed an atomic monopoly. But with the growth of the Soviet nuclear stockpile, our allies have become the real victims of our policy of withholding atomic information. They are either forced into a wasteful duplication of effort and into research long since accomplished by the United States and the U.S.S.R. or else they are obliged to rely on mili-

[58] See, for example, the Soviet note to Turkey, *New York Times*, January 24, 1957.

[59] *New York Times*, February 9, 1957.

tary establishments hopelessly at a disadvantage vis-à-vis that of the Soviet Union.

Almost as important as the possession of nuclear weapons would be the acquisition by our NATO partners of missiles, at least of intermediary range. Since most of European Russia is vulnerable to missiles with a range of 1,500 miles, the existence of this capability would place Europe in a better position to withstand the threat of a Soviet rocket attack, a threat which proved so effective during the Suez crisis. The agreement between President Eisenhower and Prime Minister Harold Macmillan to make United States missiles available to Britain is a hopeful step in a direction which could become a model for all of NATO.[60]

The possession of nuclear weapons and missiles will not by itself solve NATO's difficulties, however. On the contrary, it may become one more argument for a reduction of forces and one more temptation to stake everything on an all-out retaliatory strategy. And a strategy of massive retaliation may cause the alliance to recoil before resisting any except the most dire and unambiguous challenges. In order to escape the paralysis induced by such prospects NATO must adopt a doctrine which shows the relevance of the new weapons to a strategy less catastrophic than all-out war.

The leadership in this effort must be taken by the United States. Only the United States possesses the technical know-how which can give meaning to a European defense contribution. Only the United States possesses the retaliatory force which can furnish the shield for a local defense. Unless the United States, in its doctrine and its military establishment, demonstrates its faith in the local defense of Europe, the military effort of NATO will lack a sense of direction. There is no point in adding conventional German divisions to an Anglo-American army equipped with nuclear weapons and backed by a tactical air force which is based almost exclusively on a nuclear strategy. A logistics system of World War II vintage based

---

[60] For text of the agreement, see *New York Times*, March 25, 1957.

on a few supply centers, each completely vulnerable to nuclear attack, is highly dangerous if our strategy envisages the possibility of using nuclear weapons. NATO's present cumbersome structure is hardly suitable for the rapid re-action required by nuclear war. The conventional armies of our Continental allies may actually prove an impedi-ment on a nuclear battlefield. NATO will, therefore, have to be adapted to the nuclear period both doctrinally and organizationally. The armies of our allies, or at least that part of them earmarked for Europe, should be equipped and trained for nuclear war. And the alliance should strive to gain acceptance for a strategic doctrine which does not identify nuclear war with all-out war. NATO, in short, must seek to escape its present inconsistencies. It is either a device to defend Europe locally or an instrument to unleash the British and American strategic air forces. It cannot be both and it cannot be the former without a more realistic defense effort by our European allies.

Should our allies prove reluctant to support even a militarily revitalized NATO, it would seem time to put an end to the half-measures that have hamstrung the mili-tary effort of the alliance. In the absence of a more sub-stantial European defense effort, five American and four British divisions are too little to assure local defense and too much for internal security purposes. The presence of less than half that number would amply demonstrate our determination and insure our participation in an all-out war. In the absence of a military structure capable of achieving local defense, the protection of Europe resides essentially in the willingness of the United States and Great Britain to undertake all-out war in response to Soviet aggression. This determination could be conveyed with less ambiguity through a reduction of United States and British strength in Europe, for it would remove any assumption that an attack on Europe would be dealt with by local defense.

The North Atlantic Treaty Organization has thus come to a fork in the road. It can no longer reconcile an all-out strategy with an inadequate and half-hearted effort of local defense. It must decide soon whether NATO represents a variation on the Monroe Doctrine—defining a region which will be protected essentially by a unilateral United States guarantee—or whether it can be made to serve what has become the most productive and least costly strategy: the strategy of a local defense based on nuclear weapons.

Our European allies must realize that in the nuclear age they do not have the resources to maintain a military establishment for both limited and all-out war. Any effort to do so will reduce the over-all effectiveness without adding to their individual strength. Their most meaningful contribution is in the capability for limited war. As for us, while we should do everything we can to assure an adequate basis for the defense of Europe, anything short of an establishment capable of local defense will result in a dispersal of resources.

Much has been made of strengthening the nonmilitary side of NATO, but such proposals will remain palliatives until NATO faces up to the military facts. A defensive alliance cannot be maintained unless it develops some notion of the nature of common defense.

The willingness to undertake a local defense of Europe will be a test whether the alliance can be adapted to conditions radically changed from those that were foreseen at its initiation. The effort to call the North Atlantic Treaty Organization into being has been so considerable, that we may be tempted to overlook the fact that a strategy developed when we enjoyed an atomic monopoly is no longer adequate to a period of nuclear plenty. The free world, which has been challenged to protect its political beliefs, is also asked to demonstrate the resilience of its strategic thinking. If NATO cannot develop a strategy less catastrophic than all-out war, its determination cannot be expected to survive the perils which will inevitably confront it. It may be that neither we nor our European allies will be prepared to make the economic sacrifices required for such a course. But at least we should not confuse in our own minds the least burdensome with the most effective strategy. The result of an attempt to evade the strategic problem may be catastrophe in case of war and a steady deterioration of the cohesiveness of the alliance during periods of peace.

The shape of future strategy cannot be determined solely by ourselves or by our allies, however. Rather, our measures will be relevant only to the extent that they prove adequate to deal with the threat which makes the free world's concern with strategy so important in the first place: the revolutionary challenge of the Soviet Union and Communist China.

10

THE STRATEGY OF AMBIGUITY—
SINO-SOVIET STRATEGIC THOUGHT

WHAT IS A REVOLUTIONARY? Were the answer to this question self-evident, only the most moribund societies would ever collapse and few, if any, international orders would be overthrown. For it would then be possible to stifle, at its inception, the party or the state seeking to subvert the existing system or to remedy, in time, the situation that brought about its emergence. Instead, history reveals a strange phenomenon. Time and again states appear which boldly proclaim that their purpose is to destroy the existing structure and to recast it completely. And time and again, the powers that are the declared victims stand by indifferent or inactive, while the balance of power is overturned. Indeed, they tend to explain away the efforts of the revolutionary power to upset the equilibrium as the expression of limited aims or specific grievances until they discover—sometimes too late and always at excessive cost— that the revolutionary power was perfectly sincere all along, that its call for a new order expressed its real aspirations. So it was when the French Revolution burst on an unbelieving Europe and when Hitler challenged the system of Versailles. So it has been with the relations of the rest of the world toward the Soviet bloc.

How was it possible that from positions of extreme weakness these powers could emerge as the most powerful states of Europe and that the most recent of these challengers, the U.S.S.R., can bid for the domination of the world less than a generation after a group of die-hards were trying to hold Moscow against enemies converging from all sides?

Part of the answer is to be found in the tendency of the powers which represent the *status quo* to confront the revolutionary power with methods they learned in a more secure environment, in the difficulty they find in adjusting to the changed nature of international relations in a revolutionary international order. An international order the basic arrangements of which are accepted by all the major powers may be called "legitimate." A system which contains a power or a group of powers which rejects either the arrangements of the settlement or the domestic structure of the other states is "revolutionary." A legitimate order does not make conflicts impossible; it limits their scope. Wars may arise, but they will be fought *in the name* of the existing system and the peace will be justified as a better expression of agreed arrangements. In a revolutionary order, on the other hand, disputes have to do, not with adjustments within a given framework, but with the framework itself.

Thus, while disputes in a revolutionary period may retain a familiar form, their substance has altered significantly. In a legitimate order, disputes are blunted by a shared understanding that no alternative order is envisaged by the contestants; adjustments, therefore, are sought in order to improve the working of a system accepted by all the major powers. A revolutionary order, on the other hand, is such because a major power refuses to accept the framework of the international order or the domestic structure of other states, or both. Adjustments here have primarily a tactical significance: to prepare positions for the next test of strength. Negotiations within a legitimate order have three functions: to formulate agreements or disagreements in a manner that does not open unbridgeable schisms; to perpetuate the international system by providing a forum for making concessions; to persuade by stating a plausible reason for settlement. But, in a revolutionary period, most of these functions have changed their purpose. The emphasis of traditional diplomacy on "good faith" and "willingness to come to an agreement" is a positive handicap when it comes to dealing with a power dedicated to overthrowing the international system. For it is precisely "good faith" and "willingness to come to an agreement" which are lacking in the conduct of a revolutionary power. Diplomats can still meet, but they cannot persuade each other. Instead, diplomatic conferences become elaborate stage plays which seek to influence and win over public opinion in other nations; their purpose is less the settlement of disputes than the definition of issues for which to contend. They are less a forum for negotiation than a platform for propaganda.

While this changed function of diplomacy may be clear enough in retrospect, an understanding of it in the face of a revolutionary challenge is inhibited by the very factors which make for the spontaneity, indeed the existence, of a legitimate order. To be sure, no international order is ever stable *solely* because it is considered legitimate by its component states. The fact that each power within an international system is sovereign and that its intentions are, therefore, subject to change imposes a measure of precaution on all policy. No statesman can make the survival of his country entirely dependent on the assumed good will of another sovereign state, because one of his most effective guarantees for this will remaining good is not to tempt it by too great a disproportion of power. For this reason, there always exists in international relations the temptation to strive for absolute security, to press the search for safety to the point of eliminating all possible sources of danger. But since absolute security for one power is unattainable except by the annihilation or neutralization of all the others, it can be achieved only by a cycle of violence culminating in the destruction of the multistate system and its replacement by single-power domination. The quest for absolute security inevitably produces a revolutionary situation.

A legitimate order is distinguished by not pressing the quest for security to its limits, by its willingness to find safety in a combination of physical safeguards and mutual trust. It is legitimate not because each power is perfectly satisfied, but because it will not be so dissatisfied that it will seek its remedy in overthrowing the existing system. The confidence required for the operation of a legitimate order does not presuppose the absence of *all* tensions, but the conviction on the part of all major powers that the disputed issues do not threaten their national survival. To the extent that this measure of mutual trust is not present, the quest for absolute security will reappear and relations will tend to be based on force and the threat of force, either on war or on an armaments race.

The powers that represent the *status quo* are, therefore, at a profound psychological disadvantage vis-à-vis a revolutionary power. They have everything to gain from believing in its good faith, for the tranquillity they seek is unattainable without it. All their instincts will cause them to seek to integrate the revolutionary power into the legitimate framework, the framework to which they are used and which to them seems "natural." They will ascribe existing tensions to misunderstanding, to be removed by patience and good will: ". . . we are dealing with people who are rather unpredictable," President Eisenhower has said of the Soviet leaders, "and at times they are just practically inexplicable, so far as we are concerned. So you go along announcing your views about peace in the world, what you are striving to do . . . and then for the rest of it, you meet them from time to time, or your diplomatic representatives do, in order to see whether it is possible to ameliorate the situation. . . ." [1]

A revolutionary power confronts the legitimate order with a fearful challenge. A long period of peace leads to the temptation to trust appearances and to seek to escape the element of conjecture in policy by interpreting the motives of other powers in the most favorable and familiar manner. But against a revolutionary power, tactics of conciliation are self-defeating. Here safety can be found only in a precautionary policy which stakes an assessment of future menace against current protestations of innocence. When an established order is confronted by a revo-

---

[1] *New York Times*, January 24, 1957. (Press Conference of January 23, 1957.)

lutionary power, its survival depends on the ability to see through appearances and to keep the implied challenge from becoming overt. The world will never know what horrors it was spared from revolutions that were stifled in their infancy or indeed whether the repression of them was justified.

Since both its history and its aspirations generally keep a *status quo* power from such a course, the revolutionary power will be able to defeat its opponents by manipulating their preconceptions against them. Napoleon's conquests were made possible because the "legitimate" rulers surrendered after a lost battle according to the canons of eighteenth-century warfare; the familiar assumptions prevented them from conceiving the enormity of Napoleon's goals. Hitler could use the doctrines of his opponents in annexing Austria, because they wanted to believe that his aims were limited by the "legitimate" claim of national self-determination. And the Soviet rulers have expanded their power into the center of Europe and along the fringes of Asia by coupling each act of expansion with protestations of peace, democracy and freedom. The psychological advantage of a revolutionary state is that in order to defeat its aims the *status quo* powers must also give up the "legitimate" framework, the very pattern which to them represents the accustomed and desirable way of life.

The revolutionary power, therefore, gains a subtle advantage. If it displays any degree of psychological skill, it can present every move as the expression of limited aims or as caused by a legitimate grievance. The *status quo* powers, on the other hand, cannot be sure that the balance of power is in fact threatened or that their opponent is not sincere until he has demonstrated it, and, by the time he has done so, it is usually too late. However the physical balance may be weighted at first against the revolutionary power, this handicap is more than made up by the psychological advantage conferred by the absence of self-restraint.

In the past, conflicts between a legitimate and a revolutionary order have often had a tragic quality, for each side was unconscious of the role it was playing. To be sure, one side was attacking the *status quo* while the other defended it. But each contender spoke in the name of an absolute truth and each was wont to ascribe its victory to the superior validity of its maxims or its greater resolution. The particular dynamism of the Soviet system derives from its combination of revolutionary righteousness and psychological adeptness. Its leaders have studied not only the elements of their own doctrine—which is true of all revolutionary movements—but have consciously sought to press the psychological vulnerabilities of their opponents into their service. The liberal theory of the West preaches tolerance. Therefore, the Communists in democratic states seek to present their organization merely as one of the contending parties and claim for it the equality of democratic opportunity which it will be their first act to deny their opponents should they come to power by parliamentary means. The empiricism of the free world teaches that resistance by force is justified only against overt aggression. Therefore, the Soviet leaders graduate their moves so that the equilibrium is overturned by almost imperceptible degrees which magnify the inward doubts of the non-Soviet world. The West feels ambiguous about the use of power and the uncommitted peoples exalt peace into an absolute principle. Thus Soviet policy alternates peace offensives with threats of the dire consequences if their demands are disregarded: while Bulganin and Khrushchev, during their visit to India, were loudly protesting their love of peace, a hydrogen bomb was set off in the Soviet Union. The timing could hardly have been accidental. The free world believes that peace is a condition of static equilibrium and that economic advance is a more rational objective than foreign adventures. Therefore, the Communists appear periodically in the guise of the domestic reformer eager to spread the fruits of material advancement.

For each change of pace and tactic, the U.S.S.R. has found defenders among its victims, who justified its course not on the ground of Communist doctrine, but because it fitted in with the preconceptions of a legitimate order. The great advance of communism over the past generation has many causes, but chief among them is a spiritual crisis among its opponents. "We say to the powers," wrote Lenin long ago, "'. . . you . . . do not know what you want and . . . you are suffering from what is called a weak will which is due to your failure to understand economics and politics which we have appraised more profoundly than you.'" [2]

Whatever the validity of Lenin's statement, there is something remarkable about the reluctance of the defenders of the post-World War I "legitimate" order to believe the publicly announced aims of its declared mortal enemies. Hitler's *Mein Kampf* was ignored for a decade and a half while his intended victims spoke of taming him through the responsibilities of power. And neither Lenin's published works nor Stalin's utterances nor Khrushchev's declarations have availed against the conviction of the non-Soviet world that peace is the natural relation among states and that a problem deferred is a problem solved. Typical of these views in the 1920's was the opinion of the prominent historian, Florinsky: "The former crusaders of world revolution at any cost have exchanged their swords for machine tools and now rely more on the results of their labor than on direct action to achieve the ultimate victory of the proletariat." [3] In the 1930's, Soviet opposition to Fascism and Soviet peaceful intentions were a shibboleth, despite the fact that the U.S.S.R. was among the first great powers to make overtures to Nazi Germany.[4] During World War II there was a general conviction among Western policy-makers that after the war the U.S.S.R. would prefer to concentrate on the development of its own resources rather than engage in foreign adventures. And after the death of Stalin there took place a new outburst of speculation that a "basic" change had occurred in Soviet thinking. "The Soviet lead-

[2] V. I. Lenin, *Selected Works* (New York: International Publishers, 1943), v. 9, pp. 311-2, as quoted by Nathan Leites in *A Study of Bolshevism* (Glencoe, Ill.: The Free Press, 1953), p. 383.

[3] Michael T. Florinsky, *World Revolution and the U.S.S.R.*, p. 216, as quoted by T. A. Taracouzio, *War and Peace in Soviet Diplomacy* (New York: Macmillan, 1933), p. 129.

[4] See below, pp. 351-2.

ers," said Secretary Dulles in 1956, "are scrapping thirty years of policy based on violence and intolerance." [5]

The situation is doubly paradoxical because of the exasperation with which the Soviet leaders regularly have repudiated the notion that a change of tactics on their part implies an abandonment of their basic doctrines. ". . . if anyone thinks," Khrushchev said at the height of the "peace offensive," "that we shall forget about Marx, Engels, and Lenin, he is mistaken. This will happen when shrimps learn to whistle." [6] "We must learn the wisdom of the Bolsheviks," wrote Mao. "When our naked eyes are not enough we must avail ourselves of the aid of a telescope or microscope. The method of Marxism serves as a telescope or microscope in matters political and military." [7]

It is the insistence by the intended victims that the Bolsheviks do not "mean" what they have so often proclaimed which has given an air of unreality to the relations between the Soviet bloc and the rest of the world. The non-Communist world, for a variety of motives, has been easy prey to each new Soviet change of line because of its eagerness to integrate the Soviet power center into a legitimate system—the contingency above all others which Bolshevik doctrine explicitly rejects. The inevitable misunderstandings of revolutionary periods, which derive from the tendency of familiar terms to change their meanings, become in Soviet hands a tool to encompass their opponents' downfall.

Throughout the decades when Mao and other Chinese Communist leaders were proclaiming their devotion to Marxist-Leninist doctrine, many analysts in the West were arguing that Chinese communism was inherently different from Soviet communism. And today, in many areas of Asia at least, there is a general belief in the peaceful character of the Chinese regime based on no more solid

---

5 U.S. Department of State *Press Release No. 92*, February 25, 1956.

6 Denis Healey, "When Shrimps Learn to Whistle," *International Affairs*, v. 32 (January 1956), p. 2.

7 Mao Tse-tung, *Selected Works* (New York: International Publishers, 1955), v. 1, p. 222.

evidence than the natural desire of the peoples concerned and on the Chinese rulers' skill in using the term "peace" with all the ambiguity which attaches to it in Communist doctrine. "The theory of Marx, Engels, Lenin and Stalin is a 'universally applicable theory,' " Mao has written. "We should not regard their theory as a dogma, but as a guide to action. We should not merely learn Marxist-Leninist words and phrases, but study Marxism-Leninism as the science of revolution." [8] Yet it is precisely the revolutionary quality of Chinese communism that has most consistently been denied, lending color to Mao's contemptuous phrase: "We have a claim on the output of the arsenals of London as well as Hangyeng, and what is more, it is to be delivered to us by the enemy's own transport corps. This is the sober truth, not a joke." [9]

II

What, then, are the principles which constitute the "science of revolution?" In both Soviet and Chinese Communist thought they derive from Marxism as reinterpreted by Lenin. To be sure, many tenets of classical Marxism and even of Leninism have since been discarded or modified. But it is one thing to adapt doctrine to the tactical requirements of the moment; it is quite another to give up the belief which to Communists distinguishes theirs from all other movements: the confidence that Leninist theory will enable them to understand and to manage an inexorable historical development. For this reason, a study of Marxist-Leninist theory is not considered an abstract philosophical exercise in Soviet countries, but the prerequisite to effective action. It explains also the constant reiteration by Marxist leaders that victory is achieved only by superior *theoretical* insight.[10] In every Soviet school, whether technical or professional, a study of Marxist-Leninist theory takes up a large part of the curriculum: ". . . all those members of the Communist Party," wrote

8 Same, v. 2, p. 259.
9 Same, v. 1, p. 253.
10 Same, v. 1, p. 233; v. 2, p. 201.

Mao, "who are fairly qualified to study must study the theory of Marx, Engels, Lenin and Stalin. . . . It is impossible for a party to lead a great revolutionary movement to victory if it has no knowledge of revolutionary theory. . . ." [11]

As a result, while Communist tactics are highly flexible, every effort is made to integrate them into a doctrine presented as unchanging and inflexible. Part of the reason for the misunderstanding by the non-Soviet world of Soviet motivations is that more attention is paid to Soviet announcements meant for public consumption and couched in the simple slogans of propaganda, than to Soviet doctrinal discussions. Yet the latter are much more significant. Since the Soviet "legitimacy" is based on the claim to superior theoretical insight, every tactical move is justified as the expression of "pure" theory and every effort is made to maintain doctrinal militancy whatever the tactical requirements of the moment. From Lenin, to Stalin, to Mao, and to the current Soviet leadership, the insistence on superior historical understanding, on endless and inevitable conflict with non-Soviet states, on ultimate victory, has been unvarying. It is with these underlying beliefs, compared to which Soviet tactics are like the visible tip of the iceberg in relation to the submerged mass, that this chapter deals. It pays particular attention to Lenin and Mao, for, while they may become superseded on this point or that, they have established the basic orientation and the pattern of thinking of their society, including the attitudes of the current Soviet leadership, which, as will be seen, have not been basically changed even by the enormity of the new technology.

Marxist-Leninist theory asserts that political events are only manifestations of an underlying reality which is defined by economic and social factors. Leninism is said to enable its disciples to distinguish appearance from reality and not to be deceived by what are only symptoms, often misleading, of deep-seated economic and social factors. The "true" reality resides not in what statesmen say, but

---

11 Same, v. 2, p. 258.

in the productive process they represent. This process in all societies, except a Communist one, is characterized by a class struggle between the exploiting classes and the proletariat. To be sure, in the industrially advanced countries the struggle may sometimes be obscured by the ability to exploit colonies and "semi-colonial countries." But the respite is only temporary. For imperialism transfers the class struggle to the international scene. The very effort to escape the contradictions of the capitalist economy at home sharpens international tensions and leads inevitably to an unending cycle of conflicts and wars among the imperialist powers.[12] Thus all of political life is only a reflection of a struggle produced by economic and social changes. Statesmen are powerless to alter this fact; they can only guide it or utilize it for the ends of the dominant class.

The existence of a Communist state results, according to Leninist theory, in intensifying the contradictions of capitalism. For a "Socialist" state is not only a symbol of the possibility of revolutionary upheaval, its very existence limits the markets available to capitalism. Thus the larger the Soviet bloc, the smaller the stage on which the tensions of capitalism can work themselves out and the greater the resulting conflicts within the capitalist camp.[13] Another consequence is that, whether they are aware of it or not, capitalist states must seek to destroy the Socialist state if they are not to be destroyed by it. Thus the basic relationship between the two camps is one of inevitable conflict and whether it is hot or cold at any given moment is largely a question of tactics. Nor will statesmen be able to escape the operation of these economic laws by an act of will, for their role is determined by the economic structure of the society they represent. Conciliatory American

---

[12] See Vladimir Lenin, "Imperialism, the Highest Stage of Capitalism," in Hans J. Morgenthau and Kenneth W. Thompson, eds., *Principles and Problems of International Politics* (New York: Alfred A. Knopf, 1950), pp. 63-9.

[13] This thesis was advanced most explicitly in Stalin's last article in *Bolshevik* (October 1952). For text, see Boris Meissner and John S. Reshetar, *The Communist Party of the Soviet Union* (New York: Praeger, 1956), pp. 198-9.

statements will, therefore, appear to Soviet leaders either as hypocrisy or stupidity, ignorance or propaganda. Even when they accept the "subjective" sincerity of American statesmen, the Soviet leaders still believe them powerless to deal with the "objective" factors of American society which will make continuing conflict inevitable. Soviet statesmen consider diplomatic conferences a means to confirm an "objective" situation, and nothing is more futile than to seek to sway them by invocations of abstract justice or shared purposes.

As a result, relations between the Communist and the non-Communist world always have some of the attributes of war whatever form the contest may take at any given moment. It is not that the Soviet leadership glorifies war for its own sake; it is rather that it believes that the struggle is imposed on it by the task history has set it. Lenin wrote:

> War is a great disaster. But a social-democrat cannot analyze war apart from its historic importance. For him there can be no such thing as absolute disaster, or absolute welfare and absolute truth. He must analyze . . . the importance of war from the point of view of the interests of his class—the proletariat. . . . He must evaluate war not by the number of its casualties, but by its political consequences. Above the interests of the individuals perishing and suffering from war must stand the interests of the class. And if the war serves the interests of the proletariat . . . [it] is progress irrespective of the victims and the suffering it entails.[14]

"War," wrote Mao, "this monster of mutual slaughter among mankind will be finally eliminated through the progress of human society. . . . But there is only one way of eliminating it, namely, to oppose war by means of war, to oppose counter-revolutionary war by means of revolutionary war. . . ." [15]

The image of a constant conflict between the Communist and the non-Communist world has given a completely

---

14 V. I. Lenin, *Sochineniia* (3rd ed.; Moscow: 1935), v. 6, p. 457, as quoted by Taracouzio, cited, p. 53.

15 Mao Tse-tung, cited, v. 1, p. 179.

different meaning to the Soviet notion of war and peace. To the non-Soviet world, peace appears as an end in itself, and its manifestation is the *absence* of struggle. To the Soviet leaders, by contrast, peace is a *form* of struggle. To the nations which are heir to the liberal tradition of the West, man is an end in himself. In the Soviet concept, man is the product of a social experience, a datum to be manipulated for his own good.

The incommensurability between the two positions is all the more remarkable because both democratic beliefs and Marxism grew out of the same social experience of the industrial revolution. Because the doctrines of humanitarianism and individual dignity too often hid social inequality, the Marxists drew the conclusion that they were invented together with religion by clever capitalists as a device to confuse and enslave the proletariat. It did not occur to the Marxists that these doctrines might be sincerely held and that their potency has done more for the amelioration of the condition of the working class than the Communist Manifesto. The image of the cunning capitalists devising or manipulating philosophies, religions and systems of government in terms of their suitability for oppressing the proletariat has had several paradoxical consequences: Had the capitalist powers been as aware of their interests, as coolly calculating, as cold-bloodedly manipulating as communism asserts, the Soviet state could never have come into being or flourished. It was because the non-Communist powers refused to believe in irreconcilable antagonisms that the U.S.S.R. has emerged in the center of Europe and China has achieved a dominant position in Asia. Had the non-Soviet world used its beliefs merely as a tool in the class struggle, the colonial peoples would still be subjugated. It was because the non-Communist powers *do* believe in their own principles that their resistance to independence movements has been so indecisive. Thus the Soviet leaders in some respects have constantly overestimated their opponents, looking for devious manipulation in the most superficial gesture.

However incorrect the Communist assessment, it has given an increasing urgency to international relationships. Knowing its own motivations toward the non-Communist world, the Soviet leadership cannot credit any assertion of peaceful intention by its declared enemy. Against an opponent possessing the attributes ascribed to him by Soviet doctrine, relations have had to assume the form not only of a struggle but of a contest without quarter. "Until the final issue [between capitalism and communism] is decided," said Lenin, "the state of awful war will continue. . . . Sentimentality is no less a crime than cowardice in war." [16] "We . . . have no use for stupid scruples about benevolence, righteousness and morality in war," wrote Mao. "In order to win victory we must try our best to seal the eyes and ears of the enemy, making him blind and deaf. . . ." [17]

One way of achieving this aim has been through an unintended method, through making the most of the ambiguity inherent in Communist terminology. Because disciplined Communists see everything in relation to the class struggle, the concepts of war and peace, seemingly so unambiguous, have been turned into tools of Soviet political warfare. If wars are caused by the class struggle, and if the class struggle reveals the determining role of an exploiting class, all wars by non-Communist powers are unjust by definition. By contrast, all wars of the Soviet Union are just, since a government which has abolished the class struggle cannot fight any other kind. That peace can be achieved by war, that a war by a classless society is a form of peace—these are paradoxes dear to the heart of dialectically-trained Leninists. "The Bolsheviks hold that there are two kinds of war," wrote Stalin. "*Just* wars . . . waged to defend the people from foreign attack . . . or to liberate the people from capitalist slavery or to liberate colonies. . . . *Unjust* wars, wars of conquest waged to conquer and enslave foreign countries and foreign nations.

---

[16] Lenin, *Selected Works,* cited, v. 9, pp. 242 and 267, as quoted by Leites, cited, p. 347.

[17] Mao Tse-tung, cited, v. 2, p. 217.

Wars of the first kind the Bolsheviks supported." [18] "Wars in history," wrote Mao following Stalin, "can be divided into two kinds: just and unjust. All progressive wars are just and all wars impeding progress are unjust. We Communists are opposed to all unjust wars that impede progress, but we are not opposed to progressive, just wars. . . . We [Communists] . . . aim at peace not only in one country but throughout the world, and we not only aim at temporary peace but at permanent peace. In order to achieve this objective we must wage a life-and-death war, must be prepared to sacrifice anything. . . ." [19]

Thus peace offensives have alternated in Soviet strategy with threats of war, depending on the Soviet assessment of the tactical requirements of the moment. Since, according to Soviet theory, permanent peace can be achieved only by abolishing the class struggle and since the class struggle can be ended only by a Communist victory, any Soviet move, no matter how belligerent, advances the cause of peace while any non-Communist policy, no matter how conciliatory, serves the ends of war. While Soviet tanks were shooting down civilians in Hungary in the fall of 1956, it was the United Nations which, in Soviet propaganda, threatened peace by debating Soviet intervention. And in 1939, it was the League of Nations which threatened peace by condemning the Soviet attack on Finland. Hence, too, the constant effort to expand the Soviet sphere and to fill every vacuum; any territory in the possession of a non-Communist state is considered, by virtue of its different social structure, a danger to the peace of the Soviet bloc. Therefore, finally, the skillful use of peace offensives and disarmament talks always aimed precisely at the psychological weak point of the non-Soviet world: that it considers peace as an end in itself, an attitude which

---

[18] Joseph Stalin, *History of the Communist Party of the Soviet Union (Bolsheviks): Short Course* (New York: International Publishers, 1939), pp. 167-8, as quoted by Raymond L. Garthoff in *Soviet Military Doctrine* (Glencoe, Ill.: The Free Press, 1953), p. 38.

[19] Mao Tse-tung, cited, v. 2, p. 199.

Lenin once described as the "pitiful pacifism of the bourgeoisie." "The replacement of the slogan 'armament of the proletariat' by that of 'disarmament,' " proclaimed a thesis at the Sixth World Congress of the Comintern, "[can] serve . . . only as a revolutionary slogan. . . . The peace policy of a proletarian state in no way signifies that the Soviets have come to terms with capitalism. . . . It is merely another—in this situation a more advantageous—form of the struggle against capitalism. . . ." [20]

What is striking, therefore, about relations between the Soviet and the non-Soviet world is not the flexibility of Soviet tactics, but that essentially the same pattern of Soviet behavior should time and again raise discussion about its "sincerity" or its "novelty." The Soviet leaders have advanced variations of the same disarmament proposals since the mid-1920's. Their recurrent peace offensives have followed the same line that the export of revolution was impossible. And their periods of belligerency have had the same justification, that a capitalist encirclement was threatening the Soviet bloc. Yet each new Soviet move has been taken at face value and has produced infinite arguments over whether the Soviet Government was preparing for a "showdown" or ushering in a period of peace.

Nothing could be more irrelevant. For the one contingency which Soviet theory explicitly rules out is a static condition. Neither an all-out showdown nor a permanent peace are part of Soviet theory except as the former may be forced on them by an all-out attack like Hitler's, or the latter may come about through achieving Communist hegemony over the entire world. Rather, the Soviet concept is one of seeking to manage the inevitable flow of history, to bring about the attrition of the enemy by gradual increments and not to stake everything on a single throw of the dice. "A reckless military man relying solely upon enthusiasm," wrote Mao, "cannot but be tricked by the enemy . . . and consequently he cannot but

---

[20] Taracouzio, cited, pp. 274-5.

run his head against a brick wall. . . ." [21] "To accept battle at a time when it is obviously advantageous to the enemy and not to us is a crime," wrote Lenin.[22]

The reverse of these propositions is, of course, that failure to enter into a battle when the relation of forces is favorable is equally a crime. The choice of Soviet tactics is, therefore, determined by their assessment of the relationship of forces, and for this they believe Marxist theory gives them an incomparable tool. "The strength of Stalinist strategy consists in its basis on the correct calculation of the real relation of opportunities, forces, tendencies, regarding them not as static, but dynamic, in development." [23] Because Soviet doctrine teaches the inevitable hostility of the non-Communist world, no potential gain can be sacrificed to win an illusory good will. According to a leading Soviet theoretical journal, writing in 1953, any idea of pacifying the imperialists at the price of giving up sympathy and support of the liberation movements of other countries, or with small concessions, is merely bourgeois liberalism and a break with the theory of the class struggle.[24]

In this struggle, moreover, military actions are but one form of conflict and appropriate only to a specific relation of forces. The struggle is unchanging but its forms vary: "We Marxists," wrote Lenin, "have always been proud of the fact that by a strict calculation of the mass of forces and mutual class relations we have determined the expediency of this or that form of struggle. . . . At different moments of economic evolution, and depending on varying political, national, cultural, and other social conditions, different forms of struggle assume prominence, become the chief form of struggle, whereupon in their turn the

---

21 Mao Tse-tung, cited, v. 1, p. 185.

22 Lenin, *Selected Works*, cited, v. 10, p. 119, as quoted by Leites, cited, p. 495.

23 Major General Nikolai Talensky, "The Great Victorious Army of the Soviet Union," *Bolshevik* (February 1946), pp. 28-9, as quoted by Garthoff, cited, p. 16.

24 "Vsepobezhdaiushchaia Sila Idei Leninizma" (All-Conquering Power of the Ideas of Leninism) (editorial), *Kommunist,* no. 1 (January 1953), pp. 1-13.

secondary and supplementary forms of struggle also change their aspect." [25]

From the Soviet point of view, relations between the Soviet and non-Soviet world, therefore, reflect an equilibrium of forces in flux in which the task of the Communist leadership is to tilt the scale by constant if imperceptible pressure in the direction predetermined by the forces of history. Neither personal feelings nor considerations of abstract principle can enter into this contest. The Soviet leadership can only be profoundly suspicious of overtures that ask it to demonstrate its "good faith" by a specific concession as a prelude to a permanent settlement. If the forces have been calculated correctly, a settlement will always be possible, according to Soviet theory, and if they have been misjudged, good faith cannot act as a substitute. Soviet negotiators typically adopt a posture of belligerency or intransigence in order to squeeze the last possible gain from the existing relation of forces; and their professions of good will are always abstract, involving no practical consequences.

To the Soviet way of thinking, a settlement is not something to be achieved by the process of negotiation; rather an "objective" situation is ratified by the settlement. There is no value in making concessions. Either they are unnecessary on the basis of the relationship of forces and, therefore, a needless surrender. Or else they reflect the relationship of forces and are, therefore, not concessions, strictly speaking. Not to take advantage of a strategic opportunity is to demonstrate not moderation, but weakness.

As a result, the Soviet leaders never give up the chance to fill a vacuum, real or imagined, for the sake of winning the good will of the non-Communist world. The immense reservoir of sympathy built up during World War II was sacrificed without hesitation to obtain a bastion in Eastern Europe. The Geneva summit conference was used to perpetuate the Soviet position in East Germany and did not stand in the way of the Soviet arms deal with Egypt. Neither the "spirit of Geneva," nor the chidings of

---

25 Lenin, *Sochineniia*, cited, v. 22, p. 265 and v. 10, pp. 80-1, as quoted by Garthoff, cited, p. 19.

the uncommitted proved an obstacle to the ruthless use of Soviet force in putting down the revolt in Hungary. In every policy choice the Soviet leaders identify security with a physical relationship of forces: they cannot have any confidence in the continued good will of powers whom Soviet doctrine defines as permanently hostile.

The nature of the Soviet challenge is, therefore, inherently ambiguous. It uses the "legitimate" language of its opponents in a fashion which distorts its meaning and increases the hesitations of the other side. The belief in an inevitable historical progress leads the Soviet leaders to maintain a constant pressure just short of the challenge which they believe would produce a final showdown. To be sure, the Soviet leadership may miscalculate and thus bring on a holocaust despite its most rational calculations. But to the extent they do not miscalculate, the non-Soviet world faces the dilemma that all dividing lines between war and peace, aggression and the *status quo* are gradually eroded and in a manner which never presents a clear-cut issue. The combination of caution, persistence, and ambiguity is well illustrated by the Soviet sale of arms to Egypt. It was launched at the height of the "Geneva spirit," which was interpreted by the Soviet leaders not as a sign of relaxation of tensions, but as a measure of the free world's yearning for release from tensions, and, therefore, as opening a new strategic opportunity. It was negotiated by Czechoslovakia, in order to keep the Soviet line of retreat open in case the Western powers should react strongly. When the Soviet leaders saw that they could penetrate the Middle East without increasing the risk of counterpressures and, much less, of war, they gradually increased their commitment by increments so small that none of them seemed to justify serious alarm, until suddenly during the Suez crisis the U.S.S.R. emerged as a major Middle Eastern power, a contingency which would have been considered inconceivable a mere two years before.

The Soviet strategy of ambiguity can ultimately be countered only by a policy of precaution, by attempting to nip Soviet moves in the bud before Soviet prestige be-

comes so deeply engaged that any countermeasures increase
the risk of war. Yet a policy of precaution is the most difficult of all for *status quo* powers to implement. All their
preconceptions tempt them to wait until the Soviet threat
has become unambiguous and the danger has grown overt,
by which time it may well be too late. The Soviet leadership, therefore, presents to the West a challenge which
may be moral even more than physical. It resolves itself
ultimately into questions of how much the free world
will risk to back up its assessment of a situation without
being "certain" or whether the Soviet leaders can use the
free world's quest for certainty to paralyze its ability to act.
Many of the Soviet gains have been due in large part to a
greater moral toughness, to a greater readiness to run risks,
both physical and moral, than their opponents. And despite the moral bankruptcy of Soviet theory, which with
every passing year is demonstrated anew, the Soviet power
center has made gains which were not justified by the relation of forces but were largely due to the inward uncertainty of their declared victims.

III

The revolutionary dynamism of the U.S.S.R. and Communist China affects profoundly both the conduct of diplomacy and the conduct of war; indeed, it tends to blur
the distinction between them. To Leninist doctrine, negotiation is one tool among many others in the conduct of
the international class struggle, to be judged by its utility
in advancing Soviet objectives, but without any inherent
moral value in itself. To us, negotiation tends to be an
end in itself. To the Communists, a conference is a means
to gain time or to define the political framework of the
next test of strength or to ratify an "objective" situation.
To us, the willingness to enter a conference is in itself a
symptom of reduced tension because we believe that reasonable men sitting around a table can settle disputes in
a spirit of compromise. To the Soviet leaders, a settlement
reflects a temporary relationship of forces, inherently unstable and to be maintained only until the power balance

shifts. To us, a treaty has a legal and not only a utilitarian significance, a moral and not only a practical force. In the Soviet view, a concession is merely a phase in a continuing struggle: "Marxism-Leninism," wrote Mao, "does not allow concessions to be regarded as something purely negative. . . . Our concession, withdrawal, turning to the defensive or suspending action, *whether in dealing with allies or enemies*, should always be regarded as part of the entire revolutionary policy, as an indispensable link in the general revolutionary line. . . ." [26] To us, compromise is the very essence of the process of negotiation and we are, therefore, psychologically prepared to meet the other side at least part way as a token of good faith.

Our belief that an antagonist can be vanquished by the reasonableness of argument, our trust in the efficacy of the process of negotiation, reflect the dominant role played in our diplomacy by the legal profession and its conception of diplomacy as a legal process. But the legal method cannot be applied in a revolutionary situation, for it presupposes a framework of agreed rules within which negotiating skill is exercised. Adjustments are achieved because agreement is itself a desirable goal, because there exists a tacit agreement to come to an agreement. It is not the process of negotiation as such which accounts for the settlement of legal disputes, but a social environment which permits that process to operate. The legalistic approach is, therefore, peculiarly unsuited for dealing with a revolutionary power. Law is a legitimization of the *status quo* and the change it permits presupposes the assent of two parties. A revolutionary power, on the contrary, is revolutionary precisely because it rejects the *status quo*. It accepts a "legal" framework only as a device for subverting the existing order. Diplomacy is based on the assumption of some degree of confidence in the "good faith" of the other side. But Soviet doctrine prides itself on its ability to cut through spurious protestations of good faith to the "objective" class relations which alone furnish a real guarantee of security. "With a diplomat," wrote

[26] Mao Tse-tung, cited, v. 2, pp. 263-4. (Emphasis added.)

Stalin, "words *must* diverge from acts. . . . Words are one thing and acts something different. . . . A sincere diplomat would equal dry water, wooden iron." [27]

For these reasons it is futile to seek to deal with a revolutionary power by "ordinary" diplomatic methods. In a legitimate order, demands once made are negotiable; they are put forward with the intention of being compromised. In a revolutionary order, they are programmatic; they represent a claim for allegiance. In a legitimate order, it is good negotiating tactics to formulate maximum demands because this facilitates compromise without loss of essential objectives. In a revolutionary order, where compromise is unlikely, it is good negotiating tactics to formulate minimum demands in order to gain the advantage of advocating moderation. In a legitimate order, proposals are addressed to the opposite number at the conference table. They must, therefore, be drafted with great attention to their substantive content and with sufficient ambiguity so that they do not appear as invitations to surrender. But in a revolutionary order, the protagonists at the conference table address not so much one another as the world at large. Proposals here must be framed with a maximum of clarity and even simplicity, for their major utility is their symbolic content. In short, in a legitimate order, a conference represents a struggle to find formulas to achieve agreement; in a revolutionary order, it is a struggle to capture the symbols which move humanity.

The major weakness of United States diplomacy has been the insufficient attention given to the symbolic aspect of foreign policy. Our positions have usually been worked out with great attention to their legal content, with special emphasis on the step-by-step approach of traditional diplomacy. But while we have been addressing the Soviet leaders, they have been speaking to the people of the world. With a few exceptions we have not succeeded in dramatizing our position, in reducing a complex negotiation to its symbolic terms. In major areas of the world

---

27 Joseph Stalin, *Sochineniya* (Moscow: Gosudarstvennoe Izdatelstov Politicheskoi Literaturi, 1946), v. 2, pp. 276-7, as quoted by Leites, cited, p. 325.

the Soviets have captured the "peace offensive" by dint of the endless repetition of slogans that seemed preposterous when first advanced, but which have come to be common currency through usage. The power which has added 120 million people to its orbit by force has become the champion of anti-colonialism. The state which has utilized tens of millions of slave laborers as an integral part of its economic system appears as the champion of human dignity in many parts of the world. Neither regarding German unity, nor Korea nor the satellite orbit have we succeeded in mobilizing world opinion. But Formosa has become a symbol of American intransigence and our overseas air bases a token of American aggressiveness. We have replied to each new Soviet thrust with righteous protestations of our purity of motive. But the world is not moved by legalistic phrases, at least in a revolutionary period. This is not to say that negotiations should be conceived as mere propaganda; only that by failing to cope adequately with their psychological aspect we have given the Soviet leaders too many opportunities to use them against us.

As a result, the international debate is carried on almost entirely in the categories and at the pace established by the Soviets. The world's attention is directed toward the horror of nuclear weapons, but not toward the danger of Soviet aggression which would unleash them. The Soviet leaders negotiate when a relaxation of tension serves their purpose and they break off negotiations when it is to their advantage, without being forced to shoulder the onus for the failure. The negotiations beginning with the summit conference at Geneva can serve to illustrate these points. We were right to agree to the summit conference and to the subsequent meeting of the foreign ministers, although it would have been wiser to combine the two, and to relate a relaxation of tension to concrete political conditions. But it was not necessary to permit the Soviet leaders to build up a distinction between the President and the rest of the United States Government so that any subsequent increase in tensions could be ascribed by them to the President allegedly having succumbed to the pressure of his advisors or of the "objective" factors of the American economy.[28] Moreover, to the extent that the Soviet leaders believed the sincerity of our profession of peaceful intentions, they realized that they might make gains perhaps not otherwise open to them on the basis of the existing relation of forces. As a result, on the way back from Geneva Khrushchev and Bulganin pledged themselves to maintain their East German satellite and thereby to perpetuate the division of Germany. And shortly thereafter the world learned of the Soviet-Egyptian arms deal which marked the active entry of Soviet policy into the Middle East.

Having established its acceptance of two *de facto* governments in Germany, Soviet diplomacy could permit the foreign ministers' conference on German unity to fail completely. Indeed the very abruptness of its failure demonstrated our impotence to affect events and laid the basis for Moscow to negotiate directly with West Germany, perhaps eventually to the exclusion of the Western powers. And in the Middle East the Kremlin used its new-found enthusiasm for Arab nationalism as a means to advance ambitions which had eluded Imperial Russia. In short, what many in the non-Soviet world considered the beginning of a relaxation of tensions was used by the Kremlin as a means to attempt to overturn the world balance of power.

Thus the canons of traditional diplomacy become a subtle device of Soviet pressure. They enable the Soviet spokesmen to define the moral framework of most disputes and to shift the debate to issues of maximum embarrassment to us. It is a cardinal principle of traditional diplomacy that negotiations should concentrate on the most soluble problems, lest the holding of a conference foredoomed to failure exacerbate existing tensions. The application of this principle to a revolutionary situation enables the Kremlin to demoralize the international order still further. Since we consider negotiation as inherently valuable while the Soviet leaders refuse to negotiate except when it serves their purpose, a fundamental inequal-

---

28 For example, see Marshal Zhukov's remarks in India, *New York Times*, February 10, 1957.

ity exists in the negotiating position of the two parties. The emphasis on "soluble" problems ensures that diplomatic conferences become means for Moscow to liquidate unprofitable disputes and to shift all points of tension to the non-Soviet side of the line. The invasion of Egypt was treated more urgently in the United Nations than the suppression of the Hungarian uprising because the latter seemed less soluble, and the issue of Formosa has been kept more prominently before world opinion than has the unification of Korea or of Germany. Diplomacy in this manner becomes an instrument of political warfare, which merges insensibly into military measures if the situation warrants it.

IV

The notion that international relations reflect the class struggle also underlies the Soviet theory of war. War is not a last resort to be invoked if all else fails. Rather it is one form of a continuing struggle; its use is mandatory if the relation of forces warrants it, and resort to it should be avoided if the power constellation is unfavorable. Soviet military doctrine, therefore, rejects the notion that there is such a thing as "purely" military considerations. "War," wrote Lenin, "is part of the whole. The whole is politics. . . . Appearances are not reality. Wars are most political when they seem most military." [29]

These comments were written by Lenin as marginalia to Clausewitz, the non-Soviet thinker who has had perhaps the profoundest impact on Soviet military thought.[30] The reason is not far to seek. Despite a ponderous style and a complicated method, Clausewitz was the first truly "modern" military theorist. War, to Clausewitz, was not an isolated act but part of a continuing political process in which will, popular attitudes and the nature of objec-

---

[29] For a complete list of Lenin's marginalia and the appropriate text, see Bertholdt C. Friedl, "Cahier de Lénine No. 18674 des Archives de l'Institut Lénine à Moscow," Les Fondements Théoriques de la Guerre et de la Paix en USSR (Paris: Éditions Médicis, 1945), pp. 47-90.

[30] See Byron Dexter, "Clausewitz and Soviet Strategy," Foreign Affairs, v. 28 (October 1950), pp. 41-55.

tives play a cardinal role. "War," he wrote "can never be separated from political intercourse and if . . . this is done in any way, all the threads of the different relations are, to a certain extent, broken, and we have before us a senseless thing without an object." [31] These lines were underscored by Lenin in a volume which he inscribed: "This volume is composed of nothing but fine points." [32]

To be sure, Clausewitz' influence rests in part on the ambiguity of his method which has enabled diverse followers to find in his dicta support for divergent interpretations. Much of this ambiguity derives from his habit of first stating an idea in its extreme form, in order to trace its full logical implications, and only then bringing forward considerations which modify the application of the pure theory. In his writings the most absolute statements regarding the nature of war as an act of pure violence are found side by side with many profound and common-sense observations which mitigate the application of theory. Thus, Clausewitz' definition of the aim of war as breaking the enemy's will to resist has been taken as a point of departure in many later treatises on total war.[33] What is often overlooked is that Clausewitz also pointed out that to consider the breaking of the enemy will as a purely military problem was a hopelessly theoretical approach; that in practice the nature of war depended to a considerable extent on the objectives sought, the issues at dispute and the resolution of the protagonists.

It was precisely this dialectic quality of Clausewitz' argumentation which attracted Lenin to him. The essence of Clausewitz' teaching is his insistence that the relationship between states is a dynamic process in which war constitutes only one aspect, and even a period of peace can become an instrument for imposing a nation's will. ". . . with the conclusion of peace, a number of sparks are always extinguished which would have smouldered on quietly,

31 Carl von Clausewitz, *On War* (London: Kegan Paul, Trench, Trubner, 1940), v. 3, p. 122.

32 Friedl, cited, p. 72.

33 See for example, Dale O. Smith, *U.S. Military Doctrine: A Study and Appraisal* (New York: Duell, Sloan, and Pearce, 1955).

and the excitement of the passions abates, because all those whose minds are disposed to peace, of which in all nations and under all circumstances there is always a great number, turn themselves away completely from the road to resistance." [34] That the skillful use of peace offensives by Soviet policy has not been accidental is demonstrated by Lenin's marginalia "exactly" along this passage. And this is confirmed by another aphorism of Clausewitz on which Lenin remarked and which has been paraphrased in Soviet thought on several occasions: "The conqueror," he said, "is always a lover of peace. . . . He would like to enter our territory unopposed." [35]

The passage which most appealed to Lenin and which Stalin in 1946 emphasized as a cardinal tenet of Marxist thought concerned the relationship of war to politics. War, argued Clausewitz, can never be an act of pure violence because it grows out of the existing relations of states, their level of civilization, the nature of their alliances and the objectives in dispute. War would reach its ultimate form only if it became an end in itself, a condition which is realized only among savages and probably not even among them. For war to rage with absolute violence and without interruption until the enemy is completely defenseless is to reduce an idea to absurdity. War reveals the impact on each other of two hostile wills, which are inadequately informed about each other's intentions. This alone prevents war from being conducted as an abstract science, and it is limited furthermore by the goals which policy imposes on war.

A total war, conducted on purely military considerations, would have been to Clausewitz a contradiction in terms. In a passage heavily underlined by Lenin he wrote:

. . . War is nothing but a continuation of political intercourse, with a mixture of other means. We say mixed with other means in order thereby to maintain at the same time that this political intercourse does not cease by the War itself. . . . And how can we conceive it to be otherwise? Does

---

34 Clausewitz, cited, v. 1, p. 28.
35 Friedl, cited, p. 58.

the cessation of diplomatic notes stop the political relations between different Nations and Governments? Is not War merely another kind of writing and language for political thoughts? It has certainly a grammar of its own, but its logic is not peculiar to itself. . . . This kind of idea would be indispensable even if War was perfect War, the perfectly unbridled element of hostility. . . . But this view is doubly indispensable if we reflect that real War is no such consistent effort tending to an extreme . . . but a half-and-half thing, a contradiction in itself . . . as such, it cannot follow its own laws, but must be looked upon as a part of another whole— and this whole is policy . . . policy makes out of the all-overpowering element of War a mere instrument, it changes the tremendous battle-sword which should be lifted with both hands and the whole power of the body to strike once for all, into a light handy weapon *which is even sometimes nothing more than a rapier to exchange thrusts and feints and parries.* . . . Only through this kind of view War recovers unity; only by it can we see all Wars as things of *one* kind. . . .[36]

The intimate relation in Clausewitz' thought between policy and war was characterized by Stalin in 1946 as "having confirmed a familiar Marxist thesis." It has been paraphrased by a leading Soviet military authority: "If war is a continuation of politics, only by other means, so also peace is a continuation of struggle, only by other means."[37] And it has been quoted with approval by Mao.[38] It accounts for the Soviet preference for indirect attack—the conflict in which physical and psychological factors are combined in the proportion best calculated to produce the maximum confusion and hesitation on the part of the enemy. Buttressed by Marxist theory, this concept has been applied to Soviet military doctrine with its emphasis on morale, deception and a "main thrust" at the enemy's weakest link—all attributes which seek to place psychology and policy at the service of a strategy based on never-ending

---

36 Clausewitz, cited, v. 3, pp. 121-3. (Emphasis added.)

37 Boris M. Shaposhnikov, *Mozg Armii* (Moscow-Leningrad: Gosizdat, 1929), v. 3, p. 239, as quoted by Garthoff, cited, p. 11.

38 Mao Tse-tung, cited, v. 2, p. 202.

struggle.[39] Therefore, too, the most substantial Communist contribution to the theory of war has been in the area of limited war—the conflict in which power and policy are most intimately related, in which everything depends on gearing the psychological to the physical components of policy. Both Soviet and Chinese Communist theory emphasize the integral relationship between peace and war as alternating or combined methods for conducting a conflict; indeed, both in language and theory, the two tactics are considered almost identical.[40]

Significantly, the best theoretical statement of Communist military thought is found not in Soviet, but in Chinese writings. This is no accident. The expansion of the U.S.S.R. has been due largely to a skillful use of political warfare and to the vast opportunities created by the collapse of German power in Central Europe. Chinese communism owes its entire success, indeed its survival, to its ability to derive political benefits from military operations. The main concern of Soviet communism for the first decade and a half was the *protection* of its home base; the chief concern of Chinese communism was the *conquest* of a home base.

Written in the 1930's at the beginning of the war against Japan, Mao's essays on "Protracted War" and on "Strategic Problems of China's Revolutionary War" are remarkable for their sense of proportion and their skill in adapting the Leninist orthodoxy to Chinese conditions. They are important not only because of the light they shed on the thinking of one of the most powerful men in the world today, but also because of the consistency with which the strategy developed by Mao has been pursued by the Chinese Communists both during the civil war and in the Korean war.

Starting from the familiar Leninist doctrine that war is the highest form of struggle, Mao elaborated a theory of war which combines a high order of analytical ability with

---

[39] For a good treatment of operational Soviet doctrine see Garthoff, cited, pp. 299-408.

[40] See, for example, Stalin's explanation of the nature of political strategy entirely in military terms, Garthoff, cited, p. 13 ff.

rare psychological insight and complete ruthlessness. The key to Communist superiority Mao finds in Marxist doctrine which he compares to a telescope which permits the distinguishing of the essential from the irrelevant. He, therefore, considers a study of Marxist-Leninist-Stalinist theory a prerequisite to effective action. The essence of war, Mao asserts, resides in the intimate relation of two hostile wills which keep secrets from each other.[41] On one plane, no one knows as much about one's own actions as the enemy because correct intelligence is the key to successful military operations. On the other hand, many pressures combine to obscure the clear view which their own self-interest enjoins on military commanders. There is not only the confusion of the battle, but also the inherent deceptiveness of an analysis on the basis of purely military considerations. War reflects deep-seated factors of social structure and only by understanding them can strategy make a correct assessment. Thus theory is the indispensable handmaiden of strategy; its task is to bring the "subjective" assessment into line with "objective" factors. "Know your enemy and know yourself," said Mao, paraphrasing an old Chinese proverb, "and you can fight a hundred battles without disaster." [42]

What then did Mao's theoretical insight reveal to him? It showed a current of revolution sweeping across the world, a revolution which would receive its impetus in part from the success of Chinese communism: "The [Chinese] Communist party has led and continues to lead the stupendous, sublime, glorious and victorious revolutionary war. This war is not only the banner of China's liberation, but is pregnant with significance for world revolution. The eyes of the revolutionary masses throughout the world are upon us. . . . we will lead the Chinese revolution to its completion and also exert a far-reaching influence on the revolution in the East as well as in the whole world. Our past revolutionary wars prove that we need not only a correct Marxist political line, but also a

---

41 Mao Tse-tung, cited, v. 1, p. 175 ff.
42 Same, v. 1, p. 187.

correct Marxist military line." [43] The correct military line Mao summed up in his three propositions which he considered the prerequisite for victory: "[1] to fight resolutely a decisive engagement in every campaign or battle when victory is certain; [2] to avoid a decisive engagement in every campaign or battle when victory is uncertain; and [3] to avoid absolutely a strategic decisive engagement which stakes the destiny of the nation." [44]

The basic military strategy of Chinese communism was defined as "protracted limited war." The relationship of forces being unfavorable for waging an all-out war, the kind of war in which absolute power reigns supreme, the Communist goal has to be a series of transformations, none of them decisive in themselves, the cumulative effect of which, however, should be to change the balance of power:

> People who direct a war cannot strive for victories beyond the limit allowed by the objective conditions, but within that limit they can and must strive for victories through their conscious activity. . . . We do not advocate that any of our commanders . . . should detach himself from objective conditions and become a rash and reckless hothead, but we must encourage everyone of them to become a brave and wise general. . . . Swimming in an immense ocean of war, a commander must not only keep himself from sinking, but also make sure of reaching the opposite shore with measured strokes. Strategy and tactics as laws for directing the war constitute the art of swimming in the ocean of war.[45]

Mao's theory of war, therefore, rejects the notion of a quick, decisive war conducted on the basis of purely military considerations, which underlies so much of American strategic thought. It abounds with exhortations that the psychological equation of war is as important as the physical one; indeed that it is not strength which decides war, but the ability to use it subtly and to the enemy's maximum disadvantage. Mao mentions with approval examples from Chinese history where a superior enemy was defeated

43 Same, v. 1, p. 191.
44 Same, v. 2, p. 233.
45 Same, v. 2, pp. 201-2.

by stratagem. He recounts the story of a Chinese commander who completely disconcerted his opponent by delaying his attack beyond the point when it was expected and who turned a retreat into a rout by always permitting his opponent to withdraw to a position of further disadvantage. He places great emphasis on the ability to create illusions for the enemy and then to strike him with a surprise attack; the ability to launch a surprise attack is in fact considered directly proportionate to the ability to bring about illusions. For this reason, Mao never tires of counseling a strategy of maximum ambiguity, in which the enemy's impatience for victory is used to frustrate him. He expresses this principle in sixteen words: "Enemy advances, we retreat; enemy halts, we harass; enemy tires, we attack; enemy retreats, we pursue." [46]

His concern with winning a war through the psychological exhaustion of his opponent led Mao, like Stalin, to pay particular attention to the strategic counteroffensive. If part of the confusion of war is caused by the inadequacy of intelligence about the enemy's intentions, one way of reducing this uncertainty is to induce the enemy to advance in a predetermined direction. As the opponent advances into hostile territory he may make mistakes through overconfidence or he may become discouraged about his inability to fight a decisive engagement against an elusive hostile force. Moreover, it will then be easier to deny the enemy the information he requires to act purposefully. Sometime in the course of the enemy advance a point is usually reached at which, according to Mao, Communist psychological superiority outbalances the physical superiority of the opponent. This will particularly be true if it is possible to attack columns on the move. For then the absolute superiority of the enemy can be transformed into a relative inferiority on the battlefield. The art of warfare is to isolate enemy units, however great their combined superiority, and to defeat them in detail: "We defeat the many with the few . . . [by defeating] the few with the many—this we say to the separate units of the enemy

---

[46] Same, v. 1, p. 212.

forces that we meet on the battlefield. This is no longer a secret and the enemy in general is by now well acquainted with our habit. But he can neither deprive us of our victories nor avoid his losses, because he does not know when and where we shall strike. That we keep secret. The Red Army's operations are as a rule surprise attacks." [47]

For this reason Mao inveighs against "desperadoism" and "adventurism"—the tendency to cling to territory at all cost or the quest for a quick victory. The strength of Communist strategy, according to Mao, is precisely its willingness to accept withdrawals as long as they are related to an over-all strategic plan. The Communist superiority resides in the fact that in a protracted war the internal contradictions of the capitalist enemy are certain to mature: "The . . . objective of retreat is to induce the enemy to commit mistakes and to detect them. . . . we can skilfully induce the enemy to commit mistakes, by staging a 'feint,' as Sun Tzu called it (i.e., 'make a noise in the east but strike in the west' . . .)." [48] ". . . in order to draw the enemy into a fight unfavourable to him but favourable to us, we should often engage him when he is on the move and should look for such conditions favourable to ourselves as the advantageousness of the terrain, the vulnerability of the enemy, the presence of inhabitants who can blockade information, and fatigue and inadvertence on the part of the enemy. This means that we should allow the enemy to advance and should not grudge the temporary loss of part of our territory. . . . We have always advocated the policy of 'luring the enemy to penetrate deep'. . . ." [49]

If necessary, Chinese Communist theory maintains, even negotiations can be utilized to magnify the psychological pressure on the opponent or to deprive him of the fruits of his victory. Like a judo artist, Mao therefore proposes to paralyze the enemy when seeming to be most pliable and to use the opponent's strength to defeat him by attacking him when most off-balance. The desire of the opponent for a rapid victory is considered a sign of weak-

47 Same, v. 1, p. 242.
48 Same, v. 1, pp. 217-8.
49 Same, v. 2, pp. 223-4.

ness to be exploited by skillful Communist strategy and to be used to frustrate the enemy when success seems nearest. It requires no elaboration to note the strategy advanced by Mao in the 1930's was followed almost precisely during the Korean war.

Thus limited war is not considered by Soviet doctrine as a strategic aberration, but as a strategic opportunity. It is the form of conflict best suited to take advantage of the preconceptions and inhibitions of *status quo* powers. It permits the posing of risks in such a manner that they will always seem out of proportion to the objectives in dispute. And this strategy is given an additional impetus by the horrors of modern weapons. For against a power which is committed to an all-out strategy either by its strategic doctrine or by its weapons systems a threshold is created below which the Communists' favored strategy of ambiguity can be carried out with considerable chances of success. Mao's strategy of protracted war can be effective, after all, only against an opponent unprepared either physically or psychologically for limited war; an opponent to whom a war without total victory seems somehow beyond reason.

A war waged against Communist powers, therefore, presupposes an ability to relate the physical to the psychological balance of international relations, to find a mode of action in which power and the willingness to use it are most nearly in harmony. Mao understood that in the subtle adjustments of the psychological balance the side least eager for peace has a negotiating advantage because it can outwait, if not outfight, its opponent. Thus in any conflict with Communist powers it is important, above all, to be clear at the outset about the precise objectives of the war. *And no conditions should be sought for which one is not willing to fight indefinitely and no advance made except to a point at which one is willing to wait indefinitely. The side which is willing to outwait its opponent—which is less eager for a settlement—can tip the psychological balance, whatever the outcome of the physical battle.* The great advantage of communism has been that its doctrine of protracted conflict has made it less uncomfortable with a contest seemingly without issue than we have been with our belief in the possibility of achieving total victory.[50] In any concept of limited war, it is imperative to find a mode of operation and to create a psychological framework in which our impetuosity does not transform time into an enemy ally. Henceforth, patience and subtlety must be as important components of our strategy as power.

V

But is not a change of course possible? May not the Soviet leaders be sincere in their protestations of peaceful intentions? Have not the death of Stalin and his subsequent downgrading radically altered the situation? It is difficult to know what sincerity means where self-interest is identical with the avoidance of all-out war. So long as the "relation of forces" is not clearly in the Soviet favor, Leninist theory counsels keeping the provocation below the level which might produce a final showdown. Peaceful coexistence would thereby become the most efficient offensive tactic, the best means to subvert the existing order.

What is permanent in Soviet theory is the insistence upon the continuing struggle, not the form it takes at any given moment. Conflict between opposing social systems is inevitable, but its nature must be adapted to changing conditions. "Communists," said Stalin to H. G. Wells in 1934, "do not in the least idealize methods of violence. . . . They would be very pleased to drop violent methods if the ruling class agreed to give way to the working class." [51]

Nor is the slogan of peaceful coexistence the invention of the group which succeeded Stalin. Since 1918 it has reappeared in Soviet policy at periodic intervals. In the

---

[50] The inherent weakness of the British and French attack on Egypt was that they did not possess a legitimacy which would have enabled them to continue in possession of the Suez Canal. Even had the military operations been more successful, the legitimization of the attack made it impossible for Great Britain and France to stay, once military operations between Egypt and Israel had ceased. President Gamal Abdel Nasser had every opportunity to frustrate his opponents by outwaiting them.

[51] Joseph Stalin, "Marxism vs. Liberalism: An Interview between Joseph Stalin and H. G. Wells," 1934, as quoted by Garthoff, cited, p. 11 (f.n.)

1920's, it was ushered in by Lenin's statement: ". . . we shall make every possible concession within the limits of retaining power. . . ." [52] And it was justified in 1926 by Stalin in the only terms which make sense in Marxist doctrine: that peaceful coexistence was produced by a temporary equilibrium of forces and was justified only by tactical considerations: "A certain degree of *provisional* equilibrium [emphasis added] has been established between our country of socialist construction and the countries of the capitalist world. This equilibrium characterizes the present stage of the 'peaceful co-existence.' . . ." [53]

In the 1930's peaceful coexistence had a similar tactical significance. Notably, it followed upon an unsuccessful overture to Nazi Germany. This overture was made not because the Soviet leaders preferred Fascist Germany to the Western powers; it was simply that they saw no essential difference between the social structure of Nazi Germany and the Western democracies. The best way to protect the Soviet Union was to set the capitalist powers against each other, to deflect German energies, if at all possible, toward the West. ". . . we are far from being admirers of the Fascist régime in Germany," said Stalin soon after Hitler came to power. "The importance, however, lies not in Fascism, if for no other reason than the simple fact that Fascism in Italy, for instance, did not prevent us from establishing most cordial relations with that country. . . . We are oriented as we were before, and as we are now, . . . only toward the U.S.S.R. And if the interests of the

---

[52] Lenin, *Selected Works,* cited, v. 9, p. 242, as quoted by Leites, cited, p. 491.

[53] Joseph Stalin, *XIV S'ezd Vsesoivznoi Kommunisticheskoi Partii* (b) 18-31 Dekabria 1925 Stenograficheskii Otchel, p. 8, as quoted by Taracouzio, cited, p. 138. The Soviet notion of the motivations of the non-Communist world is also well illustrated by Stalin's reaction to the Kellogg Pact: "They talk about pacifism; they speak about peace among European states. Briand and Chamberlain are embracing each other. . . . All this is nonsense. From European history we know that every time that treaties envisaging a new arrangement of forces for new wars have been signed, these treaties have been called treaties of peace. . . . [although] they were signed for the purpose of depicting new elements of the coming war." (Same, p. 15, as quoted by Taracouzio, cited, pp. 139-40.)

Soviet Union demand that we approach one country or another . . . we shall do so without hesitation." [54]

Only when the overture to Germany had failed and it seemed as if the Soviet Union might become the first victim of the often predicted capitalist "contradictions," did the U.S.S.R. emerge as the champion of collective security. Then the League of Nations, only recently derided as an instrument of capitalist hypocrisy, became the focal point of Soviet diplomacy. As always during such periods, the international aspect of communism was played down. The "export of revolution is nonsense," said Stalin now, "each country, if it so desires, will make its own revolution." [55] And once more eager advocates in the West accepted the Soviet statements at face value and contrasted the consistent anti-Fascism of the U.S.S.R. with the vacillations of the Western powers. Had they read Stalin's statement in 1933, they would have been less shocked about the Nazi-Soviet pact: the treaty which made inevitable the war so long predicted by Soviet theory.

There was nothing inconsistent about the Nazi-Soviet pact or anything immoral in it from the Soviet point of view. It was the logical application of a policy announced by Stalin a decade previously: ". . . a great deal . . . depends on whether we shall succeed in deferring the inevitable war with the capitalist world . . . until the time . . . when the capitalists start fighting with each other. . . ." [56] Less than six months before his death, Stalin ushered in the most recent period of peaceful coexistence precisely with the argument that a period of *détente* would sharpen the conflicts among the capitalist powers whose difficulties had increased with the growth of the Communist bloc.[57]

Any policy which is based on the assumption of a change

---

[54] Stalin, *XVII S'ezd Vsesoivznoi Kommunistecheskoi Partii,* cited, p. 14, as quoted by Taracouzio, cited, pp. 181-2.

[55] Stalin, interview with Roy Howard, as quoted by Taracouzio, cited, p. 231.

[56] Stalin, *Sochineniya,* cited, v. 10, pp. 288-9, as quoted by Leites, cited, p. 501.

[57] "Economic Problems of Socialism in the U.S.S.R.," in Meissner and Reshetar, cited, p. 199.

THE STRATEGY OF AMBIGUITY

in Soviet purposes bears the burden of proving that the change now is "real," that the Soviet leadership is now interested in a basic and lasting accommodation. This would be tantamount to asserting that the Soviet leaders have ceased being Bolsheviks. The notion of an accommodation assumes an indefinite prolongation of the *status quo*. But the notion of a static condition is explicitly rejected by Communist doctrine. A genuine settlement between different social systems can come about in Marxist eyes only with the end of the class struggle. In any other situation the Communists assign themselves the task of exacerbating all tensions. Moreover, while it is easy to see how the Soviet leaders might refrain from a certain course of action because the relation of forces seemed to them unfavorable, it is difficult to find a reason for their giving up a theory which thus far has served them so well. Now that Mao rules 400 million people and China has emerged as the strongest state of Asia, why should he abandon a doctrine which seemed valid when he was reduced to 20,-000 adherents in the mountains of Yenan? Why should the Soviet leaders give up a system of analysis which has been taught in all their schools for over a generation and in whose dogmas their thought has been steeped for many decades? Why should they do so, when they see how their state has transformed itself within twenty-five years from an international outcast to a position where in the Suez crisis it could threaten with impunity to launch rocket attacks upon other great powers?

Nor is there any evidence that they have any intention of modifying the basic Soviet doctrine. *Pravda* at the close of 1956 was again insisting that the downgrading of Stalin referred only to the cult of his personality and that it did not affect the ideological posture of communism.[58] And Khrushchev maintained at the same time that when it came to fighting imperialism, all Communists were Stalinists.

Even the speech with which Khrushchev opened the Twentieth Congress of the Communist Party in February 1956, hailed in the West as opening an era of peaceful co-

---

[58] *New York Times,* December 24, 1956.

existence, was in fact a restatement of familiar Leninist doctrine. Its significance did not rest in its invocations of peace, but in the fact that after almost forty years of Communist rule the non-Soviet world had still not learned the peculiar Communist use of such terms as "peace" and "democracy." Neither the doctrine of the increasing contradictions of the capitalist economy nor of the intensified revolutionary struggle was given up by Khrushchev. On the contrary, they were reaffirmed and bolstered with quotations from Lenin.[59] To be sure, Khrushchev did not draw any explicit conclusions regarding the inevitability of war; indeed, he gave an ambiguous definition of "peaceful coexistence" hardly different in substance and almost identical in words with the "peaceful coexistence" theme of the 1920's and 1930's. But before a group trained in Marxist dialectics, it was not necessary to draw such obvious lessons. All of them knew, even if Western readers did not, what would happen if both the domestic and international contradictions of capitalism matured at the same time. Thus the most remarkable aspect of Khrushchev's speech was not its content, but that after thirty years such shopworn phraseology could still lull the non-Soviet world and be seriously debated as ushering in a new era of Soviet behavior.

Khrushchev's speech began in correct Soviet style with a description of the economic and social conditions which underlay international relationships. He contrasted the constantly improving position of the Soviet economy with a capitalist economy "developing in the direction of still greater enrichment of the monopolies, more intensive exploitation and . . . lowering of . . . living standards . . . sharpening of the competitive struggle among capitalist states, maturing of new economic crises and upheavals." He warned his listeners not to be confused by the seeming prosperity of the capitalist economy. Quoting Lenin, he emphasized that the decay of capitalism does not preclude its rapid growth: ". . . only a temporary coincidence of circumstances favorable to capitalism prevented existing

---

[59] Nikita S. Khrushchev, "Report to the Party Congress," *Current Digest of the Soviet Press*, v. 8 (March 7, 1956), pp. 4, 5, 10 and 11.

crises phenomena from developing into a deep economic crisis. . . . The capitalists and the learned defenders of their interests are circulating a 'theory' . . . [of] salvation from economic crises. The representatives of Marxist-Leninist science have [often] pointed out that this is a hollow illusion. The arms drive does not cure the disease, but drives it deeper. . . . present-day technology does not remove the contradiction, only emphasizes it. . . . Crises are inherent in the very nature of capitalism; they are inevitable." [60]

The consciousness of impending catastrophe has impelled the capitalist powers, according to Khrushchev, to resort to the inevitable expedient of forming aggressive military pacts to restore their position by military means. But the Soviet leaders were not fooled, argued Khrushchev, by the hypocrisy of calling the alliances defensive. "We know from history that, when planning a redivision of the world, the imperialist powers have always lined up military blocs. Today the 'anti-Communism' slogan is again being used . . . to cover up one power's claims for world domination." [61] Thus Khrushchev was echoing Stalin's attack on the Kellogg Pact as "depicting the new elements of the coming war."

However, there existed a basic difference between the position of the U.S.S.R. before World War II and at present: the growth of the Socialist bloc "dedicated to peace and progress." And the newly emergent peoples in Asia and Africa constituted another counterweight to imperialist war aims: "The whole course of international relations in recent years shows that great popular forces have risen to fight for the preservation of peace. The ruling imperialist circles cannot ignore this. Their more farsighted representatives are beginning to admit that the 'positions of strength' policy . . . has failed. . . . These public figures still do not venture to state that capitalism will find its grave in another world war . . . but they are already obliged to admit openly that the socialist camp is invincible." [62]

---

60 Same, pp. 4-5.
61 Same, p. 6.
62 Same, p. 7.

In short, since long-term trends were favorable a period of peaceful coexistence was tactically advisable. But as in all past periods of peaceful coexistence, Khrushchev was at pains to point out that this change of tactics did not imply a modification of revolutionary goals: "Our enemies like to depict us Leninists as advocates of violence always and everywhere. True, we recognize the need for the revolutionary transformation of capitalist society into socialist society. It is this that distinguishes the revolutionary Marxists from the reformists, the opportunists. There is no doubt that in a number of capitalist countries violent overthrow of the dictatorship of the bourgeoisie . . . [is] inevitable. But the forms of social revolution vary. . . . moreover, achieving these forms need not be associated with civil war under all circumstances. . . . The greater or lesser intensity which the struggle may assume, the use or non-use of violence in the transition to socialism depend on the resistance of the exploiters. . . . Of course, in those countries where capitalism is still strong, where it possesses a tremendous military and police machine serious resistance by reactionary forces is inevitable." [63]

Thus the capitalist powers were given the option—as indeed they had under Stalin—of surrendering peacefully. Khrushchev's speech was given particular poignancy by later events. For the only examples of the "peaceful" triumph of communism he could think of were Czechoslovakia and Hungary.

It is remarkable that this restatement of familiar doctrine should have given rise to speculation about a change of Soviet course. For only two explanations were possible for Khrushchev's speech: either Khrushchev believed it, in which case little would have changed from Stalinist days, or he thought his audience believed this particular reasoning, in which case his freedom of maneuver in making a settlement with the West would be severely circumscribed. Moreover, the speeches at the same Congress delivered by other Soviet figures such as Shepilov, Mikoyan and Molotov were, if anything, even more intransigent.

---

[63] Same, pp. 11-2.

The emerging middle class in Russia may, of course, in time ameliorate the rigors of Soviet doctrine. It has happened before in history that a revolutionary movement has lost its Messianic *élan*. But it has usually occurred only when a Messianic movement came to be opposed with equal fervor or when it reached the limit of its military strength. The Turks did not stop voluntarily at the gates of Vienna or the Arabs in southern France. Rather, a line was established because they had been defeated in battle and the decay did not set in until the West for several centuries exercised unremitting pressure to push them back. In any case, the problem for American policy is to analyze precisely what consequences would flow from a change within the Soviet Union. The history of middle-class revolutions, which in Russia would almost inevitably imply a much larger role for the military, is not too reassuring on this point. Napoleon did not lead, after all, a proletarian army, nor was Hitler a Marxist. It can be argued that a middle class deprived of Marxist theory might be even more inflexible than the present Soviet leadership. It could no longer count on the inevitable triumph of Marxism; it would no longer be able to rely on the ebb-and-flow doctrine of Communist dialectic. The bastions acquired by Stalin might, therefore, represent to it the surety of possession. To a military man a radar screen in Central Europe may seem more important than the good will of the Western powers.

To be sure, the opposite is also possible. The new middle class may prove reluctant to jeopardize its domestic gains, although in the face of our repeated protestations of our horror of war they may rate this jeopardy as rather low. But an even more important point is raised by the speculations regarding Soviet intentions: the degree to which we can afford to gear our policy to assumptions regarding the possible transformation of Soviet society. The test of policy is its ability to provide for the worst contingency; it can always escape its dilemmas by relying on history or the good will of the opposing states. A wise policy will keep under its own control all factors essential to survival. It will not count too much on changes in domestic structures of other states, particularly of avowedly revolutionary powers like the U.S.S.R. or Communist China where both the historical record and the often-repeated proclamations should inspire caution.

Moreover, there may be some prices we are unable to pay even for a domestic Soviet transformation. Perhaps a long period of peace would alter the Soviet regime. But we cannot give up the Middle East to purchase it. Perhaps a policy of inactivity on our part would magnify all the internal tensions of the Soviet system. But it may also give the Soviet leaders the breathing spell needed to overcome them and to gather forces for a renewed onslaught. There is, in short, no means of escaping the inextricable element of international relations: in a system of sovereign states, policy always has somewhat of a "precautionary" aspect. It must guard not only against current intentions of another power, but against the possibility that these intentions may change. It is risky to trust that history will accomplish what the structure of international relations imposes as the duty of statesmanship.

To be sure, the United States should utilize all opportunities to bring about a more moderate course within the Soviet bloc. But, while we should always leave open avenues for a basic change in Soviet leadership, we should have few illusions about the degree to which these can be promoted by a conciliatory American policy. For, when we have been most conciliatory, as after the Geneva summit conference, the Soviet leaders have been most insistent about feeling threatened. And they are probably sincere in these assertions. Their revolutionary quality derives, however, not from the fact that they feel threatened—a measure of threat is inherent in the relation of sovereign states—but that nothing can reassure them. Because their doctrine *requires* them to fear us, they strive for absolute security: the neutralization of the United States and the elimination of all our influence from Europe and Asia. And because absolute security for the U.S.S.R. means absolute insecurity for us, the only safe United States policy is one which is built on the assumption of a continued revolutionary struggle, even though the methods may vary with the requirements of the changing situation.

Nevertheless, the likelihood of a continuing revolutionary conflict should not be confused with the imminence of an all-out showdown. An all-out attack is the least likely form of Soviet strategy, either politically or militarily. Yet this is the kind of conflict for which our military and strategic doctrine best prepare us. From this the Soviet leaders derive two basic advantages. In the political field, we tend to look for the "pure" case of aggression which their doctrine teaches the Soviet leaders to avoid by all means. And in the military field, it causes us to look for absolute solutions in a contest which Moscow will seek to transform into a subtle blend of political, economic, psychological and, incidentally, military warfare.

We have thus been inhibited by two contradictory motivations. We have refused to take at face value the often-repeated Soviet assertions that they mean to smash the existing framework and have sought to interpret every Soviet maneuver in terms of categories which we have come to consider as "legitimate." On the other hand, we have conducted our relations with the Soviet bloc, whether military or diplomatic, as if it were possible to conceive of a terminal date to the conflict. Many of our pronouncements have given rise to the notion that an over-all diplomatic settlement is at least conceivable, and much of our military thought centers around the possibility of victory in an all-out war, which would put an end to international tensions once and for all.

Both contingencies are explicitly rejected by Communist doctrine. As long as the class struggle continues until, that is, the Communist system has triumphed all over the world, conflict between the Soviet and non-Soviet world is considered to be inevitable, although its forms may vary with the tactical requirements of the situation. Nor would Soviet doctrine counsel risking everything in an all-out showdown unless the disproportion of power in their favor became overwhelmingly clear. Thus, both the free world's quest for legitimacy and its search for absolute answers increase its vulnerability to the Soviet strategy of ambiguity: the former by taking at face value every tactical move by the Soviets; the latter by producing an excessive concern with the least likely danger.

Effective action against the Soviet threat, therefore, pre-supposes a realization that the contest with the Soviet bloc is likely to be protracted, a fact from which we cannot escape because the Soviet leaders insist on it. Both in our diplomacy and in our military policy we must be able to gear firmness to patience, and not be misled by Soviet maneuvers or by our preference for absolute solutions. The United States must study the psychology of its op-ponents as carefully as they have studied ours. We must learn that there are no purely political any more than purely military solutions and that, in the relation among states, will may play as great a role as power. We must un-derstand that the quest for certainty can only paralyze action because it will play into the hands of the Soviet strategy of ambiguity. History demonstrates that revolu-tionary powers have never been brought to a halt until their opponents stopped pretending that the revolution-aries were really misunderstood legitimists.

Everything depends, therefore, on our ability to gradu-ate our actions both in our diplomacy and in our military policy. To the extent that we succeed in seeing policy as a unity in which political, psychological, economic and military pressures merge, we may actually be able to use Soviet theory to our advantage. Soviet and Chinese Com-munist theory leave little doubt that these are not regimes which would risk everything to prevent changes adverse to them so long as their national survival is not directly af-fected. They are even less likely to stake everything to achieve a positive gain. To be sure, the Soviet leaders have sought skillfully to paralyze opposition to their pressures by creating the impression that a withdrawal from any territory once occupied by Soviet troops or in which Soviet influence has been growing, as in Egypt, is inconceivable, and that any attempt to bring it about may lead to all-out war. But both history and Soviet theory would seem to in-dicate that this is a form of atomic blackmail. One need only study the abject effort of the Politburo in the weeks before the German attack on the U.S.S.R. to achieve an accommodation to realize that, when confronted with an unfavorable relation of forces, the Communist regimes would not hesitate to apply Lenin's dictum: one step backward, two steps forward. We too often forget that, when faced with determined United States opposition, the Kremlin in 1946 withdrew its troops from Iran. And Mao has repeatedly labeled the refusal to yield when confronted with superior force as "desperadoism."

Most of the discussion in this chapter has been in terms of a Soviet doctrine developed before the first explosion of the atomic bomb. Has nuclear power brought about a change in Soviet theory? It has been remarkable how little Soviet doctrine has been affected by the horror of modern weapons. This factor has been an element both of strength and of weakness. Of strength, because during the period of our atomic monopoly it enabled the Soviet propaganda to create a psychological framework which increased our inhibitions against using them. And of potential weakness, because it may make it more difficult to integrate nuclear weapons into an effective Soviet strategy or because it may cause the Soviets to underestimate the horror of nuclear war. The Soviet effort to assess the meaning of the new technology may, therefore, give an indication of the future direction of revolutionary conflict in the nuclear age.

11

THE SOVIET UNION AND
THE ATOM

FOR ALL ITS CONFIDENCE in its skill in manipulating social forces, for all its pride in its ability to predict the course of history, the end of World War II confronted the Soviet leadership with a fearful challenge. At the precise moment when Soviet armies stood in the center of a war-wrecked Europe and Lenin's prophecies of the doom of capitalism seemed on the verge of being fulfilled, a new weapon appeared far transcending in power anything previously known. Was the dialectic of history so fragile that it could be upset by a new technological discovery? Was this to be the result of twenty years of brutal repression and deprivation and of four years of cataclysmic war that at its end the capitalist enemy should emerge with a weapon which could imperil the Soviet state as never before?

It must have been disheartening for the men in the Kremlin to enter a postwar world where the ascendancy of the U.S.S.R. as a world power, seemingly confirmed by the outcome of the conflict, was again put into question. The purely ideological problems were no less formidable. If capitalism could extricate itself from its difficulties by a new technological discovery, the structure of the economy was not as crucial as Soviet doctrine postulated; it was less fundamental in fact than the state of technology. If the predictive power of Leninism failed at so vital a point, the whole dogma based on superior prescience was put into question.

But the Soviet leadership reacted with the iron discipline it had learned during its history of militancy. It refused to recognize an inconsistency between Leninist theory and reality, for to do so would have been to give up its reason for existence. Rather, it took the position that the new developments confirmed accepted doctrine, and that the decay of capitalism, far from being arrested by the more powerful weapons at its disposal, would be accelerated by it.

Nor was this display of discipline merely an exercise in abstract theory. On the contrary, the Soviet leaders put their doctrinal training to good use in the eminently practical task of surviving as a revolutionary power. They had learned all their lives that appearances were deceiving and that a political situation reflected a combination of political, economic, psychological and military factors. They had been taught that the emphasis on any one of these factors to the exclusion of the others was self-defeating. They were convinced that superiority in one category of power could be compensated by a manipulation of the others. Thus, while Soviet leadership could not do anything immediate about our possession of the atomic bomb, it might undermine the will to use it by a worldwide campaign against the horrors of nuclear warfare. And domestically, Soviet leadership was even more sure of itself. Since the Kremlin controlled all the media of communication, it could establish the framework of thinking about nuclear matters within the Soviet Union both by withholding information and by interpreting it to fit the tactical requirements of the Soviet line.

The result was a tour de force, masterful in its comprehension of psychological factors, brutal in its consistency, and ruthless in its sense of direction. With a cold-blooded effrontery, as if no other version of reality than its own were even conceivable, through all the media and organizations at its disposal, through diplomacy and propaganda, the Kremlin advanced three related themes. One was that the decisiveness of nuclear weapons was overrated; this was designed to demonstrate that the U.S.S.R. remained predominant in the essential categories of power. A second maintained that, although not decisive, nuclear weapons were inherently in a special category of horror from other weapons and should, therefore, be banned. By means of diplomatic notes, peace congresses, resolutions and propaganda, this campaign sought to paralyze the psychological basis for the use of our most potent weapon. A third and subordinate theme was that the only legitimate use of the atom was its peaceful application, in which field the U.S.S.R. was prepared to take the lead. This position reinforced the previous one; it gave impetus to Soviet peace offensives and strengthened its appeal to the uncommitted powers.

All three themes recur in Soviet doctrine since 1945 with changes of emphasis, but little alteration in content. It is possible to distinguish two phases, however, in Soviet efforts to come to grips with the atom: the period of our atomic monopoly and the period after the Kremlin had acquired a nuclear arsenal of its own. During the former period, the Soviet leaders relied largely on their "ban-the-bomb" propaganda, which insisted that atomic bombs were as evil and horrible as they were ineffectual. With the growth of the Soviet nuclear arsenal, and especially since the death of Stalin, threats of thermonuclear retaliation have alternated with proposals to eliminate nuclear weapons. The Soviet leaders no longer rely entirely on our inhibitions; they have sought also to play on our fears. But in doing so, nuclear power became better understood by the Soviet public, and this raised a host of problems with respect to doctrinal purity, militancy and the perils of the nuclear age, which had been evaded in 1945.

II

The Soviet effort to minimize nuclear weapons was so consistent and was begun so early that it must have been planned long before the explosion of the first atomic bomb over Hiroshima. When President Truman informed Stalin during the Potsdam Conference that the United States possessed a new weapon of fearful power, he was startled by Stalin's nonchalance in acknowledging it: "The Russian Premier," wrote Truman, "showed no special interest. All he said was that he was glad to hear it and that he hoped we would make 'good use of it against the Japanese.' " [1] Against the background of the later disclosures of Soviet espionage, there can be no doubt that Stalin was well aware of the impact of what he was being told. It is almost certain, in fact, that Stalin learned of the possibility of nuclear explosions well before Truman, who was not informed of the existence of our Atomic Energy Program until he became President in April 1945. Stalin's behavior at Potsdam reflected a decision to minimize the importance of nuclear weapons in order to demonstrate the Kremlin's independence and the impossibility of intimidating it.

With the official Soviet attitude thus determined, the whole apparatus of Soviet propaganda and diplomacy went into action in support. The bombing of Hiroshima was mentioned in the Soviet press only briefly, and with no further discussion or elaboration. The end of the Far Eastern war was attributed entirely to the intervention of Soviet armies. The bombing of Nagasaki was not reported when it occurred. Although the Soviet regime was soon to launch a world-wide campaign to "ban" the use of atomic bombs, the Soviet public had to wait for nearly ten years to find out precisely what the atomic bomb was.

Moreover, whatever the uncertainties and qualms of the power which did possess the atomic bomb, Soviet propaganda knew no such hesitations. As early as September 1, 1945, less than a month after the bombing of Hiroshima and Nagasaki, the Soviet *New Times*, was ready with an official interpretation of the significance of nuclear weapons. Because the semblance of wartime harmony was still being maintained, the form chosen was one of those indirect methods so dear to the heart of Soviet strategists: an analysis of foreign press comments regarding the atomic bomb. After a brief summary of descriptions of the atomic bomb, the article turned to an examination of its implications. The atomic bomb, argued the *New Times*, had not been the decisive weapon in the war against Japan. Such a

---

[1] Harry S. Truman, *Memoirs*, v. 1, *Year of Decisions* (New York: Doubleday, 1955), p. 416.

proposition was advanced only by bankrupt Japanese mili-
tarists to obscure their ignominious defeat at the hands of
the U.S.S.R. and by "semi-Fascist" commentators in the
Western world: "The experience of the second World
War and the unsurpassed victories of the Red Army have
clearly shown that success in war is not achieved by the
one-sided development of one or the other weapon, but by
the perfection of all arms and their skillful coordina-
tion." [2] In short, nothing of particular significance had
happened at Hiroshima.

If the atomic bomb had not proved decisive against
Japan, it could obviously not be used to intimidate the
U.S.S.R. "Under the influence of the announcement of
the atomic bomb, the reactionary circles [in the United
States] . . . are inclined to stand forth unashamed in their
imperialist nakedness. They demand that the United
States should establish its domination over the world with
the atomic bomb. Apparently the lessons of history mean
nothing to those errant imperialists. They do not stop to
ponder over the debacle of Hitler's plans of world domin-
ion which, after all, were also based on the expectation
of exploiting temporary advantages in the production of
armaments." [3] But while nuclear weapons did not confer
a basic advantage, their indiscriminate destructiveness
made it all the more necessary for all "progressive" forces
to unite against their use.[4]

In this manner, the strains of subsequent Soviet nuclear
policy emerged barely three weeks after the explosion of
the first atomic bomb over Hiroshima: the relative unim-
portance of nuclear weapons, their special horror, and the
Soviet Union as the defender of the peace appealing to all
groups repelled by the prospect of atomic warfare. Stalin
was merely ratifying official dogma when, a year after the
first atomic explosion, he took his first public stand on
nuclear matters: "I do not consider the atomic bomb as

---

[2] M. Rubinstein, "The Foreign Press on the Atomic Bomb," *New Times* (published in English by the newspaper *Trud*, Moscow), no. 7(17) (September 1, 1945), p. 14.

[3] Same, p. 15.

[4] Same, p. 17.

such a serious force as several political groups incline to think it. Atomic bombs are intended to frighten people with weak nerves, but they cannot decide the outcome of a war since for this atomic bombs are completely insufficient." [5]

This theme, once sanctified by Stalin, was henceforth repeated with tiresome regularity in Soviet literature and by the Communist parties all over the world. Under the heading "atomic bomb" the official Soviet encyclopedia confined itself simply to repeating Stalin's dictum quoted above.[6] And a Chinese Communist author, in assessing the significance of the new technology, did little more than paraphrase Stalin: "The atom bomb is one of the modern weapons which possess the greatest destructive power. . . . Except for causing effects of destruction bigger than those produced by ordinary bombs, however, such a weapon can produce no other effects. The final decisive force to destroy the enemy's fighting power is still not the atom bomb but strong and vast ground troops. . . . To countries with a fighting will and with vast territories such as the Soviet Union and China, the atom bomb's usefulness is even smaller." [7]

The Soviet leadership thus maintained rigidly the "pure" doctrine that no mechanical invention could possibly disturb the foreordained course of history. Accordingly, the atomic bomb was increasingly treated as a Western propaganda trick designed as a means of blackmailing the "Socialist camp" into submission. The few Soviet discussions regarding nuclear matters which reached the public were entirely on the psychological level. Atomic warfare was not analyzed as a strategic problem. Instead, theories which had suggested that atomic warfare might change the course of history were derided. A Communist philosopher summed up the whole American discussion of nuclear matters as an effort to "frighten both imaginary

---

[5] *Pravda*, September 25, 1946.

[6] *Bol'shaia Sovetskaia Entsiklopediia* (2d. ed.; 1950), v. 3, p. 433.

[7] Teng Ch'ao, "Piercing through the Myth of Atomic War," *Mei-ti Chun-shih-shang ti Jo-tien* (The Military Weakness of American Imperialism) (Peiping: Shih-chieh Chih-shih, 1950), pp. 24-31.

opponents and one's own fellow citizens." [8] American writers were accused of exaggerating the effectiveness of the bomb, Lewis Mumford coming in for special ridicule for suggesting that after an atomic holocaust man would return to primitive conditions of life. The atomic bomb could have added little to the destruction of Stalingrad; yet still Russia had won the war.[9] And *Pravda* contributed its part to the campaign to deprecate the atom bomb by quoting unidentified reports from Tokyo that in Hiroshima only 8,481 individuals had been affected by the atomic explosion and only 7,967 in Nagasaki.[10]

The studied aloofness with respect to nuclear technology extended to the scientific achievement which had developed nuclear weapons. A book on atomic energy published in 1952 disposed of the whole question of the military use of atomic energy in three pages out of four hundred, citing Stalin's dictum that nuclear weapons could not be decisive.[11] The study stressed the alleged contribution of Russian theorists like Dmitri I. Mendeleev to atomic research; it minimized the role of Western theorists and said practically nothing about the scientists who actually produced the bomb. Indeed, Lenin's alleged contribution to atomic science was given more prominence than that of any Western scientist. Lenin had taken note of the new theories of the "destructibility of the atom, its inexhaustibility, the changeability of all forms of matter and of its movement [which were, he continued] the foundation of dialectical materialism." [12] This general line was also followed in the Soviet encyclopedia's discussion of the scientific background of atomic energy.[13]

The effort to minimize nuclear technology was accompanied by a complete blackout on news regarding Western

---

8 O. V. Trakhtenberg, " 'Sotsiologiia' Atomnoi Bomby" (The "Sociology" of the Atom Bomb), *Voprosy Filosofii*, no. 3 (1948), p. 294.

9 Same, pp. 294-5.

10 *Pravda*, January 21, 1950.

11 M. I. Korsunsky, *Atomnoe Iadro* (The Atomic Nucleus) (4th ed.; Moscow and Leningrad: Gos. Izd. Tekhniko-teoret. Lit., 1952), pp. 372-4.

12 Same, p. 61, quoted from V. I. Lenin, *Sochineniia*, v. 14 (Moscow: Gospolitizdat, 1947), p. 268.

13 *Bol'shaia Sovetskaia Entsiklopediia*, cited, p. 417.

achievements. No mention was made in the Soviet press of the following events: the United States announcement of December 1951 regarding the possibility of peaceful applications of nuclear energy; the test of Britain's first atomic bomb in October 1952; or the explosions of the United States hydrogen bomb in November 1952. It was not until 1954 that the Soviet public was permitted to see a picture of the mushroom cloud which in the West had been a symbol of the nuclear age for nearly a decade. So loath were the Soviet leaders to acknowledge the role of atomic bombs in international politics that in attacking President Truman's statement of November 1950 that, if necessary, the United States might use nuclear weapons in Korea, they did not even mention the atomic bomb, but charged him only with creating "new war hysteria." [14]

The nonchalance toward atomic matters was maintained even with respect to Soviet accomplishments in the nuclear field. The Soviet press did not report the first Soviet atomic explosion, and the world had to hear of it through an American announcement. Even then, the Soviet reaction was studiedly matter-of-fact. *Pravda* pretended surprise at the apparent excitement in the non-Soviet world about this turn of events and Andrei Y. Vyshinsky at the United Nations emphasized its peaceful and not its military implications: "We want to harness atomic energy to carry out great tasks of peaceful construction, to blast mountains, change the course of rivers. . . ." [15]

The Soviet show of indifference to its own accomplishments in the nuclear field was probably caused in part by the fear that, if flaunted too much, the atomic bomb might cause a preventive attack by the United States before the Soviet retaliatory power was fully developed. It also reflected the predominant nature played in Soviet life by doctrine. For better or worse, though more by necessity than by choice, the Soviet leadership had staked its sur-

14 For an excellent account of the Soviet regime's relations with the press, see Leo Gruliow, "What the Russians are Told," *The Reporter*, v. 12 (March 24, 1955), pp. 15-9.

15 A. Y. Vyshinsky, "Speech on Prohibition of Atomic Weapons and International Control of Atomic Energy," *Soviet News* (published by the Soviet Embassy, London), no. 2260 (November 14, 1949), p. 2.

vival as a militant revolutionary power on de-emphasizing nuclear weapons, at least through its period of maximum peril while the Soviet nuclear stockpile was small or non-existent. It would not be deflected from this course even to celebrate its own achievements.

Moreover, the Soviet position had not been simply to deprecate nuclear weapons. Such a course, though useful to maintain morale, did not supply the rationale for the activism which, according to Soviet theory, alone can ensure the success of the revolutionary movement. And Soviet leadership required a doctrine of its invincibility both for protection against imagined enemies and even more importantly to be able to continue to exert pressure on the peripheral powers of Eurasia. It was one thing, however, to assert that the atomic bomb could not be decisive by itself; it was another to maintain that the Soviet armed forces were basically superior to their opponents. But this is precisely what Soviet military doctrine set out to do. Concurrently with its campaign to minimize the implications of nuclear weapons, the Kremlin developed a strategic doctrine designed to demonstrate that it was the Soviet Union, not the United States, which possessed the decisive advantage should war break out. Soviet military doctrine found the key to its superiority in a distinction between what it defined as the "transitory" and the "constantly operating" factors of military science. The non-Soviet world might score advantages in the former category; the U.S.S.R. would nevertheless emerge victorious because of its superiority in the latter category.[16]

The distinction between transitory and permanently operating factors was not merely a dialectical quibble. It served as the basis of postwar Soviet military doctrine. It appeared in all military textbooks. It was taught at the military academies. It was repeated over and over again by all organs of Soviet propaganda. "Victory in war," wrote one Soviet author, "does not depend on 'transitory' factors, on one weapon or sudden invasion, but on certain constantly operating factors: durability of the rear, morale

16 Raymond L. Garthoff, *Soviet Military Doctrine* (Glencoe, Ill.: The Free Press, 1953), p. 34 ff.

of the army and the people, the just character of the war and the superiority of the social and economic system." [17] "Military thinking in the capitalist armies," wrote another high-ranking officer, "under the influence of unresolved class contradictions . . . displayed an erratic and extravagant predilection for the one-sided development, now of the air force (Douhet), now of the tank force (Fuller). . . . As we know all these one-sided theories and vagaries of military thought resulted for the capitalist states only in bitter disillusionment and great catastrophes." [18] According to Soviet doctrine, this one-sided development of non-Soviet military thought was no accident. It reflected the fact that capitalist leaders could not rely on their own people; they had to seek to substitute technology for manpower. "Not having reliable reserves of manpower at their disposal," wrote Marshal of Aviation Konstantin A. Vershinin in 1949, "the warmongers exaggerate the role of the Air Force out of all proportion . . . [calculating] that the people of the U.S.S.R. and of the People's Democracies will be intimidated by the so-called 'atomic' or 'push-button' war." [19]

In short, military superiority, according to Soviet military doctrine in the immediate postwar period, did not depend on technological supremacy. Indeed, a technological advance might encourage a doctrine of surprise attack which for a time was considered the most ephemeral of the "transitory" factors and was endlessly derided. Thus Soviet military doctrine, until 1953 at least, developed a strategy which was in effect a descriptive generalization of the experiences of World War II. It relied on methodical preparation and not on surprise. It preferred massed infantry attacks to sudden thrusts and battles of maneuver. It placed great stock on centralized control of the entire front and to the subordination of all arms to the land

17 M. Gusev, *Bor'ba Sovetskogo Suiuza za sokrashchenie vooruzhenii i zapreshchenie atomnogo oruzhiia* (The struggle of the Soviet Union for the reduction of arms and the prohibition of atomic weapons) (Moscow. Gospolitizdat, 1951), p. 23.

18 Major General F. Isayev, "Stalin's Military Genius," *New Times*, no. 52 (December 2, 1949), pp. 20-1.

19 "Stalinskaia Aviatsiia" (Stalinist Aviation), *Pravda*, July 17, 1949.

battle. It sought victory in incessant pressure until the inferior morale of the enemy would crumble and a breakthrough was achieved.[20]

It is remarkable that at a time when most military thinking in the United States was centered around the notion that a new war would start with a surprise attack, such a course was explicitly rejected by Soviet theory and indeed ridiculed by it. At a period when the prevalent doctrine in the United States was concerned with an all-out war decided ultimately by the attrition of industrial potential, the Soviets never tired of emphasizing the virtue of the indirect approach and of the breakthrough at the enemy's weakest link. And the breakthrough could be achieved by psychological as well as military means; the same terminology was employed interchangeably for both political and military warfare.

It is possible, of course, that these arguments were advanced simply to deceive other powers about Soviet weakness. But it is one thing for the Soviet leaders to adopt a certain propaganda line in their relations with the rest of the world; it is quite another for them consciously to mislead their entire people, and above all their military services, on a matter of life and death. It can hardly be maintained that the Soviet leaders would teach their officer corps a doctrine they knew to be erroneous, write field regulations based on principles known to be fallacious and train and equip their military services for a war they knew to be suicidal simply to mislead the outside world. On the contrary, the consistency of Soviet behavior would indicate that on questions of doctrine the Kremlin generally does mean what it says.

III

The Soviet Union possessed another advantage in the immediate postwar period: the growing conviction of the non-Soviet world, assiduously fostered by Soviet propaganda, that a nuclear war would represent an unparalleled

---

[20] For a thorough discussion of Soviet strategic and tactical doctrine drawn from Soviet field regulations, see Garthoff, cited, pp. 299-409.

catastrophe. Thus the Kremlin was in the fortunate position that every increase in the power of its opponents caused a proportionate increase in the inhibitions against using it. The Soviet leadership set about systematically to exploit this. Domestically, the Kremlin attempted to maintain its militancy by minimizing the power of nuclear weapons. Internationally, it strove to increase hesitation by emphasizing the horror of the new technology.

The policy of seeking to paralyze America's nuclear capability by undermining the psychological basis for employing it took the form of a world-wide campaign in favor of outlawing the atomic bomb as a weapon belonging to a category of special horror. In pursuance of this tactic, the Kremlin resisted all efforts to negotiate a system of international inspection. A United Nations Disarmament Commission, the majority of which was composed of non-Soviet states, was in Soviet eyes an inherently hostile organ. There was no point in making any sacrifices to an illusory good will, particularly as the first explosion of a Soviet atomic bomb was approaching and as an international inspection system would operate to perpetuate the position of the United States as the leading atomic power. Finally, there was not much symbolism in technically complex negotiations about disarmament. It was much simpler and infinitely more effective to come out flatly for a program of "banning the bomb." This would serve the dual advantage of demonstrating Soviet independence of action and focusing attention on the horror of the weapon around which America's strategy was built.

Every United States proposal in the Disarmament Commission was consequently countered by a Soviet demand that nuclear weapons be outlawed. A psychological framework was thereby created for diverting attention from the Soviet aggression which alone could unleash nuclear weapons and directing it to the horror of the new technology. "Atomic aggression" came to seem more terrible than the Soviet aggression which by our repeated declarations had to precede it. And Soviet persistence was not without effect. In every issue under dispute, from the Berlin blockade to Korea, we made clear at the outset that we would not use our most powerful weapon, because we had become convinced, probably correctly, that world opinion would not condone its use, short of an extremity which Soviet strategy tried its best to avoid.

Soviet diplomatic moves were only a part of a world-wide campaign which sought to erode the psychological basis of nuclear warfare. Within the Soviet Union this campaign was muted until 1949, lest an emphasis on the horrors of the atomic bomb demoralize the Russian people. As the Kremlin developed a nuclear stockpile of its own, references to the horrors of atomic warfare grew more frequent, although they never reached the intensity of the appeals addressed to the rest of the world. The Soviet public was constantly told, however, that the "destruction of civilization" was the goal of American "atom maniacs" willing to do anything to forestall the destruction of capitalism. Only Soviet determination was said to prevent the realization of this eventuality. In analyzing the famous "atom war" issue of *Collier's* of 1951, a Soviet journal did not take up the question of whether the portrayal was accurate but only examined the motives of the editors which it described as pathological sadism.[21]

These arguments were repeated endlessly in the Soviet effort to obtain world-wide support for its campaign to outlaw nuclear weapons. The principal tool has been the so-called "World Peace Movement." Starting with the Stockholm Peace Appeal in 1950, for which, according to Communist sources more than 500 million signatures were obtained throughout the world,[22] the Peace Movement has been conducting a well-organized campaign to stimulate mass protests and mass action against the use of nuclear weapons. Its permanent organ is the World Peace Council, headed by the French atomic scientist, Frederic Joliot-Curie, a long-time Communist sympathizer. The World Council and the various national peace councils which exist in many countries on both sides of the Iron

---

21 Joseph Clark, "Chto skryvaetsia za eleinymi rechami g-na Achesona" (What is concealed behind Mr. Acheson's unctuous speeches), *Literaturnaia Gazeta,* November 15, 1951.

22 *New Times,* no. 23 (June 5, 1954), p. 5.

Curtain have been disseminating a steady stream of arguments about the horror of nuclear warfare and the necessity of outlawing it. Besides dozens of pamphlets, they are publishing periodicals in twenty-five countries and in thirteen different languages.

It is tempting to dismiss the World Peace Movement and the strategy it represents as mere propaganda; it is also highly dangerous. The constant repetition of slogans and literature was directed at the psychological weak spots of the non-Soviet world. The West feels ambivalent about the role of force in international relations: a campaign against the horrors of nuclear warfare could only strengthen these inhibitions. The resentment against their colonial past causes many of the newly independent states to be almost desperately ready to believe the best of the Soviet Union and the worst of the West: an appeal which asked of them nothing else than to agree to the importance of peace and the horror of nuclear warfare was nearly irresistible. The Peace Movement thus enabled the Soviets to enlist the hopes and fears of many eminent men, appalled by the prospect of nuclear war, who would have had nothing to do with overt Communist efforts. The task of psychological warfare is to hamstring the opponent through his own preconceptions, and this has been precisely the Soviet strategy with respect to nuclear weapons.

Moreover, the Communists have shown their customary skill in confronting their opponents with impossible alternatives which, whether they succeed in their immediate purpose or not, define the framework of the next contest. The telegram which the Soviet-dominated East German Government sent in 1954 to its West German counterpart can serve as an example of many similar resolutions by nonofficial bodies all over the world:

> The American H-bomb tests . . . have greatly alarmed the entire peace-loving mankind. The parliaments of numerous countries—Japan, above all—have demanded the prohibition of A-bombs and other weapons of mass destruction. No country is more threatened and endangered by nuclear war than Germany. The German Parliament therefore are under an inescapable obligation to combat this terrible danger.

We therefore propose to the deputies of the West German Parliament to pass a joint resolution with the members of the Volkskammer [Parliament of East Germany] demanding a ban of weapons of mass destruction and of all experiments with them. . . .

And a similar appeal was made by the mayor of East Berlin to his counterpart in West Berlin.[23] The West German Parliament in effect was being asked either to oppose the most effective barrier to Soviet attack or to go on record as favoring atomic warfare in its own country.

These arguments, finely attuned to prevailing fears, almost imperceptibly shifted the primary concern away from Soviet aggression—the real security problem—to the immorality of the use of nuclear weapons which happened to represent the most effective means for resisting it. Because of its skill in exploiting the inhibitions of the non-Soviet world, the Soviet bloc has discovered two forms of "atomic blackmail:" the threat of the growing Soviet nuclear arsenal and an effort to deter the West by appealing to its moral inhibitions. In either case the consequence is a lowered will of resistance. The purposeful employment of the two forms of "atomic blackmail" is illustrated by the boast of an East German newspaper that the World Peace Movement had restrained the United States from using atomic weapons in Korea while the development of the Soviet hydrogen bomb had tied our hands in Indo-China.[24]

The results are not hard to find. In every crisis, from Suez to Hungary to Indo-China, the U.S.S.R. has succeeded

---

[23] *Neues Deutschland* (East Berlin), April 22, 1954.

[24] *Neue Zeitung* (East Berlin), January 25, 1955. Chinese Communist sources have advanced almost precisely the same arguments. The Communist skill in psychological matters is also demonstrated by the Chinese Communist charge during the Korean war that we were engaging in bacteriological warfare. This was probably a device to keep us from using atomic weapons or from bombing Chinese territory. Since an explicit reference to these dangers might have been construed as a confession of weakness, the Chinese accused us of bacteriological warfare which created an image of a United States ready to stoop to any baseness and thereby mobilized at least a part of Asian opinion against us. At the same time it increased our already powerful inhibitions against using weapons of mass destruction.

in shifting the onus of initiating nuclear war to us. In every situation there have been powerful advocates in the non-Soviet countries urging peace because the alternative of nuclear war seemed too terrible to contemplate. The confusion between conventional war, limited nuclear war and all-out thermonuclear war which has been the bane of NATO, while it has not been produced by Soviet maneuvers, has certainly been compounded by them. The more terrible Soviet propaganda can paint the horrors of war, even if in the guise of appeals for peace, the more likely it is to undermine the willingness to resist. In major areas of the world, "atomic" aggression has become a more invidious concept than the Soviet aggression which alone could unleash it, as is illustrated by the uproar caused by Secretary Dulles' "brink of war" statement in *Life* in January 1956. For whatever the wisdom of making the statement in the first place, Secretary Dulles left no doubt that we would go to the brink of atomic war only to counter the threat of Soviet military aggression.

While seeking to paralyze the will to resist its opponents through conjuring up the horrors of atomic war, the Kremlin did not propose to be inhibited itself by such prospects. Too great an emphasis domestically on the terrible consequences of nuclear war might give rise to the notion of a stalemate, as has indeed happened in the non-Soviet world. But a stalemate is as abhorrent to the dialectic as the admission that capitalism might save itself by means of a new technology. A stalemate implies that neither side can use force, and, if acknowledged by the Kremlin, this would have come close to giving up the doctrinal basis of militant communism. The principle that the relations between different social systems are inherently warlike and that war is always possible could not be surrendered without denying the distinguishing feature of communism, indeed the legitimization of twenty-five years of social repression.

Starting in 1949, therefore, a refinement was added to the doctrine of inevitable and protracted conflict between opposing social systems. The next war, Moscow now claimed, would produce not the destruction of civilization as such, but the destruction of capitalism. This concept was first elaborated by Georgi Malenkov on the occasion of the thirty-second anniversary of the Communist revolution (November 7, 1949); it was repeated in articles in the official party organ *Bolshevik* by Vyacheslav Molotov and Anastasy Mikoyan in subsequent months. Although it has been the subject of debate in the post-Stalin era, the idea that "only the imperialists will perish in an atomic war, but not civilization" has been explicitly reaffirmed and remains the official thesis today. It represents the theoretical justification for what Soviet behavior in every crisis has proved empirically: that the Kremlin believes it can afford to run more risks than its opponents because it is less vulnerable; or, what amounts to the same thing, that its will to victory is greater than that of its declared victims. The Soviet leadership did not propose to inhibit its freedom of action by any doctrine of the horrors of nuclear war, however useful such ideas might be to paralyze the resistance of the non-Soviet world.

IV

The Kremlin had brought off a tour de force. The Soviet Union had retained its militancy despite the United States atomic monopoly; indeed, it had transformed its relative weakness into an asset and solidified a position in the center of Europe denied the Tsars in centuries of striving. By its constant insistence that nuclear weapons were not decisive, it had maintained flexibility of action and, perhaps more importantly, Soviet armed might had come to exert an increasingly powerful pressure on the consciousness of all the countries of Eurasia, even of those who most eagerly protested their belief in Soviet peaceful intentions—and perhaps particularly those. By its world-wide campaign about the horrors of atomic warfare, the Kremlin had undermined the willingness to resist in many areas of the non-Soviet world and made very difficult the employment of the chief weapon in the Western arsenal.

All this had been accomplished, moreover, without

losing sight of essential objectives. However the Soviet regime might minimize the importance of nuclear weapons for purposes of home consumption, all energies of the Soviet state were thrown behind a "crash program" to develop nuclear weapons and a strategic air force. In less than five years the United States atomic monopoly was broken, and the Soviet nuclear arsenal was growing hand in hand with a strategic air force to deliver it. The "lead-times" to accomplish this—the time between conception and operational models—were in every case shorter than those of the United States. During the period of its greatest relative weakness when it had infinitely more to lose from a major war than its opponents, the Soviet bloc, through its iron-nerved discipline, had expanded to the fringes of Eurasia. It thereby demonstrated that in the relation among states, strength of will may be more important than power.

For all its single-minded persistence, Soviet policy was making a virtue of necessity. As long as the U.S.S.R. did not possess a nuclear stockpile of its own, it could find safety only by minimizing its importance or by conciliating powers which Soviet doctrine defined as inherently hostile. The course which was in fact adopted, while it required strong nerves, represented the sole option permitted by Communist orthodoxy. To take any other position would have been to give up the claim to invincibility on which depended so much of the domestic morale and the international prestige of the U.S.S.R. The doctrine of the "constantly operating factors" was the only means to retain militancy in the face of the United States atomic monopoly. And militancy, as Khrushchev emphasized in his speech to the Twentieth Party Congress in 1956, is what distinguishes communism from "opportunistic" socialism.

As long as nuclear weapons were difficult to manufacture and relatively scarce, there was a measure of merit in the Soviet insistence on the superiority of the "constantly operating" factors. As the Soviet nuclear stockpile grew, however, and the hydrogen bomb was about to be added to the nuclear arsenal, it became necessary to integrate the new technology more positively into Soviet doctrine. Stalin's 1946 statement had seen the Soviet Union through its period of greatest peril without the admission of weakness which would have prevented it from filling the tempting vacuum opened by World War II. But in the approaching era of nuclear plenty, atomic weapons could no longer be dismissed so cavalierly. Henceforth they would have to be integrated into Soviet theory as they were already being integrated into the Soviet armed forces. Significantly it was Stalin who again indicated the new Soviet line in one of his characteristically indirect statements, his first public pronouncement on nuclear matters since 1946. On October 3, 1951, the United States Government announced a second Soviet atomic explosion. Three days later, Stalin in an interview offered his comments on the current state of nuclear warfare, which for all their ambiguity marked a major evolution of Soviet thought on nuclear matters.

Q. What do you think about the clamor roused recently in the foreign press in connection with the testing out of an atom bomb in the Soviet Union?

A. Indeed, a test was recently made by us on a type of atom bomb. Tests on atomic bombs of various calibers will be made in the future under the plan for the defense of our country from attack from the British-American aggressive bloc.

Q. In connection with the tests on atomic bombs, public figures in the U.S. . . . shout about a threat to the security of the United States of America. Are there any grounds for such alarm?

A. There are no grounds for such alarm. Leaders of the United States of America cannot fail to know that the Soviet Union is not only against the use of the atomic weapon, but is also for its prohibition, for the cessation of its production. As is known, the Soviet Union has demanded several times the prohibition of the atomic weapon, but it has each time met the refusal of the powers of the Atlantic bloc. This means that in the event of a United States attack on our country, the ruling circles of the United States will use the atomic bomb. Precisely this circumstance compelled the Soviet Union to have the atomic weapon in order to be fully armed to meet the aggressor.[25]

Despite its characteristic obtuseness, Stalin's statement indicated a subtle shift of emphasis in familiar Soviet doctrine. The horror of atomic warfare was maintained because it remained a useful instrument to paralyze resistance, but no more was said of the fact that nuclear weapons could not be decisive. Stalin still advocated the outlawing of nuclear weapons, but the atomic bomb had ceased to be a "phantom" designed to "intimidate" and to "blackmail." It was so real, in fact, that the Soviets had felt "compelled . . . to have the atomic weapon in order to be fully armed to meet the aggressor." [26] Thus atomic weapons were officially declared a vital part of the equipment of a fully armed nation. For the first time, Soviet military doctrine was free to discuss the role of nuclear weapons in strategy.

The major impact of this new line was felt only after Stalin's death when it raised again all the problems of militancy, flexibility and doctrine which had been so resolutely avoided while the Soviet Union had not yet possessed a nuclear arsenal.

V

The growing Soviet self-confidence with respect to nuclear weapons began to emerge shortly after Stalin's death, coinciding with the first explosion of a Soviet thermonuclear bomb. In characteristic fashion, the new emphasis on Soviet nuclear might was used to usher in the period of peaceful coexistence already foreshadowed by Stalin's last public statement in the *Bolshevik* [27] and made doubly necessary by the confusion produced by the death of the dictator. Heretofore, Soviet spokesmen had very rarely boasted of Soviet powers of retaliation, partly because they did not yet exist, partly because such boasts would have

---

25 *Pravda*, October 6, 1951.

26 Same; taken from Stalin's interview of October 6, 1951. See above, p. 380.

27 See above, Chapter 10, p. 326.

contradicted the policy of minimizing the role of nuclear weapons. But now the Soviets felt strong enough to threaten the United States openly, and they possessed sufficient nuclear weapons to begin the adaptation of their military doctrine. When Malenkov, then Premier, announced on August 8, 1953, that the Soviets had set off a hydrogen bomb, he recurred to the muted threat which had already been implicit in Stalin's 1951 interview. He warned that an atomic war against the U.S.S.R. would be folly, because the Soviet Union now possessed similar weapons for retaliation so that any aggressor was certain to suffer a decisive rebuff.

In the next six months the Soviet press showed a growing willingness to treat the problem of nuclear warfare in a more realistic manner. In October 1953, Ilya Ehrenburg admitted in an article that nuclear weapons did represent a danger to the world, although he branded Secretary Dulles' statements to that effect as "ludicrous" and "exaggerated." President Eisenhower's speech of December 10, 1953, appealing for extraordinary measures to save mankind from the holocaust of a hydrogen war was reprinted in part in *Pravda*. The continued Soviet desire to retain freedom of action by not frightening its own people was reflected in the deletion of several particularly ominous passages, such as the statement that the United States possessed hydrogen bombs of millions of tons TNT equivalent. Nevertheless, the Soviet press and Soviet officials continued their references to the horrors of nuclear war on an ever increasing scale. An article in *Izvestia* (January 19, 1954) admitted that under modern conditions war "means colossal destruction." *Pravda* (January 30, 1954) welcomed the idea of a disarmament conference which would "contribute to the freeing of mankind from the terror of atomic bombing."

The mounting crescendo of dire prophecies while partly intended as a warning to the West—it coincided with the height of the crisis over Indo-China—also indicated that the new Soviet leadership stood in danger of upsetting the fine balance which Stalin had maintained between complacency and passivity, between overconfidence and loss of will. Stalin had insisted on the invincibility of the Soviet Union, but he had derived it from its superior social structure, not from a balance of terror. He, too, had invoked the horror of nuclear warfare, but primarily for foreign consumption while keeping even the most elementary facts regarding atomic weapons from the Russian people. But the use within the Soviet Union of arguments which had proved so effective in paralyzing the will to resist abroad came very close to the Western notion of a nuclear stalemate hitherto so resolutely rejected by Soviet doctrine. If the notion of a stalemate became generally accepted, the peace offensive was more than a tactical maneuver; it was a basic change in the Kremlin's view of the world. This was the issue raised by a debate which occurred in the Soviet Union in the first half of 1954, and, as was only proper in a regime legitimized by a philosophy of history, the debate concerned an abstract point regarding the nature of historical development.

A fundamental change seemed in the offing, when Premier Malenkov on March 12, 1954, apparently overthrew the concept which he had himself announced five years previously that nuclear war would mean the end only of capitalist, not of Soviet civilization. "The Soviet Government," he said suddenly, ". . . is resolutely opposed to the policy of cold war, for this is a policy of preparation for fresh world carnage, which, with modern methods of warfare, *means the ruin of world civilization.*" [28] [Emphasis added.] On March 27, 1954, this theme was repeated by a Moscow radio commentator who said that hydrogen bombs "would threaten the very existence of civilization." [29] The World Peace Council fell into line with a warning that the use of atomic weapons would result in the annihilation of man.[30] Did this mean then that the power of the hydrogen bomb had shocked the Soviet leadership into giving up its militancy? Had the enormity of modern weapons

---

28 "Speech by Comrade G. M. Malenkov," *Pravda* and *Izvestia*, March 13, 1954; cited from *Current Digest of the Soviet Press*, v. 6 (April 28, 1954), p. 8.

29 Moscow radio broadcast, March 27, 1954.

30 *New Times*, no. 15 (April 10, 1954), Supplement, p. 2.

forced it to accept the fact that war was now inconceivable? Was there now a balance between the inhibitions of the Soviet and of the non-Soviet world?

But a society finds it nearly impossible to surrender its myth, for to do so would be tantamount to giving up its image of itself; it would mean an overthrow of what has come to be considered "legitimate." To admit the possibility of a stalemate was to renounce the Marxist-Leninist dialectic of the inevitable triumph of communism. To announce an indefinitely prolonged equilibrium in the relation of forces was equivalent to surrendering the doctrine of the inherent superiority of Communist theory which could manage the inevitable conflict between social classes to its advantage. It would mean that the forces of technology were superior to the forces of history, that the class struggle could be paralyzed by technological innovations.

It is little wonder that Soviet theoretical journals throughout the early part of 1954 exhibited increasing nervousness at this turn of events. In November 1953, a Soviet economist named Gus, following the logic of some of the articles on nuclear matters which had already appeared, argued that the Marxist-Leninist law of the inevitability of war produced by capitalism remained valid, but he insisted that experience had demonstrated the possibility of paralyzing the workings of this law.[31] This thesis was immediately attacked by the head of the Department of Agitation and Propaganda who accused the unfortunate Gus of destroying Marxism in the guise of interpreting it. "There are 'theoreticians' who presume that it is possible to 'paralyze' the law discovered by Lenin of the irregularity of the political and economic development of capitalism during the epoch of imperialism with all the consequences resulting from this law. This in essence . . . acknowledges the possibility of the abolition of objective laws of the development of society. There is no need to prove that such a view has nothing in common with

---

[31] M. Gus, "Generalnaia Linia Sovetskoi Vneshnei Politiki" (The General Line of Soviet Foreign Policy), *Zvezda* (Leningrad), no. 11 (November 1953), pp. 108-9.

Marxist-Leninist science." [32] The reaction to the Gus "deviation" was a call to the faithful not to give up their militancy whatever the horrors of the new technology.

Malenkov's statement that a nuclear war would destroy civilization, that, in short, the Soviet Union was equally vulnerable as its opponents, seemed to shock the Communist party into a renewed awareness of its orthodoxy. It had not prided itself on its "activism" for over a generation to give it up at the moment of its greatest technological achievement. It had not heaped scorn on the dangers of "passivity" for an equally long period to fall into it now by means of its own doctrine. On April 26, 1954, less than two months after propounding it, in a speech to the Supreme Soviet, Malenkov was obliged to repudiate his own statement and to assert that an atomic war would lead to the breakdown of only the capitalist system.[33] *Pravda* announced the Soviet position on nuclear weapons on February 26, 1955, with finality: "Only political adventurers can think that they will succeed with the help of atomic weapons in canceling the progressive development of mankind. Weapons have never altered or canceled the laws of social development; they have never created or abolished conditions which could alter social structures of entire countries." [34]

The Party Militant had triumphed. Henceforth Communist leaders all over the world repeated with pedantic regularity the doctrine that the U.S.S.R. possessed superior freedom of action because it was less vulnerable than the capitalist world. Molotov, Mikoyan, Shepilov, Zhukov and Khrushchev defended the proposition at the Twentieth Party Congress in 1956. In France, Maurice Thorez warned his Communists not to be intimidated by American "atomic propaganda" because historical forces were on their side. In satellite East Germany, the Prime Minister, Otto Grotewohl, made the tactical advantages of the Soviet

---

32 V. Kruzhkov, "V. I. Lenin—Korifei revoliutsionnoi nauki" (V. I. Lenin—leading figure of revolutionary science), *Kommunist,* no. 1 (January 1954), p. 22.

33 *New Times,* no. 18 (May 1, 1954), Supplement, p. 9.

34 *Pravda,* February 26, 1955.

position explicit. "For us fighters against remilitarization it is *better and more correct* [emphasis added] to draw from this fact [atomic destruction] the conclusion that a third world war will destroy not us, but the imperialist forces." [35] A Soviet delegation of scientists invited by Lord Russell to an international conference in London refused, only three weeks after the Geneva summit meeting, to associate itself with a resolution which warned against nuclear war because it would mean the end of civilization; the Soviet delegation signed the resolution only after it was amended to read that nuclear war would inflict great suffering.[36]

And the Soviet leaders, whatever their momentary vacillation, guarded their orthodoxy with all the skill in doctrinal subtleties learned in a quarter century of Stalin's rule. When, on the occasion of his visit to India in December 1955, Bulganin signed a joint declaration with Nehru calling attention to the disaster of a nuclear war, he granted an interview soon after his return to Moscow to repudiate any implication of nuclear stalemate: "It is wrong to assert that inasmuch as East and West possess hydrogen weapons the possibility of a thermonuclear war is automatically excluded." [37]

Doctrinal purity had been maintained; the Soviet leadership had retained its freedom of action and defined its risks as smaller than those of its opponents. There is a tendency in the West to overlook Soviet doctrinal disputes, and their abstractness does not encourage closer examination. Yet they are the most profitable indication of Soviet intentions, far more rewarding than Soviet actions which are often deliberately designed to mislead or to lull. Since the Soviet leadership derives its claim to superiority from its theoretical insight, a doctrinal dispute in the U.S.S.R. has not only a philosophical, but an eminently practical significance. Throughout the history of Soviet commu-

---

[35] Speech to the Congress of Youth Against Remilitarization, *Neues Deutschland* (East Berlin), March 22, 1955.

[36] A. V. Topchiev, Address before the World Conference of Scientists, London, August 3, 1955, *Bulletin of the Atomic Scientists*, v. 12 (February 1956), pp. 44-5.

[37] *New Times*, no. 2 (January 5, 1956), Supplement, p. 33.

nism, almost every dispute over doctrine has reflected a disagreement on policy and almost every change of doctrine has sooner or later been translated into action.

And so it has been with the Soviet doctrine on nuclear weapons. Whether or not it was a conscious attempt to bring strategy into relationship with its willingness to take risks—and Grotewohl's statement would seem to indicate that it was—it has so worked out in practice. In every crisis, the non-Soviet world protests the horror of nuclear war and thereby reduces the strength of its negotiating position. By contrast, the Soviets do not seem so inhibited and feel free to threaten with rocket attacks on Britain and France or with dire consequences for countries accepting United States atomic support units.[38]

In fact, there seems to have grown up a tacit recognition of greater Soviet daring. When the Soviet Union was confronting difficulties in the satellite orbit, the West hastened to protest that it would neither use force against Soviet repressive efforts nor seek to enter into an alliance with any "liberated" satellite. These measures were justified with the argument that pressure by the West might cause a "desperate" Soviet Union to unleash nuclear war. But when the West confronted difficulties in the Middle East, the U.S.S.R. did not feel compelled to give similar assurances. On the contrary, it left no doubt that it was prepared to move into any vacuum; it spoke of "volunteers" and warned of rocket attacks. Obviously the Soviet leaders were less concerned that the West, in desperation, might unleash a nuclear war of its own. Thus Soviet leadership has been able to blackmail the West both with its strength and its weakness. We recoil before Soviet power but we also fear to exploit Soviet difficulties. This difference in the willingness to assume risks has been the fundamental Soviet advantage in the postwar period, nearly overcoming the bankruptcy of its social system and the instability of its leadership structure.

---

38 See, for example, the Soviet note to Turkey, *New York Times*, January 24, 1957.

VI

The eventual adaptation of Soviet military theory to nuclear weapons must be considered against this background of doctrinal militancy. For the abstract theoretical discussions had sought to overcome one of the most serious and at the same time novel problems of the nuclear age: the deterrent effect on its diplomacy of a power's own deterrent arsenal. In the past, an increase in a nation's strength resulted almost inevitably in a greater flexibility of its diplomacy. But in the nuclear period the growth in military strength tends to be accompanied by an increase in the inhibitions against its use. Because each weapons test augurs similar horrors on the other side, one of the paradoxical aspects of the nuclear age is that one of the inhibitions to decisive action has been produced by the implications of a power's own weapons technology. Insofar as a strategic doctrine could achieve it, the Kremlin meant to see to it that it would not be so inhibited.

No systematic attempt to integrate nuclear weapons into Soviet military doctrine was made until 1954. Before that time, nuclear weapons were dismissed as relatively insignificant and most discussions in military journals concerned the inherent superiority of the Soviet "constantly operating factors." As the Soviet nuclear arsenal grew, however, it became important to find a rationale for its use. In the process of developing such a theory, Soviet strategic thought began to traverse the three seemingly inevitable stages which have characterized military thought in all countries seeking to come to grips with the strategic implications of nuclear weapons: (1) an initial period of learning the essential characteristics of the new weapons which is accompanied by protestations of the still dominant traditionalists that nuclear weapons cannot alter the basic principles of strategy and tactics; (2) as the power of modern weapons becomes better understood, this is usually followed by a complete reversal: an increasing reliance on the most absolute applications of the new technology and on an almost exclusive concern with offensive retaliatory power; (3) finally, as it is realized that all-out war involves risks out of proportion to most of the issues likely to be in dispute, an attempt is made to find intermediate applications for the new technology and to bring power into harmony with the objectives for which to contend.

Once the strategic implications of nuclear technology became a fit subject for discussion in Soviet military journals, the reaction of the Soviet military, as distinguished from the political, leadership was not basically different from that of their colleagues in the West. The Soviet officers simply went through the process about five years after their Western counterparts in each phase, almost precisely reflecting the time-lag in the Soviet development of nuclear technology.

For this reason Soviet military doctrine does not seem to have reached as yet the third stage of the evolution of strategic thought with respect to nuclear weapons: that of finding subtler uses for the new technology than all-out war. Nuclear weapons have been integrated into Soviet strategic thought; but, after the initial period of denying that nuclear weapons had brought about a fundamental change in strategy or tactics, most Soviet discussions have concerned themselves with the problems of all-out war. There has been practically no published discussion of limited nuclear war. This may be due to the fact that the first priority of Soviet weapons development has to be the acquisition of a strategic arsenal and that fissionable material is not yet plentiful enough to permit a large-scale production of "small" atomic weapons. Whatever the reason, if the published discussion reflects the actual state of Soviet military thinking—and on the basis of the eminence of some of the authors it probably does—this lag in Soviet doctrine may reveal a vulnerability and a danger: a vulnerability because it may indicate Soviet difficulties in mastering the tactics of limited nuclear war and of danger because it may induce the Soviets to treat the explosion of any nuclear weapon as the prelude to all-out war.

The re-evaluation of Soviet military thought and the reorganization of the Soviet military establishment started early in 1954. For the first time the Kremlin permitted

public discussion of the characteristics of atomic weapons
and their potential destructive power. In this manner, the
Soviet public in 1954 received the same information which
the Western public had learned in 1945 concerning the
means by which atomic energy is released, the power of
the explosion, and the impact on objects in the vicinity
of the explosion.[39] The mechanism of the atomic and
hydrogen bomb was described in the same popular language which had characterized Western articles on the
subject a decade previously. Very little was said of the
hydrogen bomb; the explosion most frequently mentioned
was of the type which had destroyed Hiroshima and
Nagasaki.[40]

Concurrently with the dissemination of basic knowledge on nuclear matters, military journals began discussing the conduct of military operations under atomic
attack, another subject which had hitherto been prohibited and which presumably had not been taken up in
detail in the training of troops.[41] Most of the articles were
extremely factual and dry accounts of means by which
troops could protect themselves against the effects of
atomic explosions. All the authors emphasized that nuclear explosions need not disrupt the normal functions of

---

[39] *Krasnaia Zvezda*, spring of 1954.

[40] The dissemination of information was furthered by the publication
of a number of books and pamphlets for popular consumption. Among
them were *Atomnaia energiia i eio primenenie* (Atomic energy and its
use), by S. Petrovich and D. Didov (Moscow: Voenizdat, 1954); *Atomnaia
energiia i eio ispol'zovanie* (Atomic energy and its utilization) by I. K.
Naumenko (Moscow: DOSAFF, 1954); *Atom i atomnaia energiia* (The
atom and atomic energy), by V. A. Mezentsev (Moscow: Voenizdat, 1954).
The fact that so many of these books were published either by the military
publishing house (Voenizdat) or by the civil defense organization
(DOSAFF) indicates that the regime was slowly dropping the myth that
in the U.S.S.R. atomic energy was being used only for peaceful purposes.
This was indicated too by a review of a number of these books (appear-
ing in *Novy Mir*, April 1955, pp. 270-1), which dealt solely with the military aspects of atomic energy, even though the books themselves considered
both the military and civil applications.

[41] *Krasnaia Zvezda*, January 27, 1955, January 30, 1955, February 1,
1955; *Komsomolskaia Pravda*, June 7, 1955. These had such titles as "Radiation Checks and Activities of Troops in a Contaminated Area in Winter," "The Protection of Troops against an Atomic Attack," "The Effects
of an Atomic Explosion on Populated Areas."

an army. The major concern was to integrate atomic weapons into existing doctrine without modifying its basic characteristics.

To be sure, the articles proved that the Soviets had carefully studied Western military writings on atomic warfare. The official organ of the Red Army, in a review of a book of Colonel George Reinhardt and Lieutenant Colonel William Kintner,[42] stressed that the book contained "data and arguments which deserve careful attention." [43] The book had advocated abandoning the old concept of large mass armies and stressed the importance of small, flexible, highly maneuverable units, proposals which were the exact opposite of prevailing Soviet doctrine. Nevertheless, the main thrust of this first phase of Soviet military thought seemed to be to validate the traditional reliance on land warfare: "Soviet military art," wrote a Soviet officer, "assumes that the new means of combat, not only do not reduce, but on the contrary, enhance the part played by the foot-soldier and raises his role to a new level." [44]

As nuclear technology became more diffused, however, and better understood, the temptations of emphasizing Soviet retaliatory power proved irresistible. The West had relied too much on its own offensive arsenal not to encourage the Kremlin to seek to neutralize it by stressing the Soviet ability to retaliate. To apply "massive retaliation" in reverse became an excellent tool of Soviet political warfare, a means of paralyzing the opponent through "atomic blackmail." Starting in 1955, the Soviet leadership unleashed an ever mounting series of threats of all-out war, differing only in their ponderous Marxist jargon from the most extreme formulation of air strategy in the West. A Soviet radio commentator noted (January 31, 1955) that "according to the most optimistic estimates of authoritative circles . . . only a few hydrogen bombs would

---

42 George C. Reinhardt and William R. Kintner, *Atomic Weapons in Land Combat* (Harrisburg, Pa.: Military Service Publishing Co., 1953).

43 *Krasnaia Zvezda*, February 19, 1955.

44 Colonel F. Gavrikov, *Sovetskaia Armiia*, July 1, 1954.

be needed to ensure the destruction of Britain's principal industrial centers. Even fewer bombs would be needed in order to paralyze the vital centers of France, Belgium and Holland." [45] Major General Isayev wrote on March 5, 1955: "America's leaders have no grounds whatever for hoping that if they embarked on aggression their own country would be beyond reach of retaliation. They ought to know that the Soviet Union possesses the necessary weapons and the necessary means for swiftly delivering them to any point of the globe." [46] And Mikoyan in his speech to the Twentieth Party Congress in 1956 said that future war would be characterized by the mass use of the air force, rocket weapons and various means of mass killing such as atomic, thermonuclear, bacteriological and chemical weapons, and "the American imperialists will not be able to hide from these bombs or shelter their factories from them." [47]

In fact, one of the chief concerns of Soviet propaganda has been to prevent the United States from increasing its freedom of action by a doctrine of limited nuclear war. Soviet propaganda, both domestic and foreign, has therefore endlessly repeated that there is no such thing as a limited nuclear war, that any employment of nuclear weapons must inevitably lead to all-out war. Marshal Zhukov chose the Twentieth Party Congress as the forum for warning the West that it could not escape the consequences of Soviet "massive retaliation:" "Recently utterances of political and military figures in the United States reflect with increased frequency the idea that U.S. strategy should be based on the utilization of atomic weapons for operations on battlefields and fronts. In view of the geographical distance of America these gentlemen attach weight to the fact that atomic weapons would first be used on European territory, naturally as far from U.S. industrial centers as possible. . . . However things would not

---

[45] Moscow radio broadcast, January 31, 1955.

[46] "Fallacies of the Policy of Strength," *New Times*, no. 10 (March 5, 1955), p. 5.

[47] *Current Digest of the Soviet Press*, v. 8 (April 4, 1956), p. 8.

work out as the crafty strategists planned. Today it is impossible to fight wars and avoid counterblows. . . ." [48]

But if war depended so importantly on retaliatory power, what then had become of the "constantly operating factors?" There was a danger that the reliance on long-term trends implicit in the doctrine of the "constantly operating factors" might inhibit initiative and produce overconfidence. Such an attitude might have been acceptable when the U.S.S.R. had above all to guard against any admission of weakness. It was not equal to the opportunities and the perils of the age of nuclear plenty. As a result, the "constantly operating factors" have been slowly reinterpreted in two senses: in the direction of a greater recognition of the achievements of Western military science and in the direction of ever increasing emphasis on the role of surprise in war. The movement was launched by Marshal Vasily D. Sokolovsky, Soviet Chief of Staff, when he demanded on February 23, 1955, that there be more "creative research and bold study of the most pressing problems of military science." Such a study, argued the Marshal, should take into account the increased significance of the factor of surprise and it should include "the latest achievement not only in our country, but also abroad." [49]

The most elaborate of the new studies called for by Marshal Sokolovsky came from Marshal of Tanks P. A. Rotmistrov, one of the most original Soviet military thinkers.[50] Rotmistrov insisted that the "role of surprise attack in modern war not only is not diminishing, but, on the contrary, is growing larger." Whereas in the past the Soviet Union had nothing to fear from surprise attacks, "it must be frankly admitted that under certain circumstances surprise attack with the use of atomic and hydrogen weapons could become a deciding condition for success

---

48 *Pravda*, February 20, 1956.

49 V. D. Sokolovsky, "Nesokrushimaia Moshch' Vooruzhennykh Sil Sovetskogo Gosudarstva" (Indestructible Power of the Armed Forces of the Soviet State), *Izvestia*, February 23, 1955, p. 2.

50 Marshal P. A. Rotmistrov, "Za tvorcheskuiu razrabotku voprosov sovetskoi voennoi nauki" (For working out the problems of Soviet military science creatively), *Krasnaia Zvezda*, March 24, 1955, p. 2.

not only in the initial phases of a war, but even in its final outcome. . . . We cannot regard these events passively; we must not lull our military cadres with outdated theories; we must reveal the increasing danger of surprise attack and likewise improve the military preparedness of our Army, Navy and Air Force."

At the same time, Rotmistrov attacked two traditional Soviet dogmas which had become almost shibboleths: the reliance on the "constantly operating factors" and the doctrine, drawn from the experience of World War II, that the vastness of Soviet territory conferred immunity from attack. He criticized the exaltation of the "constantly operating factors" as purely theoretical. To be sure, capitalist countries were inferior in the "constantly operating factors," but it was self-delusion to deny that they were not improving their armaments and the morale of their soldiers. Moreover, under conditions of atomic warfare, it was possible for a short war—traditionally favored by a country inferior in social structure and morale—to be more decisive than in the past. As for the importance of space, Rotmistrov was ambivalent. He admitted that the vast expanse of Russia offered advantages over some capitalist countries with smaller territories and a higher density of population. But he insisted that the Soviet Union could no longer permit a repetition of the last war when the major battles were fought on Russian soil, and he called for a re-examination of the whole problem of space in Soviet strategy.[51]

It was an inevitable step from emphasizing the factor of surprise and the rejection of defensive war to a doctrine which stressed the importance of transferring operations into enemy territory. This was nothing new in Soviet military thought, for Soviet strategic doctrine, and for that matter political doctrine too, has always exhibited a striking preference for the offensive. Lenin had advised that "it is necessary to strive for daily successes, even if small . . . in order to retain the 'morale ascendancy'." And Stalin had

---

[51] Similar, and perhaps even more explicit arguments, were used by Lieutenant General S. Shatilov, "Bol'shaia Blagorodnaia Tema" (A Great Noble Theme), *Literaturnaia Gazeta*, May 28, 1955, p. 2.

warned against "a dangerous error called 'loss of tempo'...." [52] It was not until 1942 that the defensive was admitted to be "a normal form of combat," and even then the field regulations continued to insist that offensive combat is the basic aspect of actions by the Red Army.[53]

The new emphasis on transferring military operations onto foreign soil can, therefore, hardly be considered a doctrinal innovation, but it was given particular sharpness by references to the requirements of nuclear warfare. An article in *Red Star* insisted that the Soviet armed forces would be able to deliver an annihilating blow even in a war fought with atomic and hydrogen weapons. In such a war, Soviet strategy should strive to transfer military operations into enemy territory in order to spare the Soviet population as much as possible and to increase the inhibitions of the enemy who would presumably be reluctant to employ nuclear weapons against its own population. Because of the fact that Soviet forces would probably have to fight in enemy countries, particular attention should be paid to their morale.[54] And Marshal Alexander M. Vasilevsky wrote in *Izvestia*: "In connection with the advent of high-speed jet-propelled aviation and the existence of weapons of great destructive power, the significance of the factor of suddenness has greatly increased...." [55]

VII

Thus Soviet military thought in less than two years had come almost full cycle. From minimizing the role of nu-

---

52 Vladimir I. Lenin, *Sochineniia* (2d ed.; Moscow: The Marx-Engels-Lenin Institute for the C.C. of the CPSU (B), 1926-32), v. 21 (1929), p. 320, and Joseph Stalin, *Sochineniia* (Moscow: OGIZ, Gosizdpolit, 1946-52), v. 6 (1947), p. 159, as quoted by Garthoff, cited, p. 139.

53 *Boevoi Ustav Pekhoty* (Infantry Combat Regulations), v. 1 (1942-45), p. 12, in Garthoff, cited, p. 67.

54 Colonel P. Kashirin, "O znachenii moralnogo dukha voisk v sovremennoi voine" (The importance of moral strength of the army in contemporary war), *Krasnaia Zvezda*, May 28, 1955. See also "The Soviet General Staff Takes Stock—Changes in Soviet Military Doctrine," *The World Today*, v. 11 (November 1955), pp. 492-502.

55 A. M. Vasilevsky, "Velikaia Pobeda Sovetskogo Naroda" (The Great Victory of the Soviet People), *Izvestia*, May 8, 1955, p. 2.

clear weapons, it had come to consider them an essential, if not the primary element of strategy. From deprecating the role of surprise, it had elevated it almost to a "constantly operating factor." And it had grown to accept strategic bombing and the possibility of a devastating, short war—all notions that had heretofore been derided or rejected. What then does the new emphasis of the Soviets on nuclear weapons tell us about Soviet strategic thought and what consequences flow from it for the United States?

One of the reasons for the insistence on the new-found retaliatory power is undoubtedly a feeling of exhilaration at having emerged unscathed from an abyss. The Soviet leadership must remember the American atomic monopoly with a feeling of profound humiliation because it must have known, whatever it pretended to the outside world, that it was subject to a perhaps catastrophic blow without being able to offer a similar threat in return. And the fact that Soviet doctrine declared our intentions as inherently hostile must have added to Soviet uneasiness.

To be sure, the Soviets managed to hide their concern by an iron-nerved tour de force. But the incessant, almost gloating, references to the horror that they can now inflict on the United States may reveal an effort to "get even" retroactively for years of living on what must have seemed the brink of catastrophe. Orator after orator on the occasion of the Twentieth Party Congress in 1956 insisted that, with the development of hydrogen weapons, it was "no longer" possible to defeat the U.S.S.R.—a remarkable admission in view of the fact that any reference to the possibility of defeat would have been treated as a treasonable utterance during our atomic monopoly and an indication, perhaps, that the Soviet leadership had a better awareness of the real relationship of forces than its opponents.

Another factor is the usefulness of the present Soviet position for paralyzing the will to resist of its opponents. The more terrible Soviet propaganda can paint the consequences of another war, the more reluctant its opponents will be to resort to it, and the impact of Soviet atomic blackmail has proved none the less effective for being accomplished in the guise of peace offensives. In fact, it was not until the Soviet nuclear stockpile began to grow, that the Soviet Union derived full benefit from its tenacious campaign to outlaw nuclear weapons. For with the growth of the Soviet nuclear stockpile, the preconceptions created by peace councils, "ban-the-bomb" propaganda and Soviet invocations of the horrors of nuclear war began to serve a dual purpose: the same arguments that had hitherto enjoined self-restraint on the West could now be used to appeal to its fears. The free world which had been asked to recoil before the devastation it could inflict in a nuclear war could now be made to shrink before the destruction it might suffer. Since 1954 Soviet pronouncements have been as insistent that any resort to nuclear weapons will inevitably lead to all-out war as they had been during our atomic monopoly that nuclear weapons were horrible and ineffectual.

Since the Soviet leaders can have few doubts about the consequences of all-out thermonuclear war, this may indicate a realization that the greatest vulnerability of the Soviet armed forces is in the area of limited nuclear war. Just as during our atomic monopoly the Kremlin obscured its weakness by a show of bravado, it may now be seeking to inhibit our most effective strategy by declaring it impossible. Or else the repeated rejection of the possibility of limited nuclear war may reflect a certain backwardness in Soviet military doctrine. The reliance on the threat of all-out war may indicate that Soviet military thought is still intoxicatcd with the destructive potential of the new weapons. Some Soviet military literature—although referring to widely dispersed formations and measures to avoid the contaminating effects of radiation—gives the impression that the Soviet Union may have succumbed to the temptation of adding nuclear weapons to the existing arsenal as a more efficient explosive without the fundamental alteration of tactics which nuclear war requires. But the use of nuclear weapons simply as a form of artillery, the attempt to maintain a stabilized front and similar tactics derived from the experience of World War II would be both ineffective and extremely costly.

Of course, we cannot gear our strategy to the assumption of Soviet inadequacy. Inevitably, the Soviet armed forces will realize that nuclear war requires a new order of tactics. Nevertheless, whatever its theoretical insights, the Red Army will be at a decided disadvantage in adapting to the new conditions of warfare. Limited nuclear war, as we have seen, requires decentralized command, because it can only be conducted by relatively small, self-contained units. But Soviet military doctrine prides itself on its centralized control. In World War II, Soviet commanders were permitted only the barest minimum of initiative; their primary task was implementing plans which prescribed not only the general objective—as in American field orders—but the detailed methods for attaining it. Soviet military literature, in fact, prides itself on the "single, monolithic strategic design" of the Soviet High Command. "The deployment of troops," wrote a high-ranking Soviet officer, "can be successfully completed only when a *rigid centralized plan* . . . has been prepared." [56] In World War II, the Soviet insistence on rigid centralization made for great flexibility at the top, but extraordinary rigidity at the lower echelons. And this theory of command has been embodied also in the field regulations of 1946.

Again, in a limited nuclear war initiative is of cardinal importance, because the fluidity of operations makes it impossible to predict all contingencies in advance. Soviet military doctrine, however, while paying lip-service to initiative, discourages it in practice. Soviet doctrine distinguishes between two kinds of leadership: the first, inspiring, initiating and directing; the other, implementing and directing according to plan. The former is the task of the Politburo and the High Command, the latter the duty of all other commanders. Thus the task of subordinate commanders has in practice been limited to what the Soviet field regulations describe as "making precise plans of a higher command." Leadership, to be sure, is considered a "constantly operating factor," but it has been

---

[56] Lieutenant General V. Zlobin, *Voennaia Mysl'* (Military Thought), no. 5 (1945), as quoted by Garthoff, cited, p. 212. (Italics are Garthoff's.)

defined in terms of "organizing ability" with respect to the orders of higher headquarters.[57]

As a result, the operations of the Soviet armed forces in World War II, while often displaying great flexibility strategically, ran to stereotype tactically. Field regulations prescribed the exact location of company commanders in the rear of their troops. Field orders determined not only the direction of the attack, but the precise form it was to take. The sphere of initiative of division commanders could not have been more restricted. "Important decisions," wrote a Soviet war correspondent, *that cannot be put off for a moment* [emphasis added] must be made by the division commander himself." [58] German accounts commented on the rigidity of Soviet tactics. Divisions were prohibited from crossing the divisional boundaries and carried out this order even if it meant the destruction of a neighboring unit before their eyes. Regiments advanced on prescribed lines even into their own artillery fire. To deviate from orders was an offense punishable by court-martial if it did not succeed. To carry out even suicidal orders did not involve any stigma. "American lieutenants," wrote General Bradley, "were delegated greater authority on the Elbe than were Russian division commanders." [59]

It would, therefore, seem to the United States' advantage to adopt a strategy which places a premium on initiative and decentralized control. The more decisions Soviet commanders can be forced to improvise, the less they will be able to profit from their military tradition. The most effective means for taking advantage of the lack of initiative of subordinate Soviet commanders is by fluid operations. The best strategy for exploiting the rigidity of the Soviet command structure is that of limited nuclear war. An all-out war can be carried out according to a centralized plan with target systems and attack patterns carefully prepared in advance; this is indeed the only possible way of con-

---

[57] Garthoff, cited, p. 199.

[58] Vassili Grossman, *The Years of War* (Moscow: FLPH, 1946), p. 418, as quoted by Garthoff, cited, p. 211.

[59] Omar N. Bradley, *A Soldier's Story* (New York: Holt, 1951), p. 551.

ducting such a conflict. A conventional war permits the massing of troops and the adoption of a rigid command structure. In limited nuclear war, on the other hand, everything depends on daring and leadership of a higher order—qualities in which both by tradition and training our armed forces are likely to excel those of the U.S.S.R.

Nor will the Soviet High Command be able to escape its dilemma by an act of will. It is one thing to be theoretically aware of the importance of leadership, initiative and decentralized command; it is quite another to bring these qualities about. It has often been noted that the mere possession of a navy does not guarantee success in sea battles. In the absence of the "feel" for naval warfare produced by a long tradition, even a substantial navy may be doomed to sterility as Germany experienced in World War I and Japan in World War II. The Soviet leaders may have less difficulty in creating the equipment for limited nuclear war than in adapting the psychology of their personnel to its requirements. For nothing in Soviet society encourages initiative or produces self-reliant action spontaneously.

The Soviet Union was successful in World War II because its mode of action was well suited to the existing technology and the particular conditions of all-out conventional war. But, as has so often happened before, the very qualities which led to success given one set of conditions may become an element of weakness given another. Even assuming the maximum degree of insight on the part of Soviet leadership, it will not be easy for it to develop the qualities in the subordinate commanders that will be at a premium in a limited nuclear war. Self-reliance cannot be improvised. It exists in the American officer corps because it is drawn from a society in which individual initiative has traditionally been encouraged. By the same token, these qualities will be difficult to realize in the Soviet armed forces because nowhere in Soviet society can models for them be found. Where everything is done according to plan, there may be a tendency to reduce even initiative to stereotype. The Soviets may be able to train units for limited nuclear war, but the pattern of operation for such a conflict would not come "naturally" because the Soviet human material would possess no instinct for this kind of warfare.

Both Russian history and Soviet dogmatism would indicate that the Soviet armed forces will be more at home with mass attacks than with sharp individual clashes, more with carefully planned campaigns than with deliberately flexible operations. The history of Russian and Soviet naval warfare—and naval warfare offers the closest analogy to the tactics of limited nuclear war—demonstrates the extraordinary difficulty of adapting the Russian human material to operations different from the massive defense of the "motherland." To be sure, Soviet troops could learn the strategy of limited nuclear war just as Americans could master the principles of mass infantry attacks. But the Red Army will probably not be any more at ease with the new tactics than Americans would be in the ruthless utilization of manpower at which the Red Army excelled in World War II. A limited nuclear war does not guarantee success by itself, but it would use the sociological, technological and psychological advantages of the United States to best effect.

A familiar argument is certain to recur at this point: if limited nuclear war is to our advantage, it must be to the Soviet disadvantage, and the Soviet leadership would, therefore, adopt a strategy either of conventional or of all-out war. It is clear that the Soviet leaders cannot force us into a strategy of conventional war against our wishes. And as for the option of all-out war, it cannot be repeated often enough that the fact that the Soviets cannot profit from limited war does not mean that they can profit from all-out war. The penalties of all-out war are so evident that they leave hardly any room for miscalculation. If we behave effectively, we should be able to make it clear to even the most fanatic opponent that all-out war would be tantamount to national suicide.

One of the more hopeful aspects of the present situation may be that a gap may have been created between Soviet political and strategic doctrine; between the political preference for the indirect approach, the constant pressure, the exploitation of the psychological weak point of the opponent, and the strategic options open for achieving the political goal. Whether the gap is exploited—indeed, whether it comes into being—depends importantly on our own strategic doctrine: on our ability to break away from our own preconceptions and on our readiness to face the prospects and opportunities of limited war.

12

THE NEED FOR DOCTRINE

WHATEVER THE PROBLEM, then, whether it concerns questions of military strategy, of coalition policy, or of relations with the Soviet bloc, the nuclear age demands above all a clarification of doctrine. At a time when technology has put in our grasp a command over nature never before imagined, the value of power depends above all on the purpose for which it is to be used. The research and development programs of the military services will soon overwhelm them with a vast number of complex weapons. And the usual answer that a service can never possess a too varied capability will no longer do, for it is prohibitively expensive. In the 1930's each service had to select among perhaps two weapons systems; during World War II, this had risen to eight to ten. In the 1950's the number is over a hundred, and in the 1960's it will be in the thousands. Only a doctrine which defines the purpose of these weapons and the kind of war in which they are to be employed permits a rational choice.

Strategic doctrine transcends the problem of selecting weapons systems. It is the mode of survival of a society. For a society is distinguished from an agglomeration of individuals through its ability to act purposefully as a unit. It achieves this by reducing most problems to a standard of average performance which enables the other members of the group to take certain patterns of behavior for granted and to plan their actions accordingly. A society acquires momentum by coupling cooperative effort with specialization of functions. Its sense of direction comes to

403

expression in its strategic doctrine, which defines the challenges which it will meet in its relations with other societies and the manner of dealing with them. For society, doctrine plays the role of education for the individual: it relates seemingly disparate experiences into a meaningful pattern. By explaining the significance of events *in advance* of their occurrence, it enables society to deal with most problems as a matter of routine and reserves creative thought for unusual or unexpected situations.

The test of a strategic doctrine is whether it can establish a pattern of response—a routine—for the most likely challenges. The degree to which a society, in its relations with other groups, confronts situations which seem to it unexpected, reveals a breakdown of its strategic thought. If a society faces too many unexpected contingencies its leadership will no longer be able to draw strength from the collective effort. The routine on which its action is based will seem incongruous. The machinery for making decisions will become overloaded. This is why Machiavelli said, "Nothing is easier to effect than what the enemy thinks you will never attempt to do." An unexpected situation forces improvisation and takes away the advantage of sober calculation. While improvisation may only inhibit the best performance of an individual, it can have far more serious consequences for a society. In extreme cases, members of the group may take independent action and thereby complicate an effective over-all response. Or it may lead to panic, the inability to make any response to a challenge except by fleeing from it.

The Romans stampeded the first time they confronted Hannibal's elephants, not because the elephants were particularly effective but because the Romans had never considered a mode for dealing with such a contingency. Within a few years they had developed a "doctrine;" the charges of the beasts became an "expected" tactic to be confronted through discipline instead of through flight. In 1940, the rapid German tank thrusts demoralized the French Army above all because maneuvers of this kind had been explicitly rejected by French doctrine. A German tank force actually inferior in numbers was able to rout its opponent because French commanders possessed no concepts for dealing with it. Before the end of the war, the strategic doctrine of the allies had caught up with German tactics, and indeed improved on them. Armored warfare was transformed from a tactic of surprise into a matter of routine. Surprise can take two forms, then: an unexpected timing and an unexpected mode of action. The secret of Napoleon's victories was that he confused his enemies by the speed of his maneuvers. Conversely, it is possible to be aware that an attack is imminent and yet to be unprepared for the form it takes. In 1941, we knew that Japan was planning a military move, but our strategic doctrine did not foresee an attack on Hawaii.

The basic requirement for American security is a doctrine which will enable us to act purposefully in the face of the challenges which will inevitably confront us. Its task will be to prevent us from being continually surprised. Our doctrine must be clear about the nature of our strategic interest in the world. It must understand the mode of Soviet behavior and not make the mistake of ascribing to the Soviet leaders a pattern of action in terms of our own standards of rationality. Since our policy is so explicitly based on deterrence, our doctrine must pay particular attention to determining how the other side calculates its risks. Deterrence is achieved when the opponent cannot calculate any gain from the action we seek to prevent; and what is considered a gain is, for purposes of deterrence, determined by his criteria, not ours. Strategic doctrine, finally, must be able to assess the forces which move contemporary events and find the means for shaping them in the desired direction.

In the absence of a generally understood doctrine, we will of necessity act haphazardly; conflicting proposals will compete with each other without an effective basis for their resolution. Each problem, as it arises, will seem novel, and energies will be absorbed in analyzing its nature rather than in seeking solutions. Policies will result from countermoves to the initiatives of other powers; our course will become increasingly defensive.

Many of our problems in the postwar period have been

produced by our failure to accept the doctrinal challenge.
We have tended to ascribe our standards of reasonable
behavior to the Soviet leaders. We have had difficulty in
defining our purposes in relation to the revolutionary
forces at loose in the world. Above all, we have had a penchant for treating our problems as primarily technical and
to confuse strategy with the maximum development of
power. Our bias in favor of technology over doctrine
may derive from our tradition of the frontier and a century and a half of almost uninterrupted expansion. But
while the immediate challenges were in terms of overcoming physical obstacles, the motive force which impelled men into an unexplored continent was a strong
sense of purpose: a doctrine of independence so much
taken for granted that it was never made explicit.

One of the paradoxical lessons of the nuclear age is that
at the moment when we have at our disposal an unparalleled degree of power, we are driven to realize that the
problems of survival can be solved only in the minds of
men. The fate of the mammoth and the dinosaur serves as
a warning that brute strength does not always supply the
mechanism in the struggle for survival.

II

Of course, we do possess a strategic doctrine expressed
in the decisions of the Joint Chiefs of Staff and of the
National Security Council. But the decisions of the Joint
Chiefs and of the National Security Council give a misleading impression of unity of purpose. The officials comprising these bodies are either heads of military services in
the case of the Joint Chiefs, or heads of executive departments in the case of the National Security Council. As
administrators of complex organizations they must give
most of their attention to reducing the frictions of the
administrative machine, both within their departments
and in the relation of their departments to other agencies.
Their thoughts run more naturally to administrative
efficiency than to the elaboration of national objectives. In
the committees where national policies are developed,

they become negotiators rather than planners, and the
positions they seek to reconcile inevitably reflect a departmental point of view in which administrative or budgetary considerations play a major role. The heads of
departments do not stand above the battle of the bureaucracy; they are spokesmen for it. In fact, the departmental
viewpoint is sometimes purposely exaggerated in order to
facilitate compromise.

As a result, the conclusions of both the Joint Chiefs of
Staff and the National Security Council reflect the attainable consensus among sovereign departments rather than
a sense of direction. Because agreement is frequently
unattainable except by framing conclusions in very generalized language, decisions by the Joint Chiefs of Staff or
the National Security Council do not end serious interdepartmental disputes. Instead they shift them to an interpretation of the meaning of directives. And departments or
services whose disagreements prevented the development
of doctrine in the first place will choose the exegesis closest to their original point of view. Seeming unanimity
merely defers the doctrinal dilemma until either some
crisis or the requirements of the budgetary process force a
reconsideration under the pressure of events.

Within the Department of Defense these problems are
compounded by the obsolescent division of functions
among the services and the predominant role which is
played by fiscal considerations in setting force levels. According to the Key West agreement each service has the
primary mission of defeating its enemy counterpart: it is
the mission of the Air Force to dominate the sky, of the
Navy to control the seas, and of the Army to defeat the
enemy's ground forces.

With modern weapons, this definition of primary missions amounts to giving each service a claim to develop a
capability for total war. For the sky cannot be dominated
short of a scale of attack on the opposing retaliatory force
which will unleash an all-out conflict; control of the seas
implies the destruction of industrial facilities and supply
depots deep in enemy territory, as Admiral Burke testified

before the Symington Committee; and the Army had declared a 1,500-mile missile essential for the performance of its mission. A division of functions makes sense only if the functions in fact represent distinguishable strategic missions. If in the performance of its primary mission each service must carry out tasks inseparable from the primary mission of a sister service, energies will be increasingly absorbed in jurisdictional disputes. Nor can this problem be avoided by administrative fiat as has been demonstrated repeatedly. Interservice rivalries are inherent in the definition of missions. They result inevitably from a division of roles based on means of locomotion at a time when technology makes a mockery of such distinctions.[1]

The disputes among the services have grown so bitter, because force levels, which determine appropriations, are set on the basis of each service's primary mission. Since, in purely military terms, the primary mission cannot be achieved without defeating the enemy completely, each service will always consider its force levels inadequate and will insist that one reason for this inadequacy is a transgression by a sister service on its field of jurisdiction. Thus the setting of force levels on the basis of primary missions, when these missions represent no distinctive strategic option, inhibits an over-all approach to questions of doctrine.

The dispute between the Army and the Air Force regarding the importance of airlift provides an illustration. The significance of their dispute resides not in the arguments advanced on either side, but in the fact that in terms of the primary mission of each service it is insoluble. The Air Force, charged with defeating the enemy air arm, must look on an investment in planes of no tactical or strategic combat effectiveness as a diversion of resources. The Army, on the other hand, charged with destroying its enemy counterpart, cannot carry out its primary mission if it cannot get rapidly to the theater of combat. For it, airlift is the condition of all effective action.

The rigid division of functions among the services, therefore, prevents the consideration of airlift in terms of over-

---

1 See above, Chapter 2, pp. 58-61.

all strategy. The Army, to which the airlift is essential, is precluded by the Key West agreement from developing one, and Secretary Wilson's clarification of missions reinforces the prohibition against building up an Army air arm.[2] The Air Force, which has primary responsibility for all weapons which depend on the air as a means of locomotion, is impelled by its primary mission to consider airlift a marginal requirement. In fact, the Key West agreement precludes the Air Force from considering airlift in the only terms which are meaningful to the Army: those of strategic mobility. Thus our process of arriving at strategic decisions breaks down at the precise point where the division of functions on the basis of means of locomotion causes one service to be assigned a responsibility which is subsidiary to its primary mission, although essential to the primary mision of another service.

The intimate connection between primary mission and budgetary rewards impels our Joint Chiefs, with the best intentions in the world, to become essentially advocates of a service point of view. The Joint Chiefs have risen to their position through a lifetime of dedication to one service. They are a product of its problems, its training schools, its environment. Maintaining the morale of their service can never be far from their minds. And mastering the primary mission of each service is becoming so difficult that the effort almost inevitably inhibits a consideration of its relationship to an over-all mission; or, more accurately, it leads to a psychological distortion in which over-all strategy tends to be equated with a service's primary mission. The test of an organization is how naturally and spontaneously it enables its leadership to address itself to its most severe challenges. There is little in the organization of our national defense establishment that impels the service chiefs in a spontaneous fashion to consider over-all strategic doctrine.

Whenever the service chiefs dissent from prevailing policy they are accused of "parochialism"—as if their atti-

---

2 "Memorandum on Guided Missiles," *New York Times,* November 27, 1956.

tude were a matter of choice rather than an almost inevitable consequence of the system which has produced them. It is difficult to escape the habits of a lifetime. The manner in which a familiar pattern of thought determines reactions to new situations is illustrated by the attitude of both the German and American staffs to the emergence of missiles. In both Germany and the United States, the Air Force concentrated initially on developing what was, in effect, an unmanned bomber: the V-1 guided missile in Germany, the Talos and Snark missiles in the United States. In both Germany and the United States, the Army developed the closest approximation in the missile field to an artillery projectile: the V-2 rocket in Germany, the Honest John, Nike and Redstone missiles in the United States. In developing these weapons the services were not being consciously parochial. They simply concentrated on the things they knew best. They were doing what came naturally.

Another factor inhibiting the development of strategic doctrine is the predominance of fiscal considerations in our defense planning. This is not even always a question of deliberate choice. One of the reasons for the emphasis on fiscal policy and technology has been that the position of the advocates of economy has usually been explicit and that the pressures of technology have brooked no delay. In the process of coordinating diverse policies, which is the primary function of the National Security Council, there always exists a clear fiscal policy, largely because governmental economy is the *raison d'être* of the Bureau of the Budget and because only one agency—the Treasury Department—is responsible for setting objectives in the fiscal field. But there is rarely, if ever, an equally clear National Security policy to oppose it. On the contrary, each contending service is tempted to enlist the backing of the Treasury Department and the Bureau of the Budget by claiming that its particular strategy will help to promote governmental economy. The fiscal viewpoint, therefore, often comes to predominate by default. In a conceptual vacuum the side with the clearest and most consistent position will hold the field.

Whatever the reason, every Administration since World War II has at some time held the view that this country could not afford more than a certain sum for military appropriations, overriding the question of whether we could afford to be without an adequate military establishment and inhibiting a consideration of the standards of adequacy in the realm of strategy. Now the imposition of a budgetary ceiling is not inevitably pernicious. Removing all budgetary restrictions would inhibit doctrine even more, because it would lead each service to hoard weapons for every eventuality—as occurred to some extent during the Korean war. And the proliferation of weapons systems unrelated to doctrine will cause strategic decisions—which always involve choices—to be made in the confusion of battle. The difficulty with our present budgetary process is that by giving priority to cost over requirement, it subordinates doctrine to technology. Budgetary requests are not formulated in the light of strategic doctrine. Rather doctrine is tailored and, if necessary, invented to fit budgetary requests.

The predominance of fiscal considerations makes for doctrinal rigidity because it causes each service to be afraid that a change in doctrine will lead to a cut in appropriations. Thus in 1950, a violent controversy broke out between advocates of strategic air power and a group of scientists at the Lincoln Laboratory of the Massachusetts Institute of Technology, who were accused of advocating a cut in our retaliatory force. The remarkable thing about this dispute was that the M.I.T. group explicitly denied underrating the importance of strategic air power. They insisted that their recommendations had been solely concerned with building up our air defense. Yet the partisans of strategic air power had psychology, if not logic, on their side. Under a fixed ceiling on defense expenditures, any new appropriation was bound to lead to the reduction of existing forces; a new capability could in practice be developed only at the expense of an existing one.

As a result, budgetary pressures compound the inherent conservatism of the military and encourage a subtle form of waste. Each service pushes weapons development in every category without much regard for the program of other services, and each service seeks to obtain control over as many different weapons as possible as a form of insurance against drastic budgetary cuts in the future. Because to relinquish a weapons system may mean to relinquish the appropriations that go with it, each service has a powerful incentive to hold on to every weapon even after it has outlived its usefulness. A weapons system, no matter how obsolescent, represents a budgetary category. There is no guarantee that a replacement will find acceptance among the budgetary authorities, and in any case justifying a new item involves a long process fraught with serious danger of budgetary reduction.

While there is undoubtedly an upper limit of defense spending beyond which the injury to the economy would outweigh the gain in military strength, it is also the case that this theoretical ceiling has consistently been underestimated. In 1949, during the B-36 hearings, it was generally agreed that our economy could not support indefinitely a military budget of $14.6 billion, and yet within a year military expenditures had reached four times that amount. Since 1953 the military budget has been stabilized at around $35 billion on the same argument used for a much smaller budget in 1949, that higher expenditures would have a deleterious effect on the economy. With the steady rise since 1953 in the gross national product, the percentage devoted to defense expenditures has actually been declining. To be sure, there is no requirement that defense expenditures should rise with the gross national product. Such an approach is as mechanical as that which led to the imposition of a budgetary ceiling. It does indicate, however, that even according to the strictest canons of fiscal orthodoxy, the ceiling need not be as rigid as its advocates maintain. It also means that if the current defense budget is too low even to maintain our retaliatory force, as was argued by the chiefs of each service before the Symington Committee,[3] an increase in expenditures is essential, both to improve our readiness for all-out war and to bring about the capability for limited war described earlier.[4]

The doctrinal handicap imposed by the predominance of fiscal considerations is not compensated for by an increase in civilian control either within the Executive Branch or by Congress. Effective control over military programs is made very difficult by the fiction of the annual review of programs and by their technical complexity. The yearly review has become increasingly out of phase with the substantive realities of defense planning. The hiatus between development, procurement and operation is several years in the case of most weapons. The introduction of a new weapon into a unit implies that all units will be so equipped over a period of time. Thus the first order for B-52's logically carried with it the obligation to continue procurement until all heavy bomber wings of the Strategic Air Command were composed of jet planes. Similarly, starting the construction on an aircraft-carrier makes almost inescapable future appropriations to complete it.[5]

---

[3] The minimum estimates by each service were as follows: (U.S. Senate, *Study of Airpower,* Hearings before the Subcommittee on the Air Force of the Committee on Armed Services, 84th Cong., 2nd Sess. (Washington: GPO, 1956.)

Air Force	$23 billion	p. 1,494 (General Twining)
Navy	13 billion	p. 1,358 (Admiral Burke)
Army	12 billion	p. 1,280 (General Taylor)

Although these figures are by no means conclusive and the requests were reduced by the Secretary of Defense from $48 billion to $38 billion, the budget was held down only by deferring major new procurement. Every deferred expenditure will increase the pressure in future years either to increase the budget or to reduce forces. And no new provision was made for the limited war capabilities where we are weakest: airlift, tactical air support, and expanded and modernized ground forces.

[4] See above, Chapter 5, p. 154 ff.

[5] This difficulty is not confined to the field of defense policy although it is perhaps most evident there. The European Recovery Program (ERP), for example, was launched by an authorization for the expenditure of $15 billion over a five-year period. Although Congress was not legally bound thereby to appropriate this amount, or indeed any amount, in subsequent years, the moral obligation to continue appropriations was considerable. As a result, a new Administration and a new Congress discover very often that a large part of the current budget is already preempted by decisions made in previous years.

In these circumstances, a yearly review does not bring about effective control; it does ensure that no dispute is ever finally resolved. Each year the same arguments about the efficacy of limited war, airlift and the relative merits of carrier and strategic aviation are repeated. They are not settled until some technical development outstrips the dispute or an administrative decision allocates roles and missions which the losing service accepts only because it has every prospect of reopening the issue in the following year. In the absence of doctrinal agreement, interservice disputes can be resolved only by compromises which may define only the least unacceptable strategy or by a proliferation of missions and weapons systems.

The technical complexity of most disputes complicates civilian control and particularly Congressional control even further. Within the Department of Defense the multiplication of civilian officials, often in office for only a year or two, causes the Secretaries and Assistant Secretaries to become less agents of control than a device for legitimizing interservice disputes. Their short term in office makes it difficult, if not impossible, for them as civilians to become familiar with the subtleties of strategic problems. Instead of being able to establish a unified concept, they are largely dependent on the advice of their professional staff whose spokesmen they almost inevitably become.

As for Congressional control, the only forum where the over-all defense program can be considered is in the Appropriations Committee. A meaningful judgment by the Congress on the defense budget would require it to assess the military strength achieved by a given expenditure and to correlate this strength to an agreed set of national security objectives. Neither condition is met by current practice. To be sure, the budget is introduced by testimony of the service chiefs and their civilian superiors regarding the gravity of the international situation. But no attempt is made to show the relationship of strategy to events abroad beyond the general implication that the proposed program will ensure the security of the United States. In turn, the Congressional committees can make their judgments only in terms of a vague assessment of the international situa-

tion. They will hesitate to reduce the budget if they feel
the situation to be grave, and they will be disposed to pare
requests drastically when they think the situation is less
serious than has been represented.

Such Congressional consideration of strategic concepts
as does take place is usually produced by the dissatisfaction of some service with its budgetary allocations. The
B-36 hearings in 1949 resulted from the cancellation by
Secretary Johnson of the Navy's giant carrier, and the
Symington Committee hearings on air power in 1956 were
a reaction to the budgetary ceiling imposed on the Air
Force (and other services too) by Secretary Wilson. But
such a procedure has the disadvantage of emphasizing the
problems of one particular service and of obscuring the
real difficulties which occur in the area of overlapping
strategies.

Moreover, even the hearings explicitly addressed to the
problem of the roles and missions of the services tend to
be conducted in the familiar technical categories. Thus
during the Symington hearings, relatively little attention
was paid to the strategic concepts of the services; on the
whole, the Committee was content to take the services at
their own valuation of themselves. But a great deal of
time was spent on the relative numbers of the Soviet and
United States heavy bomber force and the relative thrust
of jet engines. To be sure, these figures are important, but
their significance depends on the strategic doctrine which
determines their role. Without a concept of war—or at
least of air war—comparative numbers mean little, and the
relative thrust of jet engines means less. The quest for
numbers is a symptom of the abdication of doctrine.

In order to create a favorable climate for their budgetary requests, the services tend to emphasize the most
ominous aspects of the United States security problem. Because of their awareness that there exists a greater recep-
tiveness for programs which seem to offer total solutions,
each service is tempted to stress the part of its mission
which poses the most absolute sanctions. Thus in 1951
the Army produced the "atomic cannon," a cumbersome,
hybrid and already obsolescent weapon, partly to gain ac-

cess to the nuclear stockpile. Similarly, after the B-36 hearings, the Navy abandoned its opposition to identifying deterrence with maximum retaliatory power. In fact, it adopted the theory as its own and in its budgetary presentations has emphasized its contribution to the strategic striking force more than its less dramatic task of antisubmarine warfare. And Congressional hearings leave little doubt that within the Air Force the Strategic Air Command has the highest prestige value.

Thus the budgetary process places a premium on the weapons systems which fit in best with the traditional preconceptions of American strategic thought. It is not that the belief in the importance of strategic striking forces is wrong; indeed, the Strategic Air Command must continue to have the first claim on our defense budget. It is simply that the overemphasis on total solutions reinforces the already powerful tendency against supplementing our retaliatory force with subtler military capabilities which address themselves to the likelier dangers and involve a less destructive strategy.

The failure to pay adequate attention to strategic doctrine inhibits not only the formulation of military policy but also the conduct of diplomacy. In order to justify appropriations before an economy-minded Congress and Bureau of the Budget, there is a tendency to paint the strategic problem in the darkest terms. Thus a vicious circle is set up: the more frightening we paint Soviet power, the more we confirm our predilection for an all-out strategy. But the more fearful the consequences of our strategy, the more reluctant will the political leadership be to invoke it. In every crisis, we are obliged to gear our measures to the availability of forces instead of having in advance geared our forces to the most likely danger. Even with respect to the forces we have available, our hesitations are multiplied because the services do not agree among themselves about strategy for either limited or for total war, but particularly for the former.

III

To be sure, many of the obstacles to the development of doctrine are inherent in the complexity of the strategic problem and in the novelty of the challenge confronting us. No previous generation has had to master so many revolutions occurring simultaneously, in ideology, in emerging new nations, in the existence of an irreconcilably hostile bloc of powers and in the rapidly changing weapons technology. The concern with technology is understandable in a situation where the penalty for a wrong guess about weapons systems may be national catastrophe. The predilection with all-out war stems almost inevitably from the fact that it is our gravest, if not our most likely, danger. It, therefore, rightly holds the first priority in our defense effort. And provision for it is so complicated, that it can easily obscure all other concerns. The fact remains that survival will depend on our ability to overcome these difficulties.

The basic challenge of any society is how it can bring its leadership to think naturally and spontaneously about the problems of greatest over-all concern. An administrative mechanism charged with developing strategic doctrine will be ineffective if nothing in the daily experience of the individuals comprising it leads them naturally to reflection about the problems of strategy. The mere fact that each high official spends a certain amount of time on the interdepartmental committees charged with producing over-all objectives is not sufficient. Strategic doctrine is not achieved merely by an apportionment of time. Its profundity depends on the ability to transcend the technical requirements of the moment.

An administrative mechanism will encourage profound strategic thought if it leads officials to reflect spontaneously about problems of doctrine, not only by fiat when they have achieved eminence but throughout their careers. This is impossible as long as there exists a mechanistic division of functions among our services which is growing increasingly unrealistic. A strategy utilizing missiles is not necessarily analogous to air strategy simply because missiles fly through the air, any more than a 1,500-mile missile is a tactical weapon because it is fired like an artillery projectile. The logic of strategy, therefore, demands a greater degree of unification among the services and above all between the Air Force and the Army whose roles and missions overlap most. This unification is as important at the lower and intermediary echelons where attitudes are formed as at the top where often little can be done except to provide a forum for well-established views.

It may well be that the separation of the Army and the Air Force in 1948 occurred two decades too late and at the precise moment when the distinction between ground and air strategy was becoming obsolescent. Instead of making the Army Air Corps independent, it would probably have been wiser to mix the two organizations more thoroughly and to develop a single service neither focused on exclusive ground nor on exclusive air strategy. Instead, the separation of the two services was achieved to the detriment of both. Different service academies, training schools and war colleges inevitably emphasize a particular aspect of our strategic problem instead of an over-all doctrine in which traditional distinctions should be disappearing, in which the Army would begin to approach the mobility of the Air Force and the Air Force to develop the relative discrimination of ground warfare.

It would still be the wisest course to move in the direction of a single service initially by amalgamating the Army and the Air Force. The Navy's strategic problems may remain sufficiently distinct not to require integration, and in any case resistance in the Navy to complete unification would be so bitter as to obviate its advantages. A unified service with a single system of service schools would force officers at a formative stage of their careers into a framework less narrowly addressed to the concerns of a particular service. Loyalty to a service which is one of the most attractive traits of the military and which now necessarily produces a rigid adherence to a service point of view could in this manner be utilized to help produce an over-all strategic doctrine.

To be sure, the officers of all services attend each other's war colleges even now. But it is one thing to attend a service school as an outsider to learn the point of view of another service; it is quite another to provide incentives from the earliest stages of an officer's career to consider strategic problems apart from the interests of a service. In a single service, a staff officer would be judged less by his skill in defending his service's point of view in the coordinating procedure of the Pentagon than by his contribution to an over-all doctrine or at least by his ability to operate within it. Loyalty to the organization would be identical with the requirements of doctrine. Doctrine would no longer be a tool of interservice rivalry but a subject to be considered on its own merits.

Complete unification among the services is probably out of the question. The traditions from which each service derives its strength would bring about overwhelming resistance to the concept of a single uniform and a single system of service schools. It may even be that a single service would be too unwieldy and would still require a subdivision according to the strategic tasks which have to be performed. It may, therefore, be best to begin reorganization by creating two basic commands, each representing a clearly distinguishable strategic mission. The Army, Navy and Air Force could continue as administrative and training units, much as the training commands *within* the various services operate today. But for all other purposes two basic organizations would be created: the Strategic Force and the Tactical Force. The Strategic Force would be the units required for all-out war. It would include the Strategic Air Command, the Air Defense Command, the units of the Army required to protect overseas bases and the units of the Navy which are to participate in the retaliatory attack. The Tactical Force would be the Army, Air Force and Navy units required for limited war. The Strategic Force would probably be under Air Force command, the Tactical Force under Army command. The training and doctrine of each Force should be uniform, and its officers should attend the same technical and service schools. The schools would continue to be administered by a parent service but the curriculum and student body should be determined by the Force commander.

Such a division would reflect the realities of the strategic situation. While the Tactical Force might be required in an all-out war and for such a purpose would come under the command of the Strategic Force, the Strategic Force should not be utilized for limited war and should be as self-contained as possible even for all-out war. The Strategic Force should not be utilized for limited war, because by training and doctrine it is not suited for it and, because its unimpaired power represents the only guarantee for the war remaining limited. If an enemy could bring about a significant attrition of the Strategic Force by means of a limited war, he would tilt the strategic balance in his favor however the limited war ended. Moreover, any utilization of the Strategic Force in a limited war might create doubts about our intentions to keep the war limited and thereby unleash a retaliatory blow.

Both the Strategic and the Tactical Forces should be self-contained, because if the Tactical Force is considered an auxiliary to an all-out strategy, we will always be tempted to conserve it for a final showdown. And, as we have seen, the training, weapons systems and doctrine for limited war differ basically from that appropriate for all-out war.[6] Moreover, the Tactical, just as the Strategic, Force should be able to accomplish its mission with the forces-in-being. It cannot afford to rely on substantial mobilization, because this might be taken by the enemy as a prelude to an all-out showdown. In any case, half-trained reserves would probably not be adequate for the speed and complexity of modern war.[7]

The division of our military establishment into a Strategic and a Tactical Force would reflect the real nature of the strategic problem we confront: the necessity for being protected against all-out war as the prerequisite of all other measures and the capability to fight limited war as

---

6 See above, Chapters 5, p. 155 ff., and 6, p. 179 ff., for a full discussion of the strategy and weapons systems implied by this organization.

7 See above, Chapter 4, pp. 93-4, and Chapter 5, p. 161, for a discussion of the importance of forces-in-being.

the form of conflict where the cost is commensurate with the issues actually under dispute.

In such an organization, too, the Joint Chiefs of Staff would change their character. They would then consist of a Chairman, the Chief of the Tactical Force, the Chief of the Strategic Force, and the Chief of Naval Operations (to represent operations such as antisubmarine warfare which do not fit into any of the above categories). Such a group would in its very nature be more oriented toward doctrine than the present Joint Chiefs of Staff. The Chief of each Force would represent an integrated strategic mission and not a means of locomotion. Since service chiefs would continue to administer the traditional services, the Chief of each Force would be freed of many of the routine problems of administration which, as Admiral Radford pointed out before the Symington Committee, make the Chairman the only member of the present group who can give his full attention to problems of over-all strategy.

The advantage of the proposed organization for the conduct of military operations is demonstrated by the fact that in every recent war we have set up joint commands reflecting the same basic concept. The new organization would create in peacetime the structure which the requirements of combat would impose on us in any case. To be sure, the same contest over appropriations as is now going on might take place between the Chiefs of the Strategic and the Tactical Forces. And there would be the same temptation to invent doctrine in support of budgetary requests. But with each Force representing a distinguishable strategic mission, self-interest and the requirements of strategic doctrine would be identical.

The change in the organization of the services should be supplemented by strengthening the organization for strategic decisions of the civilian side of the Department of Defense. At present the Secretary of Defense is at best an arbiter of doctrinal disputes. He possesses neither the staff nor the organization to shape them. Implicit in the present organization is the notion that strategic doctrine reflects "purely" military considerations. Thus the Chairman of the Joint Chiefs reports directly to the President and attends meetings of the National Security Council. Although the special relationship between the President and the Chairman of the Joint Chiefs is implicit in the fact that the President is also Commander in Chief, it has contributed to the practical autonomy of the military in matters of doctrine.

Such a separation of strategy and policy can be achieved only to the detriment of both. It causes military policy to become identified with the most absolute applications of power and it tempts diplomacy into an overconcern with finesse. Since the difficult problems of national policy are in the area where political, economic, psychological and military factors overlap, we should give up the fiction that there is such a thing as "purely" military advice. The Secretary of Defense would gain greatly from instituting some form of Strategic Advisory Council either composed of the service secretaries or by strengthening the functions now exercised by the Assistant Secretary of Defense for National Security Affairs. The Strategic Advisory Council or the Assistant Secretary of Defense should be related more closely to the deliberations of the Joint Chiefs of Staff. They might, for example, meet jointly on all issues, save purely technical matters of procurement or weapons development. Both the civilian officials and the Joint Chiefs would profit from an amalgamation of their functions. At every stage of formulation of strategy, doctrine would be considered as a combination of political, economic and military factors replacing the incongruity of the present system which seeks to compromise two incommensurables: "purely" military and "purely" political considerations.

An attempt to channel military thought toward greater concern with doctrine might also address itself to the problem of relieving the pressure inherent in the almost incessant effort of either preparing, negotiating or justifying budgets. The yearly budget review encourages irresponsibility. Almost inevitably it diverts energies from problems of over-all strategy and causes the budget to be justified in terms which flatter prevailing predilections. A great deal would be gained by an extension of the budget cycle for defense appropriations. Some constitutions which provided for a yearly review of the budget have made exceptions in the case of military appropriations. It would be a great advance if our military budget could be extended over a two-year period. Thus the military budget would coincide with the term of the House of Representatives. And, as we have seen, many of the essential commitments for major procurement in any case extend over several years.

To be sure, in its initial stages the proposed procedure might sharpen interservice rivalries because commitments would now be more fundamental. But bringing the interservice dispute into the open would produce healthy consequences in the long run. The failure to resolve doctrinal disagreements, and the pretense of harmony at each budgetary hearing, cause the conflict to rage by subterfuge, by planned leaks to newspapers or to sympathetic Congressmen. A two-year budgetary cycle would free the service chiefs from the constant pressure of short-term considerations; it might encourage planning to turn from the essentially defensive task of justifying force levels to the consideration of the purpose of force levels.

With the emergence of an agreed strategic doctrine within the Department of Defense, the whole process of formulating security objectives within the Executive Branch would gain in balance. The clear fiscal point of view could then be confronted by an explicit Department of Defense position. With a better structure for producing discussions and a longer interval between the need for preparing budgetary requests (and even in its absence), the interservice disputes would lose a great deal of their tenseness. Doctrine would then be built on the only sound basis: a realization that the task of strategy is not simply to provide the tools of war but also to utilize these tools for the purpose of war.

IV

It would be a mistake, however, to expect too much from organizational remedies. For many of the difficulties described in this chapter and in this book have been caused by national traits which are deeply ingrained in the American experience. As in all tragedies, many of our problems have been produced in spite of our good intentions and have been caused not by our worst qualities but by our best. What is at issue, therefore, is not a policy but an attitude.

Foremost among the attitudes which affect the making of our policy is American empiricism and its quest for certainty: nothing is "true" unless it is "objective," and it is not "objective" unless it is part of experience. This makes for the absence of dogmatism and for the ease of social relations. But it has pernicious consequences in the conduct of policy. Policy is the art of weighing probabilities; mastery of it lies in grasping the nuances of possibilities. To attempt to conduct it as a science must lead to rigidity. For only the risks are certain; the opportunities are conjectural. One cannot be "sure" about the implications of events until they have happened and when they have occurred it is too late to do anything about them. Empiricism in foreign policy leads to a penchant for *ad hoc* solutions. The rejection of dogmatism inclines our policy-makers to postpone committing themselves until all facts are in; but by the time the facts are in, a crisis has usually developed or an opportunity has passed. Our policy is, therefore, geared to dealing with emergencies; it finds difficulty in developing the long-range program that might forestall them.

A symptom of our search for certainty is the vast number of committees charged with examining and developing policy. The very multiplicity of committees makes it difficult to arrive at decisions in time. It tends to give a disproportionate influence to subordinate officials who prepare the initial memoranda, and it overwhelms our higher officials with trivia. Because of our cult of specialization, sovereign departments negotiate national policy among each other with no single authority, except an overburdened President, able to take an over-all view or to apply decisions over a period of time. This results in the gap previously noted between grand strategy and particular tactics, between the definition of general objectives so vague as to be truistic and the concern with immediate problems. The gap is bridged only when a crisis forces the bureaucratic machinery into accelerated action, and then the top leadership has little choice but to concur in the administrative proposals. In short, we are trying to cope with political problems by administrative means.

Our inward doubt makes for vulnerability to Soviet maneuvers in two ways: on the one hand, every Soviet change of line is taken to some extent at face value. We cannot be certain that the Soviets may not "mean" it this time until they have proved they do not; and they will try their best not to prove it until the new tactic has served its purpose. On the other hand, we have found it difficult to adjust our tactics to new situations, so that we always tend to speak in the categories of the most recent threat but one. Moreover, we hesitate not only in the face of Soviet blandishments but also before Soviet intransigence. Every Soviet aggressive move finds us debating its implications and creates pressures for deferring a showdown for the "clear" case of aggression the Soviet leaders are trying very hard not to present. The paradoxical result is that we, the empiricists, often appear to the world as rigid, unimaginative and even somewhat cynical, while the dogmatic Bolsheviks exhibit flexibility, daring and subtlety. This is because our empiricism dooms us to an essentially reactive policy that improvises a counter to every Soviet move, while the Soviet emphasis on theory gives them the certainty to act, to manuever and to run risks. The very fact of Soviet action forces us to assume the risks of countermoves and absorbs our energies in essentially defensive measures.

The willingness to act need not derive from theory, of course. Indeed, an overemphasis on theory can lead to a loss of touch with reality. In many societies—in Great Britain, for example—policy developed from a firmly held tradition of a national strategy. For more than two centuries, it was a tenet of British policy that Antwerp should not fall into the hands of a major power. This was not backed by an elaborate metaphysics but simply by a tradition of British sea power whose requirements were so generally understood that they were never debated. The absence of a tradition of foreign policy exaggerates the biases of our empiricism. As a result, we find it difficult to conduct our policy with a proper regard for the timing of measures. We tend to overlook that policy exists in time as well as in space, that a measure is correct only if it can be carried out at the proper moment. To be sure, our cumbersome administrative mechanism adds immeasurably to the problem. But in addition, our deliberations are conducted as if a course of action were eternally valid, as if a measure which might meet exactly the needs of a given moment could not backfire if adopted a year later.

For this reason, our policy lacks a feeling for nuance, the ability to come up with variations on the same theme, as the Soviet leaders have done so effectively. We consider policy-making concluded when the National Security Council has come to a decision. And, in fact, the process of arriving at a decision is so arduous and a reappraisal is necessarily so "agonizing" that we are reluctant to re-examine policies after they have outlived their usefulness. But a written statement of policy is likely to amount to a truism; the real difficulty arises in applying it to concrete situations. And, while we have often come up with proper measures, we have not found it easy to adapt our approach to changing conditions over a period of time.

Another factor shaping our attitude toward foreign affairs is our lack of tragic experience. Though we have known severe hardships, our history has been notably free of disaster. Indeed, the American domestic experience exhibits an unparalleled success, of great daring rewarded and of great obstacles overcome. It is no wonder, therefore, that to many of our most responsible men, particularly in the business community, the warnings of impending peril or of imminent disaster sound like the Cassandra cries of abstracted "egg-heads." For is not the attribute of the "egg-head" his lack of touch with reality, and does not American reality show an unparalleled wealth coupled with an unparalleled growth?

There has been much criticism of Secretaries George M. Humphrey and Charles E. Wilson for their emphasis on holding down the defense budget. But in fairness, the psychological background of their decisions should be understood. Despite all the information at their disposal, they simply cannot believe that in the nuclear age the penalty for miscalculation may be national catastrophe. They may know in their heads, but they cannot accept in their hearts, that the society they helped to build could disappear as did Rome or Carthage or Byzantium, which probably seemed as eternal to their citizens. These characteristics make for an absence of a sense of urgency, a tendency to believe that everything can be tried once and that the worst consequence mistakes can have is that we may be forced to redouble our efforts later on. The irrevocable error is not yet part of the American experience.

Related to this is our reluctance to think in terms of power. To be sure, American expansion, both economic and geographic, was not accomplished without a judicious application of power. But our Calvinist heritage has required success to display the attribute of justice. Even our great fortunes, however accumulated, were almost invariably held to impose a social obligation; the great foundation is after all a peculiarly American phenomenon. As a nation, we have used power almost shamefacedly, as if it were inherently wicked. We have wanted to be liked for our own sakes, and we have wished to succeed because of the persuasiveness of our principles rather than through our strength. Our feeling of guilt with respect to power has caused us to transform all wars into crusades, and then to apply our power in the most absolute terms. We have rarely found intermediary ways to use our power and in those cases we have done so reluctantly.

But foreign policy cannot be conducted without an awareness of power relationships. To be sure, force alone will not overcome the contemporary revolution. An imaginative diplomacy and bold programs are required if we are to identify ourselves with the aspirations of humanity. But unless we maintain at least an equilibrium of power

between us and the Soviet bloc, we will have no chance
to undertake any positive measures. And maintaining this
equilibrium may require some very difficult choices. We
are certain to be confronted with situations of extraordinary ambiguity, such as civil wars or domestic coups. Each
successive Soviet move is designed to make our moral position that much more difficult: Indo-China was more ambiguous than Korea; the Soviet arms deal with Egypt
more ambiguous than Indo-China; the Middle Eastern crisis more ambiguous than the arms deal with Egypt. There
can be no doubt that we should seek to forestall such
occurrences. But once they have occurred, we must find
the will to act and to run risks in a situation which permits only a choice among evils. While we should never
give up our principles, we must also realize that we cannot maintain our principles unless we survive.

The obverse of our reluctance to think in terms of
power has been our notion of the nature of peace. We
assume that peace is the "normal" pattern of relations
among states, that it is equivalent to a consciousness of
harmony, that it can be aimed at directly as a goal of
policy. These are truisms rarely challenged in our political debate. Both major political parties maintain that they
work for a lasting peace, even if they differ about the best
means of attaining it. Both make statements which imply
that on a certain magic day, perhaps after a four-power
conference, "peace will break out."

No idea could be more dangerous. To begin with, the
polarization of power in the world would give international relations a degree of instability even if there were
no ideological disagreement, and the present volatile state
of technology is likely to compound this sense of insecurity. Whenever peace—conceived as the avoidance of war—
has become the primary objective of a power or group of
powers, international relations have been at the mercy of
the state willing to forego peace. To entrust the fate of a
country entirely to the continued good will of another
sovereign state is an abdication of statesmanship; it means
that survival is completely dependent on factors outside
of one's own control. Peace, therefore, cannot be aimed at

directly; it is the expression of certain conditions and power relationships. It is to these relationships—not to peace as such—that diplomacy must address itself.

A power can survive only if it is willing to fight for its interpretations of justice and its conception of vital interests. Its test comes in its awareness of where to draw the line and for what issue to contend. Its adequacy to meet its challenges depends on the alternatives it poses for itself. This is why it is so crucial for the United States to become clear about the nature of our strategic interest in the world. It would be comforting if we could confine our actions to situations in which our moral, legal and military positions are completely in harmony and where legitimacy is most in accord with the requirements of survival. But, as the strongest power in the world, we will probably never again be afforded the simple moral choices on which we could insist in our more secure past. The thrust of Soviet aggression will always be directed at the weak points in our armor and to issues in which our psychological inhibitions are at a maximum. To deal with problems of such ambiguity presupposes above all a moral act: a willingness to run risks on partial knowledge and for a less than perfect application of one's principles. The insistence on absolutes either in assessing the provocation or in evaluating possible remedies is a prescription for inaction.

To be sure, to engage in nuclear war without a prayerful awareness of its consequences is to open Pandora's box. But to permit the Soviets to overturn the strategic balance because it has been jeopardized by our own lack of imagination is to compound shortsightedness with dogmatism. The price we may have to pay for a failure to take action in time may be the kind of measure which does no more than gain us a breathing spell for more positive steps. The refusal to act will ensure that the next contest will be fought on even more difficult ground.

In the process of defining our strategic interest we cannot avoid facing another fact of the nuclear age little in accord with our predilections: the difficulty, if not impossibility, of holding a perimeter of twenty thousand miles while always remaining on the defensive politically, militarily and spiritually. A major part of the perimeter encompasses countries whose traditional structures are in rapid flux. Even if we were omniscient, it would seem inevitable that in some countries forces hostile to our interests will gain ascendancy. To be sure, communism has never come to power anywhere by peaceful means. But the boundary between peace and war has been steadily eroded; and communism may well have a different meaning for the newly independent nations of Asia and the Middle East than for the countries of Western Europe. If then every addition to the Soviet orbit becomes immunized against United States influence while the Soviet bloc remains free to exacerbate all tensions within the non-Soviet world, our eventual expulsion from Asia and the Middle East, and perhaps even from Europe, will be almost inevitable.

To overcome this danger requires a more dynamic conception of world affairs. A great historical movement which is represented by the coming together of communism and the anti-colonial revolution cannot be mastered only by negative motives. A policy impelled primarily by a desire to prevent an expansion of the Soviet sphere ensures that militarily we will be forced always to fight at the point of our greatest weakness; that diplomatically we will always contest issues of maximum embarrassment to us; that spiritually we will convey an impression of uncertainty. In any conflict the side which is animated by faith in victory has a decided advantage over an opponent who wishes above all to preserve the *status quo*. It will be prepared to run greater risks because its purpose will be stronger. The advantage of initiative is that each move opens the possibility of several further steps. If carried far enough, it will force the opponent to protect itself against an ever growing number of contingencies and, therefore, to concentrate on purely defensive measures.

This does not mean preventive war. Considerations of principle would prohibit such a course apart from the enormous destructiveness of modern weapons. However, we should be as ready to profit from opportunities in the Soviet orbit as the Soviet bloc feels free to exploit all the difficulties of the non-Soviet world. In foreign policy courage and success stand in a causal relationship.

v

We thus reach our final problem: the adequacy of our leadership groups for dealing with the challenges we are likely to confront. This is an aspect of a more general problem faced by any society: where to strike a balance between the requirements of organization and the need for inspiration. Organization expresses the importance of continuity; the routine by which it operates represents a recognition that a society must be able to assimilate and utilize mediocrity. Inspiration, on the other hand, is the mechanism of growth; it is the ability to transcend a framework which has come to be taken for granted. The stability of a society depends on its skill in organization which enables it to react mechanically to "ordinary" problems and to utilize its resources to best effect. The greatness of a society derives from its willingness to chart new ground beyond the confines of routine. Without organization every problem becomes a special case. Without inspiration a society will stagnate; it will lose the ability to adapt to new circumstances or to generate new goals. The experience of a people tends to be confined to the level of its average performance. But leadership is the refusal to confine action to average performance; it is the willingness to define purposes perhaps only vaguely apprehended by the multitude. A society learns only from experience: it "knows" only when it is too late to act. But a statesman must act as if his inspirations were already experience, as if his aspiration were "truth." He must bridge the gap between a society's experience and his vision, between its tradition and its future.

In this task his possibilities are limited because there is an inherent tension between the mode of action of a bureaucracy and the pattern of statesmanship. A smoothly working bureaucracy creates the illusion of running by itself; it seeks to reduce all problems to administrative terms. The basic motivation of a bureaucracy is its quest for safety; its preference is in favor of a policy of minimum risk. A bureaucracy, therefore, tends to exaggerate the technical complexities of its problems and to seek to reduce questions of judgment to a minimum. Technical problems are susceptible to "objective" analysis, whereas questions of judgment contain too many uncertain elements. An administrative mechanism has a bias in favor of the *status quo,* however arrived at. Short of an unambiguous catastrophe, the *status quo* has the advantage of familiarity. No "objective" criteria can prove that a change of course will yield superior results. The inclination of a bureaucracy is to deny the possibility of great conception by classifying it as "unsound," "risky" or other terms which testify to a preference for equilibrium over exceptional performance. It is no accident that most great statesmen were opposed by the "experts" in their foreign offices, for the very greatness of the statesman's conception tends to make it inaccessible to those whose primary concern is with safety and minimum risk.

A society owes its vitality to its ability to strike a balance between the requirement of organization and the need for inspiration. Too much stress on organization leads to bureaucratization and the withering of imagination. Excessive emphasis on inspiration produces a tour de force without continuity or organizational stability. The best solution is a bureaucracy which runs sufficiently smoothly to take care of ordinary problems as a matter of routine, but not so pervasive as to inhibit the creative thought which is inseparable from statesmanship.

The complexities of contemporary life inhibit the establishment of this balance, however. For the mastery of any one field, whether it be politics, science, or industry, is so difficult that it discourages reflection about its relationship to other activities. The structure of most organizations is growing so intricate that learning to manipulate it tends to leave little energy for reflecting on its purpose. The ultimate in bureaucratization comes about when the internal problems of an administrative mechanism approach the complexity of the external problems with which it was designed to deal, a condition rapidly being reached in many aspects of modern life.

Thus at a moment when the capacity to think conceptually was never more important, technical problems have become so complicated that they tend to pre-empt all attention. A strong leadership group is developed when the qualities which are encouraged in reaching the top approximate the qualities required for providing effective over-all guidance. But the structure of a modern society tends to run counter to this need. The skill required in attaining eminence within a large administrative mechanism is essentially manipulative: the ability to adapt to prevailing standards and to improve efficiency within a framework which is given. But the qualities required for leadership are primarily creative: to set the framework within which administration will then operate. The patterns of thinking developed in the rise to eminence may, therefore, inhibit effectiveness once eminence has been reached. The rewards in a bureaucracy are for skill in adjusting to an equilibrium. The requirement of leadership is the ability to galvanize an organization and to prevent the equilibrium from becoming an end in itself. The incentive of an organization is specialized skill. The imperative of leadership is scope and vision which in turn may be unrecognized at lower levels because of the insufficiency of the challenge.

Many of the difficulties of our governmental apparatus are, therefore, only symptoms of challenges faced by our entire society among which our sudden emergence as the major power in the free world is perhaps the most important. The qualities of our leadership groups were formed during a century or more of primary concern with domestic development. Politics was considered a necessary evil and the primary function of the state was the exercise of police powers. Neither training nor incentives impelled our leadership groups to think in political or strategic terms. This emphasis was compounded by our empiricism with its cult of the expert and its premium on specialization.

The two professions which are most dominant in the

higher levels of Government—industry and the law—can serve as an illustration. The rewards in industry, particularly large-scale industry, are for administrative competence; they, therefore, produce a tendency to deal with conceptual problems by administrative means, by turning them over to committees of experts. And the legal profession, trained to deal with a succession of discreet individual cases, produces a penchant for *ad hoc* decisions and a resistance to the "hypothetical cases" inherent in long-range planning. Our leadership groups are, therefore, better prepared to deal with technical than with conceptual problems, with economic than with political issues. Each problem is dealt with "on its merits," a procedure which emphasizes the particular at the expense of the general and bogs down planning in a mass of detail. The absence of a conceptual framework makes it difficult for them even to identify our problems or to choose effectively among the plethora of proposals and interpretations produced by our governmental machinery.

This explains many postwar Soviet successes. Whatever the qualities of Soviet leadership, its training is eminently political and conceptual. Reading Lenin or Mao or Stalin, one is struck by the emphasis on the relationship between political, military, psychological and economic factors, the insistence on finding a conceptual basis for political action and on the need for dominating a situation by flexible tactics and inflexible purpose. And the internal struggles in the Kremlin ensure that only the most iron-nerved reach the top. Against the Politburo, trained to think in general terms and freed of problems of day-to-day administration, we have pitted leaders overwhelmed with departmental duties and trained to think that the cardinal sin is to transgress on another's field of specialization. To our leaders, policy is as a series of discrete problems; to the Soviet leaders it is an aspect of a continuing political process. As a result, the contest between us and the Soviet system has had many of the attributes of any contest between a professional and an amateur. Even a mediocre professional will usually defeat an excellent amateur, not because the amateur does not know what to do, but because he cannot react with sufficient speed and consistency. Our leaders have not lacked ability, but they have had to learn while doing, and this has imposed too great a handicap.

To be sure, many of the shortcomings of our leadership groups reflect the very qualities which make for the ease of relationships within American society. The condition for our limited Government has been the absence of basic social schisms, the regulation of many concerns not by Government fiat but by "what is taken for granted." A society can operate in this fashion only if disputes are not pushed to their logical conclusions, and if disagreements are blunted by avoiding dogmatism. And, in fact, the fear of seeming dogmatic permeates our social scene. Opinions are usually introduced with a disclaimer which indicates that the proponent is aware of their contingency and claims no superior validity for them. This produces a preference for decisions by committee, because the process of conversation permits disagreements to be discovered and adjustments made before positions have hardened. Our decision-making process is, therefore, geared to the pace of conversation; even departmental memoranda on which policy decisions are ultimately based are written with an eye to eventual compromise and not with the expectation that any of them will be accepted in their entirety.

It would be a mistake to be pessimistic. When World War II ended, no one would have supposed that the United States would assume commitments on such a world-wide scale. Our shortcomings are imposing only because of the magnitude of the threat confronting us. Moreover, the performance of the United States, for all its failings, compares favorably with that of the other nations of the non-Soviet world. Our difficulties are, therefore, only a symptom, and by no means the most obvious one, of an inward uncertainty in the free world. To be sure, by the nature of their institutions democracies cannot conduct policy as deviously, change course as rapidly or prepare their moves as secretly as dictatorships. But the crisis of the non-Soviet world lies deeper. The tragic element in foreign policy is the impossibility of escaping conjecture; after the "objective" analysis of fact there remains a residue of uncertainty about the meaning of events or the opportunities they offer. A statesman can often escape his dilemmas by lowering his sights; he always has the option to ignore the adversary's capabilities by attributing peaceful intentions to him. Many of the difficulties of the non-Soviet world have been the result of an attempt to use the element of uncertainty as an excuse for inaction. But in foreign policy certainty is conferred at least as much by philosophy as by fact. It derives from the imposition of purpose on events.

This is not to say that we should imitate Soviet dogmatism. A society can survive only by the genius that made it great. But we should be able to leaven our empiricism with a sense of urgency. And while our history may leave us not well enough prepared to deal with tragedy, it does teach us that great achievement does not result from a quest for safety. Even so, our task will remain psychologically more complex than that of the Kremlin. As the strongest and perhaps the most vital power of the free world we face the challenge of demonstrating that democracy is able to find the moral certainty to act without the support of fanaticism and to run risks without a guarantee of success.

BIBLIOGRAPHY

A comprehensive bibliography on a subject which has
aroused so much controversy would serve little purpose
because much of the literature is purely polemical. The
following titles have, therefore, been selected from among
the sources used in the preparation of this work. Wherever appropriate, a brief explanation of the significance
of books listed has been included. In the case of periodicals the title is usually an adequate indication of the
substance. A great deal of the most useful material is
contained in official documents and in Congressional
hearings. The most important of these have been listed.
The bibliography has been divided into the following
categories:

 A. Nuclear Weapons and Strategy
 B. Civil Defense
 C. International Control of Nuclear Weapons
 D. Soviet Strategy and Nuclear Weapons
 E. Technical and Scientific Aspects and Personal
  Recollections

A. NUCLEAR WEAPONS AND STRATEGY
Books
Amster, Warren. *A Theory for the Design of a Deterrent Air
Weapon System. Report* OR-P-29. San Diego, Cal.: Con-
vair, 1955. 65 p.
A brilliant paper analyzing the nature of deterrence.
Highly technical and perhaps somewhat too pat in its assumption that the ratio of destructiveness required for
deterrence can be precisely calculated for each contingency
in advance.

Baldwin, Hanson W. *Power and Politics: The Price of Security in the Atomic Age.* Claremont, Cal.: Claremont College Press, 1950. 117 p.
Series of lectures on American military and foreign policy. The recommendations are somewhat dated and not really elaborated.

———. *The Price of Power.* New York: Harper, 1948. 361 p.
Analysis of United States military problems and policy, including a discussion of atomic weapons and their implications. Somewhat dated.

Biorklund, Elis. *International Atomic Policy During a Decade.* London: Allen and Unwin, 1956. 148 p.
A history of nuclear power by a Swedish admiral. Interesting because the author is a specialist on Soviet affairs and has examined many Soviet documents.

Blackett, P. M. S. *Atomic Weapons and East-West Relations.* New York: Cambridge University Press, 1956. 103 p.
A series of lectures indicating the transformation of the author's view with respect both to nuclear weapons and the U.S.S.R. Includes a discussion about the feasibility of limiting nuclear war.

———. *Fear, War and the Bomb.* New York: McGraw-Hill, 1949. 244 p.
A highly intelligent, if dogmatic, work deprecating the importance of nuclear weapons. Highly colored by a tendency to ascribe only pure motives to the Soviet Union.

Brodie, Bernard, ed. *The Absolute Weapon: Atomic Power and World Order.* New York: Harcourt, Brace, 1946. 214 p.
A symposium about the impact of nuclear weapons on international relations and strategy. Though dated, it remains a useful and constructive work.

———. *The Atomic Bomb and American Security.* Memorandum No. 18. New Haven: Yale Institute of International Studies, 1945. 28 p.
One of the first thoughtful analytical papers about the implications of nuclear weapons.

——— and Eilene Galloway. *The Atomic Bomb and the Armed Services.* Public Affairs Bulletin No. 55. Washington: GPO, 1947. 177 p.
An analysis of the impact of nuclear weapons on the role of the Army and Navy, drawn from interviews with high-ranking officers.

Bush, Vannevar. *Modern Arms and Free Men*. New York: Simon and Schuster, 1949. 273 p.
A good discussion of the relationship between science and strategy. Rather better on the scientific than on the political plane and somewhat overoptimistic.

Buzzard, Rear Admiral Sir Anthony W., and others. *On Limiting Atomic War*. London: Royal Institute of International Affairs, 1956. 46 p.
An interesting effort to define the nature of limited nuclear war both diplomatically and militarily. Not altogether convincing.

Eliot, George Fielding, and others. *The H Bomb*. New York: Didier, 1950. 175 p.
A collection of statements and articles by such men as Stewart Alsop, Hanson Baldwin, Hans Bethe, David E. Lilienthal, Walter Lippmann and Hans Morganthau on the technological feasibility, the military advisability and the political consequences of the hydrogen bomb. Uneven.

Finletter, Thomas K. *Power and Policy*. New York: Harcourt, Brace, 1954. 408 p.
A thoughtful work by a former Secretary of the Air Force. Marred by a penchant for absolutes, but a good exposition of the strategy of all-out war.

Gaillard, Félix. *La France et l'Energie Atomique dans la Paix et dans la Guerre*. Paris: Parti Républicain Radicale et Radicale Sociale, 1954.
An exposition of the attitudes of the Radical Socialist party in opposition to a French nuclear weapons program. Typical of all French positions in 1954.

Great Britain. Ministry of Defence. *Statement on Defence* (Annual). Cmd. 9075, 9391, 9691. London: HMSO, 1954-56.
A useful record of the evolution of official British thought.

————. ————. *Defence: Outline of Future Policy*. Cmnd. 124. London: HMSO, April 1957. 10 p.

Ismay, Lord H. L. I. *NATO: The First Five Years*. Utrecht, Netherlands: Bosch, 1955. 280 p.
Useful as a reference work for the history and structure of the North Atlantic Treaty Organization.

Kaufmann, William W., ed. *Military Policy and National Security*. Princeton: Princeton University Press (for the Center of International Studies), 1956. 274 p.
A somewhat uneven symposium on such problems as the importance of military potential, alliances and limited war.

———. *The Requirements of Deterrence.* Memorandum No. 7. Princeton: Center of International Studies, 1954. 23 p.
A thoughtful pamphlet criticizing the doctrine of massive retaliation. Particularly strong in its analytical portions.

Knorr, Klaus. *Euratom and American Policy: A Conference Report.* Princeton: Center of International Studies, Princeton University, 1956. 22 p.
An analysis by a study group of the Center of International Studies of the economic and political issues raised by Euratom for its West European participants and the United States.

Liddell Hart, Basil Henry. *Defense of the West.* New York: William Morrow, 1950. 335 p.
An uneven analysis of strategy in the nuclear period. A good section about the need for a more flexible organization of the services, particularly of the Army.

Miksche, Colonel F. O. *Atomic Weapons and Armies.* New York: Praeger, 1955. 222 p.
An analysis of the use of nuclear weapons in tactical operations. Thoughtful, but a good example of a strategic concept which adds nuclear weapons to existing tactics simply as a more efficient explosive.

Osgood, Robert Endicott. *Limited War: the Challenge to American Strategy.* Chicago: University of Chicago Press, 1957. 364 p.
A very good study of the problems of limited war both historically and in relation to contemporary strategy.

Parson, Nels A., Jr. *Guided Missiles in War and Peace.* Cambridge, Mass.: Harvard University Press, 1956. 161 p.
A technical description of missiles available or in prospect.

Possony, Stefan T. *Strategic Air Power: The Pattern of Dynamic Security.* Washington: Infantry Journal Press, 1949. 313 p.
A very good discussion of the principles of air strategy, but it does full justice only to the problem of all-out war.

Reinhardt, George C. *American Strategy in the Atomic Age.* Norman, Okla.: University of Oklahoma Press, 1955. 236 p.
A rather sketchy advocacy of a strategy to overcome the bipolarization of the world.

——— and William R. Kintner. *Atomic Weapons in Land Combat.* Harrisburg, Pa.: Military Service Publishing Co., 1953. 182 p.

A fairly technical, but very original analysis of the tactics appropriate to nuclear weapons.

Slessor, Sir John. *Strategy for the West.* New York: Morrow, 1954. 180 p.
A somewhat superficial exposition of air strategy, centered around strategic bombing forces.

Smith, Dale O. *U.S. Military Doctrine: A Study and Appraisal.* New York: Duell, Sloan and Pearce, 1955. 256 p.
A defense of "massive retaliation." Stronger on passion than on analysis.

U.S. Atomic Energy Commission. *In the Matter of J. Robert Oppenheimer.* Transcript of Hearing before Personnel Security Board. Washington: GPO, 1954. 992 p.

U.S. House. Committee on Armed Services. *The National Defense Program—Unification and Strategy.* Hearings, 81st Cong., 1st sess. Washington: GPO, 1949. 639 p.

———. Subcommittee of the Committee on Appropriation. *Military Establishment Appropriation Bill for 1947.* Hearings, 79th Cong., 2d sess. Washington: GPO, 1946. pp. 400-430. (Statement of General Spaatz.)

———. ———. *Department of the Army Appropriations for 1956.* Hearings, 84th Cong., 1st sess., on H.R. 6042. Washington: GPO, 1955. 1,538 p.

———. ———. *Department of the Navy Appropriations for 1956.* Hearings, 84th Cong., 1st sess., on H.R. 6042. Washington: GPO, 1955. 1,241 p.

U.S. President. *Report to Congress on the Mutual Security Program for the Six Months Ended June 30, 1954.* Washington: GPO, 1954. 63 p.

U.S. Senate. Committee on Armed Services. *National Defense Establishment—Unification of the Armed Services.* Hearings, 80th Cong., 1st sess., on S. 758. Washington: GPO, 1947. 2 parts.

———. ———. *Universal Military Training.* Hearings, 80th Cong., 1st sess. Washington: GPO, 1948. 1,122 p.

———. Committee on Armed Services and Committee on Foreign Relations. *Military Situation in the Far East.* Hearings, 82nd Cong., 1st sess. Washington: GPO, 1951. 5 parts.

———. Committee on Foreign Relations. *Statements of . . . John Foster Dulles and Adm. Arthur Radford . . . on Foreign Policy and Its Relation to Military Programs.* Hearings, 83d Cong., 2d sess. Washington: GPO, 1954. 51 p.

———. Subcommittee on the Air Force of the Committee on

Armed Services. *Study of Airpower.* Hearings, 84th Cong., 2d sess. Washington: GPO, 1956. 23 parts.

Weinstein, Adelbert. *Keiner Kann den Krieg Gewinnen.* Bonn: Schimmelbusch, 1955. 68 p.

An analysis of the impact of nuclear weapons on strategy by the military correspondent of a leading German newspaper. Shortsighted and nationalistic, but a good indication of the psychological problems raised by the prospect of nuclear warfare among our allies.

Periodicals

✓ Acheson, Dean G. "Instant Retaliation: the Debate Continued," *New York Times,* March 28, 1954, sec. 6, p. 13.

"Atlantic Report on the World Today: Deterrence Doctrine," *Atlantic Monthly,* v. 195 (May 1955), p. 4.

Attlee, Clement R. "The Political Problem," *Bulletin of the Atomic Scientists,* v. 10 (October 1954), pp. 327-8.

Baldwin, Hanson W. "Postscript on the Revolt of the Admirals; B-36 Bomber," *Time,* v. 65 (February 21, 1955), p. 28.

"Basic Airpower Debate Shapes Up," *Aviation Week,* v. 62 (January 3, 1955), p. 21.

Berkner, Lloyd V., and others. "United States Military Policy," Special Issue, *Current History,* v. 26 (May 1954), pp. 257-301.

"British Missile Details Revealed," *Aviation Week,* v. 62 (March 21, 1955), p. 17.

Brodie, Bernard. "Navy Department Thinking on the Atomic Bomb," *Bulletin of the Atomic Scientists,* v. 3 (July 1947), pp. 177-80, 198-9.

——. "Some Notes on the Evolution of Air Doctrine," *World Politics,* v. 7 (April 1955), pp. 349-70.

——. "Strategic Bombing: What It Can Do," *Reporter,* v. 3 (August 15, 1950), pp. 28-31.

——. "War Department Thinking on the Atomic Bomb," *Bulletin of the Atomic Scientists,* v. 3 (June 1947), pp. 150-5.

Bush, Vannevar. "What's Wrong at the Pentagon?" *Collier's,* v. 130 (December 27, 1952), pp. 131-5.

Buzzard, Sir Anthony W. "Graduated Deterrence," *World Politics,* v. 8 (January 1956), pp. 228-37.

Carney, Robert B. "Carney: New U.S. Carrier Is Built for the Future" (Excerpt from an Address, December 11, 1954),

U.S. News and World Report, v. 37 (December 17, 1954), p. 101.

Churchill, Winston. "Defense Through Deterrents," *Vital Speeches of the Day,* v. 21 (March 15, 1955), pp. 1090-4.

Dulles, John Foster. "Policy for Security and Peace," *Foreign Affairs,* v. 32 (April 1954), pp. 353-64.

——. "The Evolution of Foreign Policy" (Address, Council on Foreign Relations, January 12, 1954), *The Department of State Bulletin,* v. 30 (January 25, 1954), pp. 107-10.

Eisenhower, Dwight D. "National Security and the Defense of Freedom" (Address, National Junior Chamber of Commerce, June 10, 1953), *The Department of State Bulletin,* v. 28 (June 22, 1953), pp. 863-5.

Finletter, Thomas K. "New Look at Air Policy," *Atlantic Monthly,* v. 192 (September 1953), pp. 25-30.

"Forrestal Opens New Carrier Era," *Aviation Week,* v. 61 (December 20, 1954), pp. 13-7.

Fox, William T. R. " 'Middle Run' Planning: Atomic Energy and International Relations," *Bulletin of the Atomic Scientists,* v. 4 (August 1948), pp. 227-32.

"Graduated Deterrence," *The Economist* (London), v. 177, (November 5, 1955), pp. 457-8.

Healey, Denis. "The Atom Bomb and the Alliance," *Confluence,* v. 5 (April 1956), pp. 70-8.

——. "The Bomb that Didn't Go off," *Encounter* (London), (July 1955), pp. 5-9.

Hetherington, Alastair. "Sir Winston Orders a Bomb," *Reporter,* v. 12 (March 24, 1955), pp. 11-5.

Kennan, George F. "Illusion of Security," *Atlantic Monthly,* v. 194 (August 1954), pp. 31-4.

Killian, James R., Jr. and A. G. Hill. "For a Continental Defense," *Atlantic Monthly,* v. 192 (November 1953), pp. 37-41.

Knorr, Klaus. "Defense for Atomic War," *Bulletin of the Atomic Scientists,* v. 11 (March 1955), pp. 77-81, 84.

Lapp, Ralph E. "Does the Superbomb Add to our Security?" *Reporter,* v. 10 (May 11, 1954), pp. 10-3.

Lay, James S., Jr. "National Security Council's Role in the U.S. Security and Peace Program," *World Affairs,* v. 115 (Summer 1952), pp. 37-9.

Leghorn, Colonel Richard S. "No Need to Bomb Cities to Win War," *U.S. News and World Report,* v. 38 (January 28, 1955), pp. 79-94.

Liddell Hart, Basil Henry. "All Military Knowledge Is Now Useless," *News Chronicle* (London), March 1, 1955.

——. "Military Strategy versus Common Sense," *The Saturday Review*, v. 39 (March 3, 1956), pp. 7-8.

Lincoln, George A. "Factors Determining Arms Aid," *Academy of Political Science, Proceedings*, v. 25 (May 1953), pp. 263-72.

McMahon, Brian. "Atomic Weapons and the National Defense," *Congressional Record*, 82nd Cong., 1st sess., v. 97 (September 18, 1951), pp. 496-501. (Daily edition.)

Middleton, Drew. "NATO Changes Direction," *Foreign Affairs*, v. 31 (April 1953), pp. 427-40.

Millis, Walter. "Military Problems of the New Administration," *Foreign Affairs*, v. 31 (January 1953), pp. 215-24.

Montgomery of Alamein, Bernard Law. "What the Next War Will Be Like," (Address, November 29, 1954), *U.S. News and World Report*, v. 37 (December 17, 1954), pp. 94-9.

Morgenthau, Hans J. "Another Great Debate: the National Interest of the United States," *American Political Science Review*, v. 46 (December 1952), pp. 961-88.

——. "The Political and Military Strategy of the United States," *Bulletin of the Atomic Scientists*, v. 10 (October 1954), pp. 323-7.

Morton, Thruston B. "Advancing Peace Through Collective Security," *The Department of State Bulletin*, v. 32 (February 7, 1955), pp. 215-21.

Murphy, Robert D. "The Interrelationship of Military Power and Foreign Policy," *The Department of State Bulletin*, v. 31 (August 30, 1954), pp. 291-4.

——. "The Soldier and the Diplomat," *Foreign Service Journal* (Washington), v. 29 (May 1952), pp. 17-9, 49-50.

Niemeyer, Gerhart. "1964: After Ten Years of Coexistence," *U.S. News and World Report*, v. 37 (December 10, 1954), pp. 40-6.

Nitze, Paul H. "Atoms, Strategy and Policy," *Foreign Affairs*, v. 34 (January 1956), pp. 187-98.

——. *Impact of New Weapons on Political and Strategic Problems of the West*. June 1955. (Unpublished paper delivered at meeting of Nobel Institute at Oslo.)

Oppenheimer, J. Robert. "Atomic Weapons and American Policy," *Foreign Affairs*, v. 31 (July 1953), pp. 525-35.

Phillips, Thomas R. "The Atomic Revolution in Warfare,"

Bulletin of the Atomic Scientists, v. 10 (October 1954), pp. 315-7.

Polanyi, Karl. "Whither Civilization? British Thinkers Ponder the Atomic Age," *Commentary* (London), v. 2 (September 1946), pp. 280-5.

Radford, Admiral Arthur W. "Defense for the Long Haul" (Address, National Press Club, December 14, 1953), *Vital Speeches of the Day*, v. 20 (January 1, 1953), pp. 171-3.

———. "We Give Military Advice Only" (Interview), *U.S. News and World Report*, v. 38 (February 25, 1955), pp. 42-8, 50.

Reinhardt, George C. and William R. Kintner. "The Need for a National Staff," *U.S. Naval Institute Proceedings*, v. 78 (July 1952), pp. 720-7.

———. "The Tactical Side of Atomic Warfare," *Bulletin of the Atomic Scientists*, v. 11 (February 1955), pp. 53-8.

Sherwin, C. W. "Securing Peace Through Military Technology," *Bulletin of the Atomic Scientists*, v. 12 (May 1956), pp. 159-64.

Slessor, Sir John. "The Great Deterrent and Its Limitations," *Bulletin of the Atomic Scientists*, v. 12 (May 1956), pp. 140-6.

———. "The H-Bomb or Graduated Deterrence," *International Affairs* (London), v. 32 (April 1956), pp. 158-65.

Slichter, Sumner H. "Rearmament: Too Much, Too Soon," *Atlantic Monthly*, v. 189 (January 1952), pp. 49-51.

Spaatz, Carl. "Supercarriers, A Sharp Point of View in the Raging Debate," *Newsweek*, v. 45 (January 3, 1955), pp. 20-1.

Stimson, Henry L. "The Decision to Use the Atomic Bomb," *Harper's*, v. 194 (February 1947), pp. 97-107.

Strauss, Lewis L. "We're Ahead of the Soviets on the H-Bomb," *U.S. News and World Report*, v. 37 (December 17, 1954), pp. 58-67.

Symington, W. Stuart. "The Intercontinental Ballistic Missile," *Congressional Record*. 83rd Cong., 1st sess., v. 100 (July 21, 1954), pp. 10,707-15. (Daily edition.)

Wilmot, Chester. "If NATO Had to Fight," *Foreign Affairs*, v. 31 (January 1953), pp. 200-14.

Wilson, Charles E. "Wilson Explains Program to Gain Maximum Defense without Waste," *New York Herald Tribune*, October 12, 1954.

——— and Dwight D. Eisenhower. "Adapting U.S. Military Strength to Meet Changing World Conditions" (Exchange of Correspondence), *The Department of State Bulletin,* v. 32 (January 17, 1955), pp. 87-8.

Wright, Quincy. "World Politics," *Air Affairs* (Washington), v. 1 (March 1947), pp. 334-418.

Wolfers, Arnold. "Superiority in Nuclear Weapons: Advantages and Limitations," *The Annals of the American Academy of Political and Social Science,* v. 290 (November 1953), pp. 7-15.

———. "Could a War in Europe Be Limited?" *Yale Review,* v. 45 (Winter 1956), pp. 214-228.

B. CIVIL DEFENSE

Books

Associated Universities, Inc. *Report of the Project East River.* New York, 1952.

Government-sponsored study of United States vulnerability to atomic attack and recommendations to build up adequate civil defense. A fundamental work.

U.S. House. Subcommittee of the Committee on Government Operations. *Civil Defense for National Survival.* Hearings, 84th Cong., 2d sess. Washington: GPO, 1956. 7 v.

———. ———. *24th Intermediate Report.* Hearings, Report No. 2946. Washington: GPO, 1956. 103 p.

U.S. National Security Resources Board. *Civil Defense Against Atomic Warfare: A Selected Reading List.* Washington: GPO, 1950. 24 p.

———. *Damage from Atomic Explosion and Design of Protective Structures.* Washington: GPO, 1950. 32 p.

U.S. President's Air Policy Commission. *Survival in the Air Age.* Washington: GPO, 1948. 166 p.

U.S. Senate. Subcommittee on Civil Defense of the Committee on Armed Services. *Civil Defense Program.* Hearings, 84th Cong., 1st sess. Washington: GPO, 1955, 377 p.

U.S. Strategic Bombing Survey. *Final Report Covering Air-Raid Protection and Allied Subjects in Japan.* Washington: GPO, 1947. 248 p.

Periodicals

Air Force Association. "Survival in the Hydrogen Age," *Bulletin of the Atomic Scientists,* v. 11 (January 1955), pp. 29-34.

Baldwin, Hanson W. "What Kind of Defense in the Atomic Age," *New York Times,* May 17, 1953, sec. 6.

Kaysen, Carl. "The Vulnerability of the U.S. to Atomic Attack," *World Politics,* v. 6 (January 1954), pp. 190-208.

Lapp, Ralph E. "Atomic Bomb Explosions—Effects on an American City," *Bulletin of the Atomic Scientists,* v. 4 (February 1948), pp. 49-54.

———. "The Strategy of Civil Defense," *Bulletin of the Atomic Scientists,* v. 6 (August-September 1950), pp. 241-3.

Teller, Edward. "If an H-Bomb Hits——," *U.S. News and World Report,* v. 40 (March 2, 1956), pp. 42-3.

C. INTERNATIONAL CONTROL OF NUCLEAR WEAPONS

Books

Bolté, Charles G. *The Price of Peace: A Plan for Disarmament.* Boston: The Beacon Press, 1956. 108 p.

A passionate plea for disarmament by a former member of the U.S. Mission to the United Nations, marred by a self-righteous tone and a total unconcern with technical and political problems.

Fox, William T. R. "International Control of Atomic Weapons," in Bernard Brodie, ed., *The Absolute Weapon: Atomic Power and World Order.* New York: Harcourt, Brace, 1946. pp. 169-203.

A very thoughtful, though somewhat dated, discussion regarding the problems of international control of the atom.

Moch, Jules. *Human Folly: To Disarm or Perish?* Translated by Edward Hyams, London: Gollancz, 1955. 222 p.

An intelligent plea for total disarmament which avoids, however, the difficult issues of control and inspection in a world relying to an ever greater extent on the peaceful uses of nuclear technology.

Osborn, Frederick. *Atomic Impasse, 1948.* A Collection of Speeches. Washington: GPO, 1948. 48 p.

A collection of speeches by the Deputy U.S. representative to the U.N. Atomic Energy Commission in defense of the Baruch plan.

Smyth, H. D., and others. *Symposium on Atomic Energy and Its Implications.* Proceedings of the American Philosophical Society. Philadelphia: American Philosophical Society, 1946. 79 p.

Papers by leading scientists and political scientists, such as
Smyth, Oppenheimer, Fermi, Viner, Shotwell and Compton, on the scientific origins and the impact of atomic energy.

U.N. Atomic Energy Commission. *International Control of
Atomic Energy: The First Report of the United Nations
Atomic Energy Commission to the Security Council.* U.S.
Department of State. U.S. and U.N. Report Series, no. 8.
Washington: GPO, 1947. 101 p.

———. *International Control of Atomic Energy and the Prohibition of Atomic Weapons.* U.S. Department of State. International Organization and Conference Series III, no.
41. Washington: GPO, 1949. 90 p.

———. *Scientific and Technical Aspects of the Control of
Atomic Energy.* New York: Department of Public Information, 1946. 42 p.

U.S. Atomic Energy Commission. *Semiannual Report.* Washington: GPO, 1947-1956.

U.S. Department of State. *International Control of Atomic
Energy, Growth of a Policy.* Washington: GPO, 1946.
281 p.

A summary record of the official declarations and proposals
relating to the international control of atomic energy made
between August 6, 1945 and October 15, 1946. Primarily
useful for background of disarmament negotiations.

U.S. Joint Committee on Atomic Energy. *The Hydrogen
Bomb and International Control: Technical and Background Information.* Washington: GPO, 1950. 41 p.

U.S. Representative on the United Nations Disarmament
Commission. *United States Efforts Toward Disarmament.*
Report to the President by the Deputy U.S. Representative, U.S. Department of State, International Organizations
and Conference Series III, no. 89. Washington: GPO,
1953. 42 p.

Periodicals

Cavers, David F. "Atomic Controls in Disarmament Planning," *Bulletin of the Atomic Scientists,* v. 8 (March 1952),
pp. 84-7.

———. "The Arms Stalemate Ends," *Bulletin of the Atomic Scientists,* v. 11 (January 1955), pp. 9-12.

Dulles, Allen W. "Disarmament in the Atomic Age," *Foreign
Affairs,* v. 25 (January 1947), pp. 204-16.

Haskins, Caryl P. "Atomic Energy and American Foreign Policy," *Foreign Affairs*, v. 24 (July 1946), pp. 591-609.

Hodgson, P. E. "International Control of Atomic Energy," *Bulletin of the Atomic Scientists*, v. 11 (February 1955), p. 63.

Kaufmann, William W. "Disarmament and American Foreign Policy," *Foreign Policy Reports*, v. 26 (September 1, 1950), pp. 89-92.
Considers the political value and effectiveness of some of the various disarmament plans suggested by Americans, specifically by Senators McMahon and Tydings.

Oppenheimer, J. Robert. "International Control of Atomic Energy," *Foreign Affairs*, v. 26 (January 1948), pp. 239-52.

Russell, Bertrand. "World Conference of Scientists," *Bulletin of the Atomic Scientists*, v. 12 (February 1956), pp 41-3.

Urey, Harold Clayton. "An Alternative Course for the Control of Atomic Energy," *Bulletin of the Atomic Scientists*, v. 3 (June 1947), pp. 139-42.

D. SOVIET STRATEGY AND NUCLEAR WEAPONS

Books

DeWitt, Nicholas. *Soviet Professional Manpower: Its Education, Training, and Supply*. Washington: National Science Foundation, 1955. 400 p.
A splendid analysis of Soviet efforts to increase the level of technical competence of their society and of the tremendous strides made in this respect.

Ely, Colonel Louis B. *The Red Army Today*. 3rd ed. Harrisburg, Pa.: Military Service Publishing Co., 1953. 272 p.
An interesting description of the Red Army organization, training and tactics. Somewhat dated since it was written before the Soviet Union had developed a tactical nuclear capability.

Friedl, Bertholdt C. *Les Fondements Théoriques de la Guerre et de la Paix en U.R.S.S.* Paris: Editions Médicis, 1945. 203 p.
Lenin's marginalia to Clausewitz, together with the text he annotated.

Garthoff, Raymond L. *Soviet Military Doctrine*. Glencoe, Ill.: The Free Press, 1953. 587 p.
A good study of Soviet military doctrine. The relation of Soviet military doctrine to Soviet political doctrine is

well handled. Extensive bibliography, including primary sources.

Gusev, M. *Bor'ba Sovetskogo Soiuza za sokrashchenie vooruzhenii i zapreshchenie atomonogo oruzhiia* (The struggle of the Soviet Union for the reduction of arms and the prohibition of atomic weapons). Moscow: Gospolitizdat, 1951.
For discussion, see Chapter 11.

Korsunsky, M. I. *Atomnoe Iadro* (The Atomic Nucleus). 4th ed. Moscow and Leningrad: Gos. Izd. Tekhniko-teoret. Lit., 1952.
For discussion, see Chapter 11.

Lee, Asher. *The Soviet Air Force.* New York: Harper, 1950. 207 p.
An interesting description of the Soviet Air Force. Primarily useful for its historical sections and views on Soviet training and tactics. Its technical sections have been overtaken by events.

Leites, Nathan. *A Study of Bolshevism.* Glencoe, Ill.: The Free Press, 1953. 639 p.
A very useful study of Soviet doctrine drawing on primary sources to an extent which sometimes obscures the analysis.

Lenin, V. I. *Selected Works.* New York: International Publishers, 1943. 2 v.

Liddell Hart, Basil Henry, ed. *The Red Army.* New York: Harcourt, Brace, 1956. 480 p.
A composite image of the Soviet Army, strategy and logistics by soldiers and scholars. Shows the Soviet armed forces to be highly formidable.

Mao Tse-tung. *Selected Works.* New York: International Publishers, 1954. 3 v.
A collection of writings by the leader of Chinese communism. Brilliant and very significant for the light they shed on Chinese Communist thought and its heavy dependence on Soviet theory.

Meissner, Boris and John S. Reshetar. *The Communist Party of the Soviet Union.* New York: Praeger, 1956. 276 p.
A useful collection of documents bearing on events in the U.S.S.R. since 1952.

Mezentsev, V. A. *Atom i atomnaia energiia* (The atom and atomic energy). Moscow: Voenizdat, 1954.
One of a series of books on atomic energy published by Soviet military and civil defense organizations after 1953

when the Soviet regime was dropping the myth that atomic energy was being used only for peaceful purposes.

Naumenko, I. K. *Atomnaia energiia i eio ispol'zovanie* (Atomic energy and its utilization). Moscow: DOSAFF, 1954.
For discussion, see Chapter 11.

Petrovich, S. and D. Didov. *Atomnaia energiia i eio primenenie* (Atomic energy and its use). Moscow: Voenizdat, 1954.

Stockwell, Richard E. *Soviet Air Power.* New York: Pageant Press, 1956. 238 p.
A useful survey of Soviet air power with an appendix of illustrations including description and performance of the latest Soviet plane types.

Taracouzio, T. A. *War and Peace in Soviet Diplomacy.* New York: Macmillan, 1940. 354 p.
A highly interesting study of Soviet notions of war and peace and the manner in which political and military strategy merge in Soviet thought.

U.S. Joint Committee on Atomic Energy. *Soviet Atomic Espionage.* Washington: GPO, 1951. 222 p.

Periodicals

Baldwin, Hanson W. "Russia Can Be Beaten Without A-Bomb," *New York Times,* January 5, 1955.

Dexter, Byron. "Clausewitz and Soviet Strategy," *Foreign Affairs,* v. 29 (October 1950), pp. 41-55.

Finletter, Thomas K. "When Russia Is Ready," *Atlantic Monthly,* v. 194 (September 1954), pp. 29-34.

Gruliow, Leo. "What the Russians Are Told About Atomic and Hydrogen Weapons," *Reporter,* v. 12 (March 24, 1955), p. 15-9.

Healey, Denis. "Cominform and World Communism," *International Affairs* (London), v. 24 (July 1948), pp. 339-49.

Isayev, F. "Stalin's Military Genius," *New Times* (Moscow), no. 52 (December 21, 1949).

Kashirin, Colonel P. "O znachenii moralnogo dukha voisk v sovremennoi voine" (The importance of moral strength of the army in contemporary war), *Krasnaia Zvezda* (Moscow), May 28, 1955.

"Speech by Comrade G. M. Malenkov," *Pravda* and *Izvestia,* March 13, 1954. Translated in *Current Digest of the Soviet Press,* v. 6 (April 28, 1954), pp. 6-8.

Rotmistrov, Marshal P. "Za tvorcheskuiu razrabotku vopro-

sov sovetskoi voennoi nauki" (For working out the problems of Soviet military science creatively), *Krasnaia Zvezda*
(Moscow), March 24, 1955.

Rubinstein, M. "The Foreign Press on the Atomic Bomb,"
New Times (Moscow), no. 7 (17) (September 1, 1945).

Sokolovsky, V. "Nesokrushimaia Moshch' Vooruzhennykh Sil
Sovetskogo Gosudarstva" (Indestructible Power of the
Armed Forces of the Soviet State), *Izvestia*, February 23,
1955.

"The Soviet General Staff Takes Stock—Changes in Soviet Military Doctrine," *The World Today*, v. 11 (November 1955),
pp. 492-502.

Trakhtenberg, O. V. " 'Sotsiologiia' Atomnoi Bomby" (The
"Sociology" of the Atom Bomb), *Voprosy Filosofii* (Moscow), no. 3, 1948.

Zhukov, Georgii, "On Western Policy and Soviet Armed
Forces," *Current Digest of the Soviet Press*, v. 8 (April 18,
1956), pp. 10-11, 37.

E. TECHNICAL AND SCIENTIFIC ASPECTS

Books

Bradley, David. *No Place to Hide.* Boston: Little, 1948. 182 p.
Account by a participant of the first Bikini experiments
which tested weapons now considered "small-yield."

Compton, Arthur Holly. *Atomic Quest: A Personal Narrative.*
New York: Oxford University Press, 1956. 370 p.
Account of the development of the atomic bomb and of
the personalities involved. A balanced and fair account.

Darrow, Karl K. *Atomic Energy.* New York: Norman Wait
Harris Foundation, 1948. 80 p.
An attempt to explain nuclear physics to the layman.

Dean, Gordon. *Report on the Atom.* New York: Knopf, 1953.
321 p.
A thoughtful survey of the United States atomic energy
program from the mining of uranium to the construction
of the weapons with some reflections on strategy and the
peaceful uses of the atom by the former chairman of the
Atomic Energy Commission.

Hecht, Selig. *Explaining the Atom.* New York: The Viking
Press, 1947. 205 p.
A rather technical explanation of the atomic bomb.

India. Publications Division. *Nuclear Explosions and their Effects*. Delhi: National Printing Works, 1956. 184 p.
A fairly technical description of the effects of thermonuclear explosions based largely on United States and Japanese sources all leading up to the conclusion that nuclear bomb tests should be stopped. (Foreword to this effect by Jawaharlal Nehru.)

Lapp, Ralph E. *Atoms and People*. New York: Harper, 1956. 304 p.
An interesting account of the development of both the atom and the hydrogen bomb with a description of some of the personalities involved and their relationships. Much less useful on problems of strategy where the desirable and the possible are not always sufficiently distinguished.

Laurence, William Leonard. *Dawn Over Zero*. New York: Knopf, 1946. 274 p.
The story of the Manhattan Engineering Project which produced the first atomic bomb by the science reporter of the *New York Times*. Not too technical.

————. *The Hell Bomb*. New York: Knopf, 1951. 198 p.
A good discussion of the scientific and political problems involved in producing the H-Bomb.

Pierls, R. E. and M. L. E. Oliphant. "The Scientific and Technical Backgrounds," in *Atomic Energy: Its International Implications*, a discussion by a Chatham House Study Group. London: Royal Institute of International Affairs, 1948. pp. 29-41.
A discussion of steps taken in the practical realization of the release of atomic energy. Contains an interesting chapter on the exchange of information between Great Britain and the United States in the early stages of our atomic energy program.

Smyth, Henry DeWolf. *Atomic Energy for Military Purposes*. Princeton: Princeton University Press, 1945. 264 p.
The official report on the development of the A-bomb under the auspices of the United States Government, 1940-45. A highly technical but extremely able account of scientific knowledge on which the A-bomb projects were based.

The Effects of Atomic Weapons. Washington: The Combat Forces Press, 1950. 456 p.
Detailed and official presentation of the effects of atomic bombs. Most complete treatment of the subject. Fairly technical.

U.S. Department of State. *Science and Foreign Relations; International Flow of Scientific and Technological Information,* by Lloyd V. Berkner. General Foreign Policy Series No. 30. Washington: International Science Policy Survey Group, 1950. 170 p.

U.S. Senate. *Atoms for Peace Manual.* S. Doc. 55. Washington: GPO, 1955. 615 p.

A compilation of official materials on international cooperation for peaceful uses of atomic energy. December 1953-July 1955.

——. Special Committee on Atomic Energy. *Atomic Energy Act of 1946.* Hearings, 79th Cong., 2d sess., on S. 1717. Washington: GPO, 1946. pt. 3.

——. Report, April 19, 1946. S. Rept. 1211. Washington: GPO, 1946. 125 p.

U.S. Strategic Bombing Survey. *The Effects of Atomic Bombs on Hiroshima and Nagasaki.* Washington: GPO, 1946. 46 p.

Wendt, Gerald. *You and the Atom.* New York: Morrow, by arrangement with UNESCO, 1956. 95 p.

A lay explanation of atomic energy: sources of raw materials, reactors, radioactivity, use of atomic energy for peaceful purposes. Contains a helpful table of definitions of the most frequently used scientific terms.

Periodicals

"Biological Effects of Atomic Radiation," National Academy of Sciences, Report of the Genetics Committee. *New York Times,* June 13, 1956.

Dean, Gordon. "The Role of Atomic Energy in the World Economy," *Bulletin of the Atomic Scientists,* v. 6 (June 1951), pp. 185-8.

Eisenhower, Dwight D. "Atomic Power for Peace" (Address, U.N. General Assembly, December 8, 1953), *The Department of State Bulletin,* v. 29 (December 21, 1953), pp. 847-51.

Lapp, Ralph E. "Radioactive Fall-Out," *Bulletin of the Atomic Scientists,* v. 11 (February 1955), pp. 45-51.

Libby, Willard F. "Radioactive Fall-out," *Bulletin of the Atomic Scientists,* v. 11 (September 1955), pp. 256-60.

Muller, H. J. "How Radiation Changes the Genetic Constitution," *Bulletin of the Atomic Scientists,* v. 11 (November 1955), pp. 329-38.

Rotblat, J. "The Hydrogen-Uranium Bomb," *Bulletin of the Atomic Scientists,* v. 11 (May 1955), pp. 171-2, 177.

Strauss, Lewis L. "The Truth About Radioactive Fall-out," *U.S. News and World Report,* v. 38 (February 25, 1955), pp. 35-6, 38.

Westergaard, Mogens. "Man's Responsibility to His Genetic Heritage," *Bulletin of the Atomic Scientists,* v. 11 (November 1955), pp. 318-28.

INDEX